Course Student Guide

to accompany

Transitions Throughout the
Life Span

Fourth Edition

Richard O. Straub

Coast
LEARNING SYSTEMS

Coast Community College District

Ding-Jo H. Currie, Chancellor, Coast Community College District
Loretta P. Adrian, President, Coastline Community College
Dan C. Jones, Executive Dean, Office of Instructional Systems Development
Laurie R. Melby, Director of Production
Lynn M. Dahnke, Marketing Director
Judy Garvey, Director, E-Media & Publishing
Robert D. Nash, Director, Instructional Designer & Faculty Support
Wendy Sacket, E-Media & Publishing Project Coordinator
Linda Wojciechowski, Senior E-Media & Publishing Assistant
Thien Vu, E-Media & Publishing Assistant

The course *Transitions Throughout the Life Span* is produced by the Coast Community
College District in cooperation with Worth Publishers and KOCE-TV, Channel 50.

ISBN-10: 1-4292-3451-2
ISBN-13: 978-1-4292-3451-1

Worth Publishers
41 Madison Avenue
New York, NY 10010
www.worthpublishers.com

Contents

Introduction

To the Student

Welcome to *Transitions Throughout the Life Span*. This course has been designed to cover the concepts, vocabulary, and subjects that are typical of an on-campus, college-level human development course. This course introduces the development process in three distinct categories or domains—biosocial, cognitive, and psychosocial.

While most people achieve developmental milestones, each person will take his or her own unique path. The twenty-six half-hour video lessons feature an assortment of real-life examples, historical footage, and an array of subject-matter experts. Throughout this course we will emphasize how the development principles you will be learning can be used to improve the quality of your everyday life, as well as those around you.

As with any college-level course, this course has a textbook, a student guide, assignments, and tests. In lieu of classroom lectures, however, you will be watching half-hour video programs. The designers, academic advisors, and producers of this course have produced an engaging and comprehensive course that will entertain you as you learn about the fascinating subject of human development.

Course Components

The Course Student Guide

This course student guide is an integral part of *Transitions Throughout the Life Span*. Think of it as your "road map." This guide gives you a starting point for each lesson, as well as directions and exercises that will help you successfully navigate your way through each lesson. Reading this guide will provide you with the information that you normally would receive in the classroom if you were taking this course on campus. Each lesson in this course student guide includes the following components:

- **Preview:** An overview of the lesson that informs you of the importance of the subject you are about to study and gives you a brief snapshot of the upcoming video lesson.

- **Prior Course Knowledge:** A list of concepts, theories, terms, and other knowledge presented in previous lessons that you should recall in order to prepare for the current lesson.

- **Learning Objectives:** Your instructional goals for the lesson, which will guide your reading, viewing, thinking, and studying. Upon completing each lesson, you should be able to satisfy each of the learning objectives. (Hint: Instructors often develop test questions directly from learning objectives.)

- **Reading Assignment:** Description of page numbers and sections in the textbook that should be read for each lesson.

- **Viewing Assignment:** Instructions on which video lesson to view, as well as mention of each segment within the video lesson.

- **Summary:** A summary of the lesson—to be read after reading the textbook and viewing the video lesson—that clarifies key points.

- **Key Terms:** Much of education is learning the meaning of new terms and concepts. It is important to be able to define each of the key terms and concepts for each lesson.

- **Practice Questions:** These self-test questions (multiple-choice, matching, and true-false questions) help you review and master basic facts and definitions presented in each lesson.

- **Applying Your Knowledge:** These self-test questions (multiple-choice) help you evaluate your understanding of the lesson's broader and conceptual material and its application to real-world situations.

- **Answer Key:** Answers to the key terms and self-test items are conveniently located at the end of each lesson so that you can get immediate feedback. After completing the Key Terms section and other self-tests, be sure to check the Answer Key to make sure you correctly understand the material.

- **Lesson Review:** This chart has been designed to act as a study tool to help you achieve each learning objective. It lists pages in the textbook, segments in the video lesson, and sections in the course student guide where you can find more information on each objective. Use this tool to master concepts and skills that you feel are your weak points.

The Textbook

This course student guide has been written to accompany the textbook *The Developing Person Through the Life Span*, eighth edition, by Kathleen Stassen Berger (Worth Publishers, 2012). In much the same way as the course lessons, the textbook is complete with real-life stories—some funny, some dramatic, others quite personal. This textbook allows you to learn about human development by observing and hearing about the lives of real, ordinary people. You will repeatedly discover how the study of human development can enrich the life of everyone who takes the time to look deeply into the science of human development and behavior.

Video Programs

Each of the video lessons features a real-life situation—a story line that will help you recognize and appreciate how development affects the lives of ordinary people. The award-winning producers and directors at Coast Learning Systems have brought together top professionals from various fields of psychology and development to help explain different aspects of human development.

How to Take a Distance Learning Course

If this is your first experience with distance learning, welcome. Distance learning courses are designed for busy people whose situation or schedules do not permit them to take a traditional on-campus course.

This course student guide is designed to help you study effectively and learn the material presented in both the textbook and the video lessons. To complete a distance learning course successfully, you will need to schedule sufficient time to read the textbook, watch each video lesson, and study the materials outlined in this guide. In conjunction with your instructor, this guide will provide you with:

- directions on how to take this course.
- study recommendations.
- a preview for each lesson.
- a set of learning objectives for each lesson.
- a list of key terms and concepts for each lesson.
- several different types of study activities and self-tests for each lesson.

The course student guide is a complement to the textbook and the video lessons. It is not a substitute. You will not be able to complete this course successfully unless you purchase and read the textbook, watch the video program—and study. By following the instructions in this guide, you should be able to easily master the learning objectives for each lesson.

To complete this course successfully, you will need to:

- contact your instructor to find out about any course requirements, time lines, meetings, and scheduled exams.
- purchase a copy of the course textbook.
- read and study the textbook.
- view each video lesson in its entirety.
- understand the key terms and concepts presented in this guide.
- be able to satisfy the learning objectives for each lesson.
- complete the self-tests.
- complete any additional assignments your instructor may require.

Even though you do not have scheduled classes to attend each week on campus, please keep in mind that this is a college-level course. It will require the same amount of work as a traditional, classroom version of this course and at the same level of difficulty. As a distance learner, however, it will be up to you alone to keep up with your deadlines. It's important that you schedule enough time to read, study, review, and reflect.

Do your best to keep up with the work. In a distance learning course, it's very difficult to catch up if you allow yourself to get behind schedule. We strongly recommend that you set aside specific times each week for reading, viewing the videos, completing assignments, and studying for quizzes and exams. You will be more likely to succeed if you make a formal study schedule and stick to it.

When you watch each video program, try to do so without any interruptions. If you are interrupted, you may miss an important point. If possible, view the videos in a recorded mode so you can stop the tape and take notes. Also, take some time immediately after watching the video to reflect on what you have just seen. This is an excellent time to discuss the lesson with a friend or family member. Your active thinking and involvement will promote your success.

It is our goal to give you a good, basic understanding of the field of human development. This course will provide you with all the basic information required for a college-level introductory class in human development.

Minds are like parachutes; they only function when open.
—Thomas R. Dewar

And, don't forget to always check with your instructor. He or she will explain the specific course requirements for your assigned class. We sincerely hope you enjoy your introduction to the discipline of human development.

Study Recommendations

Everyone has his or her own unique learning style. Some people learn best by reading alone the first thing each morning, others by discussing ideas with a group of friends, still others by listening to experts and taking notes. While there is no "best" way to learn, psychologists and educators have identified several things you can do that will help you study and learn more effectively.

One of the advantages of distance learning is that you have many choices for how you study. You can tailor this course to fit your "best" way to learn. Below are several study tips. These are proven methods that will help you learn and retain what you are studying. Please take the time to read through this list. You will discover that by using one or more of these techniques you can significantly improve your ability to learn and remember new information.

Open your mind: One of the major obstacles to learning new information is that new information often differs from what we already "know." For example, if you believe that obesity is caused by depression, it will be difficult for you to learn about new information that reveals that there is no cause-and-effect relationship between obesity and depression. To learn, you need to have an open mind. We are not suggesting you simply believe everything you are told. We want you to think critically about what you are told. However, be cautious and guard against letting old beliefs or opinions stop you from learning anything new.

Reduce interference: One of the major reasons for forgetting information is that new information interferes with other information. When you are studying more than one subject at a time, you are increasing the likelihood of interference occurring. If possible, try to study one thing at a time. If you must take multiple subjects, try to take courses with very different subjects, such as art and psychology or math and history. For example, it would not be a good idea to take Human Development and Introduction to Psychology during the same semester. Of course, visiting with friends, watching television, listening to the radio, or any distraction while you are studying will also interfere with your ability to learn new information. When you engage in these types of activities during or just after studying, you risk letting the information you have just learned interfere with other information. Give yourself time to absorb new information.

Don't cram: You probably already know that staying up all night cramming for an exam the following morning is not a good way to study. The opposite of cramming is, in fact, one of the best ways to study. Spacing out your studying into smaller and more frequent study periods will improve retention. Instead of studying for six hours in one evening, you will learn more and retain more if you study one hour per night for six nights.

Reduce stress: In addition to being bad for your health, stress is bad for learning. Stress and anxiety interfere with learning. You will learn more and enjoy it more if you are relaxed when you study. One of the most effective ways of relaxing that does not interfere with learning is exercise. A good brisk walk or run before you settle in to study is a good prescription for success. Ideally, you would study some, take a break, then get some exercise while you think about what you have just learned. And later, when you are relaxed, return and study some more.

Be a Smart Student: Most top students have one thing in common. They all have excellent study habits. Students who excel have learned, or were fortunate enough to have someone teach them, how to study effectively. There is no magic formula for successful studying. However, there are a few universal guidelines.

Do make a commitment to yourself to learn.

Don't let other people interrupt you when you are studying.

Do make a study schedule and stick to it.

Don't study when you are doing something else, like watching television.

Do create a specific place to study.

Don't study if you are tired, upset, or overly stressed.

Do exercise and relax before you study.

Don't study for extended periods of time without taking a break.

Do give yourself ample time to study.

Don't complain that you have to go study.

Do take a positive approach to learning.

Make the most of your assignments: You will master this material more effectively if you make a commitment to completing all your assignments. The lessons will make more sense to you, and you will learn more, if you follow these instructions:

- Set aside a specific time to view, read, and study each lesson.
- Before you view each video lesson, read the Preview and Learning Objectives outlined in this guide.
- Read the assigned textbook pages for the lesson you are studying.
- View the video lesson.
- Review the Key Terms. Check your understanding of all unfamiliar terms in the glossary notes in the textbook.
- Complete the Practice Questions for each lesson.

Think about what you have learned: You are much more likely to remember new information if you use it. Remember that learning is not a passive activity. Learning is active. As soon as you learn something, try to repeat it to someone or discuss it with a friend. If you will think about what you just learned, you will be much more likely to retain that information. The reason we remember certain information has to do mostly with (1) how important that information is to us, and (2) whether or not we actively use the information. For example, if you suffer from headaches and the textbook or video is discussing various headache remedies, this information will be valuable to you. Because of your personal interest in this subject, you will have little difficulty remembering this information. What do you do, however, when you need to learn some information that is not personally valuable or interesting to you? The best way to remember this type of information is to reinforce it—and the best reinforcer is actively using the information.

Get feedback on what you are studying: Study alone, learn with others. You need feedback to help reinforce learning. Also, feedback helps make sure you correctly understand the information. The study activities and self-tests in this guide are specifically designed to give you feedback and reinforce what you are learning. The more time and practice you devote to learning, the better you will be at remembering that information. When you take a self-test, make sure you immediately check your answers with the answer key. Don't wait and check your answers later. If you miss a question, review that section of the textbook to reinforce the correct understanding of the material.

A good gauge of how well you understand some information is your ability to explain that information to another person. If you are unable to explain some term or concept to a friend, you probably will need to review and study that term or concept further.

Contact your instructor: If you are having an especially difficult time with learning some information, contact your instructor. Your instructor is there to help you. Often a personal explanation will do wonders in helping you clear up a misunderstanding. Your instructor wants to hear from you and wants you to succeed. Don't hesitate to call, write, e-mail, or visit your instructor.

Some students do better with study groups; others do better studying alone. If study groups are helpful to you, let your instructor know of your preference. However, be aware that study groups are not a substitute for studying alone. Study groups often turn into friendly chats and not much actually gets learned. So, remember that study groups are not a substitute for individual effort.

Learn it well: Retention is the key to long-term knowledge. One of the best methods to increase your retention is to overlearn material. It is a common mistake to think that just because you can answer a question or give a brief definition of a term or concept, you really know and will remember that term or concept. Think back about how many things you have already "learned." How much do you really remember? Much of what we learn is quickly forgotten. If you want to really learn some information, learn it in a way that you will not forget it—overlearn it.

Overlearning is simple. After you have learned a fact or new word, spend an additional ten or fifteen minutes actively reviewing that fact or word. You will be amazed how much this will increase your long-term retention.

Enjoy learning: You do not need to suffer to learn. In fact, the opposite is true. You will learn more if you enjoy learning. If you have the attitude that "I hate to study" or "schoolwork is boring," you are doing yourself a real disservice.

You will progress better and learn more if you adopt a positive attitude about learning and studying. Since you are choosing to learn, you will be well served by also choosing to enjoy the adventure.

We are sure you will enjoy *Transitions Throughout the Life Span.*

Acknowledgments

Several of the individuals responsible for the creation of this course are listed on the copyright page of this book. In addition, appreciation is expressed for these contributions:

Members of the Course Advisory Committee

The following gifted scholars, professionals, and teachers helped focus the approach and content of the video lessons, faculty manual, and course student guide to ensure accuracy, academic validity, accessibility, significance, and instructional integrity.

Pauline Abbott, Ed.D., California State University, Fullerton
Mary Belcher, M.A., Orange Coast College
Joyce Bishop, Ph.D., Golden West College
Fredda Blanchard-Fields, Ph.D., Georgia Institute of Technology
Michael Catchpole, Ph.D., R. Psych., North Island College, British Columbia, Canada
Chuansheng Chen, Ph.D., University of California, Irvine
Donald Cusumano, Ph.D., St. Louis Community College
Linda Flickinger, M.A., St. Clair County Community College
Andrea R. Fox, M.D., M.P.H., University of Pittsburgh and VA Pittsburgh Healthcare System
Ellen Greenberger, Ph D., University of California, Irvine
Jutta Heckhausen, Ph.D., University of California, Irvine
Sally Hill, M.A., Bakersfield College
Sandra J. McDonald, M.S., Sierra College
Mary K. Rothbart, Ph.D., University of Oregon
Susan Siaw, Ph.D., California State Polytechnic University, Pomona
Barbara W. K. Yee, Ph.D., University of South Florida
Judy Yip, Ph.D., University of Southern California
Elizabeth Zelinski, Ph.D., University of Southern California

Lead Academic Advisors

Roberta Beam, M.A., Tyler Junior College
Amy Himsel, M.A., University of California, Irvine
Doug Hughey, M.A., Mt. San Antonio College
Jeanne Ivy, M.S., L.P.A., Tyler Community College
Phyllis Lembke, M.A., Coastline Community College
Robert D. Nash, M.S., Ed., Coast Learning Systems

Course Production Team

Vanessa Chambers, Jason Daley, Sharon Dymmel, Liz Ervin, Jim Jackson, Becky Koppenhaver, Alejandro Lopez, Dorothy McCollom, Laurie R. Melby, Salma Montez, Evelyn Moore, Harry Ratner, Greg Rogers, Mike Rust, Wendy Moulton-Tate, Charlie Powell, and the many other talented people who helped make the programs.

The Developing Person

Lesson 1

Introduction:
Theories of Development

Preview

The first lesson of this course introduces the **scientific study of human development**, beginning with a brief introduction to the scientific method, a description of the domains into which development is often divided, a description of the scope of the field, and an overview of the major **developmental theories** that have guided research over the past century. A philosopher once said that "nothing is more practical than a good theory," and such has proven to be the case in developmental psychology. Theories help psychologists organize large amounts of information and focus their research on specific, testable ideas about development.

In an effort to organize this course, human development has been divided into three major domains: biosocial, cognitive, and psychosocial. The **biosocial domain** includes all the growth and change that occur in a person's body, and the genetic, nutritional, and health factors that affect that growth and change. The **cognitive domain** includes all the mental processes that are used to obtain knowledge or to become aware of the environment. It includes all the processes people use to think, decide, and learn. The **psychosocial domain** includes development of emotions, temperament, and social skills. The influence of family, friends, the community, the culture, and the larger society are particularly central to this domain. Very few factors, however, belong exclusively to one domain or another. Each aspect of development is related to all three domains.

Several major themes are introduced in this lesson that will be woven into lessons throughout the course, including the idea that development is influenced as much by external factors as by internal factors. This theme, framed initially by philosophers many years ago, continues to drive the field today as researchers weigh the relative contributions of biological factors (such as heredity) and environmental factors (such as learning) in development.

The impact of external factors on development is revealed in the many contexts in which development occurs (such as the family), as well as the many contexts that have an influence on society at large (such as culture). Each of us as individuals is affected by, and affects, other individuals (such as family members and friends) and groups of individuals (such as the neighborhood and community). Furthermore, our development is also affected by the influence of larger systems in the environment (such as ethnicity and culture.)

A third theme of the lesson and course is that development is a lifelong process. Although some early theorists believed that our personalities and fates are fully shaped by the end of childhood, developmental psychologists today recognize that people continue to grow and change from the day they are born until the day they die.

Learning Objectives

Use this information to guide your reading, viewing, thinking, and studying. After successfully completing this lesson, you should be able to:

1. Discuss the role genes play in the nature–nurture debate, and their role in developmental timing and genetic vulnerability.
2. Define the life-span perspective of development, and identify five characteristics or principles of development.
3. Identify and describe the three domains into which human development is often separated.
4. Describe the ecological-systems approach to human development, and explain how this approach leads to an understanding of the overlapping contexts in which people develop.
5. Discuss the three broad, overlapping contexts that affect development throughout the life span.
6. Define developmental theory, and describe how developmental theories help explain human behavior and development.
7. Discuss the major focus of psychoanalytic theories, and describe the conflicts that occur during Freud's stages of psychosexual development.
8. Describe the crises of Erikson's theory of psychosocial development, and contrast them with Freud's stages.
9. Discuss the major focus of behaviorism, and explain the basic principles of classical and operant conditioning.
10. Discuss social learning theory as an extension of learning theory.
11. Identify the primary focus of cognitive theory, and briefly describe Piaget's stages of cognitive development as well as the process that, according to Piaget, guides human development.
12. Explain what is meant by information processing and how it can be applied to the study of human development.
13. Discuss the basic ideas of Vygotsky and the sociocultural theory of development.
14. Discuss the universal perspective, and describe the difference between humanism and evolutionary theory.
15. Summarize the contributions and criticisms of the major developmental theories, and explain the eclectic perspective of contemporary developmentalists.

📖 **Read** Chapter 1, "Introduction," pages 3–18; and Chapter 2, "Theories of Development," pages 33–59.

⏮ **View** the video for Lesson 1, "The Developing Person."

Segment 1: *Contexts and Systems*

Segment 2: *Theories of Development*

Segment 3: *The Life-Span Perspective*

Summary

The scientific study of human development is the science that seeks to understand how and why people change with increasing age, and how and why they remain the same. Those interested in human development use a scientific approach, which will be described at depth in the next lesson, to study such questions as the nature–nurture debate, the timing of critical and sensitive periods, and the role genetic vulnerability plays in the unfolding of an individual's life.

The study of human development is done within a **life-span perspective** that recognizes the fact that development is lifelong, multidirectional, multicontextual, multicultural, multidisciplinary, and plastic. Human development is also multidimensional in that it includes many dimensions of many domains. The three major domains of development include the **biosocial domain** (brain and body as well as changes in them and the social influences that guide them), the **cognitive domain** (thought processes, perceptual abilities, and language mastery, as well as the educational institutions that encourage them), and the **psychosocial domain** (emotions, personality, and interpersonal relationships with family, friends, and the wider community).

According to Urie Bronfenbrenner's **ecological-systems approach**, human development is supported by systems at four nested levels: the microsystem (immediate social setting), the mesosystem (connections among various microsystems), the exosystem (the community structures and local educational, medical, employment, and communications systems that directly affect the various microsystems and indirectly affect everyone in those microsystems), and the macrosystem (cultural values, political philosophies, economic patterns, and social conditions). The larger perspective fostered by the ecological approach makes it imperative that development be understood in its social context—its historical, cultural, ethnic, and socioeconomic contexts.

Scientific investigations into human development is guided by theories, even as the studies themselves investigate the theories. The theories fall into several categories, based on the aspect of human behavior or development on which they focus.

Psychoanalytic theory interprets human development in terms of intrinsic drives and motives, many of which are irrational and unconscious. According to Sigmund Freud, development progresses through five psychosexual stages; at each stage, sexual interest and pleasure is focused on a particular part of the body—the mouth during infancy (the oral stage), the anus during early childhood (the anal stage), and the genitalia later in the preschool years (the phallic stage). Following a five- or six-year stage of sexual latency, the individual enters the fifth stage, the genital stage, which lasts throughout adulthood.

In his psychosocial theory of human development, Erik Erikson proposed eight developmental stages, each of which is characterized by a particular challenge, or developmental crisis (for example, young adults are faced with the challenge of establishing intimate relationships). Erikson emphasized each person's interactions in the social environment and the importance of family and cultural influences in determining how well-prepared individuals are to meet and resolve these crises.

Proponents of **behaviorism (learning theory)** formulated laws of behavior that are presumed to operate at every age. As demonstrated by Ivan Pavlov, classical conditioning involves learning by association: the subject comes to associate a neutral stimulus with a meaningful response. In operant conditioning, proposed by B. F. Skinner, the individual learns that a particular behavior produces a particular consequence. **Social learning theory** emphasizes the ways in which people learn new behaviors by observing and imitating, or **modeling**, the behavior of other people they consider admirable, powerful, or similar.

Cognitive theory focuses on the structure and development of the individual's thought processes and their effect on his or her understanding of the world—focusing on how children's thinking differs from adults' thinking. Jean Piaget viewed cognitive development as a process that follows a universal sequence of age-related periods: sensorimotor, preoperational, concrete operational, and formal operational. According to Piaget, each individual strives for **cognitive equilibrium**—that is, a state of mental balance achieved through the development of mental concepts that explain his or her experiences.

Sociocultural theory seeks to explain individual knowledge, development, and competencies in terms of the guidance, support, and structure provided by the broader cultural context. Lev Vygotsky believed that the development of cognitive competencies results from social interaction between children and more mature members of the society in what has been called an "apprenticeship in thinking."

The universal perspective focuses on the shared impulses and common needs of all humans. For instance, humanism, which was proposed by Abraham Maslow, holds that all humans have five basic needs that exist in a hierarchy; the bottom needs must be met before the top needs become of importance, and a person will trade a higher need to satisfy a need at a lower level of the hierarchy. Carl Rogers, on the other hand, focused on the common need for respect, appreciation and unconditional positive regard.

Another universal perspective is evolutionary theory, which is based on the work by Charles Darwin and focuses on the role selective adaptation plays in guiding our behavior. According to evolutionary theory, any genetic variation that increases the likelihood that offspring will reproduce will be favored, and passed down through the generations as an adaptation.

These many theories complement one another, as each emphasizes a somewhat different aspect of development and, as such, is too restricted to account for the diversity of human behavior. **Psychoanalytic theory** calls attention to the importance of early childhood experiences and "hidden dramas" that influence daily life. **Behaviorism** highlights the effect of the immediate environment on behavior. **Cognitive theory** promotes a greater understanding of how intellectual processes and thinking affect our behavior. **Sociocultural theory** reminds us that development is embedded in a rich and multifaceted cultural context. Universal theories focus upon those traits and behaviors humans have in common, regardless of place or time.

Developmentalists agree that the interaction between nature and nurture is the crucial influence on any particular aspect of development at any point in time during the life span. Today, most developmentalists take an **eclectic perspective**; instead of limiting themselves to only one school of thought, they apply insights drawn from various theoretical views.

📖   **Review all reading assignments for this lesson.**

💻   **As assigned by your instructor, complete the optional online component for this lesson.**

Key Terms

Using your own words, write a brief definition or explanation of each of the following terms on a separate piece of paper.

1. science of human development
2. nature
3. nurture
4. critical period
5. sensitive period
6. dynamic-systems theory
7. life-span perspective
8. ecological-systems approach
9. cohort
10. socioeconomic status (SES)
11. ethnic group
12. race
13. biosocial domain
14. cognitive domain
15. psychosocial domain *Erikson*
16. mirror neurons
17. developmental theory
18. psychoanalytic theory *Freud*
                           Erikson

19. behaviorism (learning theory)
20. conditioning
21. classical conditioning
22. operant conditioning
23. reinforcement
24. social learning theory
25. modeling
26. self-efficacy
27. cognitive theory *Jean Piaget*
28. cognitive equilibrium
29. information processing
30. sociocultural theory *Vygotsky*
31. apprenticeship in thinking
32. zone of proximal development
33. humanism
34. selective adaptation
35. eclectic perspective

Practice Questions I

Multiple-Choice Questions

1. The science of human development is defined as the study of
   a. how and why people change or remain the same over time.
   b. psychosocial influences on aging.
   c. individual differences in learning over the life span.
   d. all of the above.

2. The cognitive domain of development includes
   a. perception.
   b. thinking.
   c. language.
   d. all of the above.

3. Changes in height, weight, and bone thickness are part of the _____ domain.
    a. cognitive
    b. biosocial
    c. psychosocial
    d. physical

4. Psychosocial development focuses primarily on personality, emotions, and
    a. intellectual development.
    b. sexual maturation.
    c. relationships with others.
    d. perception.

5. The ecological-systems approach to developmental psychology focuses on the
    a. biochemistry of the body systems.
    b. cognitive domain only.
    c. internal thinking processes.
    d. overall environment of development.

6. Researchers who take a life-span perspective on development focus on
    a. the sources of continuity from the beginning of life to the end.
    b. the sources of discontinuity throughout life.
    c. the "nonlinear" character of human development.
    d. all of the above.

7. During the 1960s, American society tilted toward a youth culture. This is a vivid example of the effect of the _____ on society.
    a. "baby boom" cohort
    b. biosocial domain
    c. cognitive domain
    d. microsystem

8. A developmentalist who is interested in studying the influences of a person's immediate environment on his or her behavior is focusing on which system?
    a. mesosystem
    b. macrosystem
    c. microsystem
    d. exosystem

9. Socioeconomic status (SES) is determined by a combination of variables, including
    a. age, education, and income.
    b. income, ethnicity, and occupation.
    c. income, education, and occupation.
    d. age, ethnicity, and occupation.

10. The purpose of a developmental theory is to
    a. provide a broad, coherent view of the complex influences on human development.
    b. offer guidance for practical issues encountered by parents, teachers, and therapists.
    c. generate testable hypotheses about development.
    d. do all of the above.

11. Which developmental theory emphasizes the influence of unconscious drives and motives on behavior?
    a. psychoanalytic
    b. learning
    c. cognitive
    d. sociocultural

12. Which of the following is the correct order of the psychosexual stages proposed by Freud?
    a. oral stage; anal stage; phallic stage; latency; genital stage
    b. anal stage; oral stage; phallic stage; latency; genital stage
    c. oral stage; anal stage; genital stage; latency; phallic stage
    d. anal stage; oral stage; genital stage; latency; phallic stage

13. Erikson's psychosocial theory of human development describes
    a. eight crises all people are thought to face.
    b. four psychosocial stages and a latency period.
    c. the same number of stages as Freud's, but with different names.
    d. a stage theory that is not psychoanalytic.

14. An American psychologist who explained complex human behaviors in terms of operant conditioning was
    a. Lev Vygotsky.
    b. Ivan Pavlov.
    c. B. F. Skinner.
    d. Jean Piaget.

15. Pavlov's dogs learned to salivate at the sound of a bell because they associated the bell with food. Pavlov's experiment with dogs was an early demonstration of
    a. classical conditioning.
    b. operant conditioning.
    c. positive reinforcement.
    d. social learning.

16. The nature–nurture controversy considers the degree to which traits, characteristics, and behaviors are the result of
    a. early or lifelong learning.
    b. genes or heredity.
    c. heredity or experience.
    d. different historical concepts of childhood.

17. Modeling, an integral part of social learning theory, is so called because it
    a. follows the scientific model of learning.
    b. molds character.
    c. follows the immediate reinforcement model developed by Albert Bandura.
    d. involves people's patterning their behavior after that of others.

18. According to which theorist must the basic needs of survival and safety be met before higher needs such as belonging and achievement can be pursued?
    a. B. F. Skinner
    b. Ivan Pavlov
    c. Jean Piaget
    d. Abraham Maslow

19. Which developmental theory stresses the role of selective adaptation?
    a. learning
    b. evolutionary
    c. cognitive
    d. sociocultural

20. Which is the correct sequence of stages in Piaget's theory of cognitive development?
    a. sensorimotor, preoperational, concrete operational, formal operational
    b. sensorimotor, preoperational, formal operational, concrete operational
    c. preoperational, sensorimotor, concrete operational, formal operational
    d. preoperational, sensorimotor, formal operational, concrete operational

21. When an individual's existing understanding no longer fits his or her present experiences, the result is called
    a. a psychosocial crisis.
    b. equilibrium.
    c. disequilibrium.
    d. negative reinforcement.

22. The zone of proximal development refers to the
    a. control process by which information is transferred from the sensory register to working memory.
    b. influence of a pleasurable stimulus on behavior.
    c. range of skills a child can exercise with assistance but cannot perform independently.
    d. mutual interaction of a person's internal characteristics, the environment, and the person's behavior.

23. Nature is to nurture as
    a. *tabula rasa* is to blank slate.
    b. Jean Rousseau is to John Locke.
    c. B. F. Skinner is to Ivan Pavlov.
    d. Urie Bronfenbrenner is to Kurt Lewin.

24. The information processing approach can help developmentalists determine when
    a. a child is malnourished.
    b. operant conditioning has occurred.
    (c) cognitive processes are impaired.
    d. genetic vulnerability explains a key behavior.

Matching Items
Match each definition or description with its corresponding term.

Terms
25. ___F___ psychoanalytic theory
26. ___K___ nature
27. ___A___ learning theory
28. ___C___ social learning theory
29. ___H___ cognitive theory
30. ___D___ nurture

31. ___G___ sociocultural theory
32. ___E___ conditioning
33. ___B___ sensitive period
34. ___I___ modeling
35. ___J___ humanism

Descriptions or Definitions
a. emphasizes the impact of the immediate environment on behavior
b. a period during which learning can occur
c. emphasizes that people learn by observing others
d. environmental influences that affect development
e. a process of learning, as described by Pavlov or Skinner
f. emphasizes the "hidden dramas" that influence behavior
g. emphasizes the cultural context in development
h. emphasizes how our thoughts shape our actions
i. the process whereby a person learns by imitating someone else's behavior
j. emphasizes the goodness of people and the commonality of their needs
k. traits that are inherited

Practice Questions II

Multiple-Choice Questions

1. When developmentalists discuss the "context" of individual development, they are referring to
   a. microsystem and mesosystem.
   b. exosystem.
   c. macrosystem.
   (d.) microsystem, mesosystem, exosystem, and macrosystem.

2. People often mistakenly believe that most developmental changes
   a. originate within each individual as a result of genetic factors.
   b. take place in a larger social context.
   c. are temporary.
   d. occur in the same way in all people.

3. According to the ecological-systems approach, the macrosystem would include
   a. the peer group.
   b. the community.
   c. cultural values.
   d. the family.

4. A cohort is defined as a group of people
   a. of similar national origin.
   b. who share a common language.
   c. born within a few years of each other.
   d. who share the same religion.

5. Which developmental theorist has been criticized for suggesting that every child, in every culture, in every nation, passes through certain fixed stages?
   a. Sigmund Freud
   b. Erik Erikson
   c. Jean Piaget
   d. all of the above

6. Of the following terms, the one that does **NOT** describe a stage of Freud's theory of childhood sexuality is
   a. phallic.
   b. oral.
   c. anal.
   d. sensorimotor.

7. We are more likely to imitate the behavior of others if we particularly admire and identify with them. This belief finds expression in
   a. stage theory.
   b. sociocultural theory.
   c. social learning theory.
   d. Pavlov's experiments.

8. According to Erikson, an adult who has difficulty establishing a secure, mutual relationship with a life partner might never have resolved the crisis of
   a. initiative versus guilt.
   b. autonomy versus shame.
   c. intimacy versus despair.
   d. trust versus mistrust.

9. Who would be most likely to agree with the statement, "Anything can be learned"?
   a. Jean Piaget
   b. Lev Vygotsky
   c. John Watson
   d. Erik Erikson

10. Classical conditioning is to _____ as operant conditioning is to _____.
    a. Skinner; Pavlov
    b. Watson; Vygotsky
    c. Pavlov; Skinner
    d. Vygotsky; Watson

11. Learning theorists have found that they can often solve a person's seemingly complex psychological problem by
    a. analyzing the patient.
    b. admitting the existence of the unconscious.
    c. altering the environment.
    d. administering well-designed punishments.

12. According to Piaget, an infant first comes to know the world through
    a. sucking and grasping.
    b. naming and counting.
    c. preoperational thought.
    d. instruction from parents.

13. According to Piaget, the stage of cognitive development that generally characterizes preschool children (2 to 6 years old) is the
    a. preoperational stage.
    b. sensorimotor stage.
    c. oral stage.
    d. psychosocial stage.

14. In Piaget's theory, cognitive equilibrium refers to
    a. a state of mental balance.
    b. a kind of imbalance that leads to cognitive growth.
    c. the ultimate stage of cognitive development.
    d. the first stage in the processing of information.

15. You teach your dog to "speak" by giving her a treat each time she does so. This is an example of
    a. classical conditioning.
    b. respondent conditioning.
    c. reinforcement.
    d. modeling.

16. A child who must modify an old idea in order to incorporate a new experience is using the process of

    a. assimilation.

    b. accommodation.

    c. cognitive equilibrium.

    d. guided participation.

17. Which of the following is a common criticism of sociocultural theory?

    a. It places too great an emphasis on unconscious motives and childhood sexuality.

    b. Its mechanistic approach fails to explain many complex human behaviors.

    c. Development is more gradual than its stages imply.

    d. It neglects developmental processes that are not primarily social.

18. A major pioneer of the sociocultural perspective was

    a. Jean Piaget.

    b. Albert Bandura.

    c. Lev Vygotsky.

    d. Ivan Pavlov.

19. Stimulus is to response as

    a. action is to reaction.

    b. reaction is to action.

    c. nature is to nurture.

    d. nurture is to nature.

20. Many fields, including education, neuroscience, psychology, and anthropology, contribute to the science of development. This is

    a. multidirectional.

    b. multicontextual.

    c. multicultural.

    d. multidisciplinary.

21. Body strength increases during early life and then begins to decline with age. This is an example of

    a. multidirectionality.

    b. multicontextuality.

    c. multicultural influence.

    d. multidisciplinarity.

22. Change is ongoing and can occur at any point throughout the life span. This is representative of

    a. multidirectionality.

    b. continuity.

    c. plasticity.

    d. the life-span perspective.

23. Fingers and toes develop during a _____ in development.
   a. critical period
   b. pause
   c. sensitive period
   d. surge

True or False Items

Write T (for true) or F (for false) on the line in front of each statement.

24. __T__ Behaviorists study what people actually do, not what they might be thinking.

25. __T__ Erikson's eight developmental stages are centered not on a body part but on each person's relationship to the social environment.

26. __F__ Most developmentalists agree that the nature–nurture controversy has been laid to rest.

27. __T__ Information processing refers to an analogy between the human mind and a computer.

28. __F__ Humanists like Abraham Maslow and Carl Rogers focus on humanity's tendency to commit evil acts.

29. __F__ According to Piaget, a state of cognitive equilibrium must be attained before cognitive growth can occur.

30. __T__ In part, cognitive theory examines how an individual's understandings and expectations affect his or her behavior.

31. __F__ According to Piaget, children begin to think only when they reach preschool age.

32. __T__ Most contemporary researchers have adopted an eclectic perspective on development.

Applying Your Knowledge

1. Dr. Ramirez conducts research on the psychosocial domain of development. She is most likely to be interested in a child's
   a. perceptual abilities.
   b. brain-wave patterns.
   c. emotions.
   d. use of language.

2. Jamal is writing a paper on the role of the social context in development. He would do well to consult the writings of
   a. Jean Piaget.
   b. Sigmund Freud.
   c. Urie Bronfenbrenner.
   d. B. F. Skinner.

3. Dr. Wong looks at human development in terms of the individual's supporting ecosystems. Evidently, Dr. Wong subscribes to the _____ approach.
    a. psychosocial
    b. ecological-systems
    c. biosocial
    d. cognitive

4. When we say that the idea of old age as we know it is a "social construction," we are saying that
    a. the idea is built on the shared perceptions of members of society.
    b. old age has only recently been regarded as a distinct period of life.
    c. old age cannot be defined.
    d. the idea is based on a well-tested hypothesis.

5. Many songbirds inherit a genetically programmed species song that enhances their ability to mate and establish a territory. The evolution of such a trait is an example of
    a. selective adaptation.
    b. disequilibrium.
    c. accommodation.
    d. assimilation.

6. When a pigeon is rewarded for producing a particular response and so learns to produce that response to obtain rewards, psychologists describe this chain of events as
    a. operant conditioning.
    b. classical conditioning.
    c. modeling.
    d. reflexive actions.

7. Dr. Cleaver notices that a baby waves his arms when his mother smiles. According to the information processing analogy, the mother's smile is the baby's _____ and the waving arms are the _____.
    a. output; input
    b. response; conditioning
    c. zone of proximal development; apprenticeship in thinking
    d. input; output

8. Which of the following is the best example of the apprenticeship in thinking?
    a. After watching her mother change her baby sister's diaper, four-year-old Brandy changes her doll's diaper.
    b. To help her son learn to pour liquids, Linda engages him in a bathtub game involving pouring water from cups of different sizes.
    c. Seeing his father shaving, three-year-old Jack pretends to shave by rubbing whipped cream on his face.
    d. After reading a recipe in a magazine, Kyle gathers ingredients from the cupboard.

9. A child who calls all furry animals "doggie" will experience cognitive
_____ when she encounters a hairless breed for the first time. This
may cause her to revamp her concept of "dog" in order to _____ the
new experience.

   a. disequilibrium; accommodate

   b. disequilibrium; assimilate

   c. equilibrium; accommodate

   d. equilibrium; assimilate

10. A confirmed neo-Freudian, Dr. Thomas strongly endorses the views of Erik
Erikson. She would be most likely to disagree with Freud regarding the
importance of

   a. unconscious forces in development.

   b. irrational forces in personality formation.

   c. early childhood experiences.

   d. sexual urges in development.

11. After watching several older children climbing around a new jungle gym,
five-year-old Jennie decides to try it herself. Which of the following best
accounts for her behavior?

   a. classical conditioning

   b. modeling

   c. apprenticeship in thinking

   d. reinforcement

12. I am 8 years old, and although I understand some logical principles, I have
trouble thinking about hypothetical concepts. According to Piaget, I am in the
_____ stage of development.

   a. sensorimotor

   b. preoperational

   c. concrete operational

   d. formal operational

13. Two-year-old Bjorn has a simple understanding for "dad," and so each time he
encounters a man with a child, he calls him "dad." When he learns that these
other men are not "dad," Bjorn experiences

   a. conservation.

   b. cognition.

   c. equilibrium.

   d. disequilibrium.

14. Most adults become physiologically aroused by the sound of an infant's
laughter. These interactive reactions, in which caregivers and babies elicit
responses in each other,

   a. help ensure the survival of the next generation.

   b. do not occur in all human cultures.

   c. are the result of conditioning very early in life.

   d. are more often found in females than in males.

15. The school psychologist believes that each child's developmental needs can be understood only by taking into consideration the child's broader social and cultural background. Evidently, the school psychologist is working within the _____ perspective.

    a. psychoanalytic
    b. humanistic
    c. social learning
    d. sociocultural

16. Four-year-old Rashad takes great pride in successfully undertaking new activities. Erikson would probably say that Rashad is capably meeting the psychosocial challenge of

    a. trust versus mistrust.
    b. initiative versus guilt.
    c. industry versus inferiority.
    d. identity versus role confusion.

17. Dr. Bazzi's developmental research draws upon insights from several theoretical perspectives. Evidently, Dr. Bazzi is working from a(n) _____ perspective.

    a. cognitive
    b. learning
    c. eclectic
    d. sociocultural

18. Dr. Ivey believes that development is a lifelong process of gradual and continuous growth. Based on this information, with which of the following theories would Dr. Ivey most likely agree?

    a. Piaget's cognitive theory
    b. Erikson's psychosocial theory
    c. Freud's psychoanalytic theory
    d. learning theory

19. Professor Villa believes that self-respect and self-esteem are only possible if a person has enough to eat and a safe place to sleep. Professor Villa is evidently an advocate of

    a. behaviorism.
    b. humanism.
    c. evolutionary theory.
    d. cognitive theory.

20. Cassandra is deathly afraid of snakes but will dash across the street in heavy traffic, even though she is more likely to be injured in traffic than by a snake. Cassandra is displaying

    a. selective adaptation.
    b. operant conditioning.
    c. classical conditioning.
    d. apprenticeship in thinking.

Answer Key

Key Terms

1. The science of human development is the science that seeks to understand how and why people change, and how and why they remain the same, as they grow older. (p. 4; video lesson, segment 3; objective 2)

2. Nature refers to all the traits, capacities, and limitations that a person inherits at the moment of conception. (p. 5; video lesson, introduction; objective 1)

3. Nurture refers to all the environmental influences that affect a person's development following the moment of conception. (p. 5; video lesson, introduction; objective 1)

4. A critical period is a time when a particular type of developmental growth in body or behavior must happen if it is ever going to happen. (p. 6; objective 1)

5. A sensitive period is a time when a certain type of development is most likely to occur, although it may still happen later. (p. 6; objective 1)

6. Dynamic-systems theory describes a process in which changes within a person or group are systematically connected to each other. That means that each aspect of a person's development can potentially affect all other aspects. (p. 8; objectives 2 & 4)

7. The life-span perspective on human development recognizes that human growth is lifelong and characterized by both continuity (as in personality) and discontinuity (as in the number of brain cells). (p. 10; video lesson, segment 3; objective 2)

8. According to Urie Bronfenbrenner's ecological-systems approach or model, human development is supported by systems at four nested levels: the microsystem, the mesosystem, the exosystem, and the macrosystem. (pp. 11–12; video lesson, segment 1; objective 4)

9. A cohort is a group of people who, because they were born within a few years of each other, experience many of the same historical and social emotions. (p. 12; objective 5)

10. An individual's socioeconomic status (SES) is determined by his or her income, education, place of residence, and occupation. (p. 12; objective 5)

11. An ethnic group is a collection of people who share certain attributes, such as national origin, religion, ancestry, and/or language and who, as a result, tend to identify with each other and have similar daily encounters with the social world. (p. 14; objective 4)

12. Race is a social construction that was originally based on biological differences between people whose ancestors came from different regions of the world. (pp. 14–15; objective 4)

13. The biosocial domain is concerned with brain and body changes and the social influences that guide them. (p. 15; objective 3)

14. The cognitive domain is concerned with thought processes, perceptual abilities, and language mastery, and the educational institutions that encourage these aspects of development. (p. 15; objective 3)

15. The psychosocial domain is concerned with emotions, personality, and interpersonal relationships with family, friends, and the wider community. (p. 15; objective 3)

16. Mirror neurons are brain cells that respond to actions performed by someone else, as if the observer had done that action. Mirror neuron

Lesson 1/Introduction: Theories of Development

research provides an example of how developmental psychology benefits from an interdisciplinary approach. (p. 16; objectives 2 & 3)

17. A developmental theory is a systematic statement of principles and generalizations that explains behavior and development and provides a framework for future research. (p. 33; video lesson, segment 2; objective 6)

18. Psychoanalytic theory interprets human development in terms of intrinsic drives and motives, many of which are irrational and unconscious. (pp. 36–37; objective 7) *Freud, Erikson*

19. Behaviorism (learning theory) emphasizes the sequences and processes of conditioning that underlie most of human and animal behavior. (p. 40; objective 9)

20. Conditioning is the learning process that occurs either through the association of two stimuli (classical conditioning) or through the use of positive or negative reinforcement or punishment (operant conditioning). (pp. 40–41; objective 9)

21. Classical conditioning is the learning process in which a meaningful stimulus (such as the smell of food to a hungry animal) is connected with a neutral stimulus (such as the sound of a tone) that had no special meaning before conditioning (p. 40; objective 9)

22. Operant conditioning is the learning process by which a particular action is followed by something desired (which makes the person or animal more likely to repeat the action) or by something unwanted (which makes the action less likely to be repeated). (p. 41; objective 9)

23. Reinforcement is the process by which the consequences of a particular behavior strengthen the behavior, making it more likely that the behavior will be repeated. (p. 41; video lesson, segment 2; objective 9)

24. An extension of behaviorism, social learning theory emphasizes that people often learn new behaviors through observation and imitation of other people. (pp. 41–42; video lesson, segment 2; objectives 9 & 10)

25. Modeling refers to the process by which we observe other people's behavior and then pattern our own after it. (pp. 41–42; video lesson, segment 2; objective 10)

26. Self-efficacy is a person's belief that he or she is effective. According to social learning theory, it can motivate people to change. (p. 42; objective 10)

27. Cognitive theory emphasizes that the way people think and understand the world shapes their perceptions, attitudes, and actions. (p. 45; video lesson, segment 2; objective 11)

28. In Piaget's theory, cognitive equilibrium is a state of mental balance, in which a person's thoughts about the world seem not to clash with each other or with his or her experiences. (p. 46; video lesson, segment 2; objective 11)

29. Information processing is a perspective that compares human thinking processes, by analogy, to computer analysis of data, including sensory input, connections, stored memories, and output. (p. 47; objective 12)

new theory 30. Sociocultural theory seeks to explain development as the result of a dynamic interaction between developing persons and their surrounding culture. (p. 48; objective 13)

31. An apprenticeship in thinking is Vygotsky's term for how cognition is stimulated and developed in people by older and more skilled members of society. (p. 49; objective 13)

32. According to Vygotsky, developmental growth occurs when mentors draw children into the zone of proximal development, which is the range of skills

the child can exercise with assistance but cannot perform independently. (pp. 49–50; objective 13)

(33) Humanism is a theory that stresses the potential of all humans for good and the belief that all people have the same basic needs, regardless of culture, gender, or background. (p. 51; objective 14)

(34) Selective adaptation is the evolutionary process through which useful genes that enhance survival become more frequent within populations. (p. 53; objective 14)

35. Developmentalists who work from an eclectic perspective accept elements from several theories, instead of adhering to only a single perspective. (p. 57; video lesson, segment 3; objective 15)

Practice Questions I

Multiple-Choice Questions

1. a. is the correct answer. (video lesson, segment 3; objective 2)

   b. & c. are incorrect. The study of development is concerned with a broader range of phenomena, including biosocial aspects of development, than these answers specify.

2. d. is the correct answer. (objective 3)

3. b. is the correct answer. (objective 3)

   a. is incorrect. This domain is concerned with thought processes.

   c. is incorrect. This domain is concerned with emotions, personality, and interpersonal relationships.

   d. is incorrect. This is not a domain of development.

4. c. is the correct answer. (objective 3)

   a. is incorrect. This falls within the cognitive and biosocial domains.

   b. is incorrect. This falls within the biosocial domain.

   d. is incorrect. This falls within the cognitive domain.

5. d. is the correct answer. This approach sees development as occurring within four interacting levels, or environments. (video lesson, segment 1; objective 4)

6. d. is the correct answer. (video lesson, segment 3; objective 1)

7. a. is the correct answer. (objective 4)

   b. is incorrect. The biosocial domain is concerned with brain and body changes.

   c. is incorrect. The cognitive domain is concerned with thought processes in individuals and the factors that influence them.

8. c. is the correct answer. (objective 4)

   a. is incorrect. This refers to systems that link one microsystem to another.

   b. is incorrect. This refers to cultural values, political philosophies, economic patterns, and social conditions.

   d. is incorrect. This includes the community structures that affect the functioning of smaller systems.

9. c. is the correct answer. (objective 5)

10. d. is the correct answer. (video lesson, segment 2; objective 6)

11. a. is the correct answer. (video lesson, segment 2; objective 7)

    b. is incorrect. Learning theory emphasizes the influence of the immediate environment on behavior.

c. is incorrect. Cognitive theory emphasizes the impact of conscious thought processes on behavior.

d. is incorrect. Sociocultural theory emphasizes the influence on development of social interaction in a specific cultural context.

12. a. is the correct answer. (objective 7)

13. a. is the correct answer. (video lesson, segment 2; objective 8)

b. & c. are incorrect. Whereas Freud identified five stages of psychosexual development, Erikson proposed eight psychosocial stages.

d. is incorrect. Although his theory places greater emphasis on social and cultural forces than Freud's did, Erikson's theory is nevertheless classified as a psychoanalytic theory.

14. c. is the correct answer. (video lesson, segment 2; objective 9)

15. a. is the correct answer. In classical conditioning, a neutral stimulus—in this case, the bell—is associated with a meaningful stimulus—in this case, food. (video lesson, segment 2; objective 9)

b. is incorrect. In operant conditioning, the consequences of a voluntary response determine the likelihood of its being repeated. Salivation is an involuntary response.

c. & d. are incorrect. Positive reinforcement and social learning pertain to voluntary, or operant, responses.

16. c. is the correct answer. (objective 1)

a. is incorrect. These are both examples of nurture.

b. is incorrect. Both of these refer to nature.

d. is incorrect. The impact of changing historical concepts of childhood on development is an example of how environmental forces (nurture) shape development.

17. d. is the correct answer. (video lesson, segment 2; objective 10)

a. & c. are incorrect. These can be true in all types of learning.

b. is incorrect. This was not discussed as an aspect of developmental theory.

18. d. is the correct answer. The hierarchy is often referred to as Maslow's hierarchy of needs. (objective 14)

a. & c. are incorrect. Sociocultural and learning theories focus almost entirely on environmental factors (nurture) in development.

b. is incorrect. Cognitive theory emphasizes the developing person's own mental activity but ignores genetic differences in individuals.

19. b. is the correct answer. (objective 14)

20. a. is the correct answer. (video lesson, segment 2; objective 11)

21. c. is the correct answer. (objective 11)

a. is incorrect. This refers to the core of Erikson's psychosocial stages, which deals with people's interactions with the environment.

b. is incorrect. Equilibrium occurs when existing schemes do fit a person's current experiences.

d. is incorrect. Negative reinforcement is the removal of a stimulus as a consequence of a desired behavior.

22. c. is the correct answer. (objective 13)

a. is incorrect. This describes attention.

b. is incorrect. This describes positive reinforcement.

d. is incorrect. This describes reciprocal determinism.

23. b. is the correct answer. Locke believed that the mind at birth is a *tabula rasa,* or "blank slate," onto which learning (nurture) leaves its mark. Rousseau emphasized the natural (biological) goodness of human beings. (video lesson, introduction; objective 1)

24. c. is the correct answer. Using computer processing as an analogy for thinking can help identify where there is an impairment. (objective 12)

Matching Items

25. f (video lesson, segment 2; objective 7)
26. k (video lesson, introduction; objective 1)
27. a (video lesson, segment 2; objective 9)
28. c (video lesson, segment 2; objective 10)
29. h (objective 11)
30. d (video lesson, introduction; objective 1)
31. g (objective 13)
32. e (objective 9)
33. b (objective 1)
34. i (video lesson, segment 2; objective 10)
35. j (objective 14)

Practice Questions II

Multiple-Choice Questions

1. d. is the correct answer. (objectives 4 & 5)
2. a. is the correct answer. (objective 2)

   b. is incorrect. This is the emphasis of the newer, ecological-systems approach.

   c. & d. are incorrect. The textbook does not suggest that people commonly make these assumptions.

3. c. is the correct answer. (video lesson, segment 1; objective 4)

   a. & d. are incorrect. These are part of the microsystem.

   b. is incorrect. This is part of the exosystem.

4. c. is the correct answer. (objective 5)

   a., b., & d. are incorrect. These are attributes of an ethnic group.

5. d. is the correct answer. (video lesson, segment 2; objective 14)

6. d. is the correct answer. This is one of Piaget's stages of cognitive development. (video lesson, segment 2; objective 7)

7. c. is the correct answer. (video lesson, segment 2; objective 10)

8. d. is the correct answer. (video lesson, segment 2; objective 8)

9. c. is the correct answer. (objective 9)

   a. is incorrect. Piaget formulated a cognitive theory of development.

   b. is incorrect. Vygotsky formulated a sociocultural theory of development.

   d. is incorrect. Erikson formulated a psychoanalytic theory of development.

10. c. is the correct answer. (video lesson, segment 2; objective 9)

11. c. is the correct answer. (video lesson, segment 2; objective 9)

    a. & b. are incorrect. These are psychoanalytic approaches to treating psychological problems.

    d. is incorrect. Learning theorists generally do not recommend the use of punishment.

12. a. is the correct answer. These behaviors are typical of infants in the sensorimotor stage. (video lesson, segment 2; objective 11)

b., c., & d. are incorrect. These are typical of older children.

13. a. is the correct answer. (video lesson, segment 2; objective 11)

b. is incorrect. The sensorimotor stage describes development from birth until age 2.

c. is incorrect. This is a psychoanalytic stage described by Freud.

d. is incorrect. This is not the name of a stage; "psychosocial" refers to Erikson's stage theory.

14. a. is the correct answer. (objective 11)

b. is incorrect. This describes disequilibrium.

c. is incorrect. This is formal operational thinking.

d. is incorrect. Piaget's theory does not propose stages of information processing.

15. c. is the correct answer. (video lesson, segment 2; objective 8)

a. & b. are incorrect. Teaching your dog in this way is an example of operant, rather than classical (respondent), conditioning.

d. is incorrect. Modeling involves learning by imitating others.

16. b. is the correct answer. (objective 11)

a. is incorrect. Assimilation occurs when new experiences do not clash with existing ideas.

c. is incorrect. Cognitive equilibrium is mental balance, which occurs when ideas and experiences do not clash.

d. is incorrect. This is Vygotsky's term for the process by which a mentor engages a child in shared learning activities.

17. d. is the correct answer. (objectives 13 & 15)

a. is incorrect. This is a common criticism of psychoanalytic theory.

b. is incorrect. This is a common criticism of learning theory.

c. is incorrect. This is a common criticism of psychoanalytic and cognitive theories that describe development as occurring in a sequence of stages.

18. c. is the correct answer. (objective 13)

19. a. is the correct answer. (video lesson, segment 2; objective 9)

b. is incorrect. This answer would have been correct had the question read "Response is to stimulus as…"

c & d. are incorrect. Nature and nurture refer to internal and external influences on development, respectively.

20. d. is the correct answer. (objective 2)

21. a. is the correct answer. (objective 2)

22. c. is the correct answer. (objective 2)

23. a. is the correct answer. (objective 1)

True or False Items

24. T (video lesson, segment 2; objective 9)

25. T (video lesson, segment 2; objective 8)

26. F Although most developmentalists believe that nature and nurture interact in shaping development, the practical implications of whether nature or nurture plays a greater role in certain abilities keep the controversy alive. (video lesson, introduction; objective 1)

27. T   This is information processing by definition. (objective 13)

28. F   The humanists see human beings as being inherently good. (objective 14)

29. F   On the contrary, disequilibrium often fosters greater growth. (objective 11)

30. T   (video lesson, segment 2; objective 11)

31. F   The hallmark of Piaget's theory is that, at every age, individuals think about the world in unique ways. (video lesson, segment 2; objective 11)

32. T   (video lesson, segment 3; objective 15)

Applying Your Knowledge

1. c. is the correct answer. (objective 3)

   a. & d. are incorrect. These pertain to the cognitive domain.

   b. is incorrect. This pertains to the biosocial domain.

2. c. is the correct answer. (video lesson, segment 1; objective 4)

   a. is incorrect. Piaget is notable in the area of cognitive development.

   b. is incorrect. Freud was a pioneer of psychoanalysis.

   d. is incorrect. Skinner is notable in the history of learning theory.

3. b. is the correct answer. (video lesson, segment 1; objective 4)

   a., c., & d. are incorrect. These are the three domains of development.

4. a. is the correct answer. (objective 6)

5. a. is the correct answer. (objective 14)

   b. is incorrect. This term describes the confusion that may happen during a new experience.

   c. & d. are incorrect. These terms describe the processes by which cognitive concepts incorporate (assimilate) new experiences or are revamped (accommodated) by them.

6. a. is the correct answer. This is an example of operant conditioning because a response recurs due to its consequences. (video lesson, segment 2; objective 9)

   b. & d. are incorrect. In classical conditioning, the individual learns to associate a neutral stimulus with a meaningful stimulus.

   c. is incorrect. In modeling, learning occurs through the observation of others, rather than through direct exposure to reinforcing consequences, as in this example.

7. d. is the correct answer. (objective 13)

   a. is incorrect. The terms are reversed.

   b. is incorrect. These terms refer to behaviorism.

   c. is incorrect. These terms refer to sociocultural learning.

8. b. is the correct answer. (objective 13)

   a. & c. are incorrect. These are both examples of modeling.

   d. is incorrect. Guided participation involves the coaching of a mentor. In this example, Kyle is simply following written directions.

9. a. is the correct answer. (objective 11)

   b. is incorrect. Because the dog is not furry, the child's concept of dog cannot incorporate (assimilate) the discrepant experience without being revamped.

c. & d. are incorrect. Equilibrium exists when ideas (such as what a dog is) and experiences (such as seeing a hairless dog) do not clash.

10. d. is the correct answer. (video lesson, segment 2; objective 8)

11. b. is the correct answer. Evidently, Jennie has learned by observing the other children at play. (video lesson, segment 2; objective 10)

    a. is incorrect. Classical conditioning is concerned with the association of stimuli, not with complex responses, as in this example.

    c. is incorrect. The apprenticeship in thinking involves the interaction of a mentor and a child.

    d. is incorrect. Reinforcement is a process for getting a response to recur.

12. c. is the correct answer. (video lesson, segment 2; objective 11)

13. d. is the correct answer. When Bjorn experiences something that conflicts with his existing understanding, he experiences disequilibrium. (objective 11)

    a. is incorrect. Conservation is the ability to recognize that objects do not change when their appearances change.

    b. is incorrect. Cognition refers to all mental activities associated with thinking.

    c. is incorrect. If Bjorn's thinking were in equilibrium, all men would be "dad"!

14. a. is the correct answer. (objective 1)

    b. & c. are incorrect. Infant social reflexes and adult caregiving impulses occur in all cultures (b), which indicates that they are the product of nature rather than nurture (c).

    d. is incorrect. The textbook does not address the issue of gender differences in infant reflexes or caregiving impulses.

15. d. is the correct answer. (objective 13)

16. b. is the correct answer. (video lesson, segment 2; objective 8)

    a. is incorrect. According to Erikson, this crisis concerns younger children.

    c. & d. are incorrect. In Erikson's theory, these crises concern older children.

17. c. is the correct answer. (video lesson, segment 3; objective 15)

    a., b., & d. are incorrect. These are three of the many theoretical perspectives upon which someone working from an eclectic perspective might draw.

18. d. is the correct answer. (video lesson, segment 2; objectives 6 & 9)

    a., b., & c. are incorrect. Each of these theories emphasizes that development is a discontinuous process that occurs in stages.

19. b. is the correct answer. (objective 14)

20. a. is the correct answer. (objective 14)

Lesson Review

Lesson 1

Introduction
Theories of Development

Please Note: Use this matrix to guide your study and achieve the learning objectives of this lesson. It will also help you to view the video, which defines and demonstrates important concepts and skills as they relate to everyday life.

Learning Objective	Textbook	Course Student Guide	Video Lesson
1. Discuss the role genes play in the nature–nurture debate, their role in developmental timing, and genetic vulnerability.	pp. 5–7	Key Terms: 2, 3, 4, 5; Practice Questions I: 6, 16, 23, 26, 30, 33; Practice Questions II: 23, 26; Applying Your Knowledge: 14.	Introduction
2. Define the life-span perspective of development, and identify five characteristics or principles of development.	pp. 10–18	Key Terms: 1, 6, 7, 16; Practice Questions I: 1; Practice Questions II: 2, 20, 21, 22.	Segment 3: *The Life-Span Perspective*
3. Identify and describe the three domains into which human development is often separated.	pp. 15–16	Key Terms: 13, 14, 15, 16; Practice Questions I: 2, 3, 4; Applying Your Knowledge: 1.	
4. Describe the ecological-systems approach human development, and explain how this approach leads to an understanding of the overlapping contexts in which people develop.	pp. 11–12	Key Terms: 6, 8, 11, 12; Practice Questions I: 5, 7, 8; Practice Questions II: 1, 3; Applying Your Knowledge: 2, 3.	Segment 1: *Contexts and Systems*
5. Discuss the three broad, overlapping contexts that affect development throughout the life span.	pp. 12–15	Key Terms: 9, 10; Practice Questions I: 9; Practice Questions II: 1, 4.	
6. Define developmental theory, and describe how developmental theories help explain human behavior and development.	pp. 33–36, 56–57	Key Terms: 17; Practice Questions I: 10; Applying Your Knowledge: 4, 18.	

Learning Objective	Textbook	Course Student Guide	Video Lesson
7. Discuss the major focus of psychoanalytic theories, and describe the conflicts that occur during Freud's stages of psychosexual development.	pp. 36–37, 39	Key Terms: 18; Practice Questions I: 11, 12, 25; Practice Questions II: 6.	Segment 2: Theories in Development
8. Describe the crises of Erikson's theory of psychosocial development, and contrast them with Freud's stages.	pp. 37–38	Practice Questions I: 13; Practice Questions II: 8, 15, 25; Applying Your Knowledge: 10, 16.	Segment 2: Theories in Development
9. Discuss the major focus of behaviorism, and explain the basic principles of classical and operant conditioning.	pp. 39–41	Key Terms: 19, 20, 21, 22, 23, 24; Practice Questions I: 14, 15, 27, 32; Practice Questions II: 9, 10, 11, 19, 24; Applying Your Knowledge: 6, 18.	Segment 2: Theories in Development
10. Discuss social learning theory as an extension of learning theory.	pp. 41–42	Key Terms: 24, 25, 26; Practice Questions I: 17, 28, 34; Practice Questions II: 7; Applying Your Knowledge: 11.	Segment 2: Theories in Development
11. Identify the primary focus of cognitive theory, and briefly describe Piaget's stages of cognitive development as well as the process that, according to Piaget, guides human development.	pp. 45–47	Key Terms: 27, 28; Practice Questions I: 20, 21, 29; Practice Questions II: 12, 13, 14, 16, 29, 30, 31; Applying Your Knowledge: 9, 12, 13.	Segment 2: Theories in Development
12. Explain what is meant by information processing and how it can be applied to the study of human development.	pp. 47–48	Key Terms: 29; Practice Questions I: 24.	
13. Discuss the basic ideas of Vygotsky and the sociocultural theory of development.	pp. 48–51	Key Terms: 30, 31, 32 Practice Questions I: 22, 31; Practice Questions II: 17, 18, 27; Applying Your Knowledge: 7, 8, 15.	
14. Discuss the universal perspective, and describe the difference between humanism and evolutionary theory.	pp. 51–56	Key Terms: 33, 34; Practice Questions I: 18, 19, 35; Practice Questions II: 5, 28; Applying Your Knowledge: 5, 19, 20.	
15. Summarize the contributions and criticisms of the major developmental theories, and explain the eclectic perspective of contemporary developmentalists.	pp. 56-57	Key Terms: 35; Practice Questions II: 17, 32; Applying Your Knowledge: 17.	

A Scientific Approach

Lesson 2

Developmental Study as a Science

Preview

The scientific study of human development is the science that seeks to understand how and why people change with increasing age, and how and why they remain the same. Central to this science is the set of principles and procedures scientists use to produce the most objective results possible. Lesson 2 discusses these principles and procedures, beginning with the **scientific method** and including **scientific observation**, correlational research, **experiments**, and **surveys**. To study people over time, developmentalists have created several research designs: cross-sectional, longitudinal, and cross-sequential. As these methods are described, several classic developmental psychology studies are summarized.

The final section of the lesson discusses the ethics of research with humans. In addition to ensuring confidentiality and safety, developmentalists who study children are especially concerned that the benefits of research outweigh the risks.

Prior Course Knowledge that Will Be Used in this Lesson

This course lesson focuses primarily on research methods, drawing on material from each of the three domains of development. Recall from Chapter 1 that the three domains of development include the biosocial domain (brain and body as well as changes in them and the social influences that guide them), the cognitive domain (thought processes, perceptual abilities, and language mastery, as well as the educational institutions that encourage them), and the psychosocial domain (emotions, personality, and interpersonal relationships with family, friends, and the wider community). All three domains are important at every age, and each of the domains is affected by the other two.

Learning Objectives

Use this information to guide your reading, viewing, thinking, and studying. After successfully completing this lesson, you should be able to:

1. List and describe the basic steps of the scientific method.
2. Describe scientific observation and correlation as research strategies, noting at least one advantage (or strength) and one disadvantage (or weakness) of each.
3. Describe the components of an experiment, and discuss the main advantage and some of the limitations of this research method.
4. Describe surveys and case studies, noting at least one advantage (or strength) and one disadvantage (or weakness) of each.
5. Describe three basic research designs used by developmental psychologists.
6. Distinguish between quantitative and qualitative research, and discuss the strengths and weaknesses of each.
7. Discuss the code of ethics that should be followed by researchers in the field of developmental psychology.

📖 **Read Chapter 1, "Introduction," pages 4–5 (The Scientific Method), and pages 19–30.**

⏮ **View the video for Lesson 2, "A Scientific Approach."**

Segment 1: *The Scientific Method*

Segment 2: *Research Methods*

Segment 3: *Studying Changes over Time*

Summary

The **scientific method** consists of five basic steps: (1) formulate a research question, (2) develop a **hypothesis**, (3) test the hypothesis, (4) draw conclusions, and (5) make the findings available. **Replication** of research findings verifies the findings and leads researchers to more definitive and extensive conclusions.

Because the variables in research are numerous, it is difficult to determine whether all the relevant ones have been identified in a particular investigation. Developmentalists deal with both intrapersonal variation, which occurs from day to day in each person, and interpersonal variation, which occurs between people or groups.

In designing research, scientists are concerned with four issues: validity, accuracy, generalizability, and usefulness. There are many ways to test hypotheses. One method is **scientific observation** of people in their natural environment or in a laboratory setting. Observation is limited in that it tells us only if two variables are correlated.

Correlation is a statistical term indicating that two variables are related, or vary together. **Experiments** can reveal cause-and-effect relationships by allowing experimenters to observe whether a change in an **independent variable** affects some specific behavior, or **dependent variable**. Experiments are not, however, without their limitations. Even if subjects behave normally in an experiment, their performance may not be applicable to the real world.

The scientific **survey** is especially vulnerable to bias: the phrasing of the questions may affect the responses obtained; people may give answers they think the researcher wants to hear or the answers they think will make them look a certain way in the researcher's eyes.

In **cross-sectional research**, groups of people who are different in age but similar in all other important ways are compared on the characteristic that is of interest to the researcher(s). One limitation of cross-sectional research is that it is always possible that some variable other than age differentiates the groups. In **longitudinal research**, the same people are studied over a period of time. Longitudinal research is particularly useful in studying developmental trends that occur over a long age span.

Both longitudinal and cross-sectional researchers must bear in mind that research on a single cohort may not be valid for people developing in an earlier or later cohort. In **cross-sequential research**, several groups of people at different ages (cross-sectional component) are followed over time (longitudinal component).

There are some cautions when conducting scientific research. One is that, while correlation shows a relationship, it doesn't necessarily mean one variable causes the other. Another is to consider the strengths and weakness of the type of data that has been gathered. Quantitative data fits neatly into categories and statistical analysis, but may miss subtleties. Qualitative data is effective in situations of diversity and complexity, but is vulnerable to personal bias and is hard to replicate.

Another caution is ethics—when studying people, scientists take special care to ensure that participation is voluntary and harmless and that the study's benefits outweigh its costs. Sometimes scientists conduct a meta-analysis, or a compilation of data from many other sources, so that no participants are directly involved.

📖　　**Review all reading assignments for this lesson.**

💻　　**As assigned by your instructor, complete the optional online component for this lesson.**

Key Terms

Using your own words, write a brief definition or explanation of each of the following terms on a separate piece of paper.

1. empirical
2. scientific method
3. replication
4. cohort
5. scientific observation
6. experiment
7. independent variable
8. dependent variable
9. experimental group
10. comparison group
11. survey
12. cross-sectional research
13. longitudinal research
14. cross-sequential research
15. correlation
16. code of ethics
17. Instructional Review Board (IRB)
18. quantitative research
19. qualitative research
20. hypothesis
21. variable
22. attachment
23. the Strange Situation
24. random assignment

Practice Questions I

Multiple-Choice Questions

1. The scientific study of human development is defined as the study of
   a. how and why people change or remain the same over time.
   b. psychosocial influences on aging.
   c. individual differences in learning over the life span.
   d. all of the above.

2. A hypothesis is a
   a. conclusion.
   b. prediction to be tested.
   c. statistical test.
   d. correlation.

3. In an experiment testing the effects of group size on individual effort in a tug-of-war task, the number of people in each group is the
   a. hypothesis.
   b. independent variable.
   c. dependent variable.
   d. level of significance.

4. Which research method would be most appropriate for investigating the relationship between parents' religious beliefs and their attitudes toward middle school sex education?
   a. experimentation
   b. longitudinal research
   c. naturalistic observation
   d. the survey

5. Developmentalists who carefully observe the behavior of schoolchildren during recess are using a research method known as
   a. a longitudinal study.
   b. cross-sectional research.
   c. scientific observation.
   d. cross-sequential research.

6. In an experiment to determine the effects of attention on memory, memory is the
   a. control condition.
   b. intervening variable.
   c. independent variable.
   d. dependent variable.

7. The emotional tie that develops between an infant and his or her primary caregiver is called
   a. self-awareness.
   b. synchrony.
   c. affiliation.
   d. attachment.

8. Harry Harlow found that when monkeys were reared in social isolation, they would seek
   a. contact comfort as much as nourishment.
   b. nourishment over contact comfort.
   c. the company of other monkeys that had been socially isolated.
   d. no food, water, or nourishment of any kind.

9. If shoe size and IQ are negatively correlated, which of the following is true?
   a. People with large feet tend to have high IQs.
   b. People with small feet tend to have high IQs.
   c. People with small feet tend to have low IQs.
   d. IQ is unpredictable based on a person's shoe size.

10. To protect participants, scientists who study human development are bound by
    a. a code of ethics.
    b. a code of honor.
    c. a chain of bonds.
    d. none of the above.

11. A study using numerical data that can be analyzed using statistical methods is called
    a. qualitative research.
    b. correlation.
    c. replication.
    d. quantitative research.

12. When conducting a qualitative study, a researcher must be aware of
    a. the possible influence of personal bias when gathering the data.
    b. the need for a control or comparison group.
    c. the desire for results that are significant.
    d. the necessity that cohorts should be in the same group.

Matching Items
Match each definition or description with its corresponding term.

Terms
13. ___F___ cross-sequential
14. ___C___ correlation
15. ___G___ scientific observation
16. ___B___ hypothesis

17. ___A___ scientific method
18. ___E___ cross-sectional
19. ___D___ longitudinal research

Definitions or Descriptions
a. a general procedural model that helps researchers remain objective
b. a testable prediction regarding development
c. a statistical measure of relationship between two variables
d. research study retesting one group of people at several different times
e. research study comparing people of different ages at the same time
f. research study that follows groups of people of different ages over time
g. unobtrusively watching and recording of the behavior of a group of research subjects

Practice Questions II

Multiple-Choice Questions

1. Professor Cohen predicts that because "baby boomers" grew up in an era that promoted independence and assertiveness, people in their 40s and 50s will respond differently to a political survey than will people in their 20s and 30s. The professor's prediction regarding political attitudes is an example of a(n)

   a. meta-analysis.
   b. hypothesis.
   c. independent variable.
   d. dependent variable.

2. A cohort is defined as a group of people

   a. of similar national origin.
   b. who share a common language.
   c. born within a few years of each other.
   d. who share the same religion.

3. In a test of the effects of noise, groups of students performed a proofreading task in a noisy or a quiet room. To what group were students in the noisy room assigned?

   a. experimental
   b. control
   c. randomly assigned
   d. dependent

4. If developmentalists discovered that poor people are happier than wealthy people are, this would indicate that wealth and happiness are
   a. unrelated.
   b. positively correlated.
   c. negatively correlated.
   d. causally related.

5. In an experiment testing the effects of noise level on mood, mood is the
   a. hypothesis.
   b. independent variable.
   c. dependent variable.
   d. scientific observation.

6. Which of the following research strategies would be best for determining whether alcohol causes impairments to memory?
   a. case study
   b. observation
   c. survey
   d. experiment

7. Well-conducted surveys measure attitudes using _____ phrasing.
   a. random
   b. experimental
   c. highly controlled
   d. unbiased

8. Which of the following research methods does **NOT** belong with the others?
   a. case study
   b. survey
   c. experiment
   d. observation

9. Repeating a study, using the same procedures on another group of participants, to verify or refute the original study's conclusions is called
   a. variable controlling.
   b. replication.
   c. representative sampling.
   d. stratification.

10. In a test of the effects of noise, groups of students performed a proofreading task in a noisy or a quiet room. To what condition were students in the quiet room exposed?
   a. experimental
   b. comparison
   c. randomly assigned
   d. dependent

11. The Instructional Review Board (IRB)
    a. decides if a study should be published.
    b. hires researchers to conduct studies.
    c. ensures that a code of ethics is followed during research.
    d. decides what studies should be replicated.

Matching Items

Match each definition or description with its corresponding term.

Terms

12. _____F_____ independent variable   16. _____C_____ experimental group
13. _____H_____ dependent variable   17. _____B_____ comparison group
14. _____G_____ experiment   18. _____A_____ quantitative research
15. _____E_____ replicate   19. _____D_____ survey

Definitions or Descriptions

    a. a study that gathers numerical data
    b. the "treatment-absent" condition in an experiment
    c. the "treatment-present" condition in an experiment
    d. the research strategy in which a representative sample of individuals is questioned
    e. to repeat an experiment to check the reliability of its results
    f. the variable manipulated in an experiment
    g. to test a hypothesis in a controlled situation
    h. the variable measured in an experiment

Applying Your Knowledge

1. When researchers find that the results of a study are statistically significant, this means
    a. they may have been caused purely by chance.
    b. it is unlikely they could be replicated.
    c. it is unlikely they could have occurred by chance.
    d. that the sample population was representative of the general population.

2. If height and weight are correlated, which of the following is true?
    a. There is a cause-and-effect relationship between height and weight.
    b. A person's height is related to his or her weight.
    c. Height and weight are completely unrelated.
    d. None of the above statements are true.

3. To study the effects of temperature on mood, Dr. Sanchez had students fill out questionnaires in very warm or very cool rooms. What was the independent variable?

   a. the number of subjects assigned to each group

   b. the students' responses to the questionnaire

   c. the room temperature

   d. the subject matter of the questions

4. Esteban believes that high doses of caffeine slow a person's reaction time. To test his belief, he has five friends each drink three 8-ounce cups of coffee and then measures their reaction time on a learning task. What is wrong with Esteban's research strategy?

   a. No independent variable is specified.

   b. No dependent variable is specified.

   c. There is no control condition.

   d. There is no provision for replication of the findings.

5. Which of the following is an example of longitudinal research?

   a. A researcher compares how many different age groups perform on a memory test.

   b. A researcher compares how the same group of people, at different ages, performs on a test of memory.

   c. An investigator compares the performance of an experimental group and a control group of subjects on a memory test.

   d. A researcher compares the performance of several different age groups on a test of memory as each group is tested repeatedly over a period of years.

6. For her developmental psychology research project, Lakia decides she wants to conduct lengthy interviews with seniors who have recently lost their spouses. Her research project is

   a. quantitative research.

   b. an experiment.

   c. unethical.

   d. qualitative research.

7. Dr. Weston is comparing research findings for a group of 30-year-olds with findings for the same individuals at age 20, as well as with findings for groups who were 30 in 1990. Which research method is she using?

   a. longitudinal research

   b. cross-sectional research

   c. case study

   d. cross-sequential research

8. A psychologist studies the play behavior of third-grade children by watching groups during recess at school. Which research technique is being used?

   a. correlation

   b. case study

   c. experimentation

   d. naturalistic observation

Answer Key

Key Terms

1. Information is considered empirical when it is based on scientific data from experiments, surveys, and other research methods. (p. 4; objective 1)

2. The scientific method is a general procedural model that helps researchers remain objective as they study behavior. The five basic steps of the scientific method are (1) formulate a research question; (2) develop a hypothesis; (3) test the hypothesis; (4) draw conclusions; and (5) make the findings available. (p. 4; video lesson, segment 1; objective 1)

3. To replicate a test of a research hypothesis is to repeat it and obtain the same results using a different but related set of subjects or procedures in order to test its validity. (p. 4; objective 1)

4. A cohort is a group of people who, because they were born within a few years of each other, experience many of the same historical and social conditions. (p. 12; video lesson, segment 3; objective 5)

5. Scientific observation is the unobtrusive watching and recording of subjects' behavior in a situation that is being studied, either in the laboratory or in a natural setting. (p. 19; video lesson, segment 2; objective 2)

6. The experiment is the research method in which an investigator tests a hypothesis in a controlled situation in which the relevant variables are limited and can be manipulated by the experimenter. (p. 20; video lesson, segment 2; objective 3)

7. The independent variable is the variable that is manipulated in an experiment. (p. 20; video lesson, segment 2; objective 3)

8. The dependent variable is the variable that is being studied in an experiment. (p. 20; video lesson, segment 2; objective 3)

   Example: In the study of the effects of a new drug on memory, the subjects' memory is the dependent variable.

9. The experimental group of an experiment is one in which subjects are exposed to the independent variable being studied. (p. 20; video lesson, segment 2; objective 3)

10. The comparison group (also known as control group) of an experiment is one in which the treatment of interest, or independent variable, is withheld so that comparison to the experimental group can be made. (p. 20; video lesson, segment 2; objective 3)

11. The scientific survey is the research method in which information is collected from a large number of people, either through written questionnaires or through interviews. (p. 21; video lesson, segment 2; objective 4)

12. In cross-sectional research, groups of people who differ in age but share other important characteristics are compared with regard to the variable under investigation. (pp. 21–22; video lesson, segment 3; objective 5)

13. In longitudinal research, the same group of individuals is studied over a period of time to measure both change and stability as they age. (p. 22; video lesson, segment 3; objective 5)

14. Cross-sequential research follows a group of people of different ages over time, thus combining the strengths of the cross-sectional and longitudinal methods. (p. 25; objective 5)

15. Correlation is a statistical term that merely indicates whether two variables are related to each other such that one is likely (or unlikely) to occur when the other occurs or one is likely to increase (or decrease) when the other increases (or decreases). (p. 26; video lesson, segment 2; objective 2)

16. Developmental psychologists and other scientists work from a code of ethics, which is a set of moral principles that guides their research. (p. 27; video lesson, segment 3; objective 7)

17. The Instructional Review Board (IRB) is a group that exists within most educational and medical institutions to ensure that research follows established guidelines and remains ethical. (p. 27; objective 7)

18. Quantitative research is research that provides data that can be expressed with numbers, such as ranks or scales. (p. 27; objective 6)

19. Qualitative research is research that considers qualities instead of quantities. Descriptions of particular conditions and participants' expressed ideas are often part of qualitative studies. (p. 27; objective 6)

20. In the scientific method, a hypothesis is a specific, testable prediction regarding development. (p. 4; video lesson, segment 1; objective 1)

21. A variable is any quantity, characteristic, or action that can take on different values within a group of individuals or a single individual. (video lesson, segment 2; objective 3)

22. Attachment refers to the relationship between an infant and his or her caregiver. (video lesson, segment 1; objective 5)

23. The Strange Situation is a laboratory research procedure used to measure an infant's attachment to his or her caregiver. (video lesson, segment 2; objective 5)

24. Random assignment is the procedure of assigning participants to the experimental and control conditions of an experiment by chance in order to minimize preexisting differences between the groups. (video lesson, segment 2; objective 3)

Practice Questions I

Multiple-Choice Questions

1. a. is the correct answer. (video lesson, introduction; objective 2)

   b. & c. are incorrect. The study of development is concerned with a broader range of phenomena, including biosocial aspects of development, than these answers specify.

2. b. is the correct answer. (video lesson, segment 1; objective 1)

3. b. is the correct answer. (video lesson, segment 2; objective 3)

   a. is incorrect. A possible hypothesis for this experiment would be that the larger the group, the less hard a given individual will pull.

   c. is incorrect. The dependent variable is the measure of individual effort.

   d. is incorrect. Significance level refers to the numerical value specifying the possibility that the results of an experiment could have occurred by chance.

4. d. is the correct answer. (video lesson, segment 2; objective 4)

   a. is incorrect. Experimentation is appropriate when one is seeking to uncover cause-and-effect relationships; in this example, the researcher is only interested in determining whether the parents' beliefs predict their attitudes. Experimenters cannot manipulate religious beliefs.

   b. is incorrect. Longitudinal research would be appropriate if the researcher sought to examine the development of these attitudes over a long period of time.

   c. is incorrect. Mere observation would not allow the researcher to determine the attitudes of the subjects.

5. c. is the correct answer. (video lesson, segment 2; objective 2)

   a. is incorrect. In this method, a group of subjects is studied over a period of time.

   b. & d. are incorrect. In these research methods, two or more groups of subjects are studied and compared.

6. d. is the correct answer. (video lesson, segment 2; objective 3)

   a. is incorrect. The control condition is the comparison group, in which the experimental treatment is absent.

   b. is incorrect. Memory is the dependent variable in this experiment.

   c. is incorrect. Attention is the independent variable, which is being manipulated.

7. d. is the correct answer. (video lesson, segment 1; objective 5)

   a. is incorrect. Self-awareness refers to the infant's developing sense of "me and mine."

   b. is incorrect. Synchrony, which will be discussed in a later lesson, describes the coordinated inaction between infant and caregiver.

   c. is incorrect. Affiliation describes the tendency of people at any age to seek the companionship of others.

8. a. is the correct answer. (video lesson, segment 1; objective 5)

9. b. is the correct answer. (video lesson, segment 2; objective 2)

   a. & c. are incorrect. These answers would have been correct had the question stated that there is a *positive* correlation between shoe size and IQ. Actually, there is probably no correlation at all!

10. a. is the correct answer. (objective 7)

11. d. is the correct answer. (objective 6)

    a. is incorrect. It refers to narrative data that is used for descriptive studies.

    b. is incorrect. Correlation is a way to analyze quantitative data, not a type of study.

    c. is incorrect. Replication refers to repeating a study to see if it will yield a similar conclusion.

12. a. is the correct answer. (objective 6)

    b., c., & d. are incorrect. They are associated with quantitative, not qualitative, studies.

Matching Items

13. f (objective 5)
14. c (video lesson, segment 2; objective 2)
15. g (video lesson, segment 2; objective 2)
16. b (video lesson, segment 1; objective 1)
17. a (video lesson, segment 1; objective 1)
18. e (video lesson, segment 3; objective 5)
19. d (video lesson, segment 3; objective 5)

Practice Questions II

Multiple-Choice Questions

1. b. is the correct answer. (video lesson, segment 1; objective 1)

   a. is incorrect. In a meta-analysis, the results of a number of separate research studies are combined.

   c. & d. are incorrect. Variables are treatments (independent) or behaviors (dependent) in experiments, which this situation clearly is not.

2. c. is the correct answer. (video lesson, segment 3; objective 5)

   a., b., & d. are incorrect. These are attributes of an ethnic group.

3. a. is the correct answer. The experimental group is the one in which the variable or treatment—in this case, noise—is present. (video lesson, segment 2; objective 3)

   b. is incorrect. Students in the quiet room would be in the control condition.

   c. is incorrect. Presumably, all students in both groups were randomly assigned to their groups.

   d. is incorrect. The word *dependent* refers to a kind of variable in experiments; groups are either experimental or control.

4. c. is the correct answer. (video lesson, segment 2; objective 2)

   a. is incorrect. Wealth and happiness clearly are related.

   b. is incorrect. This answer would be correct if wealthy people were found to be happier than poor people.

   d. is incorrect. Correlation does not imply causation.

5. c. is the correct answer. (video lesson, segment 2; objective 3)

   a. is incorrect. Hypotheses make specific, testable predictions.

   b. is incorrect. Noise level is the independent variable.

   d. is incorrect. Scientific observation is a research method in which subjects are watched, while their behavior is recorded unobtrusively.

6. d. is the correct answer. In an experiment, it would be possible to manipulate alcohol consumption and observe the effects, if any, on memory. (video lesson, segment 2; objective 3)

   a., b., & c. are incorrect because only by directly controlling the variables of interest can a researcher uncover cause-and-effect relationships.

7. d. is the correct answer (objective 4)

8. c. is the correct answer. Only experiments can reveal cause-and-effect relationships; the other methods can only describe relationships. (video lesson, segment 2; objectives 2 & 3)

9. b. is the correct answer. (video lesson, segment 2; objective 3)

   a., c., & d. are incorrect. None of these terms describes precautions taken in setting up groups for experiments.

10. b. is the correct answer. The comparison condition is the one in which the treatment—in this case, noise—is absent. (video lesson, segment 2; objective 3)

    a. is incorrect. Students in the noisy room would be in the experimental condition.

    c. is incorrect. Presumably, all students in both groups were randomly assigned. Random assignment is a method for establishing groups, rather than a condition.

    d. is incorrect. The word "dependent" refers to a kind of variable in experiments; conditions are either experimental or comparison.

11. c. is the correct answer. (objective 7)

    a., b., & d. are incorrect. Other entities make these decisions.

Matching Items

12. f (video lesson, segment 2; objective 3)

13. h (video lesson, segment 2; objective 3)

14. g (video lesson, segment 2; objective 3)

15. e (objective 1)

16. c (video lesson, segment 2; objective 3)

Lesson 2/Developmental Study as a Science

17. b (video lesson, segment 2; objective 3)
18. a (objective 6)
19. d (video lesson, segment 2; objective 4)

Applying Your Knowledge

1. c. is the correct answer. (objective 1)
2. b. is the correct answer. (video lesson, segment 2; objective 2)
3. c. is the correct answer. (video lesson, segment 2; objective 3)
4. c. is the correct answer. In order to determine the effects of caffeine on reaction time, Esteban needs to measure reaction time in a control, or comparison, group that does not receive caffeine. (video lesson, segment 2; objective 3)

   a. is incorrect. Caffeine is the independent variable.

   b. is incorrect. Reaction time is the dependent variable.

   d. is incorrect. Whether or not Esteban's experiment can be replicated is determined by the precision with which he reports his procedures, which is not an aspect of research strategy.
5. b. is the correct answer. (video lesson, segment 3; objective 5)

   a. is incorrect. This is an example of cross-sectional research.

   c. is incorrect. This is an example of an experiment.

   d. is incorrect. This type of study is not described in the textbook.
6. d. is the correct answer. (objective 6)
7. d. is the correct answer. (objective 5)

   a. & c. are incorrect. In these research methods, only one group of subjects is studied.

   b. is incorrect. Dr. Weston's design includes comparison of groups of people of different ages over time.
8. d. is the correct answer. (video lesson, segment 2; objective 2)

Lesson Review

Lesson 2

Developmental Study as a Science

Please Note: Use this matrix to guide your study and achieve the learning objectives of this lesson. It will also help you to view the video, which defines and demonstrates important concepts and skills as they relate to everyday life.

Learning Objective	Textbook	Course Student Guide	Video Lesson
1. List and describe the basic steps of the scientific method.	pp. 4–5	Key Terms: 1, 2, 3, 20; Practice Questions I: 2, 16, 17; Practice Questions II: 1, 15; Applying Your Knowledge: 1.	Segment 1: *The Scientific Method*
2. Describe scientific observation and correlation as research strategies, noting at least one advantage (or strength) and one disadvantage (or weakness) of each.	pp. 19–20, 26–27	Key Terms: 5, 15; Practice Questions I: 1, 5, 9, 14, 15; Practice Questions II: 4, 8; Applying Your Knowledge: 2, 8.	Introduction Segment 2: *Research Methods*
3. Describe the components of an experiment, and discuss the main advantage and some of the limitations of this research method.	p. 20	Key Terms: 6, 7, 8, 9, 10, 21, 24; Practice Questions I: 3, 6; Practice Questions II: 3, 5, 6, 8, 9, 10, 12, 13, 14, 16, 17; Applying Your Knowledge: 3, 4.	Segment 2: *Research Methods*
4. Describe surveys and case studies, noting at least one advantage (or strength) and one disadvantage (or weakness) of each.	p. 21	Key Terms: 11; Practice Questions I: 4; Practice Questions II: 7, 19.	Segment 2: *Research Methods*
5. Describe three basic research designs used by developmental psychologists.	pp. 21–25	Key Terms: 4, 12, 13, 14, 22, 23; Practice Questions I: 7, 8, 13, 18, 19; Practice Questions II: 2; Applying Your Knowledge: 5, 7.	Segment 1: *The Scientific Method* Segment 2: *Research Methods* Segment 3: *Studying Changes over Time*

Learning Objective	Textbook	Course Student Guide	Video Lesson
6. Distinguish between quantitative and qualitative research, and discuss the strengths and weaknesses of each.	p. 27	Key Terms: 18, 19; Practice Questions I: 11, 12; Practice Questions II: 18; Applying Your Knowledge: 6.	
7. Discuss the code of ethics that should be followed by researchers in the field of developmental psychology.	pp. 27–29	Key Terms: 16, 17; Practice Questions I: 10 Practice Questions II: 11.	

Nature and Nurture: The Dance of Life

Lesson 3

The Beginnings:
Heredity and Environment

Preview

Much is determined at the moment of conception, when a sperm and ovum unite to initiate the developmental processes that will culminate in the birth of a new human being. The genetic legacies of the mother and father influence virtually everything about the developing person—including physical attributes, such as gender and appearance, as well as intellectual and personality characteristics.

Lesson 3 describes the fusion of the ovum and the sperm and the biological mechanisms by which normal, and sometimes abnormal, **chromosomes** and **genes** are transmitted to the developing person. The reading assignment and program emphasize that although the direction a person's life takes is strongly influenced by **heredity**, its ultimate course depends on the interaction of many biological and environmental factors—that is, on both nature and nurture.

Lesson 3 also discusses the benefits of **genetic counseling** for prospective parents who are at risk of giving birth to children with genetic disorders. Prenatal diagnosis of genetic disorders has been greatly facilitated by recent advances in genetic testing techniques, allowing prospective parents to make more informed decisions about the risks of childbearing.

Prior Course Knowledge that Will Be Used in this Lesson

This lesson focuses primarily on the biosocial domain of development. Recall from Chapter 1 that the biosocial domain is the part of human development that includes all the growth and changes that occur in a person's body, and the genetic, nutritional, and health factors that affect that growth and change. Remember, too, that although the division of human development into three domains makes it easier to study, development is holistic rather than piecemeal: Every aspect of human behavior reflects all three domains.

Learning Objectives

Use this information to guide your reading, viewing, thinking, and studying. After successfully completing this lesson, you should be able to:

1. Identify the mechanisms of heredity, and explain how sex is determined.

2. Discuss genetic continuity and diversity, and distinguish between monozygotic and dizygotic twins.

3. Differentiate genotype from phenotype, and explain the polygenic and multifactorial nature of human traits.

4. Explain the additive and nonadditive patterns of genetic interaction, and give examples of the traits that result from each type of interaction.

5. Discuss X-linked genes in terms of genotype and phenotype.

6. Explain how scientists distinguish the effects of genes and environment on development.

7. Identify some environmental variables that affect genetic inheritance, and describe how a particular trait, such as susceptibility to shyness (inhibition) or alcoholism, might be affected.

8. Explain the incidence of gene disorders, and discuss at least three such disorders.

9. Describe five groups of prospective parents who should seek genetic testing and counseling.

10. Explain the major methods of prenatal diagnosis, noting the advantages of each.

📖 **Read Chapter 3, "Heredity and Environment," pages 61–87.**

⏮ **View the video for Lesson 3, "Nature and Nurture: The Dance of Life."**

>> Segment 1: *The Beginning of Development*

>> Segment 2: *The Twin Perspective*

>> Segment 3: *From Genotype to Phenotype*

>> Segment 4: *Genetic and Chromosomal Abnormalities*

Summary

Conception occurs when the male **gamete** (or sperm) penetrates the membrane of the female gamete (the ovum); the gametes then fuse, and their genetic material combines to form the one-celled **zygote**. Within hours, the zygote initiates human development through the processes of duplication and division. Soon after, differentiation begins. Each body cell created from these processes carries an exact copy of the zygote's genetic instructions.

Genes, the basic units of **heredity**, are discrete segments of a **chromosome**, which is a DNA (deoxyribonucleic acid) molecule. Every human body cell, except the sperm and ovum, has 23 pairs of chromosomes (one chromosome in each pair from each parent). The sperm and ovum receive only one member of each chromosome pair when cells divide to produce gametes, and thus have only 23 single chromosomes each. The **twenty-third pair** of chromosomes, which determines sex, is designated **XY** in the male and **XX** in the female. The critical factor in the determination of the zygote's sex is which sperm reaches the ovum first, a Y sperm, creating a boy, or an X sperm, creating a girl.

Approximately once in every 270 pregnancies a single zygote splits into two separate identical cells that develop into genetically identical individuals, or **monozygotic twins**, who have the potential for developing the same physical appearance and psychological characteristics, and the same vulnerability to specific diseases. Dizygotic, or fraternal, twins occur about once in every sixty births. **Dizygotic twins** begin life as two separate zygotes and share no more genes than any other siblings (about 50 percent). The number of multiple births has doubled in many nations because of the increased use of fertility drugs and other methods of helping infertile couples.

Most traits are polygenic—that is, affected by many genes—and multifactorial—that is, influenced by many factors, including environmental factors. **Genotype** refers to the sum total of all the genes a person inherits. **Phenotype** refers to the sum total of all the genes that are actually expressed. In genetic terms, people are **carriers** of their unexpressed genes.

The various genes underlying height and skin color, for example, interact in an additive pattern: The phenotype in question reflects the sum of all the genes involved. Less commonly, genes interact in a nonadditive fashion. Genes that have a controlling influence over weaker, recessive genes are called dominant genes. Hundreds of physical characteristics follow this **dominant–recessive pattern** (a nonadditive pattern). Note that recessive genes are not always completely suppressed by their dominant gene counterparts, an outcome called incomplete dominance.

Many human characteristics are epigenetic; that is, genes do not act alone in the development of those characteristics. Rather, the characteristics encoded in genes develop or fail to develop as the result of outside factors. Certain environmental influences (such as injury, temperature extremes, drug abuse, and crowding) can impede genetic development, whereas others (nourishing food, loving care, and play) can facilitate it. When social scientists discuss the effects of the **environment** on the individual, they are referring to everything that can interact with the person's genetic inheritance at every point of life, from the first prenatal days to the last breath. Environment, as broadly defined, affects every human characteristic.

Scientists use twin research to identify genetic influences because for any given characteristic, if monozygotic twins are much more alike than dizygotic twins, it seems likely that genes play a significant role in the appearance of that trait. Another approach is to compare adopted children with both their biological and adoptive parents. Adopted children, however, are often placed in families that are similar to their birth families; thus, shared culture rather than shared genes may account for similarities. The best way to separate the effects of genes and environment is to study identical twins who have been separated at birth and raised in different families (to control for the fact that identical twins in a given family tend to be treated much more alike than dizygotic twins are).

About 5–10 percent of all zygotes have too few or too many chromosomes. Most are spontaneously aborted. Once in every 200 births, however, a baby is born with a chromosomal abnormality that leads to a recognizable syndrome.

Although most known genetic disorders are dominant, recessive and multifactorial disorders claim many more victims. Among the more common recessive genetic disorders are cystic fibrosis, thalassemia, and sickle-cell anemia. For most of human history, couples at risk for having a child with a genetic problem did not know it. **Genetic counseling** is a means by which couples can learn more about their genes and make informed decisions about childbearing.

Genetic counseling is strongly recommended for individuals who have a parent, sibling, or child with a genetic condition; couples who have a history of spontaneous abortion, stillbirth, or infertility; couples who are from the same ethnic group or subgroup; and women over age 34. Couples who have a high probability of producing a baby with a serious genetic condition have several alternatives— from avoiding pregnancy to adoption to considering abortion. In cases where the consequences of a disease are variable, the decision making is often more difficult.

📖   **Review all reading assignments for this lesson.**

💻   **As assigned by your instructor, complete the optional online component for this lesson.**

Key Terms

Using your own words, write a brief definition or explanation of each of the following terms on a separate piece of paper.

1. DNA (deoxyribonucleic acid)
2. chromosome
3. genes
4. allele
5. genome
6. zygote
7. gamete
8. genotype
9. homozygous
10. heterozygous
11. 23rd pair
12. XX
13. XY
14. stem cells
15. monozygotic (MZ) twins
16. dizygotic (DZ) twins
17. assisted reproductive technology (ART)
18. in vitro fertilization (IVF)
19. phenotype
20. polygenic
21. multifactorial
22. epigenetic
23. Human Genome Project
24. dominant–recessive pattern
25. carrier
26. X-linked gene
27. heritability
28. Down syndrome (trisomy-21)
29. fragile X syndrome
30. genetic counseling
31. phenylketonuria (PKU)
32. dominant gene
33. recessive gene
34. heredity
35. environment
36. amniocentesis
37. gene therapy

Practice Questions I

Multiple-Choice Questions

1. When a sperm and an ovum merge, a one-celled _____ is formed.
   a. zygote
   b. reproductive cell
   c. gamete
   d. monozygote

2. Genes are discrete segments that provide the biochemical instructions that each cell needs to
   a. become a zygote.
   b. maintain its chromosomes.
   c. manufacture a specific protein.
   d. increase its deoxyribonucleic acid.

3. In the male, the twenty-third pair of chromosomes is designated
_____; in the female, this pair is designated _____.
   a. XX; XY
   b. XY; XX
   c. XO; XXY
   d. XXY; XO

4. Since the twenty-third pair of chromosomes in females is XX, each ovum carries an
   a. XX zygote.
   b. X zygote.
   c. XY zygote.
   d. X chromosome.

5. When a zygote splits, the two identical, independent clusters that develop become
   a. dizygotic twins.
   b. monozygotic twins.
   c. fraternal twins.
   d. trizygotic twins.

6. In scientific research, the best way to separate the effects of genes and the environment is to study
   a. dizygotic twins.
   b. adopted children and their biological parents.
   c. adopted children and their adoptive parents.
   d. monozygotic twins raised in different environments.

7. Most of the known genetic disorders are
   a. dominant.
   b. recessive.
   c. seriously disabling.
   d. sex-linked.

8. When we say that a characteristic is multifactorial, we mean that
   a. many genes are involved.
   b. many environmental factors are involved.
   c. many genetic and environmental factors are involved.
   d. the characteristic is polygenic.

9. Genes are segments of molecules of
   a. genotype.
   b. deoxyribonucleic acid (DNA).
   c. karyotype.
   d. phenotype.

10. The potential for genetic diversity in humans is so great because
    a. there are approximately 8 million possible combinations of chromosomes.
    b. when the sperm and ovum unite, genetic combinations not present in either parent can be formed.
    c. just before a chromosome pair divides during the formation of gametes, genes cross over, producing recombinations.
    d. of all the above reasons.

11. A chromosomal abnormality routinely tested for at birth is
    a. the XXY chromosomal pattern.
    b. near-sightedness.
    c. fragile X syndrome.
    d. phenylketonuria (PKU).

12. DNA "junk"
    a. makes people sick.
    b. affects how genes work.
    c. causes genetic disorders.
    d. is composed of proteins.

13. Babies born with trisomy-21 (Down syndrome) are often
    a. born to older parents.
    b. unusually aggressive.
    c. abnormally tall by adolescence.
    d. blind.

14. To say that a trait is polygenic means that
    a. many genes make it more likely that the individual will inherit the trait.
    b. it is influenced by many genes.
    c. the trait is multifactorial.
    d. most people carry genes for the trait.

15. Some genetic diseases are recessive, so the child cannot inherit the condition unless both parents
    a. have Kleinfelter syndrome.
    b. carry the same recessive gene.
    c. have XO chromosomes.
    d. have the disease.

Matching Items

Match each definition or description with its corresponding term.

Terms

16. ___B___ gametes
17. ___G___ chromosome
18. ___A___ genotype
19. ___H___ phenotype
20. ___E___ dizygotic

21. ___F___ epigenetic
22. ___I___ fragile X syndrome
23. ___D___ carrier
24. ___C___ zygote

Definitions or Descriptions

a. a person's entire genetic inheritance
b. sperm and ovum
c. the first cell of the developing person
d. a person who has a recessive gene in his or her genotype that is not expressed in the phenotype
e. fraternal twins
f. a term referring to environmental factors that affect genes and genetic expression
g. a DNA molecule
h. the behavioral or physical expression of genetic potential
i. a chromosomal abnormality

Practice Questions II

Multiple-Choice Questions

1. Which of the following provides the best broad description of the relationship between heredity and environment in determining height?
   a. Heredity is the primary influence, with environment affecting development only in severe situations.
   b. Heredity and environment contribute equally to development.
   c. Environment is the major influence on physical characteristics.
   d. Heredity directs the individual's potential and environment determines whether and to what degree the individual reaches that potential.

2. Research studies of monozygotic twins who were raised apart suggest that
   a. virtually every human trait is affected by both genes and environment.
   b. only a few psychological traits, such as emotional reactivity, are affected by genes.
   c. most traits are determined by environmental influences.
   d. most traits are determined by genes.

3. Males with fragile X syndrome are
   a. feminine in appearance.
   b. less severely affected than females.
   c. frequently retarded intellectually.
   d. unusually tall and aggressive.

4. A pair of genes whose base pairs are identical is called
   a. homozygous.
   b. heterozygous.
   c. multifactorial.
   d. recessive.

5. Dizygotic twins result when
   a. a single egg is fertilized by a sperm and then splits.
   b. a single egg is fertilized by two different sperm.
   c. two eggs are fertilized by two different sperm.
   d. either a single egg is fertilized by one sperm or two eggs are fertilized by two different sperm.

6. In humans, the molecules of DNA that are arranged by twenty-three complementary pairs are called
   a. zygotes.
   b. genes.
   c. chromosomes.
   d. ova.

7. Shortly after the zygote is formed, it begins the processes of duplication and division. Each resulting new cell has
   a. the same number of chromosomes as was contained in the zygote.
   b. half the number of chromosomes as was contained in the zygote.
   c. twice, then four times, then eight times the number of chromosomes as was contained in the zygote.
   d. all the chromosomes except those that determine sex.

8. If an ovum is fertilized by a sperm bearing a Y chromosome,
   a. a female will develop.
   b. cell division will cease.
   c. a male will develop.
   d. spontaneous abortion will occur.

9. When the male cells in the testes and the female cells in the ovaries divide to produce gametes, the process differs from that in the production of all other cells. As a result of the different process, the gametes have
   a. one rather than both members of each chromosome pair.
   b. twenty-three chromosome pairs.
   c. X but not Y chromosomes.
   d. chromosomes from both parents.

Lesson 3/The Beginnings: Heredity and Environment

10. Genotype is to phenotype as _____ is to
    _____.
    a. genetic potential; physical expression
    b. physical expression; genetic potential
    c. sperm; ovum
    d. gamete; zygote

11. The genes that influence height and skin color interact according to the
    _____ pattern.
    a. dominant–recessive
    b. X-linked
    c. additive
    d. nonadditive

12. X-linked recessive genes explain why some traits seem to be passed from
    a. father to son.
    b. father to daughter.
    c. mother to daughter.
    d. mother to son.

13. According to the textbook, the effects of the environment on genetic inheritance include
    a. direct effects, such as nutrition, climate, and medical care.
    b. indirect effects, such as the individual's broad economic, political, and cultural context.
    c. irreversible effects, such as those resulting from brain injury.
    d. everything that can interact with the person's genetic inheritance at every point of life.

True or False Items
Write T (for true) or F (for false) on the line in front of each statement.

14. __T__ Most human characteristics are multifactorial, caused by the interaction of genetic and environmental factors.

15. __F__ Less than 10 percent of all zygotes have harmful genes or an abnormal chromosomal makeup.

16. __F__ Research suggests that susceptibility to alcoholism is at least partly the result of genetic inheritance.

17. __T__ The human reproductive cells (ova and sperm) are called gametes.

18. __F__ Only a very few human traits are polygenic.

19. __T__ A couple should probably seek genetic counseling if several earlier pregnancies ended in spontaneous abortion.

20. __F__ Many genetic conditions are recessive; thus, a child will have the condition even if only the mother carries the gene.

21. __T__ Two people who have the same phenotype may have a different genotype for a trait such as eye color.

22. __T__ When cells divide to produce reproductive cells (gametes), each sperm or ovum receives only twenty-three chromosomes, half as many as the original cell.

Applying Your Knowledge

1. Some men are color-blind because they inherit a particular recessive gene from their mother. That recessive gene is carried on the
   a. X chromosome.
   b. XX chromosome pair.
   c. Y chromosome.
   d. X or Y chromosome.

2. If your parents are much taller than your grandparents, the explanation probably lies in
   a. genetics.
   b. environmental factors.
   c. better family planning.
   d. good genetic counseling.

3. If a dizygotic twin develops schizophrenia, the likelihood of the other twin experiencing serious mental illness is much lower than is the case with monozygotic twins. This suggests that
   a. schizophrenia is caused by genes.
   b. schizophrenia is influenced by genes.
   c. environment is unimportant in the development of schizophrenia.
   d. monozygotic twins are especially vulnerable to schizophrenia.

4. A person's skin turns yellow-orange as a result of a carrot-juice diet regimen. This is an example of
   a. an environmental influence.
   b. an alteration in genotype.
   c. polygenic inheritance.
   d. incomplete dominance.

5. The personality trait of inhibition (shyness) seems to be partly genetic. A child who inherits the genes for shyness will be shy
   a. under most circumstances.
   b. only if shyness is the dominant gene.
   c. if the environment does not encourage greater sociability.
   d. if he or she is raised by biological rather than adoptive parents.

6. One of the best ways to distinguish the relative influence of genetic and environmental factors on behavior is to compare children who have
   a. the same genes and environments.
   b. different genes and environments.
   c. similar genes and environments.
   d. the same genes but different environments.

7. When identical twins have been reared apart, researchers have generally found
   a. strong behavioral and psychological similarities.
   b. strong behavioral, but not necessarily psychological, similarities.
   c. striking behavioral and psychological differences.
   d. that it is impossible to predict how such twins will develop.

8. Emily and Jim, who both have a history of alcoholism in their families, are concerned that the child they hope to have will inherit a genetic predisposition to alcoholism. Based on information presented in the text, what advice should you offer them?
   a. "Stop worrying, alcoholism is only weakly genetic."
   b. "It is almost certain that your child will become alcoholic."
   c. "Social influences, such as the family and peer environment, play a critical role in determining whether alcoholism is expressed."
   d. "Wait to have children until you are both middle aged, in order to see if the two of you become alcoholic."

9. A cell that is capable of becoming any kind of cell is called a(n)
   a. allele.
   b. gamete.
   c. stem cell.
   d. zygote.

10. Genetically, Evan's potential height is 6' 0". Because he did not receive a balanced diet, however, he grew to only 5' 9". Evan's actual height is an example of a
    a. recessive gene.
    b. dominant gene.
    c. genotype.
    d. phenotype.

11. Shannon inherited a gene from her mother that, regardless of her father's contribution to her genotype, will be expressed in her phenotype. Evidently, the gene Shannon received from her mother is a(n) _____ gene.
    a. polygenic
    b. recessive
    c. dominant
    d. X-linked

Answer Key

Key Terms
1. DNA (deoxyribonucleic acid) is a nucleic acid molecule that determines our inherited characteristics by encoding the information needed to synthesize proteins and regulate all aspects of cellular metabolism. (p. 62; video lesson, segment 1; objective 1)
2. Chromosomes are molecules of DNA that contain the genes organized in precise sequences. (p. 62; video lesson, segment 1; objective 1)

3. Genes are discrete segments of a chromosome, which is a DNA molecule, that are the basic units of heredity. (p. 62; video lesson, segment 1; objective 1)

4. A normal alteration is called an allele, one of several possible letter sequences that some genes have. Note that everyone has one allele or another of those variable genes. (p. 62; objective 1)

5. A genome is the full set of chromosomes, with all the genes they contain, that make up the genetic material of an organism. (p. 62; objective 1)

6. The zygote (a term derived from the Greek word for "joint") is the fertilized egg, that is, the one-celled organism formed during conception by the fusion of sperm and ovum. (p. 63; video lesson, segment 2; objective 1)

7. Gametes are the human reproductive cells. (p. 63; objective 1)

8. The sum total of all the genes a person inherits—his or her genetic potential—is called the genotype. (p. 64; video lesson, segment 3; objective 3)

9. Homozygous is a term referring to two genes of one pair that are exactly the same in every letter of their code. Most gene pairs are homozygous. (p. 64; objective 1)

10. Heterozygous is a term referring to two genes of one pair that may differ in some way. Typically, one allele has only a few base pairs that differ from the other member of the pair. (p. 65; objective 1)

11. The 23rd pair of chromosomes determines the individual's sex, among other things. (p. 65; objective 1)

12. XX is a twenty-third pair that consists of two X-shaped chromosomes, one from the mother and one from the father. (p. 65; objective 1)

13. XY is a twenty-third pair that consists of one X-shaped chromosome from the mother and one Y-shaped chromosome from the father. (p. 65; objective 1)

14. Stem cells are cells from which any other specialized type of cell can form. (p. 67; objective 1)

15. Monozygotic, or identical, twins develop from one zygote that splits in two, producing two genetically identical zygotes. (p. 68; video lesson, segment 2; objective 2)

16. Dizygotic, or fraternal, twins develop from two separate ova fertilized by different sperm at roughly the same time, and therefore are no more genetically similar than ordinary siblings. (p. 68; video lesson, segment 2; objective 2)

   Memory aid: A fraternity is a group of two (di) or more nonidentical individuals.

17. Assisted reproductive technology (ART) is a general term for the techniques designed to help infertile couples conceive and then sustain a pregnancy. (p. 69; objective 1)

18. In vitro fertilization (IVF) is fertilization that takes place outside a woman's body. The procedure involves mixing sperm with ova that have been surgically removed from the woman's ovary. If a zygote is produced, it is inserted into the woman's uterus, where it may implant and develop into a baby. (p. 69; objective 1)

19. The actual physical or behavioral expression of a genotype, the result of the interaction of the genes with each other and with the environment, is called the phenotype. (p. 71; video lesson, segment 3; objective 3)

20. Most human traits, especially psychological traits, are polygenic traits; that is, they are affected by many genes. (p. 71; objective 3)

21. Most human traits are also multifactorial traits—that is, influenced by many factors, including genetic and environmental factors. (p. 71; objective 3)

   Memory aid: The roots of the words polygenic and multifactorial give their meaning: poly means "many" and genic means "of the genes"; multi means "several" and factorial obviously refers to factors.

22. Epigenetic is a term referring to environmental factors that affect genes and genetic expression. (p. 71; objective 3)

23. The Human Genome Project is an international effort to map the complete genetic code. (p. 72; objective 2)

24. A dominant–recessive pattern involves the interaction of a pair of alleles in such a way that the phenotype reveals the influence of one allele (the dominant gene) more than that of the other (the recessive gene). (p. 73; objective 4)

25. A person who has a recessive gene in his or her genotype that is not expressed in his or her phenotype is called a carrier of that gene. (p. 73; objective 4)

26. X-linked genes are genes that are located only on the X chromosome. Since males have only one X chromosome, they are more likely than females to have the characteristics determined by these genes in their phenotype. (p. 73; objective 5)

27. Heritability is a statistic that indicates what percentage of the variation in a particular trait within a particular population, in a particular context and era, can be traced to genes. (p. 76; objective 7)

28. Down syndrome (trisomy-21) is a chromosomal disorder in which there is an extra chromosome at site 21. Most people with Down syndrome have distinctive physical and psychological characteristics, including a rounded face, short stature, and mental slowness. (p. 79; objective 8)

29. The fragile X syndrome is a single-gene disorder in which part of the X chromosome is attached by such a thin string of molecules that it seems about to break off. Although the characteristics associated with this syndrome are quite varied, some mental deficiency is relatively common. (p. 82; objective 9)

30. Genetic counseling involves a variety of tests through which couples can learn more about their genes, and can thus make informed decisions about their childbearing and child-rearing future. (p. 82; video lesson, segment 4; objective 9)

31. Phenylketonuria (PKU) is a genetic disorder in which a child's body is unable to metabolize the amino acid, phenylalanine. Unless the infant immediately begins a special diet, the resulting buildup of phenylalanine in body fluids causes brain damage, progressive mental retardation, and other symptoms. (p. 83; objective 8)

32. The dominant gene is the stronger of an interacting pair of alleles whose influence is more evident in the phenotype. (video lesson, segment 3; objective 4)

33. The recessive gene is the weaker of an interacting pair of alleles whose influence is less evident in the phenotype. (video lesson, segment 3; objective 4)

34. Heredity refers to the transmission of traits and predispositions from parent to child through the genes. (video lesson, introduction; objective 6)

35. When social scientists discuss the effects of the environment on genes, they are referring to everything—from the impact of the immediate cell environment on the genes to the multitude of elements in the outside world, such as nutrition, climate, family interactions, and the cultural context—

that can interact with the person's genetic inheritance at every point of life. (video lesson, segment 2; objective 6)

36. Amniocentesis is a prenatal diagnostic procedure in which a sample of amniotic fluid is withdrawn by syringe and tested to determine if the developing fetus is healthy. (video lesson, segment 4; objective 10)

37. Gene therapy (also called genetic engineering) involves the altering of an organism's genetic instructions through the insertion and addition of normal genes by way of a blood transfusion, bone marrow transplant, or direct insertion into a cluster of cells. (video lesson, segment 4; objective 10)

Practice Questions I

Multiple-Choice Questions

1. a. is the correct answer. (video lesson, segment 2; objective 1)

   b. & c. are incorrect. The reproductive cells (sperm and ova), which are also called gametes, are individual entities.

   d. is incorrect. Monozygote refers to one member of a pair of identical twins.

2. c. is the correct answer. (video lesson, segment 1; objective 1)

   a. is incorrect. The zygote is the first cell of the developing person.

   b. is incorrect. Chromosomes are molecules of DNA that carry genes.

   d. is incorrect. DNA molecules contain genetic information.

3. b. is the correct answer. (objective 1)

4. d. is the correct answer. When the gametes are formed, one member of each chromosome pair splits off; because in females both are X chromosomes, each ovum must carry an X chromosome. (objective 1)

   a., b., & c. are incorrect. The zygote refers to the merged sperm and ovum that is the first new cell of the developing individual.

5. b. is the correct answer. Mono means "one." Thus, monozygotic twins develop from one zygote. (video lesson, segment 2; objective 2)

   a. & c. are incorrect. Dizygotic, or fraternal, twins develop from two (di) zygotes.

   d. is incorrect. A trizygotic birth would result in triplets (tri), rather than twins.

6. d. is the correct answer. In this situation, one factor (genetic similarity) is held constant while the other factor (environment) is varied. Therefore, any similarity in traits is strong evidence of genetic inheritance. (video lesson, segment 2; objective 6)

7. a. is the correct answer. (video lesson, segment 4; objective 9)

   c. & d. are incorrect. Most dominant disorders are neither seriously disabling, nor sex-linked.

8. c. is the correct answer. (objective 3)

   a., b., & d. are incorrect. Polygenic means "many genes"; multifactorial means "many factors," which are not limited to either genetic or environmental ones.

9. b. is the correct answer. (video lesson, segment 1; objective 1)

   a. is incorrect. Genotype is a person's genetic potential.

   c. is incorrect. A karyotype is a picture of a person's chromosomes.

   d. is incorrect. Phenotype is the actual expression of a genotype.

10. d. is the correct answer. (video lesson, segment 1; objective 2)

11. d. is the correct answer. (objective 8)

   a., b., & c. are chromosomal abnormalities that are not tested for at birth because they do not immediately threaten the life of the infant.

12. b. is the correct answer. (objective 6)

13. a. is the correct answer. (objective 8)

14. b. is the correct answer. (objective 3)

15. b. is the correct answer. (video lesson, segment 3; objective 9)

   a. & c. are incorrect. These abnormalities involve the sex chromosomes, not genes.

   d. is incorrect. In order for an offspring to inherit a recessive condition, the parents need only be carriers of the recessive gene in their genotypes; they need not actually have the disease.

Matching Items

16. b (objective 3)

17. g (video lesson, segment 1; objective 1)

18. a (video lesson, segment 3; objective 3)

19. h (video lesson, segment 3; objective 3)

20. e (video lesson, segment 2; objective 2)

21. f (objective 6)

22. i (objective 8)

23. d (objective 7)

24. c (objective 3)

Practice Questions II

Multiple-Choice Questions

1. d. is the correct answer. (objectives 3 & 6)

2. a. is the correct answer. (video lesson, segment 2; objective 2)

3. c. is the correct answer. (objective 8)

   a. is incorrect. Physical appearance is usually normal in this syndrome.

   b. is incorrect. Males are more frequently and more severely affected.

   d. is incorrect. This is true of the XYY chromosomal abnormality, but not the fragile X syndrome.

4. a. is the correct answer. (objective 1)

5. c. is the correct answer. (video lesson, segment 2; objective 2)

   a. is incorrect. This would result in monozygotic twins.

   b. is incorrect. Only one sperm can fertilize an ovum.

   d. is incorrect. A single egg fertilized by one sperm would produce a single offspring or monozygotic twins.

6. c. is the correct answer. (video lesson, segment 2; objective 1)

   a. is incorrect. Zygotes are fertilized ova.

   b. is incorrect. Genes are the smaller units of heredity that are organized into sequences on chromosomes.

   d. is incorrect. Ova are female reproductive cells.

7. a. is the correct answer. (video lesson, segment 1; objective 1)

8. c. is the correct answer. The ovum will contain an X chromosome, and with the sperm's Y chromosome, will produce the male XY pattern. (video lesson, segment 1; objective 1)

   a. is incorrect. Only if the ovum is fertilized by an X chromosome from the sperm will a female develop.

   b. is incorrect. Cell division will occur regardless of whether the sperm contributes an X or a Y chromosome.

   d. is incorrect. Spontaneous abortions are likely to occur when there are chromosomal or genetic abnormalities; the situation described is perfectly normal.

9. a. is the correct answer. (objective 1)

   b. & d. are incorrect. These are true of all body cells except the gametes.

   c. is incorrect. Gametes have either X or Y chromosomes.

10. a. is the correct answer. Genotype refers to the sum total of all the genes a person inherits; phenotype refers to the actual expression of the individual's characteristics. (video lesson, segment 3; objective 3)

11. c. is the correct answer. (objective 4)

12. d. is the correct answer. X-linked genes are located only on the X chromosome. Because males inherit only one X chromosome, they are more likely than females to have these characteristics in their phenotype. (objective 5)

13. d. is the correct answer. (objective 7)

True or False Items

14. T (objective 3)

15. T Five to ten percent of all zygotes have an odd number of chromosomes. (objective 8)

16. T (objective 7)

17. T (objective 1)

18. F (objective 3)

19. T (video lesson, segment 4; objective 9)

20. F A trait from a recessive gene will be part of the phenotype only when the person has two recessive genes for that trait. (video lesson, segment 4; objective 4)

21. T (video lesson, segment 3; objective 3)

22. T (objective 1)

Applying Your Knowledge

1. a. is the correct answer. (objective 5)

   b. is incorrect. The male genotype is XY, not XX.

   c. & d. are incorrect. The mother contributes only an X chromosome.

2. b. is the correct answer. This trend in increased height has been attributed to improved nutrition and medical care. (objective 7)

   a., c., & d. are incorrect. It is unlikely that these factors account for height differences from one generation to the next.

3. b. is the correct answer. Since monozygotic twins are genetically identical, while dizygotic twins share only 50 percent of their genes, greater similarity of traits between monozygotic twins suggests that genes are an important influence. (video lesson, segment 2; objective 7)

a. & c. are incorrect. Even though schizophrenia has a strong genetic component, it is not the case that if one twin has schizophrenia the other also automatically does. Therefore, the environment, too, is an important influence.

d. is incorrect. This does not necessarily follow.

4. a. is the correct answer. (video lesson, segment 3; objective 3)

b. is incorrect. Genotype is a person's genetic potential, established at conception.

c. is incorrect. Polygenic inheritance refers to the influence of many genes on a particular trait.

d. is incorrect. Incomplete dominance refers to the phenotype being influenced primarily, but not exclusively, by the dominant gene.

5. c. is the correct answer. (objective 7)

a. & b. are incorrect. Research on adopted children shows that shyness is affected by both genetic inheritance and the social environment. Therefore, if a child's environment promotes socializing outside the immediate family, a genetically shy child might grow up much less timid socially than he or she would have been with less outgoing parents.

d. is incorrect. Either biological or adoptive parents are capable of nurturing, or not nurturing, shyness in their children.

6. d. is the correct answer. To separate the influences of genes and environment, one of the two must be held constant. (video lesson, segment 2; objective 6)

a., b., & c. are incorrect. These situations would not allow a researcher to separate the contributions of heredity and environment.

7. d. is the correct answer. (video lesson, segment 2; objective 6)

8. c. is the correct answer. (objective 7)

a. is incorrect. Some people's inherited biochemistry makes them highly susceptible to alcoholism.

b. is incorrect. Despite a strong genetic influence, the environment plays a critical role in the expression of alcoholism.

d. is incorrect. Not only is this advice unreasonable, but it might increase the likelihood of chromosomal abnormalities in the parents' sperm and ova.

9. c. is the correct answer. (objective 1)

10. d. is the correct answer. (objectives 3 & 4)

a. & b. are incorrect. Genes are discrete segments of a chromosome.

c. is incorrect. Genotype refers to genetic potential.

11. c. is the correct answer. (objective 5)

a. is incorrect. There is no such thing as a "polygenic gene." Polygenic means "many genes."

b. is incorrect. A recessive gene paired with a dominant gene will not be expressed in the phenotype.

d. is incorrect. X-linked genes may be dominant or recessive.

Lesson Review

Lesson 3

The Beginnings
Heredity and Environment

Please Note: Use this matrix to guide your study and achieve the learning objectives of this lesson. It will also help you to view the video, which defines and demonstrates important concepts and skills as they relate to everyday life.

Learning Objective	Textbook	Course Student Guide	Video Lesson
1. Identify the mechanisms of heredity, and explain how sex is determined.	pp. 61–70	Key Terms: 1, 2, 3, 4, 5, 6, 7, 9, 10, 11, 12, 13, 14, 17, 18; Practice Questions I: 1, 2, 3, 4, 9, 17; Practice Questions II: 4, 6, 7, 8, 9, 17, 22; Applying Your Knowledge: 9.	Segment 1: *The Beginning of Development* Segment 2: *The Twin Perspective*
2. Discuss genetic continuity and diversity, and distinguish between monozygotic and dizygotic twins.	pp. 62, 68–69	Key Terms: 15, 16, 23; Practice Questions I: 5, 10, 20; Practice Questions II: 2, 5.	Segment 2: *The Twin Perspective*
3. Differentiate genotype from phenotype, and explain the polygenic and multifactorial nature of human traits.	pp. 71–72	Key Terms: 8, 19, 20, 21, 22; Practice Questions I: 8, 14, 16, 18, 19, 24; Practice Questions II: 1, 10, 14, 18, 21; Applying Your Knowledge: 4, 10.	Segment 3: *From Genotype to Phenotype*
4. Explain the additive and nonadditive patterns of genetic interaction, and give examples of the traits that result from each type of interaction.	pp. 72–74	Key Terms: 24, 25, 32, 33; Practice Questions II: 11, 20; Applying Your Knowledge: 10.	Segment 3: *From Genotype to Phenotype* Segment 4: *Genetic and Chromosomal Abnormalities*
5. Discuss X-linked genes in terms of genotype and phenotype, and explain the concept of genetic imprinting.	p. 74	Key Terms: 26; Practice Questions II: 12; Applying Your Knowledge: 1, 11.	
6. Explain how scientists distinguish the effects of genes and environment on development.	pp. 75, 77–78	Key Terms: 34, 35; Practice Questions I: 6, 12, 21; Practice Questions II: 1; Applying Your Knowledge: 6, 7.	Introduction Segment 2: *The Twin Perspective*

Learning Objective	Textbook	Course Student Guide	Video Lesson
7. Identify some environmental variables that affect genetic inheritance, and describe how a particular trait, such as susceptibility to shyness (inhibition) or alcoholism, might be affected.	pp. 71–72, 75–77	Key Terms: 27; Practice Questions I: 23; Practice Questions II: 13, 16; Applying Your Knowledge: 2, 3, 5, 8.	Segment 2: *The Twin Perspective*
8. Explain the incidence of gene disorders, and discuss at least three such disorders.	pp. 78–82	Key Terms: 28, 31; Practice Questions I: 11, 13, 22; Practice Questions II: 3, 15.	
9. Describe five groups of prospective parents who should seek genetic testing and counseling.	pp. 82–85	Key Terms: 29, 30; Practice Questions I: 7, 15; Practice Questions II: 19.	Segment 3: *From Genotype to Phenotype* Segment 4: *Genetic and Chromosomal Abnormalities*
10. Explain the major methods of prenatal diagnosis, noting the advantages of each.		Key Terms: 36, 37.	Segment 4: *Genetic and Chromosomal Abnormalities*

* The video for this lesson offers an excellent description of these concepts.

The Wondrous Journey

Lesson 4

The Beginnings:
Prenatal Development and Birth

Preview

Anticipating the birth of a child is one of life's most enriching experiences. As the video for this lesson begins, we meet Sandra and Darrin in the anxious moments just before Sandra gives birth. The personal experiences of this young family throughout Sandra's pregnancy and delivery form the backdrop for the lesson's exploration of prenatal development and birth.

The period of prenatal development is a time of incredibly rapid growth during which the emerging person develops from a single cell into a fully functioning individual. This lesson describes that development, along with some of the problems that can occur—including prenatal exposure to disease, drugs, and other hazards—and the factors that moderate the risks of that exposure.

A person's birth marks the most radical transition of the entire life span. No longer sheltered from the outside world, the newborn becomes a separate human being who begins life almost completely dependent upon its caregivers. This lesson also examines the process of birth, its possible variations and problems, and the parent–newborn bonding process.

As you complete this video, recall your experiences with pregnancy or those of someone you know. (You may want to interview that person during your study of this lesson.) What did the mother look and feel like during the early, middle, and final stages of this pregnancy? What sort of prenatal care did she receive? What did she do to stay healthy? For example, what did she eat and how did she exercise? Did she smoke, drink alcohol, or take any medications during the pregnancy? Was the baby born close to the "due date"? What was the birthing experience like? Where did the mother have the baby, in what type of facility? Did she have any surgical procedures performed? If so, which ones? Were there any complications during birth? If so, what were they, and how were the mother and baby treated? Did the mother and father both get to hold and bond with the baby in the first few hours after birth? Did the mother experience any depression in the days and weeks after birth? If so, how was she treated?

Prior Course Knowledge that Will Be Used in this Lesson

- This lesson focuses primarily on the biosocial domain of development. Recall from Lesson 1 that biosocial development includes all the growth and changes that occur in a person's body, as well as the genetic, nutritional, and health factors that can affect that growth and change.

- This lesson begins with the development of the zygote after conception. Remember from Lesson 3 that conception occurs when the male's sperm and female's ovum unite. The resulting cell, called a zygote, then develops through a process of duplication and division.

- This lesson will also return to the epigenetic systems theory introduced in Lesson 1. Recall that the basic tenet of this theory is that our development is shaped not only by our genetics or by the environment in which we live, but rather by the interaction between the two. Nature *and* nurture make us who we are. This is just as true for prenatal development (before birth) as it is for postnatal development (after birth).

Learning Objectives

Use this information to guide your reading, viewing, thinking, and studying. After successfully completing this lesson, you should be able to:

1. Describe the significant developments of the germinal period.

2. Describe the significant developments of the embryonic period.

3. Describe the significant developments of the fetal period, noting the importance of the age of viability, and the fetus's various responses to its immediate environment (the womb).

4. Define teratology, and identify at least five teratogens.

5. Outline the effects of teratogens on the developing embryo or fetus, and describe protective steps that can be taken to moderate the risk of exposure.

6. Distinguish among low-birthweight, preterm, and small for gestational age (SGA) infants; and identify the causes of low birthweight, focusing on the relationship of poverty to low birthweight.

7. Describe the normal process of birth, specifying the events of each stage.

8. Describe the tests used to assess the newborn's condition at birth.

9. Describe the options available for medical attention during the birthing process, and discuss the pros and cons of medical assistance and traditional birthing practices.

10. Explain the causes of cerebral palsy, and discuss the special needs of high-risk infants.

11. Explain the concept of parent–newborn bonding and the current view of most developmentalists regarding early bonding in humans.

📖 **Read Chapter 4, "Prenatal Development and Birth," pages 89–119.**

⏮ **View the video for Lesson 4, "The Wondrous Journey."**

Segment 1: *The First Trimester*

Segment 2: *Risk Reduction*

Segment 3: *The Second Trimester*

Segment 4: *The Third Trimester*

Summary

The first two weeks of prenatal development are called the **germinal period**. Within hours after conception, the one-celled zygote begins the process of cell division and growth as it travels down the fallopian tube. The **embryonic period** begins as the organism begins differentiating into three layers of tissue that will become the various body systems. At the end of the first month, the cardiovascular system is functioning; the eyes, ears, nose, mouth, and arm and leg buds start to form; and the embryo is about one-fifth of an inch (just 6 millimeters) long. By the end of the second month, the developing organism weighs about 1 gram, is 1 inch long, and has all the basic organs (except the sex organs) and features of a human being. During the third month, the **fetal period** begins, and the sex organs begin to take shape.

The crucial factor in the fetus's attaining the **age of viability**, beginning at about 22 to 24 weeks, is neurological maturation, which is essential to the regulation of the basic body functions of breathing, sucking, and sleeping. By 28 weeks, the typical fetus weighs about 1,300 grams (3 pounds) and has a greater than 50 percent chance of survival outside the womb.

Teratology is a science of risk analysis which attempts to evaluate what factors can make prenatal harm more (or less) likely to occur. Three crucial factors that determine whether a specific teratogen will cause harm, and of what nature, are the timing of exposure, the amount of exposure, and the developing organism's genetic vulnerability to damage from the substance. Although each body structure has its own **critical period** during which it is most susceptible to teratogenic damage, for **behavioral teratogens** that affect the brain and nervous system the entire prenatal period is critical. Teratogens can also include conditions, such as maternal malnutrition and extreme levels of stress. Some **teratogens** have a cumulative effect on the developing individual. For other teratogens, there is a **threshold effect**; that is, the substance is virtually harmless until exposure reaches a certain frequency or dosage. However, the **interaction effect** of teratogens taken together may make them more harmful at lower dosage levels than they would be individually.

A major, preventable health hazard for the fetus is **low birthweight**, defined as birthweight that is less than 2,500 grams (5.5 pounds). Babies that weigh less than 3 pounds (1,500 grams) are classified as **very low birthweight**, while those that weigh less than 2 pounds (1,000 grams) are classified as **extremely low birthweight**. Infants who are born more than three weeks early are called **preterm**. Others, born close to the due date but weighing less than most full-term neonates, are called **small for gestational age (SGA)**.

The normal birth begins at about the 266th day after conception, when the fetus's brain signals the release of hormones that trigger uterine contractions in the mother. Labor usually lasts eight to twelve hours in first births and four to seven hours in subsequent births, but this can vary greatly. The **Apgar scale** is used to assign a score between 0 and 2 to the neonate's heart rate, breathing, muscle tone, color, and reflexes at one minute after birth and again at five minutes. A score of 7 or better indicates the newborn is not in danger; below 7, that the infant needs help in establishing normal breathing; and below 4, that the baby is in critical condition and needs immediate medical attention. Very few newborns score an immediate perfect 10, but most readily adjust to life outside the womb.

The quality of the birth experience depends on many factors, including the mother's preparation for birth, the support provided by others, and the nature and degree of medical assistance. Birth complications are much more likely if a fetus is at risk because of low weight, **preterm** birth, genetic abnormality, or teratogenic exposure, or because the mother is unusually young, old, or small, or in poor health. **Cerebral**

palsy, for example, which was once thought to be solely caused by birth procedures (such as excessive analgesia or misapplied forceps), is now known to result from a combination of factors, including genetic vulnerability, exposure to teratogens, and **anoxia** (lack of oxygen) during birth.

The popular term **parent–infant bond** is used to emphasize the tangible as well as intangible attachment between parent and child in the early moments after birth. In many animals, early contact between mother and infant can be crucial to bonding. Most developmentalists now believe that the importance of early contact between a human mother and child has been overly popularized and that the events right after birth are just one episode in a long-term process of bonding and development.

📖 **Review all reading assignments for this lesson.**

💻 **As assigned by your instructor, complete the optional online component for this lesson.**

Key Terms

Using your own words, write a brief definition or explanation of each of the following terms on a separate piece of paper.

1. germinal period
2. embryonic period
3. fetal period
4. implantation
5. embryo
6. fetus

7. ultrasound
8. age of viability
9. Apgar scale
10. cesarean section (c-section)
11. doula
12. teratogens
13. behavioral teratogens
14. threshold effect
15. fetal alcohol syndrome (FAS)
16. low-birthweight (LBW) infant
17. very low-birthweight (VLBW)

18. extremely low-birthweight (ELBW)
19. preterm
20. small for gestational age (SGA)
21. cerebral palsy
22. anoxia
23. Brazelton Neonatal Behavioral Assessment Scale (NBAS)
24. reflex
25. couvade
26. parental alliance
27. postpartum depression
28. parent–infant bond
29. kangaroo care
30. placenta
31. critical period
32. interaction effect
33. amniotic fluid
34. spina bifida

Practice Questions I

Multiple-Choice Questions

1. The first two weeks after conception are called the
   a. embryonic period.
   b. placental period.
   c. fetal period.
   d. germinal period.

2. Implantation occurs during the
   a. embryonic period.
   b. germinal period.
   c. uterine period.
   d. fetal period.

3. By the eighth week after conception, the embryo has almost all the basic organs **EXCEPT** the
   a. skeleton.
   b. elbows and knees.
   c. sex organs.
   d. fingers and toes.

4. The most critical factor in attaining the age of viability is development of the
   a. placenta.
   b. eyes.
   c. brain.
   d. skeleton.

5. Neural-tube defects, such as spina bifida, have been linked to a deficiency of _____ in an expectant mother's diet.
   a. vitamin A
   b. zinc
   c. guanine
   d. folic acid

6. An embryo begins to develop male sex organs if _____, and female sex organs if _____.
   a. genes on the Y chromosome send a biochemical signal; no signal is sent from an X chromosome
   b. genes on the Y chromosome send a biochemical signal; genes on the X chromosome send a signal
   c. genes on the X chromosome send a biochemical signal; no signal is sent from an X chromosome
   d. genes on the X chromosome send a biochemical signal; genes on the Y chromosome send a signal

7. A teratogen
    a. cannot cross the placenta during the period of the embryo.
    b. is usually inherited from the mother.
    c. can be counteracted by good nutrition most of the time.
    d. may be a virus, drug, chemical, radiation, or environmental pollutants.

8. Among the characteristics of babies born with fetal alcohol syndrome are
    a. slowed physical growth and behavior problems.
    b. addiction to alcohol and methadone.
    c. deformed arms and legs.
    d. blindness.

9. The birth process begins
    a. when the fetus moves into the right position.
    b. when the uterus begins to contract at regular intervals to push the fetus out.
    c. about eight hours (in the case of firstborns) after the uterus begins to contract at regular intervals.
    d. when the baby's head appears at the opening of the vagina.

10. The Apgar scale is administered
    a. only if the newborn is in obvious distress.
    b. once, just after birth.
    c. usually twice, 1 minute and 5 minutes after birth.
    d. every two minutes for several hours.

11. Most newborns weigh about
    a. 5 pounds.
    b. 6 pounds.
    c. 7.5 pounds.
    d. 8.5 pounds.

12. Low-birthweight babies born near the due date but weighing substantially less than they should
    a. are classified as preterm.
    b. are called small for gestational age.
    c. usually have no sex organs.
    d. have undeveloped hands and feet.

13. Approximately 1 out of every 4 low-birthweight births in the United States is caused by maternal use of
    a. alcohol.
    b. tobacco.
    c. crack cocaine.
    d. household chemicals.

14. The idea of a parent–infant bond in humans arose from
    a. observations in the delivery room.
    b. data on adopted infants.
    c. animal studies.
    d. studies of disturbed mother–newborn pairs.

Matching Items

Match each definition or description with its corresponding term.

Terms

15. ___J___ embryonic period   21. ___G___ NBAS

16. ___C___ fetal period   22. ___A___ critical period

17. ___H___ placenta   23. ___D___ ultrasound

18. ___K___ preterm   24. ___F___ fetal alcohol syndrome

19. ___B___ reflex   25. ___I___ germinal period

20. ___E___ couvade

Definitions or Descriptions

a. term for the period during which a developing baby's body parts are most susceptible to damage

b. an unlearned, involuntary action or movement

c. the age when viability is attained

d. an image formed by high-frequency sound waves

e. symptoms of pregnancy and birth experienced by fathers

f. characterized by abnormal facial characteristics, slowed growth, behavior problems, and mental retardation

g. the Brazelton Neonatal Behavioral Assessment Scale, an evaluation of a newborn's reflexes

h. the life-giving organ that nourishes the embryo and fetus

i. when implantation occurs

j. the prenatal period when all major body structures begin to form

k. refers to a baby born three or more weeks early

Practice Questions II

Multiple-Choice Questions

1. Kangaroo care
    a. poses a suffocation hazard.
    b. requires an infant seat.
    c. helps infants to thrive.
    d. lowers an infant's body temperature.

2. Which of the following reflects, in order, the correct sequence of prenatal stages of development?

   a. embryo; germinal; fetal

   b. germinal; fetal; embryo

   c. germinal; embryo; fetal

   d. ovum; fetal; embryo

3. Tetracycline, retinoic acid, and most hormones

   a. can be harmful to the human fetus.

   b. have been proven safe for pregnant women after the embryonic period.

   c. will prevent spontaneous abortions.

   d. are safe when used before the fetal period.

4. One of the first teratogens to be recognized, possibly causing deafness, blindness, and brain damage if the fetus is exposed early during the pregnancy, is

   a. rubella (German measles).

   b. anoxia.

   c. acquired immune deficiency syndrome (AIDS).

   d. neural-tube defect.

5. The Apgar scale and the Brazelton Neonatal Behavioral Assessment Scale are similar in that they

   a. are tests performed on a fetus.

   b. have a ten-point scale.

   c. determine the need for a cesarean section.

   d. assess a newborn's functioning.

6. A newborn is classified as low birthweight if he or she weighs less than

   a. 7 pounds.

   b. 6 pounds.

   c. 5.5 pounds.

   d. 4 pounds.

7. A newborn weighing 2 pounds at birth would be classified as

   a. low birthweight.

   b. very low-birthweight.

   c. extremely low-birthweight.

   d. none of the above.

8. Mothers who _____ during pregnancy are most likely to give birth to infants who are small for gestational age (SGA).

   a. smoke

   b. are malnourished

   c. drink alcohol

   d. are HIV positive

9. Which Apgar score indicates that a newborn is in normal health?

    a. 4

    b. 5

    c. 6

    d. 7

10. Many low-birthweight babies are born to teenage mothers. This is primarily because teen mothers

    a. are less well nourished.

    b. have less education.

    c. have bodies that are too young to support a healthy pregnancy.

    d. are all of the above.

11. The critical period for preventing physical defects appears to be

    a. the period of the zygote.

    b. the embryonic period.

    c. only the third trimester.

    d. the entire pregnancy.

True or False Items

Write T (for true) or F (for false) on the line in front of each statement.

12. _____ Fathers can experience some of the symptoms of pregnancy.

13. _____ Eight weeks after conception, the embryo has formed almost all the basic organs.

14. _____ In general, behavioral teratogens have the greatest effect during the period of the embryo.

15. _____ The effects of cigarette smoking during pregnancy remain highly controversial.

16. _____ The Apgar scale is used to measure vital signs such as heart rate, breathing, and reflexes.

17. _____ Newborns usually cry on their own, moments after birth.

18. _____ Research shows that immediate mother–newborn contact at birth is necessary for the normal emotional development of the child.

19. _____ Low-birthweight babies are more likely than other children to experience developmental difficulties in early childhood.

20. _____ Cesarean sections are rarely performed in the United States today because of the resulting danger to the fetus.

21. _____ Beginning at the 28th week, a fetus can hear and react to sounds outside the womb.

Applying Your Knowledge

1. Babies born to mothers who are powerfully addicted to a psychoactive drug are most likely to suffer from
   a. structural problems.
   b. behavioral problems.
   c. both a and b.
   d. neither a nor b.

2. I am about 1 inch long and 1 gram in weight. I have all of the basic organs (except sex organs) and features of a human being. What am I?
   a. a zygote
   b. an embryo
   c. a fetus
   d. an indifferent gonad

3. Elizabeth and Ethan report to their neighbors that, 5 weeks after conception, a sonogram of their child-to-be revealed female sex organs. The neighbors are skeptical of their statement because
   a. sonograms are never administered before the ninth week.
   b. sonograms only reveal the presence or absence of male sex organs.
   c. the fetus does not begin to develop female sex organs until about the ninth week.
   d. it is impossible to determine that a woman is pregnant until six weeks after conception.

4. Five-year-old Christopher can't sit quietly and concentrate on a task for more than a minute. Dr. Smith, who is a teratologist, suspects that Christopher may have been exposed to _____ during prenatal development.
   a. human immunodeficiency virus
   b. a behavioral teratogen
   c. rubella
   d. lead

5. Megan and John, who are of British descent, are hoping to have a child. Dr. Snook asks for a complete nutritional history and is particularly concerned when she discovers that Megan may have a deficiency of folic acid in her diet. Dr. Snook is probably worried about the risk of _____ in the couple's offspring.
   a. FAS
   b. brain damage
   c. neural-tube defects
   d. FAE

6. Three-year-old Taylor was born underweight and premature. Today, he is small for his age. His doctor suspects that

    a. Taylor is a victim of fetal alcohol syndrome.
    b. Taylor suffers from fetal alcohol effects.
    c. Taylor's mother smoked heavily during her pregnancy.
    d. Taylor experienced anoxia during birth.

7. Which of these fetuses is most likely to experience serious prenatal damage?

    a. a male whose 15-year-old mother has an unusually stressful home life
    b. a female whose mother did not begin to receive prenatal care until the second month of her pregnancy
    c. a female whose 30-year-old mother is on welfare
    d. a male whose mother was somewhat undernourished early in the pregnancy

8. Fetal alcohol syndrome is common in newborns whose mothers were heavy drinkers during pregnancy, whereas newborns whose mothers were moderate drinkers may suffer fetal alcohol effects. This finding shows that to assess and understand risk we must know

    a. the kind of alcoholic beverage (for example, beer, wine, or whiskey).
    b. the level of exposure to the teratogen.
    c. whether the substance really is teratogenic.
    d. the timing of exposure to the teratogen.

9. Your sister and brother-in-law, who are about to adopt a one-year-old, are worried that the child will never bond with them. What advice should you offer?

    a. Tell them that, unfortunately, this is true; they would be better off waiting for a younger child who has not yet bonded.
    b. Tell them that, although the first year is a biologically determined critical period for attachment, there is a fifty-fifty chance that the child will bond with them.
    c. Tell them that bonding is a long-term process between parent and child that is determined by the nature of interaction throughout infancy, childhood, and beyond.
    d. Tell them that if the child is female, there is a good chance that she will bond with them, even at this late stage.

10. Which of the following newborns would be most likely to have problems in body structure and functioning?

    a. Josh, whose Apgar score is 6.
    b. Christina, whose Apgar score is 7.
    c. Kingsley, whose Apgar score is 3.
    d. Corey, whose Apgar score is 5.

11. At birth, Pierre was classified as small for gestational age. It is likely that Pierre

    a. was born in a rural hospital.
    b. suffered several months of prenatal malnutrition.
    c. was born in a large city hospital.
    d. comes from a family with a history of such births.

12. Of the following, who is most likely to give birth to a low-birthweight child?

    a. twenty-one-year-old Lynn, who lives in the North

    b. twenty-five-year-old Thien, who lives in Vietnam

    c. sixteen-year-old Lori, who lives in a remote, rural part of the United States

    d. thirty-year-old Wendy, who lives in southern California

13. An infant born 266 days after conception, weighing 4 pounds, would be designated as which of the following?

    a. a preterm infant

    b. a low-birthweight infant

    c. a small-for-gestational-age infant

    d. b and c

14. A mother is astonished to find that her baby can grasp a doctor's fingers tightly enough to be lifted. The doctor is determining the newborn's

    a. Apgar score.

    b. reflexes.

    c. Brazelton Neonatal Behavioral Assessment Score.

    d. reflexes and Brazelton Neonatal Behavioral Assessment Score.

Answer Key

Key Terms

1. The first two weeks of development, characterized by rapid cell division and the beginning of cell differentiation, are called the germinal period. (p. 89; video lesson, segment 1; objective 1)

   Memory aid: A germ cell is one from which a new organism can develop. The germinal period is the first stage in the development of the new organism.

2. The embryonic period is the third through the eighth week of prenatal development, when the rudimentary forms of all anatomical structures develop. (p. 89; video lesson, segment 1; objective 2)

3. From the ninth week until birth is the fetal period, when the organs grow in size and complexity. (p. 89; video lesson, segment 1; objective 3)

4. Implantation is the process by which the outer cells of the organism burrow into the uterine lining and rupture its blood vessels to obtain nourishment and trigger the bodily changes that signify the beginning of pregnancy. (p. 90; video lesson, segment 1; objective 1)

   Memory aid: Neural means "of the nervous system." The neural tube is the precursor of the central nervous system.

5. Embryo is the name for the developing organism from approximately three through eight weeks past conception. (p. 91; objective 2)

6. Fetus is the name for the developing organism from eight weeks after conception through birth. (p. 92; objective 3)

7. An ultrasound, also called a sonogram, is an image of a fetus (or an internal organ) produced by using high-frequency sound waves. (p. 92; objective 3)

8. About twenty-two weeks after conception, the fetus attains the age of viability, at which point it has at least some slight chance of survival outside the uterus if specialized medical care is available. (p. 93; video lesson, segment 3; objective 3)

9. Newborns are rated at one and then at five minutes after birth according to the Apgar scale. This scale assigns a score of 0, 1, or 2 to each of five characteristics: heart rate, breathing, muscle tone, color, and reflexes. A score of 7 or better indicates that all is well. (p. 97; video lesson, segment 4; objective 8)

10. In a cesarean section, the fetus is removed from the mother surgically. (p. 98; objective 9)

11. A doula helps a woman with the birthing process. In modern society, a doula often works with the hospital staff to assist the mother through labor and delivery. (p. 100; objective 9)

12. Teratogens are external agents and conditions, such as viruses, bacteria, drugs, chemicals, stressors, and malnutrition, that can cause damage to the developing organism. (p. 102; video lesson, segment 2; objective 4)

13. Behavioral teratogens tend to damage the brain and nervous system, impairing the future child's intellectual and emotional functioning. (p. 103; objective 5)

14. A threshold effect is the harmful effect of a substance that occurs when exposure to it reaches a certain level. (p. 104; video lesson, segment 2; objective 5)

15. Prenatal alcohol exposure may cause fetal alcohol syndrome (FAS), which includes abnormal facial characteristics, slowed physical growth, behavior problems, and mental retardation. Likely victims are those who are genetically vulnerable and whose mothers drink three or more drinks daily during pregnancy. (p. 108; objective 5)

16. Newborns who weigh less than 2,500 grams (5.5 pounds) are called low-birthweight (LBW) infants. Such infants are at risk for many immediate and long-term problems. (p. 110; video lesson, segment 3; objective 6)

17. A very low-birthweight (VLBW) infant is born weighing less than 3 lbs., 5 oz. (p. 113; objective 6)

18. An extremely low-birthweight (ELBW) infant is born weighing less than 2 lbs., 3 oz. (p. 110; objective 6)

19. Infants who are born three or more weeks before the due date are called preterm. (p. 111; objective 6)

20. Infants who weigh substantially less than they should, given how much time has passed since conception, are called small for gestational age (SGA), or small-for-dates. (p. 111; objective 6)

21. Cerebral palsy is a muscular control disorder caused by damage to the brain's motor centers during or before birth. (p. 112; objective 10)

22. Anoxia is a temporary lack of fetal oxygen during the birth process that, if prolonged, can cause brain damage or even death. (p. 112; video lesson, segment 4; objective 10)

23. The Brazelton Neonatal Behavioral Assessment Scale (NBAS) is a test often administered to newborns that measures responsiveness and records 46 behaviors, including 20 reflexes. (p. 113; objective 8)

24. A reflex is an unlearned, involuntary action or movement that responds to a stimulus. A reflex occurs without conscious thought. (p. 113; objective 8)

25. Couvade describes those symptoms of pregnancy and birth that are experienced by fathers. (p. 115; objective 11)

26. A parental alliance develops between a mother and a father because of their mutual commitment to their children; as a result, the parents agree to cooperate and support each other in their shared parental roles. (p. 116; objective 11)

Lesson 4/The Beginnings: Prenatal Development and Birth   **75**

27. Postpartum depression is a profound feeling of sadness and inadequacy sometimes experienced by new mothers. (p. 116; objective 11)

28. The term parent–infant bond describes the strong feelings of attachment between parent and child in the early moments of their relationship together. (p. 116; video lesson; objective 11)

29. Kangaroo care is a type of care provided to newborns where the mother holds the infant on her chest, often between her breasts, for at least an hour a day. This type of care has had notable benefits in improving the sleep patterns, stability, and health of low birthweight infants. (p. 117; objectives 6 & 11)

30. The placenta is the organ that connects the mother's circulatory system with that of her growing embryo, providing nourishment to the developing organism and removing wastes. (video lesson, segment 1; objective 1)

31. The first eight weeks, as well as the last months, of pregnancy are often called the critical period, because teratogenic exposure during these time periods can produce malformations of basic body organs and structure. (video lesson, segment 2; objective 5)

32. An interaction effect occurs when one teratogen intensifies the harmful effects of another. (video lesson, segment 2; objective 5)

33. Amniotic fluid is a clear, slightly yellowish liquid that surrounds the unborn child (fetus) during pregnancy, protecting and cushioning its development. (video lesson, segment 1; objective 7)

34. Spina bifida (or cleft spine) is a birth defect that results from the failure of the spine to close properly during the first month of pregnancy. Research has shown that folic acid (a common B vitamin) is one factor that can reduce the risk of having a baby with neural tube defects such as spina bifida. (video lesson, segment 2; objective 5)

Practice Questions I

Multiple-Choice Questions

1. d. is the correct answer. (video lesson, segment 1; objective 1)

   a. is incorrect. The period of the embryo is from the third through the eighth week after conception.

   b. is incorrect. This term, which refers to the germinal period, is not used in the lesson.

   c. is incorrect. The period of the fetus is from the ninth week until birth.

2. b. is the correct answer. (objective 1)

3. c. is the correct answer. The sex organs do not begin to take shape until the fetal period. (objective 2)

4. c. is the correct answer. (video lesson, segment 3; objective 3)

5. d. is the correct answer. (objectives 4 & 5)

6. a. is the correct answer. (objective 3)

7. d. is the correct answer. (video lesson, segment 2; objective 4)

   a. is incorrect. In general, teratogens can cross the placenta at any time.

   b. is incorrect. Teratogens are agents in the environment, not heritable genes (although susceptibility to individual teratogens has a genetic component).

   c. is incorrect. Although nutrition is an important factor in healthy prenatal development, the textbook does not suggest that nutrition alone can usually counteract the harmful effects of teratogens.

8. a. is the correct answer. (objective 5)

9. b. is the correct answer. (video lesson, segment 4; objective 7)

10. c. is the correct answer. (video lesson, segment 4; objective 8)
11. c. is the correct answer. (objective 6)
12. b. is the correct answer. (objective 6)
13. b. is the correct answer. (objective 6)
14. c. is the correct answer. (video lesson, segment 4; objective 11)

Matching Items
15. j (video lesson, segment 1; objective 2)
16. c (video lesson, segment 1; objective 3)
17. h (video lesson, segment 1; objective 1)
18. k (objective 6)
19. b (objective 8)
20. e (objective 11)
21. g (objective 11)
22. a (video lesson, segment 2; objective 5)
23. d (objective 3)
24. f (objective 4)
25. i (video lesson, segment 1; objective 1)

Practice Questions II

Multiple-Choice Questions
1. c. is the correct answer. (objective 11)
2. c. is the correct answer. (video lesson, segment 1; objectives 1, 2, & 3)
3. a. is the correct answer. (objective 4)
4. a. is the correct answer. (objective 4)
5. d. is the correct answer. (video lesson, segment 4; objective 8)
6. c. is the correct answer. (video lesson, segment 4; objective 6)
7. c. is the correct answer. (objective 7)
8. a. is the correct answer. (objective 7)
9. d. is the correct answer. (video lesson, segment 4; objective 8)
10. a. is the correct answer. (objective 6)
11. b. is the correct answer. (video lesson, segment 2; objective 5)

True or False Items
12. T (objective 11)
13. T (video lesson, segment 1; objective 2)
14. F Behavioral teratogens can affect the fetus at any time during the prenatal period. (video lesson, segment 2; objective 4)
15. F There is no controversy about the damaging effects of smoking during pregnancy; tobacco is a dangerous teratogen. (objective 5)
16. T (video lesson, segment 4; objective 8)
17. T (objective 8)
18. F Though highly desirable, mother–newborn contact at birth is not necessary for the child's normal development or for a good parent-child relationship. Many opportunities for bonding occur throughout childhood. (video lesson, segment 4; objective 11)
19. T (objective 6)

20. F   Approximately one in four births in the United States are now cesarean. (objectives 9 & 10)
21. T   (objective 3)

Applying Your Knowledge

1. b. is the correct answer. (objective 5)
2. b. is the correct answer. (video lesson, segment 1; objectives 1, 2, & 3)

   a. is incorrect. The zygote is the fertilized ovum.

   c. is incorrect. The developing organism is designated a fetus starting at the ninth week.

   d. is incorrect. The indifferent gonad is the mass of cells that will eventually develop into female or male sex organs.
3. c. is the correct answer. (objective 3)
4. b. is the correct answer. (objectives 4 & 5)

   a. is incorrect. This is the virus that causes AIDS.

   c. is incorrect. Rubella may cause blindness, deafness, and brain damage.

   d. is incorrect. The textbook does not discuss the effects of exposure to lead.
5. c. is the correct answer. (video lesson, segment 2; objective 5)

   a. is incorrect. FAS is caused in infants by the mother-to-be drinking three or more drinks daily during pregnancy.

   b. is incorrect. Brain damage is caused by the use of social drugs during pregnancy.

   d. is incorrect. FAE is caused in infants by the mother-to-be drinking 1 ounce of alcohol per day.
6. c. is the correct answer. (video lesson, segment 2; objective 6)
7. a. is the correct answer. (objectives 3 & 4)
8. b. is the correct answer. (objectives 4 & 5)
9. c. is the correct answer. (video lesson, segment 4; objective 11)

   a. & b. are incorrect. Bonding in humans is not a biologically determined event limited to a critical period, as it is in many other animal species.

   d. is a correct. There is no evidence of any gender differences in the formation of the parent–infant bond.
10. c. is the correct answer. If a neonate's Apgar score is below 4, the infant is in critical condition and needs immediate medical attention. (video lesson, segment 4; objective 8)
11. b. is the correct answer. (objective 6)

    a., c., & d. are incorrect. Prenatal malnutrition and maternal tobacco use are the most common causes of a small-for-dates neonate.
12. c. is the correct answer. (objective 6)

    a., b., & d. are incorrect. The incidence of low birthweight is higher among teenaged mothers.
13. d. is the correct answer. (objective 6)

    a. is incorrect. At 266 days, this infant is full term.
14. d. is the correct answer. (video lesson, segment 4; objective 8)

Lesson Review

Lesson 4

The Beginnings
Prenatal Development and Birth

Please Note: Use this matrix to guide your study and achieve the learning objectives of this lesson. It will also help you to view the video, which defines and demonstrates important concepts and skills as they relate to everyday life.

Learning Objective	Textbook	Course Student Guide	Video Lesson
1. Describe the significant developments of the germinal period.	pp. 89–91	Key Terms: 1, 4, 30; Practice Questions I: 1, 2, 17, 25; Practice Questions II: 2; Applying Your Knowledge: 2.	Segment 1: *The First Trimester*
2. Describe the significant developments of the embryonic period.	pp. 91–92	Key Terms: 2, 5; Practice Questions I: 3, 15; Practice Questions II: 2, 13; Applying Your Knowledge: 2.	Segment 1: *The First Trimester*
3. Describe the significant developments of the fetal period, noting the importance of the age of viability, and the fetus's various responses to its immediate environment (the womb).	pp. 92–95	Key Terms: 3, 6, 7, 8; Practice Questions I: 4, 6, 16, 23; Practice Questions II: 2, 21; Applying Your Knowledge: 2, 3, 7.	Segment 1: *The First Trimester*; Segment 3: *The Third Trimester*
4. Define teratology, and identify at least five teratogens.	pp. 102–107	Key Terms: 12; Practice Questions I: 5, 7, 24; Practice Questions II: 3, 4, 14; Applying Your Knowledge: 4, 7, 8.	Segment 2: *Risk Reduction*
5. Outline the effects of teratogens on the developing embryo or fetus, and describe protective steps that can be taken to moderate the risk of exposure.	pp. 102–108	Key Terms: 13, 14, 15, 31, 32, 34; Practice Questions I: 5, 8, 22; Practice Questions II: 11, 15; Applying Your Knowledge: 1, 4, 5, 8.	Segment 2: *Risk Reduction*

Learning Objective	Textbook	Course Student Guide	Video Lesson
6. Distinguish among low-birthweight, preterm, and small-for-gestational-age (SGA) infants, and identify the causes of and treatments for low birthweight.	pp. 110–112	Key Terms: 16, 17, 18, 19, 20, 29; Practice Questions I: 11, 12, 13, 18; Practice Questions II: 6, 10, 19; Applying Your Knowledge: 6, 11, 12, 13.	Segment 2: *Risk Reduction* Segment 3: *The Second Trimester*
7. Describe the normal process of birth, specifying the events of each stage.	p. 96	Key Terms: 33; Practice Questions I: 9; Practice Questions II: 7, 8.	Segment 4: *The Third Trimester*
8. Describe the test used to assess the newborn's condition at birth.	pp. 97, 113–114	Key Terms: 9, 23, 24; Practice Questions I: 10, 19; Practice Questions II: 5, 9, 16, 17; Applying Your Knowledge: 10, 14.	Segment 4: *The Third Trimester*
9. Describe the options available for medical attention during the birthing process, and discuss the pros and cons of medical intervention and traditional birthing practices.	pp. 97–101	Key Terms: 10, 11; Practice Questions II: 20.	
10. Explain the causes of cerebral palsy, and discuss the special needs of high-risk infants.	pp. 112–113	Key Terms: 21, 22; Practice Questions II: 20.	Segment 4: *The Third Trimester*
11. Explain the concept of parent–infant bonding and the current view of most developmentalists regarding early bonding in humans.	pp. 114–117	Key Terms: 25, 26, 27, 28, 29; Practice Questions I: 14, 20, 21; Practice Questions II: 1, 12, 18; Applying Your Knowledge: 9.	Segment 4: *The Third Trimester*

Grow, Baby, Grow!

Lesson 5

The First Two Years:
Biosocial Development

Preview

This is the first of a three-lesson unit that describes the developing person from birth to age 2 in terms of biosocial, cognitive, and psychosocial development. The biosocial domain is the part of human development that includes all the growth and changes that occur in a person's body and the genetic, nutritional, and health factors that affect that growth and change. It also includes the social, cultural, and environmental factors that affect biological development.

The lesson begins with observations on the overall growth and health of infants, including their size and shape and the importance of immunizations during the first two years. A discussion of brain growth and development follows, including how a child's experiences can affect his or her brain development. At birth, the brain contains more than 100 billion nerve cells, or **neurons**, but the networks of nerve fibers that interconnect them are incomplete. During the first few years of a child's life, extensive growth occurs in these neural pathways, enabling the emergence of new capabilities in each domain of development.

The lesson then turns to a discussion of how babies move and control their bodies and the ages at which the average infant advances in ability. Vision and hearing are discussed next, along with research on infant **perception**. The final section discusses the importance of nutrition during the first two years and the consequences of severe **malnutrition**. During the video lesson, pediatricians and developmental psychologists provide expert commentary.

Prior Course Knowledge that Will Be Used in this Lesson

This is the first lesson to focus on the biosocial domain of development. Remember, although the division of human development into three domains makes it easier to study, development is holistic rather than piecemeal: Every aspect of human behavior reflects all three domains. You may also wish to review the material on epigenetic factors in Lesson 3.

Learning Objectives

Use this information to guide your reading, viewing, thinking, and studying. After successfully completing this lesson, you should be able to:

1. Describe the size and proportions of an infant's body, and discuss how babies change during the first two years and how their bodies compare with those of adults.

2. Discuss the reasons public health officials recommend immunizations for infants.

3. Describe the ways in which the brain changes or matures during infancy.

4. Discuss the role of experience in brain development.

5. Describe the basic reflexes of the newborn and distinguish between gross motor skills and fine motor skills.

6. Describe the basic pattern of motor-skill development, and discuss variations in the timing of motor-skill acquisition.

7. Distinguish between sensation and perception, and describe the extent and development of an infant's perceptual abilities using the sense of vision as an example.

8. Describe the nutritional needs of infants and toddlers.

9. Distinguish between protein-calorie malnutrition and undernutrition, identify the potential effects of these conditions on babies, and discuss methods of prevention.

📖 **Read Chapter 5, "The First Two Years: Biosocial Development," pages 121–151, and review pages 113–114 of Chapter 4, "Prenatal Development and Birth."**

⏮ **View the video for Lesson 5, "Grow, Baby, Grow!"**

    Segment 1: *Physical Growth and Health*

    Segment 2: *Brain Growth and Development*

    Segment 3: *Basic Reflexes and Motor Skills*

    Segment 4: *Infant Nutrition*

Summary

Biosocial development during the first two years is so rapid that infants often seem to change before their parents' very eyes. The newborn seems top-heavy in body proportions, with its head being one-fourth of total body length (in comparison to one-eighth of body length in an adult). By age two, the average toddler's body weight is about one-fifth adult weight and body length has increased to about one-half adult height.

Brain development is also rapid during infancy. By age two, the brain has attained about 75 percent of its adult weight, and there has been a fivefold increase in the density of **dendrite** networks in the **cortex**. As the brain develops, brain waves and physiological states become more cyclical and distinct.

The newborn's motor ability is limited to reflexes. By 6 months, most babies can reach, grab, and hold onto dangling objects. The average child can walk with assistance at 9 months, stand momentarily at 10 months, and take steps unassisted at 12 months. Although all healthy infants develop the same **motor skills** in the same sequence, the age at which these skills are acquired varies greatly from infant to infant. Variations in the acquisition of motor skills can be attributed in part to inherited factors, such as activity level, rate of physical maturation, and body type. Environmental factors, such as medical care, nutrition, and patterns of infant care, are also influential. Note that the video for Lesson 5 draws a distinction between reflexes, which are involuntary responses to stimuli, and motor skills, which require voluntary participation.

At birth, both **sensation** and **perception** are apparent. Vision is the least well developed of the senses. Newborns can focus better on objects that are between 4 and 30 inches away. By 6 months, visual acuity approaches 20/20, and infants can use both eyes to track moving objects well. In contrast, hearing is comparatively acute in the newborn. Newborns can differentiate their mother's voice from those of other women; by 1 month, they can perceive differences between very similar sounds.

For its nutritional benefits, breast milk is the ideal food for most babies. It is always sterile and at body temperature, contains more essential vitamins and iron than cow's milk, is more digestible, and provides the infant with the mother's immunity to disease. Immunizations also provide immunity to many devastating diseases. The primary cause of **protein-calorie malnutrition** in developing countries is early cessation of breast-feeding. Severe deficiency can cause **marasmus** in infants and **kwashiorkor** in toddlers. In developed countries, severe infant **malnutrition** is unusual; more prevalent is **undernutrition**. Social and/or family problems are often responsible for undernutrition in developed countries.

📖   **Review all reading assignments for this lesson.**

💻   **As assigned by your instructor, complete the optional online component for this lesson.**

Key Terms

Using your own words, write a brief definition or explanation of each of the following terms on a separate piece of paper.

1. head-sparing
2. percentile
3. rapid eye movement (REM) sleep
4. co-sleeping
5. neuron
6. cortex
7. axon
8. dendrites
9. synapses
10. transient exuberance
11. experience-expectant
12. experience-dependent
13. prefrontal cortex
14. shaken baby syndrome
15. self-righting
16. sensation
17. perception
18. binocular vision
19. motor skills
20. gross motor skills
21. fine motor skills
22. protein-calorie malnutrition
23. stunting
24. wasting
25. marasmus
26. kwashiorkor
27. metabolism
28. enriched environment
29. reflexes
30. sucking reflex
31. rooting reflex
32. breathing reflex
33. pincer grasp
34. undernutrition
35. failure-to-thrive
36. malnutrition

Practice Questions I

Multiple-Choice Questions

1. Stunting occurs when
   a. a baby is swaddled.
   b. a child receives inadequate nutrition.
   c. a child walks too early.
   d. both parents are stunted.

2. Compared to the first year, growth during the second year
   a. proceeds at a slower rate.
   b. continues at about the same rate.
   c. includes proportionately more insulating fat.
   d. usually demonstrates drop-offs in percentile ranking.

3. Norms among nations suggest that the earliest walkers in the world are infants from
   a. Western Europe.
   b. the United States.
   c. Uganda.
   d. Eastern Europe.

4. The interaction between inherited and environmental factors is responsible for
   a. variation in the age at which infants master specific motor skills.
   b. physical growth, but not the development of motor skills.
   c. the fact that babies in the United States walk earlier than do Ugandan babies.
   d. the fact that infants master motor skills more slowly today than they did fifty years ago.

5. The development of binocular vision at about 14 weeks results in
   a. a sudden improvement in the ability to focus the two eyes in a coordinated manner to see one image.
   b. the rapid development of distance vision.
   c. the refinement of the ability to discriminate colors.
   d. both a and b.

6. Proportionally, the head of the infant is about _____ of total body length; the head of an adult is about _____ of total body length.
   a. one-fourth; one-third
   b. one-eighth; one-fourth
   c. one-fourth; one-eighth
   d. one-third; one-fourth

7. Compared with formula-fed infants, breast-fed infants tend to have
   a. greater weight gain.
   b. fewer allergies and digestive upsets.
   c. less frequent feedings during the first few months.
   d. more social approval.

8. Marasmus and kwashiorkor are caused by
    a. bloating.
    b. protein-calorie deficiency.
    c. living in a developing country.
    d. poor family food habits.

9. Immunizations
    a. are credited with saving millions of lives.
    b. should be avoided until a child is two.
    c. provide immunity against various diseases.
    d. do both a and c.

10. Which of the following allows toddlers to begin walking?
    a. brain maturation
    b. practice
    c. muscle strength
    d. all of the above

11. Which of the following is true of motor-skill development in healthy infants?
    a. It follows the same basic sequence the world over.
    b. It occurs at different rates from individual to individual.
    c. It follows norms that vary from one ethnic group to another.
    d. All of the above are true.

12. Most of the nerve cells that a human brain will ever possess are present
    a. at conception.
    b. about 1 month following conception.
    c. at birth.
    d. at age 5 or 6.

Matching Items
Match each definition or description with its corresponding term.

Terms
13. ____J____ neurons
14. ____F____ dendrites
15. ____D____ kwashiorkor
16. ____A____ marasmus
17. ____G____ gross motor skill

18. ____B____ fine motor skill
19. ____H____ stunting
20. ____E____ sucking reflex
21. ____C____ protein-calorie malnutrition
22. ____I____ transient exuberance

Definitions or Descriptions
a. protein deficiency during the first year in which growth stops and body tissues waste away
b. picking up an object
c. the most common serious nutrition problem of infancy
d. protein deficiency during toddlerhood

e. newborns suck anything that touches their lips

f. nerve fibers that allow communication among neurons

g. running or jumping

h. the failure of children to grow to a normal height for their age due to malnutrition

i. the phenomenal increase in neural connections over the first 2 years

j. nerve cells

Practice Questions II

Multiple-Choice Questions

1. Dendrite is to axon as neural _____ is to neural _____.
   a. input; output
   b. output; input
   c. myelin; synapse
   d. synapse; myelin

2. Two benefits of immunizations are that they
   a. increase growth rates.
   b. provide immunity for the child.
   c. stop the spread of disease.
   d. do b & c.

3. Most babies can reach for, grasp, and hold onto an object by about the _____ month.
   a. second
   b. sixth
   c. ninth
   d. fourteenth

4. Activity level, rate of physical maturation, and how fat the infant is affect the age at which an infant walks and acquires other motor skills. They are examples of
   a. norms.
   b. environmental factors.
   c. inherited factors.
   d. the interaction of environment and heredity.

5. During the first weeks of life, babies seem to focus reasonably well on
   a. little in their environment.
   b. objects at a distance of 4 to 30 inches.
   c. objects at a distance of 1 to 3 inches.
   d. objects several feet away.

6. An advantage of breast milk over formula is that it
   a. is always sterile and at body temperature.
   b. contains traces of medications ingested by the mother.
   c. can be given without involving the father.
   d. contains more protein and vitamin D than does formula.

7. The primary cause of malnutrition in developing countries is
   a. formula feeding.
   b. inadequate food supply.
   c. disease.
   d. early cessation of breast-feeding.

8. Climbing is to using a crayon as _____ is to _____.
   a. fine motor skill; gross motor skill
   b. gross motor skill; fine motor skill
   c. reflex; fine motor skill
   d. reflex; gross motor skill

9. Breast milk
   a. is more digestible than formula.
   b. changes in composition as a baby gets older.
   c. may not contain enough vitamin D.
   d. involes all of the above.

10. A common cause of undernutrition in young children is
    a. ignorance of the infant's nutritional needs.
    b. the absence of socioeconomic policies that reflect the importance of infant nutrition.
    c. problems in the family, such as maternal depression.
    d. all of the above.

11. Neurotransmitters are chemical messengers that diffuse across the
    a. axon.
    b. myelin sheath.
    c. dendrite.
    d. synaptic gap.

12. Crawling is an example of
    a. a gross motor skill.
    b. a fine motor skill.
    c. a reflex.
    d. cognitive development.

True or False Items

Write T (for true) or F (for false) on the line in front of each statement.

13. _____ Gross motor skills develop before fine motor skills.

14. _____ Infants of all ethnic backgrounds develop the same motor skills at approximately the same age.

15. _____ The typical two-year-old is almost one-fifth its adult weight and one-half its adult height.

16. _____ Vision is better developed than hearing in most newborns.

17. _____ More than 25 percent of children worldwide suffer from malnutrition.

18. _____ Infants typically grow about one inch per month during the first year.

19. _____ Over the first two years, the infant's metabolic activity decreases steadily.

Applying Your Knowledge

1. Alicia, age 5, is of normal height but is severely underweight. Alicia is
   a. developing optimally.
   b. wasted but not stunted.
   c. is stunted but not wasted.
   d. is displaying a normal variation.

2. The brain development that permits seeing and hearing in human infants appears to be
   a. totally dependent upon genetic programming, present at birth.
   b. totally dependent upon visual and auditory experiences in the first few months.
   c. "fine-tuned" by visual and auditory experiences in the first few months.
   d. independent of both genetic and environmental influences.

3. Dan has 20/400 vision and is able to discriminate subtle sound differences. Dan most likely
   a. is a preterm infant.
   b. has brain damage in the visual processing areas of the cortex.
   c. is a newborn.
   d. is slow-to-mature.

4. A baby turns her head and starts to suck when her receiving blanket is brushed against her cheek. The baby is displaying the
   a. sucking reflex.
   b. rooting reflex.
   c. Babinski reflex.
   d. Moro reflex.

5. Sensation is to perception as _____ is to _____.
    a. hearing; seeing
    b. detecting a stimulus; making sense of a stimulus
    c. making sense of a stimulus; detecting a stimulus
    d. tasting; smelling

6. Three-week-old Nathan should have the least difficulty focusing on the sight of
    a. stuffed animals on a bookshelf across the room from his crib.
    b. his mother's face as she holds him in her arms.
    c. the checkerboard pattern in the wallpaper covering the ceiling of his room.
    d. the family dog as it dashes into the nursery.

7. Geneva has been undernourished throughout childhood. It is likely that she will be
    a. smaller and shorter than her genetic potential would dictate.
    b. slow in intellectual development.
    c. less resistant to disease.
    d. all of the above.

Answer Key

Key Terms
1. Head-sparing is a phenomenon in which the brain is biologically protected when malnutrition temporarily affects body growth. (p. 124; objectives 1 & 9)

2. A percentile denotes where the child falls on a given norm, compared to the rest of the population. Percentiles range from 1 to 100, so a child at the 50th percentile is average compared to others of the same age. (p. 124; objective 1)

3. Rapid eye movement (REM) sleep is characterized by rapid brain activity, dreams, and movements of the eyes. The amount of time we spend in REM sleep is greatest in infancy, and declines across development. (p. 125; objective 3)

4. Also referred to as bed-sharing, co-sleeping occurs when parents and their children (usually infants) sleep in the same bed. (p. 126; objective 3)

5. A neuron, or nerve cell, is the main component of the central nervous system. (p. 127; video lesson, segment 2; objective 3)

6. The cortex is the thin outer layer of the brain that is involved in the voluntary, cognitive aspects of the mind. (p. 128; objective 3)

    Memory aid: Cortex in Latin means "bark." As bark covers a tree, the cortex is the "bark of the brain."

7. An axon is the nerve fiber extension that sends impulses from one neuron to the dendrites of other neurons. (p. 128; video lesson, segment 2; objective 3)

8. Dendrites are nerve fiber extensions that receive the impulses transmitted from other neurons via their axons. (p. 128; video lesson, segment 2; objective 3)

9. A synapse is the point at which the axon of a sending neuron meets the dendrites of a receiving neuron. At that point, brain chemicals called neurotransmitters carry the impulse from axon to dendrites. (p. 128; objective 3)

10. Transient exuberance is the dramatic increase in neural connections that occurs in an infant's brain over the first two years of life. (p. 129; video lesson, segment 2; objective 3)

11. The term experience-expectant refers to brain functions that require basic common experiences in order to develop. (p. 131; objective 4)

12. The term experience-dependent refers to brain functions that depend on particular, variable experiences that occur in some families but not in others. (p. 131; objective 4)

13. The prefrontal cortex is the last region of the brain to reach maturity. It is involved with planning, decision making, and emotion regulation, and it is largely inactive in infants. (p. 132; objective 4)

14. Shaken baby syndrome is a condition brought about by the forceful shaking of an infant, often in an attempt by adults to stop the child from crying. This shaking breaks connections between neurons and ruptures blood vessels in the brain, usually resulting in long-term damage. (p. 132; objective 4)

15. Self-righting refers to the natural tendency for an individual to compensate for a deficit in development. For example, a child who does not have stimulating toys will be motivated to seek out and play with any object that is available. (p. 132; objective 4)

16. Sensation is the process by which a sensory system detects a particular stimulus. (p. 134; objective 7)

17. Perception is the mental processing of sensory information, when the brain interprets a sensation (p. 134; objective 7)

18. Binocular vision is the ability to use both eyes together to focus on a single object. (p. 136; objective 7)

    Memory aid: Bi- indicates "two"; ocular means something pertaining to the eye. Binocular vision is vision for "two eyes."

19. Motor skills are physical skills that involve large body movements, such as waving the arms, walking, and jumping (gross motor skills), and small body movements, such as picking up a coin or drawing (fine motor skills). (p. 137; video lesson, segment 3; objective 5)

20. Gross motor skills are physical abilities that demand large body movements, such as climbing, jumping, or running. (p. 137; video lesson, segment 3; objective 5)

21. Fine motor skills are physical abilities that require precise, small movements, such as picking up a coin. (p. 138; video lesson, segment 3; objective 5)

22. Protein-calorie malnutrition results when a person does not consume enough nourishment to thrive. (p. 147; objective 9)

23. Stunting is the failure of children to grow to a normal height for their age due to severe and chronic malnutrition. (p. 147; objective 9)

24. Wasting is the tendency for children to be severely underweight for their age as a result of malnutrition. (p. 148; objective 9)

25. Marasmus is a disease caused by severe protein-calorie deficiency during the first year of life. Growth stops, body tissues waste away, and the infant dies. (p. 148; objective 9)

26. Kwashiorkor is a disease caused by protein-calorie deficiency during toddlerhood. The child's face, legs, and abdomen swell with water, sometimes making the child appear well fed. Other body parts are degraded, including the hair, which becomes thin, brittle, and colorless. (p. 149; objective 9)

27. Metabolism refers to the physical and chemical processes in the body that promote growth and sustain life. (video lesson, segment 2; objective 3)

28. An enriched environment is one that provides the developing child with a highly nurturing and stimulating atmosphere in which to grow and learn. (video lesson, segment 2; objective 4)

29. Reflexes are involuntary physical responses to specific stimuli. (video lesson, segment 3; objective 5)

30. The sucking reflex is the involuntary tendency of newborns to suck anything that touches their lips. This reflex fosters feeding. (video lesson, segment 3; objective 5)

31. The rooting reflex, which helps babies find a nipple, causes them to turn their heads and start to suck when something brushes against their cheek. (video lesson, segment 3; objective 5)

32. The breathing reflex is an involuntary physical response that ensures that the infant has an adequate supply of oxygen and discharges carbon dioxide. (video lesson, segment 3; objective 5)

33. The pincer grasp is when the thumb and forefinger are used together to hold an object. (video lesson, segment 3; objective 5)

34. Undernutrition is a nutritional problem in which a child is noticeably underweight or short in stature compared to the norms. (video lesson, segment 4; objective 9)

35. Failure-to-thrive is undernutrition that involves a child who lives in an adequately nourished community but is not exhibiting normal childhood weight gain. (video lesson, segment 4; objective 9)

36. Malnutrition (referred to as protein-calorie malnutrition in the textbook) occurs when a child does not consume the appropriate nutrients (of any kind) that it needs to grow and develop. (p. 147; video lesson, segment 4; objective 9)

Practice Questions I

Multiple-Choice Questions

1. b. is the correct answer. (objective 9)

2. a. is the correct answer. (objective 1)

3. c. is the correct answer. (objective 6)

4. a. is the correct answer. (objective 6)

    b. is incorrect. Inherited and environmental factors are important for both physical growth and the development of motor skills.

    c. is incorrect. On average, Ugandan babies walk earlier than do babies in the United States.

    d. is incorrect. In fact, just the opposite is true.

5. a. is the correct answer. (objective 7)

6. c. is the correct answer. (video lesson, segment 1; objective 1)

7. b. is the correct answer, because breast milk is more digestible than cow's milk or formula. (video lesson, segment 4; objective 8)

    a., c., & d. are incorrect. Breast- and bottle-fed babies do not differ in these attributes.

8. b. is the correct answer. (objective 9)

9. d. is the correct answer. (objective 2)

10. d. is the correct answer. (objective 6)

11. d. is the correct answer. (objective 6)

12. c. is the correct answer. (objective 3)

Matching Items

13. j (video lesson, segment 2; objective 3)
14. f (video lesson, segment 2; objective 3)
15. d (objective 9)
16. a (objective 9)
17. g (video lesson, segment 3; objective 5)
18. b (video lesson, segment 3; objective 5)
19. h (objective 9)
20. e (video lesson, segment 3; objective 5)
21. c (objective 9)
22. i (video lesson, segment 2; objective 3)

Practice Questions II

Multiple-Choice Questions

1. a. is the correct answer. (video lesson, segment 2; objective 3)
2. d. is the correct answer. (objective 2)
3. b. is the correct answer. (objective 6)
4. d. is the correct answer. (objective 6)
5. b. is the correct answer. (objective 7)
6. a. is the correct answer. (video lesson, segment 4; objective 8)

   b. is incorrect. If anything, this is a potential disadvantage of breast milk over formula.

   c. is incorrect. So can formula.

   d. is incorrect. Breast milk contains more iron, vitamin C, and vitamin A than cow's milk; it does not contain more protein and vitamin D, however.

7. d. is the correct answer. (objective 9)
8. b. is the correct answer. (video lesson, segment 3; objective 5)

   c. & d. are incorrect. Reflexes are involuntary responses; climbing and using a crayon are both voluntary responses.

9. d. is the correct answer. (video lesson, segment 4; objective 8)
10. d is the correct answer. (objective 9)
11. d. is the correct answer. (objective 3)
12. a. is the correct answer. (video lesson, segment 3; objective 5)

True or False Items

13. F   Gross motor skills and fine motor skills develop together, each in its own time. (objective 5)
14. F   Although all healthy infants develop the same motor skills in the same sequence, the age at which these skills are acquired can vary greatly from infant to infant. (objective 6)
15. T   (objective 1)
16. F   Vision is relatively poorly developed at birth, whereas hearing is well developed. (objective 7)
17. T   (objective 9)
18. T   (video lesson, segment 1; objective 1)

19. F Metabolic activity increases, partly as a result of the dramatic growth occurring in the brain. (video lesson, segment 2; objective 3)

Applying Your Knowledge

1. b. is the correct answer. (objective 9)

2. c. is the correct answer. (objective 4)

   a. is incorrect. If this were true, research would show that restriction had no effect on sensory abilities.

   b. is incorrect. If this were true, sensory restriction would cause much more serious impairment than it does.

   d. is incorrect. Sensory restriction research demonstrates that both genetic and environmental factors are important in the development of sensory abilities.

3. c. is the correct answer. (objective 7)

4. b. is the correct answer. (video lesson, segment 3; objective 5)

   a. is incorrect. This is the reflexive sucking of newborns in response to anything that touches their lips.

   c. is incorrect. This is the response that infants make when their feet are stroked.

   d. is incorrect. In this response to startling noises, newborns fling their arms outward and then bring them together on their chests as if to hold on to something.

5. b. is the correct answer. (objective 7)

   a. & d. are incorrect. Sensation and perception operate in all of these sensory modalities.

6. b. is the correct answer. This is true because, at birth, focusing is best for objects between 4 and 30 inches away. (objective 7)

   a., c., & d. are incorrect. Newborns have very poor distance vision; each of these situations involves a distance greater than the optimal focus range.

7. d. is the correct answer. (video lesson, segment 4; objective 9)

Lesson Review

Lesson 5

The First Two Years
Biosocial Development

Please Note: Use this matrix to guide your study and achieve the learning objectives of this lesson. It will also help you to view the video, which defines and demonstrates important concepts and skills as they relate to everyday life.

Learning Objective	Textbook	Course Student Guide	Video Lesson
1. Describe the size and proportions of an infant's body, and discuss how babies change during the first two years and how their bodies compare with those of adults.	pp. 123–124	Key Terms: 1, 2; Practice Questions I: 2, 6; Practice Questions II: 15, 18.	Segment 1: *Physical Growth and Health;*
2. Discuss the reasons public health officials recommend immunizations for infants.	pp. 141–143	Practice Questions I: 9; Practice Question II: 2.	
3. Describe the ways in which the brain changes or matures during infancy.	pp. 125–130	Key Terms: 3, 4, 5, 6, 7, 8, 9, 10, 27, 28; Practice Questions I: 12, 13, 14, 22; Practice Questions II: 1, 11, 19.	Segment 2: *Brain Growth and Development*
4. Discuss the role of experience in brain development.	pp. 130–134	Key Terms: 11, 12, 13, 14, 15; Applying Your Knowledge: 2.	Segment 2: *Brain Growth and Development;*
5. Describe the basic reflexes of the newborn and distinguish between gross motor skills and fine motor skills.	pp. 113–114, 137–138	Key Terms: 19, 20, 21, 29, 30, 31, 32, 33; Practice Questions I: 17, 18, 20; Practice Questions II: 8, 12, 13; Applying Your Knowledge: 4.	Segment 3: *Basic Reflexes and Motor Skills*
6. Describe the basic pattern of motor-skill development, and discuss variations in the timing of motor-skill acquisition.	pp. 137–140	Practice Questions I: 3, 4, 10, 11; Practice Questions II: 3, 4, 14.	

Learning Objective	Textbook	Course Student Guide	Video Lesson
7. Distinguish between sensation and perception, and describe the extent and development of an infant's perceptual abilities using the sense of vision as an example.	pp. 134–137	Key Terms: 16, 17, 18; Practice Questions I: 5; Practice Questions II: 5, 16; Applying Your Knowledge: 3, 5, 6.	
8. Describe the nutritional needs of infants and toddlers.	pp. 144–147	Practice Questions I: 7; Practice Questions II: 6, 9.	Segment 4: Infant Nutrition
9. Distinguish between protein-calorie malnutrition and undernutrition, identify the potential effects of these conditions on babies, and discuss methods of prevention.	pp. 147–149	Key Terms: 1, 22, 23, 24, 25, 26, 34, 35, 36; Practice Questions I: 1, 8, 15, 16, 19, 21; Practice Questions II: 7, 10, 17; Applying Your Knowledge: 1, 7.	Segment 4: Infant Nutrition

The Little Scientist

Lesson 6

The First Two Years:
Cognitive Development

Preview

Lesson 6 is the first of the course lessons to focus on the domain of *cognition,* by which we mean the mental processes involved in thinking. The lesson focuses on the various ways in which infant cognitive development is revealed: through perception (which, as you'll recall from Lesson 5, refers to the mental processing of sensory information), memory, intelligence, and language development. The lesson begins with a description of infant perception and the influential theory of **affordances**. Central to this theory is the idea that infants gain cognitive understanding of their world through affordances, that is, opportunities to perceive and interact with the objects and environments around them.

The lesson also discusses the key cognitive elements needed by infants to structure their environment. Using the **habituation** procedure, researchers have found that the speed with which infants recognize familiarity and seek something novel is related to later cognitive skill. It points out the importance of memory to cognitive development.

This video lesson, "The Little Scientist," outlines Jean Piaget's theory of **sensorimotor intelligence**, which maintains that infants think exclusively with their senses and motor skills. Piaget's six stages of sensorimotor intelligence are examined.

Finally, the lesson turns to the most remarkable cognitive achievement of the first two years, the acquisition of language. Beginning with a description of the infant's first attempts at language, the video and chapter follow the sequence of events that leads to the child's ability to utter two-word sentences. The lesson concludes with an examination of language learning as teamwork involving babies and adults, who, in a sense, teach each other the unique human process of verbal communication.

As you complete this lesson, think about a baby you know (and/or interview the child's parents, if time allows). Would you describe this child as a smart baby? How does this infant express his or her intelligence? Observe how this child reacts to new stimuli and assimilates new information. Study the child's usual environment. What objects, people, and situations does the child typically encounter that could afford him or her the opportunity to learn? What kinds of things can this baby remember, and under what circumstances? How far has this child's language advanced relative to other babies of the same age? What were his or her first vocalizations and/or first words? Speculate on how one could encourage language development in this child.

Prior Course Knowledge that Will Be Used in this Lesson

- This lesson will return to Piaget's theory of cognitive development (Lesson 1) with a discussion of sensorimotor intelligence. (Recall that Piaget's theory specifies four major periods):

  1. **Sensorimotor (birth to 2 years)** ← **The First Two Years**
  2. Preoperational (2 to 6 years)
  3. Concrete Operational (7 to 11 years)
  4. Formal Operational (12 years through adulthood)

- You may wish to review the theories of B. F. Skinner and Lev Vygotsky (Lesson 1). They will come up again as the textbook and video lesson discuss how babies acquire language and what caregivers can do to help.

- In the section on perception, the textbook will refer to the importance of brain growth and development (Lesson 5). You may wish to review terms such as cortex, axons, and dendrites.

Learning Objectives

Use this information to guide your reading, viewing, thinking, and studying. After successfully completing this lesson, you should be able to:

1. Explain the Gibsons' contextual view of perception, and relate it to the idea of affordances, giving examples of affordances perceived by infants.
2. Explain what object permanence is, how it is tested in infancy, and what these tests reveal.
3. Discuss research findings on infant memory and infants' understanding of cause-and-effect relationships.
4. Identify and describe Piaget's stages of sensorimotor intelligence, and give examples of the behavior associated with each stage.
5. Describe language development during the first two years, and identify its major hallmarks.
6. Contrast the theories of Skinner and Chomsky regarding early language development, and explain current views on language learning.
7. Explain the importance of child-directed speech, and identify its main features.

📖 **Read Chapter 6, "The First Two Years: Cognitive Development," pages 153–177.**

⏮ **View the video for Lesson 6, "The Little Scientists."**

Segment 1: *Sensorimotor Intelligence*

Segment 2: *Language Development*

Summary

During the first two years of life, cognitive development proceeds at a phenomenal pace as the infant is transformed from a baby who can know its world only through a limited set of basic reflexes into a toddler capable of imitating others, anticipating and remembering events, and pretending. According to Jean Piaget—often called the "father of cognitive development"—infants learn about their environment by using their senses and motor skills (**sensorimotor intelligence**). They begin by using and then adapting their reflexes (Stages 1 and 2); soon thereafter they become aware of their own and others' actions and reactions, and this awareness guides their thinking (Stage 3). By the end of the first year, they are able to set and achieve simple goals (Stage 4). During the second year, toddlers discover new ways to achieve their goals, first by actively experimenting with objects and actions (Stage 5) and then by manipulating mental images of objects and behaviors (Stage 6). Most significant among the advances of infancy is the development of language. By age 2, the average toddler has a relatively large vocabulary and is able to converse effectively with others.

By 3 months, infants have begun to organize their perceptual experience by identifying the boundaries of separate three-dimensional objects. One way young infants learn to deduce the boundaries of objects is by observing how the parts of the object move together through space. During the first 6 months, infants also establish a rudimentary understanding of perceptual constancy, the awareness that the size or shape of an object remains the same despite changes in its appearance due to a change in its location.

Infants' ability to coordinate sensory systems indicates extensive cognitive processing of perceptual information. Both intermodal perception (associating information from one sensory modality with information from another) and cross-modal perception (using information from one sensory modality to imagine something in another) are evident in the first months of life.

The remarkable speed and ease of infants' perceptual accomplishments have led some researchers to conclude that many of these basic perceptual skills are innate, or that infants are biologically endowed with the capacities to quickly acquire these abilities. Infants conceptualize their world in increasingly more meaningful ways that are relevant to their day-to-day encounters with objects and people.

Although standard Piagetian tasks suggest that infants do not search for hidden objects until about 8 months of age, studies using the habituation technique demonstrate that infants as young as 3.5–4.5 months have a basic understanding of **object permanence** long before they can demonstrate this on a hidden-object task. Infants as young as 3 months are capable of anticipating what will occur next in a sequence of events they have observed repeatedly. By 9 months, infants can show **deferred imitation** of a model whose actions they had observed a day earlier.

Infants are well equipped to learn language from birth, partly because of innate readiness and partly because of their auditory experiences during the final prenatal months. All children follow the same sequence of accomplishments in early language development, although their timing may vary considerably. They become competent first in language function (to understand and be understood) and later in language structure. At every stage of development—including the preverbal stage when infants use cries, cooing, **babbling**, and gestures to communicate—children understand much more than they are capable of expressing.

Toddlers differ in their vocabulary growth: some learn mainly naming words (referential), while others learn a higher proportion of words that facilitate social interaction (expressive). Toddlers initially show underextension of word meanings: words are applied more narrowly than they should be. Overextension, or overgeneralization, of a small set of words to inappropriate objects indicates that language development is proceeding normally, with the child forming and testing linguistic hypotheses. The first words, used as one-word sentences, occur by about 1 year, and the first two-word sentence at about 21 months.

📖 **Review all reading assignments for this lesson.**

💻 **As assigned by your instructor, complete the optional online component for this lesson.**

Key Terms

Using your own words, write a brief definition or explanation of each of the following terms on a separate piece of paper.

1. sensorimotor intelligence
2. primary circular reactions
3. secondary circular reactions
4. object permanence
5. tertiary circular reactions
6. little scientist
7. deferred imitation
8. habituation
9. fMRI
10. information-processing theory
11. affordance
12. visual cliff
13. dynamic perception
14. people preference
15. reminder session
16. child-directed speech
17. babbling
18. naming explosion
19. holophrase
20. grammar
21. language acquisition device (LAD)
22. mental combinations
23. reduplicative babbling
24. semantics
25. intonation

Practice Questions I

Multiple-Choice Questions

1. In general terms, the Gibsons' concept of affordances emphasizes the idea that the individual perceives an object in terms of its

   a. economic importance.
   b. physical qualities.
   c. function or use to the individual.
   d. role in the larger culture or environment.

2. According to Piaget, when a baby repeats an action that has just triggered a pleasing response from his or her caregiver, a stage _____ behavior has occurred.

   a. one
   b. two
   c. three
   d. six

3. Sensorimotor intelligence begins with a baby's first

   a. attempt to crawl.
   b. reflex actions.
   c. primary circular reaction.
   d. adaptation of a reflex.

4. Piaget and the Gibsons would most likely agree that
   a. perception is largely automatic.
   b. language development is biologically predisposed in children.
   c. learning and perception are active cognitive processes.
   d. it is unwise to "push" children too hard academically.

5. By the end of the first year, infants usually learn how to
   a. accomplish simple goals.
   b. manipulate various symbols.
   c. construct mental combinations.
   d. pretend.

6. When an infant begins to understand that objects exist even when they are out of sight, she or he has begun to understand the concept of object
   a. displacement.
   b. importance.
   c. permanence.
   d. location.

7. Today, most cognitive psychologists view language acquisition as
   a. primarily the result of imitation of adult speech.
   b. a behavior that is determined primarily by biological maturation.
   c. a behavior determined entirely by learning.
   d. determined by both biological maturation and learning.

8. Children around the world
   a. attain language skills according to ethnically specific timetables.
   b. follow virtually the same sequence of early language development.
   c. routinely develop the same depth of linguistic ability despite cultural differences.
   d. attain language skills in a very different sequence because of cultural differences.

9. The average baby speaks a few words at about
   a. 6 months.
   b. 9 months.
   c. 12 months.
   d. 24 months.

10. A single word used by toddlers to express a complete thought is
   a. a holophrase.
   b. child-directed speech.
   c. reduplicative babbling.
   d. intonation.

11. A distinctive form of language, with a particular pitch, structure, and other elements, that adults use in talking to infants is called
    a. a holophrase.
    b. the LAD.
    c. child-directed speech.
    d. conversation.

12. A toddler who taps on the computer's keyboard after having observed her mother sending e-mail earlier in the day is demonstrating
    a. assimilation.
    b. accommodation.
    c. deferred imitation.
    d. dynamic perception.

Matching Items
Match each definition or description with its corresponding term.

Terms
13. ___D___ mental combinations
14. ___E___ affordances
15. ___C___ object permanence
16. ___G___ sensorimotor intelligence
17. ___A___ babbling
18. ___F___ holophrase
19. ___B___ dynamic perception
20. ___H___ reduplicative babbling

Definitions or Descriptions
a. repetitive utterance of certain syllables
b. perception that focuses on movement and change
c. the realization that something that is out of sight continues to exist
d. trying out actions mentally
e. opportunities for interaction that an object or place offers
f. a single word used to express a complete thought
g. thinking using the senses and motor skills
h. a type of babbling in which a baby puts two syllables together and repeats them over and over

Practice Questions II

Multiple-Choice Questions

1. Stage five (12 to 18 months) of sensorimotor intelligence is best described as
   a. first acquired adaptations.
   b. the period of the "little scientist."
   c. procedures for making interesting sights last.
   d. new means through symbolization.

2. Which of the following is **NOT** evidence of dynamic perception during infancy?

   a. Babies prefer to look at things in motion.

   b. Babies form simple expectations of the path that a moving object will follow.

   c. Babies use movement cues to discern the boundaries of objects.

   d. Babies quickly grasp that even though objects look different when seen from different viewpoints, they are the same objects.

3. Recent research suggests that the concept of object permanence

   a. fades after a few months.

   b. is a skill some children never acquire.

   c. may occur earlier and more gradually than Piaget recognized.

   d. involves pretending as well as mental combinations.

4. An infant in the sensorimotor stage who consistently attempts to suck her own thumb is exhibiting

   a. primary circular reactions.

   b. secondary circular reactions.

   c. perseveration.

   d. emotional maladjustment.

5. For Noam Chomsky, the "language acquisition device" refers to

   a. the human predisposition to acquire language.

   b. the portion of the human brain that processes speech.

   c. the vocabulary of the language the child is exposed to.

   d. all of the above.

6. The first stage of sensorimotor intelligence lasts until

   a. infants can anticipate events that will fulfill their needs.

   b. infants begin to adapt their reflexes to the environment.

   c. object permanence has been achieved.

   d. infants are capable of thinking about past and future events.

7. Piaget was incorrect in his belief that infants under 8 months do not have

   a. object permanence.

   b. intelligence.

   c. goal-directed behavior.

   d. all of the above.

8. The purposeful actions that begin to develop in sensorimotor stage four are called

   a. reflexes.

   b. affordances.

   c. goal-directed behaviors.

   d. mental combinations.

9. What is the correct sequence of language development in babies?
    a. crying, babbling, cooing, first word
    b. crying, cooing, babbling, first word
    c. crying, babbling, first word, cooing
    d. crying, cooing, first word, babbling

10. Compared with hearing babies, deaf babies
    a. are less likely to babble.
    b. are more likely to babble.
    c. begin to babble vocally at about the same age.
    d. begin to babble manually at about the same age as hearing babies begin to babble vocally.

11. According to Skinner, children acquire language
    a. as a result of an inborn ability to use the basic structure of language.
    b. through reinforcement and conditioning.
    c. mostly because of biological maturation.
    d. in a fixed sequence of predictable stages.

Matching Items
Match each definition or description with its corresponding term.

Terms
12. ___I___ goal-directed behavior
13. ___C___ information-processing theory
14. ___K___ intonation
15. ___A___ reminder session
16. ___H___ little scientist
17. ___B___ grammar
18. ___E___ naming explosion
19. ___D___ habituation study
20. ___J___ deferred imitation
21. ___F___ LAD
22. ___L___ semantics
23. ___G___ child-directed speech

Definitions or Descriptions
a. an experience intended to help a person recollect something
b. rules of word order, verb forms, and all other methods used to communicate meaning
c. theory of human cognition that compares thinking to the ways in which a computer analyzes data
d. a technique for studying whether infants can detect a difference between two objects or events
e. dramatic increase in vocabulary that begins at about 18 months
f. a hypothetical device that facilitates language development
g. also called "motherese" or "baby talk"
h. Piaget's term for the stage-five toddler
i. purposeful actions
j. an infant's act of copying behavior witnessed hours or days earlier
k. the cadence, tone, or emphasis of speech
l. the underlying meaning of words

Applying Your Knowledge

1. According to Skinner's theory, an infant who learns to delight his father by saying "da-da" is probably benefiting from
   a. social reinforcers, such as smiles and hugs.
   b. tertiary circular reaction.
   c. habituation.
   d. an innate ability to use language.

2. Six-month-old Juan shows visible excitement over a new mobile over his crib. After a few weeks, he is much less interested in the mobile. This is evidence of
   a. maturation.
   b. habituation.
   c. complication.
   d. overextension.

3. About nine months after speaking his or her first words, the typical child will
   a. have a vocabulary of around 50 words.
   b. begin to speak in holophrases.
   c. put words together to form rudimentary sentences.
   d. do all of the above.

4. A twenty-month-old girl who is able to try out various actions mentally without having to actually perform them is learning to solve simple problems by using
   a. dynamic perception.
   b. object permanence.
   c. intermodal perception.
   d. mental combinations.

5. A baby who repeats an action that has triggered a reaction in a parent is demonstrating an ability that typically occurs in which stage of sensorimotor development?
   a. Stage 1
   b. Stage 2
   c. Stage 3
   d. Stage 4

6. A baby who realizes that a rubber duck that has fallen out of the tub must be somewhere on the floor has certainly achieved
   a. object permanence.
   b. intermodal perception.
   c. mental combinations.
   d. cross-modal perception.

7. As soon as her babysitter arrives, twenty-one-month-old Christine holds on to her mother's legs and, in a questioning manner, says "bye-bye." Because Christine clearly is "asking" her mother if she is leaving, her utterance can be classified as

   a. babbling.

   b. an overextension.

   c. a holophrase.

   d. subject-predicate order.

8. The six-month-old infant's continual repetition of sound combinations such as "ba-ba-ba" is called

   a. cooing.

   b. reduplicative babbling.

   c. a holophrase.

   d. an overextension.

9. Like most Korean toddlers, Chun has acquired a greater number of words for _____ than her North American counterparts, who tend to acquire more words for _____.

   a. objects; social interactions

   b. social interactions; objects

   c. people; actions

   d. actions; people

Answer Key

Key Terms

1. Piaget's stages of sensorimotor intelligence (from birth to about 2 years old) are based on his theory that infants think exclusively with their senses and motor skills. (p. 153; video lesson, segment 1; objective 4)

2. In Piaget's theory, primary circular reactions are a type of feedback loop involving the infant's own body, in which infants take in experiences (such as sucking and grasping) and try to make sense of them. (p. 154; objective 4)

3. Secondary circular reactions are a type of feedback loop involving the infant's responses to objects and other people. (p. 155; objective 4)

4. Object permanence is the understanding that objects continue to exist even when they cannot be seen, touched, or heard. (p. 155; video lesson, segment 1; objective 2)

5. In Piaget's theory, tertiary circular reactions are the most sophisticated type of infant feedback loop, involving active exploration and experimentation. (p. 157; objective 4)

6. "Little scientist" is Piaget's term for the stage-five toddler who learns about the properties of objects in his or her world through active experimentation. (p. 157; video lesson, segment 1; objective 4)

7. Deferred imitation is the ability to witness, remember, and later copy a behavior that has been witnessed. (p. 157; video lesson, segment 1; objectives 3 & 4)

8. Habituation is the process of becoming so familiar with a stimulus that it no longer triggers the responses it did when it was originally experienced. (p. 158; objective 4)

9. Functional magnetic resonance imaging (fMRI) is a new imaging technique in which the brain's magnetic properties are measured to reveal changes in activity levels in various parts of the brain. (p. 158; objective 4)

10. Information-processing theory is a theory of human cognition that compares thinking to the ways in which a computer analyzes data, through the processes of input, programming, and output. (p. 160; objective 4)

11. Affordances are perceived opportunities for interacting with objects in the environment. Infants perceive sucking, grasping, noisemaking, and many other affordances of objects at an early age. (p. 161; objective 1)

12. A visual cliff is an apparent (but not actual) drop between one surface and another. (p. 161; objective 1)

13. Dynamic perception is perception that is primed to focus on movement and change. (p. 162; objective 2)

14. People preference refers to infants' innate attraction to other humans, as evidenced through infants' perceptual choices. (p. 162; objective 1)

15. A reminder session involves the experiencing of some aspect of an event that may trigger the entire memory of the event. (p. 164; objective 3)

16. Child-directed speech is a form of speech used by adults when talking to infants. Its hallmark is exaggerated expressiveness; it employs more questions, commands, and repetitions and fewer past tenses, pronouns, and complex sentences; it uses simpler vocabulary and grammar; it has a higher pitch and more low-to-high fluctuations. It is also known as "baby talk" or "motherese." (p. 168; video lesson, segment 2; objective 7)

17. Babbling, which begins at 6 or 7 months, is characterized by the extended repetition of certain syllables (such as "ma-ma"). (p. 168; video lesson, segment 2; objective 5)

18. The naming explosion refers to the dramatic increase in the infant's vocabulary that begins at about 18 months of age. (p. 169; objective 6)

19. Another characteristic of infant speech is the use of the holophrase, in which a single word is used to convey a complete thought. (p. 169; objective 5)

20. The grammar of a language includes rules of word order, verb forms, and all other methods used to communicate meaning apart from words themselves. (p. 171; objective 6)

21. According to Chomsky, children possess an innate language acquisition device (LAD) that enables them to acquire language, including the basic aspects of grammar. (p. 174; video lesson, segment 2; objective 6)

22. In Piaget's theory, mental combinations are sequences of actions that are carried out mentally. Mental combinations enable stage-six toddlers to begin to anticipate and solve problems without resorting to trial-and-error experiments. (video lesson, segment 1; objective 4)

23. Reduplicative babbling is a form of speech in which babies, at about seven to nine months, string together two syllables and repeat them over and over. (video lesson, segment 2; objective 5)

24. Semantics refers to the set of rules by which we derive meaning from the spoken sounds in a given language; also, the study of the meaning of words. (video lesson, segment 2; objective 5)

25. Intonation refers to the cadence, tone, or emphasis of a given utterance. Babies learn a great deal about intonation, including how to adjust the intonation of their sounds to change the meaning of an utterance. (video lesson, segment 2; objective 5)

Practice Questions I

Multiple-Choice Questions

1. c. is the correct answer. (objective 1)

2. c. is the correct answer. (video lesson, segment 1; objective 4)

3. b. is the correct answer. This was Piaget's most basic contribution to the study of infant cognition—that intelligence is revealed in behavior at every age. (video lesson, segment 1; objective 4)

4. c. is the correct answer. (objectives 1 & 4)

   b. is incorrect. This is Chomsky's position.

   d. is incorrect. This issue was not discussed in the textbook.

5. a. is the correct answer. (video lesson, segment 1; objective 4)

   b. & c. are incorrect. These abilities are not acquired until children are much older.

   d. is incorrect. Pretending is associated with stage six (18 to 24 months).

6. c. is the correct answer. (video lesson, segment 1; objective 2)

7. d. is the correct answer. This is a synthesis of the theories of Skinner and Chomsky. (video lesson, segment 2; objective 6)

8. b. is the correct answer. (video lesson, segment 2; objective 5)

   a., c., & d. are incorrect. Children the world over, and in every Piagetian stage, follow the same sequence and approximately the same timetable for early language development.

9. c. is the correct answer. (video lesson, segment 2; objective 5)

10. a. is the correct answer. (objective 5)

    b. is incorrect. Child-directed speech is the speech adults use with infants.

    c. is incorrect. Reduplicative babbling is a form of speech in which babies, at about seven to nine months, string together two syllables and repeat them over and over.

    d. is incorrect. Intonation refers to the cadence, tone, or emphasis of a given utterance. Babies learn a great deal about intonation, including how to adjust the intonation of their sounds to change the meaning of an utterance.

11. c. is the correct answer. (video lesson, segment 2; objective 7)

    a. is incorrect. A holophrase is a single word uttered by a toddler to express a complete thought.

    b. is incorrect. According to Noam Chomsky, the LAD, or language acquisition device, is an innate ability in humans to acquire language.

    d. is incorrect. These characteristic differences in pitch and structure are precisely what distinguish child-directed speech from regular conversation.

12. c. is the correct answer. (video lesson, segment 1; objective 3)

    a. & b. are incorrect. In Piaget's theory, these refer to processes by which mental concepts incorporate new experiences (assimilation) or are modified in response to new experiences (accommodation).

d. is incorrect. Dynamic perception is perception that is primed to focus on movement and change.

Matching Items

13. d (video lesson, segment 1; objective 4)
14. e (objective 1)
15. c (video lesson, segment 1; objective 2)
16. g (video lesson, segment 1; objective 4)
17. a (video lesson, segment 2; objective 5)
18. f (objective 5)
19. b (objective 5)
20. h (video lesson, segment 2; objective 5)

Practice Questions II

Multiple-Choice Questions

1. b. is the correct answer. (video lesson, segment 1; objective 4)

   a. & c. are incorrect. These are stages two and three.

   d. is incorrect. This is not one of Piaget's stages of sensorimotor intelligence.

2. d. is the correct answer. (objective 2)
3. c. is the correct answer. (video lesson, segment 1; objective 2)
4. a. is the correct answer (objective 4)
5. a. is the correct answer. Chomsky believed this device is innate. (video lesson, segment 2; objective 6)
6. b. is the correct answer. (video lesson, segment 1; objective 4)

   a. & c are incorrect. Both of these occur later than stage one.

   d. is incorrect. This is a hallmark of stage six.

7. a. is the correct answer. (video lesson, segment 1; objective 2)
8. c. is the correct answer. (video lesson, segment 1; objective 4)

   a. is incorrect. Reflexes are involuntary (and therefore unintentional) responses.

   b. is incorrect. Affordances are perceived opportunities for interaction with objects.

   d. is incorrect. Mental combinations are actions that are carried out mentally, rather than behaviorally. Moreover, mental combinations do not develop until a later age, during sensorimotor stage six.

9. b. is the correct answer. (video lesson, segment 2; objective 5)
10. d. is the correct answer. (objective 6)

    a. & b. are incorrect. Hearing and deaf babies do not differ in the overall likelihood that they will babble.

    c. is incorrect. Deaf babies begin to babble vocally several months later than hearing babies do.

11. b. is the correct answer. (video lesson, segment 2; objective 6)

    a., c., & d. are incorrect. These views on language acquisition describe the theory offered by Noam Chomsky.

Matching Items

12. i (video lesson, segment 1; objective 4)
13. c (objective 4)
14. k (video lesson, segment 2; objective 5)
15. a (objective 3)
16. h (video lesson, segment 1; objective 4)
17. b (objective 6)
18. e (objective 6)
19. d (objective 4)
20. j (objective 4)
21. f (video lesson, segment 2; objective 6)
22. l (video lesson, segment 2; objective 5)
23. g (video lesson, segment 2; objective 7)

Applying Your Knowledge

1. a. is the correct answer. The father's expression of delight is clearly a reinforcer in that it has increased the likelihood of the infant's vocalization. (video lesson, segment 2; objective 6)

   b. & c. are incorrect.

   d. is incorrect. This is Chomsky's viewpoint; Skinner maintained that language is acquired through learning.

2. b. is the correct answer. (objective 3)

3. c. is the correct answer. (video lesson, segment 2; objective 5)

   a. is incorrect. At 18 months of age, most children have much smaller vocabularies.

   b. is incorrect. Speaking in holophrases is typical of younger infants.

4. d. is the correct answer. (video lesson, segment 1; objective 4)

   a. is incorrect. Dynamic perception is perception primed to focus on movement and change.

   b. is incorrect. Object permanence is the awareness that objects do not cease to exist when they are out of sight.

   c. is incorrect. Intermodal perception is the ability to associate information from one sensory modality with information from another.

5. c. is the correct answer. (video lesson, segment 1; objective 4)

6. a. is the correct answer. Before object permanence is attained, an object that disappears from sight ceases to exist for the infant. (video lesson, segment 1; objective 2)

   b. is incorrect. Intermodal perception is the ability to associate information from one sensory modality with information from another.

   c. is incorrect. Mental combinations are actions that are carried out mentally.

   d. is incorrect. Cross-modal perception is the ability to use information from one sensory modality to imagine something in another.

7. c. is the correct answer. (objective 5)

   a. is incorrect. Because Christine is expressing a complete thought, her speech is much more than babbling.

b. is incorrect. An overextension is the application of a word the child knows to an inappropriate context, such as "doggie" to all animals the child sees.

d. is incorrect. The ability to understand subject-predicate order emerges later, when children begin forming two-word sentences.

8. b. is the correct answer. (video lesson, segment 2; objective 5)

a. is incorrect. Cooing is the pleasant-sounding utterances of the infant at about 2 months.

c. is incorrect. The holophrase occurs later and refers to the toddler's use of a single word to express a complete thought.

d. is incorrect. An overextension, or overgeneralization, is the application of a word to an inappropriate context, such as "doed" for the past tense of "do."

9. b. is the correct answer. (objective 6)

c. & d. are incorrect.

Lesson Review

Lesson 6

The First Two Years
Cognitive Development

Please Note: Use this matrix to guide your study and achieve the learning objectives of this lesson. It will also help you to view the video, which defines and demonstrates important concepts and skills as they relate to everyday life.

Learning Objective	Textbook	Course Student Guide	Video Lesson
1. Explain the Gibsons' contextual view of perception, and relate it to the idea of affordances, giving examples of affordances perceived by infants.	pp. 160–163	Key Terms: 11, 12, 14; Practice Questions I: 1, 4, 14.	
2. Explain what object permanence is, how it is tested in infancy, and what these tests reveal.	pp. 155–156	Key Terms: 4, 13; Practice Questions I: 6, 15; Practice Questions II: 2, 3, 7; Applying Your Knowledge: 6.	Segment 1: *Sensorimotor Intelligence*
3. Discuss research findings on infant memory and infants' understanding of cause-and-effect relationships.	pp. 163–165	Key Terms: 7, 15; Practice Questions I: 12; Practice Questions II: 15; Applying Your Knowledge: 2.	Segment 1: *Sensorimotor Intelligence*
4. Identify and describe Piaget's stages of sensorimotor intelligence, and give examples of the behavior associated with each stage.	pp. 153–159	Key Terms: 1, 2, 3, 5, 6, 7, 8, 9, 10, 22; Practice Questions I: 2, 3, 4, 5, 13, 16; Practice Questions II: 1, 4, 6, 8, 12, 13, 16, 19, 20; Applying Your Knowledge: 4, 5.	Segment 1: *Sensorimotor Intelligence*
5. Describe language development during the first two years, and identify its major hallmarks.	pp. 166–171	Key Terms: 17, 19, 23, 24, 25; Practice Questions I: 8, 9, 10, 17, 18, 19, 20; Practice Questions II: 9, 14, 22; Applying Your Knowledge: 3, 7, 8.	Segment 2: *Language Development*

Learning Objective	Textbook	Course Student Guide	Video Lesson
6. Contrast the theories of Skinner and Chomsky regarding early language development, and explain current views on language learning.	pp. 172–175	Key Terms: 18, 20, 21; Practice Questions I: 7; Practice Questions II: 5, 10, 11, 17, 18, 21; Applying Your Knowledge: 1, 9.	Segment 2: *Language Development*
7. Explain the importance of child-directed speech, and identify its main features.	p. 168	Key Terms: 16; Practice Questions I: 11; Practice Questions II: 23.	Segment 2: *Language Development*

Getting to Know You

Lesson 7

The First Two Years:
Psychosocial Development

Preview

Lesson 7 explores the emotional and social life of the developing person during the first two years. It begins with a description of the infant's emerging emotions and how they reflect increasing cognitive abilities. Newborns are innately predisposed to sociability, and are capable of expressing distress, sadness, contentment, and many other emotions, as well as responding to the emotions of other people.

This lesson also explores the social context in which a baby's emotions develop. By referencing their caregivers' signals, infants learn when and how to express their emotions. As **self-awareness** develops, many new emotions emerge, including embarrassment, shame, guilt, and pride. Parents who communicate effectively with their children are more responsive and tend to have children who are more skilled in communicating with others.

This lesson also presents the theories of Sigmund Freud and Erik Erikson that help us understand how the infant's emotional and behavioral responses begin to take on the various patterns that form personality. Important research on the nature and origins of **temperament**, which affects virtually every characteristic of the individual's developing personality, is also considered. Babies are not born with fully developed personalities. Instead, they come equipped with a basic set of temperamental tendencies in emotional expressiveness, activity level, and attention that, through their interactions with caregivers and others, are molded to form personality.

The final section of the lesson examines emotions and relationships from the perspective of parent–infant interaction. Videotaped studies of parents and infants, combined with laboratory studies, have greatly expanded our understanding of psychosocial development. In the video lesson, experts explain how the intricate patterns of parent–child interaction help infants learn to express and read emotions and promotes **attachment** to caregivers. Developmental psychologist Mary Ainsworth describes an experimental procedure she developed to measure the quality of attachment. The lesson concludes with a discussion of the impact of early day care on psychosocial development.

Prior Course Knowledge that Will Be Used in this Lesson

- The developmental theories of Sigmund Freud and Erik Erikson (from Lesson 1) will be used to help explain psychosocial development during the school years.

- Recall (from Lesson 1) that Freud's theory specifies five major stages of **psychosexual development**, during which the sensual satisfaction associated with the mouth, anus, or genitals is linked to the major developmental needs and challenges that are associated with that stage. This lesson focuses on the first two stages:

    1. **Oral Stage (birth to 1 year)**
    2. **Anal Stage (1 to 3 years)**
    3. Phallic Stage (3 to 6 years)
    4. Latency Stage (7 to 11 years)
    5. Genital Stage (adolescence through adulthood)

- Recall (from Lesson 1) that Erik Erikson's theory specifies eight stages of **psychosocial development**, each of which is characterized by a particular challenge, or **developmental crisis**, that is central to that stage of life and must be resolved. This lesson focuses on the first two stages:

    1. **Trust versus Mistrust (birth to 1 year)**
    2. **Autonomy versus Shame and Doubt (1 to 3 years)**
    3. Initiative versus Guilt (3 to 6 years)
    4. Industry versus Inferiority (7 to 11 years)
    5. Identify versus Role Confusion (adolescence)
    6. Intimacy versus Isolation (adulthood)
    7. Generativity versus Stagnation (adulthood)
    8. Integrity versus Despair (adulthood)

Learning Objectives

Use this information to guide your reading, viewing, thinking, and studying. After successfully completing this lesson, you should be able to:

1. Describe the basic emotions expressed by infants during the first days and months.
2. Describe the main developments in the emotional life of the child between 6 months and 2 years.
3. Discuss the concepts of social referencing and social learning, including their development and role in shaping later emotions.
4. Discuss the links between an infant's emerging self-awareness and his or her continuing emotional development.
5. Describe how Freud's psychosexual stages can be used to explain the origins and development of personality.
6. Discuss how Erikson's psychosocial stages can be used to explain the origins and development of personality.
7. Define and describe the concept of temperament, discuss its development as an interaction of nature and nurture, and explain the significance of research on temperament for parents and caregivers.
8. Describe the synchrony of parent–infant interaction during the first year, and discuss its significance for the developing person.
9. Define attachment, explain how it is measured and how it is influenced by context, and discuss the long-term consequences of secure and insecure attachment.

10. Discuss the potential effects of day care on a baby's development, and identify the factors that define high-quality day care.

📖   **Read Chapter 7, "The First Two Years: Psychosocial Development," pages 179–204.**

⏮   **View the video for Lesson 7, "Getting to Know You."**

    Segment 1: *Development through Crises*

    Segment 2: *Attachment*

    Segment 3: *Attachment and Day Care*

Summary

Contemporary developmentalists have revised a number of the traditional views of psychosocial development. It was once believed, for example, that infants did not have any real emotions. Researchers now know, however, that in the very first days and weeks of life, infants express and sense many emotions, including fear, anger, happiness, and surprise. Over the first two years, emotions change from a basic set of reactions to complex, self-conscious responses as infants become increasingly independent.

In the traditional view of personality development, the infant was seen as a passive recipient of the personality created almost entirely by the actions of his or her primary caregivers. Yet it is now apparent that many aspects of **temperament** are present in infants at birth and that active caregiver-infant interaction within a secure and nurturing environment is a central factor in the child's psychosocial development. During infancy, increasing independence, which Sigmund Freud explains in terms of the oral and anal stages, marks this development. Erik Erikson explains it in terms of "**trust versus mistrust**" and "**autonomy versus shame and doubt**."

A key factor in this psychosocial development is **attachment**—the affectional tie between infants and their primary caregivers. In infants the world over, attachment develops at about 7 months, when babies first become aware that other people stay in existence even when they're out of sight. **Secure attachment** helps ensure that the relatively helpless infant receives the adult care he or she needs in order to survive, and it sets the stage for the child's increasingly independent exploration of the world. By age 2, the toddler has a distinct personality that is the product of the social context and the innate temperament of the young infant.

📖   **Review all reading assignments for this lesson.**

💻   **As assigned by your instructor, complete the optional online component for this lesson.**

Key Terms

Using your own words, write a brief definition or explanation of each of the following terms on a separate piece of paper.

1. social smile
2. stranger wariness
3. separation anxiety
4. self-awareness
5. temperament
6. goodness of fit
7. trust versus mistrust
8. autonomy versus shame and doubt
9. social learning
10. working model
11. ethnotheory
12. proximal parenting
13. distal parenting
14. synchrony
15. still face technique
16. attachment
17. secure attachment (type B)
18. insecure-avoidant attachment (type A)
19. insecure-resistant/ambivalent attachment (type C)
20. disorganized attachment (type D)
21. Strange Situation
22. social referencing
23. family day care
24. center day care
25. proximity-seeking behaviors
26. contact-maintaining behaviors
27. insecure attachment

Practice Questions I

Multiple-Choice Questions

1. One of the first emotions that can be discerned in infancy is
   a. shame.
   b. distress.
   c. guilt.
   d. pride.

2. The social smile begins to appear
   a. at about 6 weeks.
   b. at about 8 months.
   c. after stranger wariness has been overcome.
   d. after the infant has achieved a sense of self.

3. An infant's fear of being left by the mother or other caregiver, called
_____, peaks at about _____.

   a. separation anxiety; 9 or 10 months
   b. stranger wariness; 8 months
   c. separation anxiety; 8 months
   d. stranger wariness; 14 months

4. Social referencing refers to

   a. parenting skills that change over time.
   b. changes in community values regarding, for example, the acceptability of using physical punishment with small children.
   c. the support network for new parents provided by extended family members.
   d. the infant response of looking to trusted adults for emotional cues in uncertain situations.

5. Psychologists who favored the _____ perspective believed that the personality of the child was virtually "created" through reinforcement and punishment.

   a. psychoanalytic
   b. behaviorism
   c. psychosocial
   d. epigenetic

6. Freud's oral stage corresponds to Erikson's crisis of

   a. orality versus anality.
   b. trust versus mistrust.
   c. autonomy versus shame and doubt.
   d. secure versus insecure attachment.

7. Erikson feels that the development of a sense of trust in early infancy depends on the quality of the

   a. infant's food.
   b. child's genetic inheritance.
   c. relationship with caregiver.
   d. introduction to toilet training.

8. The increased tendency of toddlers to express frustration and anger is most closely linked to new developments in their cognitive abilities, especially those related to

   a. goal-directed actions.
   b. social referencing.
   c. self-awareness.
   d. stranger wariness.

9. "Easy," "slow to warm up," and "difficult" are descriptions of different
   a. forms of attachment.
   b. types of temperament.
   c. types of parenting.
   d. toddler responses to the Strange Situation.

10. Research studies of infant caregiving have found all of the following statements to be true **EXCEPT**:
    a. When both parents work outside the home, child care tends to be shared equally by mothers and fathers.
    b. Fathers can provide the emotional and cognitive nurturing that children need.
    c. Divorced fathers spend less time caring for infants than married fathers do.
    d. Contemporary fathers spend more time with their children than fathers did in 1970.

11. Synchrony is a term that describes
    a. the carefully coordinated interaction between parent and infant.
    b. a mismatch of the temperaments of parent and infant.
    c. a research technique involving videotapes.
    d. the concurrent evolution of different species.

12. The emotional tie that develops between an infant and his or her primary caregiver is called
    a. self-awareness.
    b. synchrony.
    c. affiliation.
    d. attachment.

13. An important effect of secure attachment is the promotion of
    a. self-awareness.
    b. curiosity and self-directed behavior.
    c. dependency.
    d. all of the above.

14. The sight of a friendly human face is most likely to produce a smile in a _____-month-old.
    a. three
    b. six
    c. nine
    d. twelve

True or False Items

Write T (for true) or F (for false) on the line in front of each statement.

F 15. __T__ Most developmentalists think that infants must learn to be sociable. *tendency towards sociability*

F 16. __T__ The major difference between a six-month-old and a twelve-month-old is that emotions become less intense. *become more intense and are manifested more often and consistently*

17. __T__ A baby at 11 months is likely to display both stranger wariness and separation anxiety.

18. __T__ Emotional development is affected by cognitive development.

19. __F__ A securely attached toddler is most likely to stay close to his or her mother even in a familiar environment.

20. __F__ Current research shows that the majority of infants in day care are insecurely attached.

21. __F__ Temperament is genetically determined and is unaffected by environmental factors.

22. __T__ Self-awareness enables toddlers to be self-critical and to feel guilt.

T 23. __F__ Insecurely attached children display at least three different patterns of attachment behavior.

F 24. __T__ Developmental psychologists express the greatest concerns about the early mental health of children who display insecure-resistant attachment. *insecure-disorganized attachment*

25. __T__ Studies show that the influence of center child care can be both positive and negative.

Practice Questions II

Multiple-Choice Questions

1. Infants give their first real smiles, called _____, when they are about _____ of age.
   a. play smiles; 3 months
   b. play smiles; 6 weeks
   c. social smiles; 3 months
   d. social smiles; 6 weeks

2. Freud's anal stage corresponds to Erikson's crisis of
   a. autonomy versus shame and doubt.
   b. trust versus mistrust.
   c. orality versus anality.
   d. identity versus role confusion.

3. Not until the sense of self begins to emerge do babies realize that they are seeing their own faces in the mirror. This realization usually occurs

    a. shortly before 3 months.

    b. at about 6 months.

    c. between 15 and 24 months.

    d. after 24 months.

4. Infants who are placed in day care are most likely to become insecurely attached if they are in day care more than 20 hours a week, if the day care quality is poor, and if

    a. their mothers are insensitive.

    b. they come from broken homes.

    c. they have a difficult temperament.

    d. their own parents were insecurely attached.

5. Emotions such as shame, guilt, embarrassment, and pride emerge at the same time that

    a. the social smile appears.

    b. aspects of the infant's temperament can first be discerned.

    c. self-awareness begins to emerge.

    d. parents initiate toilet training.

6. In the second six months, stranger wariness is a

    a. result of insecure attachment.

    b. result of social isolation.

    c. normal emotional response.

    d. setback in emotional development.

7. The caregiving environment can affect a child's temperament through

    a. the child's temperamental pattern and the demands of the home environment.

    b. parental expectations.

    c. both a and b.

    d. neither a nor b.

8. Compared to children who are insecurely attached, those who are securely attached are

    a. more independent.

    b. more curious.

    c. more sociable.

    d. characterized by all of the above.

9. The later consequences of secure and insecure attachment for children are

    a. subject to change due to the child's current rearing circumstances.

    b. irreversible, regardless of the child's current rearing circumstances.

    c. more significant in girls than in boys.

    d. more significant in boys than in girls.

10. A child that makes brushing motions after watching his mother brush her teeth is demonstrating
    a. a desire for good hygiene.
    b. an oral stage.
    c. autonomy versus shame and doubt.
    d. social learning.

11. Compared with mothers, fathers are more likely to
    a. engage in noisier, more boisterous play.
    b. encourage intellectual development in their children.
    c. encourage social development in their children.
    d. read to their toddlers.

12. Unlike Freud, Erikson believed that
    a. problems arising in early infancy can last a lifetime.
    b. experiences later in life can alter the effects of early experiences.
    c. the first two years of life are fraught with potential conflict.
    d. all of the above are true.

Matching Items

Match each theorist, term, or concept with its corresponding description or definition.

Theorists, Terms, or Concepts

13. _____ temperament
14. _____ Erik Erikson
15. _____ the Strange Situation
16. _____ synchrony
17. _____ trust versus mistrust
18. _____ Sigmund Freud
19. _____ social referencing
20. _____ autonomy versus shame and doubt
21. _____ self-awareness
22. _____ Mary Ainsworth
23. _____ proximity-seeking behaviors
24. _____ contact-maintaining behaviors

Descriptions or Definitions

a. looking to caregivers for emotional cues
b. the crisis of infancy
c. the crisis of toddlerhood
d. approaching, following, and climbing
e. theorist who described psychosexual stages of development
f. researcher who devised a laboratory procedure for studying attachment
g. laboratory procedure for studying attachment
h. the relatively consistent, basic dispositions inherent in a person
i. clinging and resisting being put down
j. coordinated interaction between parent and infant
k. theorist who described psychosocial stages of development
l. a person's sense of being distinct from others

Applying Your Knowledge

1. In laboratory tests of attachment, when the mother returns to the playroom after a short absence, a securely attached infant is most likely to

    a. cry and protest the mother's return.

    b. climb into the mother's lap, then leave to resume play.

    c. climb into the mother's lap and stay there.

    d. continue playing without acknowledging the mother.

2. After a scary fall, eighteen-month-old Joey looks to his mother to see if he should cry or laugh. Joey's behavior is an example of

    a. proximity-seeking behavior.

    b. social referencing.

    c. insecure attachment.

    d. the crisis of trust versus mistrust.

3. Which of the following is a clear sign of an infant's attachment to a particular person?

    a. The infant turns to that person when distressed.

    b. The infant protests when that person leaves a room.

    c. The infant may cry when strangers appear.

    d. All of the above are signs of infant attachment.

4. If you had to predict a newborn baby's temperament "type" solely on the basis of probability, which classification would be the most likely?

    a. easy

    b. slow to warm up

    c. difficult

    d. There is not enough information to make a prediction.

5. One way in which infant psychosocial development has changed is that today

    a. many infants have their first encounters with other infants at a younger age.

    b. parental influence is less important than it was in the past.

    c. social norms are nearly the same for the sexes.

    d. infants tend to have fewer social encounters than in the past.

6. Ethan's mother left him alone in the room for a few minutes. When she returned, Ethan seemed indifferent to her presence. According to Mary Ainsworth's research with children in the Strange Situation, Ethan is probably

    a. a normal, independent infant.

    b. an abused child.

    c. insecurely attached.

    d. securely attached.

7. Mary and Chris, who are first-time parents, are concerned because their one-month-old baby has a high activity level. They are worried that they are doing something wrong. You inform them that their child is probably that way because

    a. they are reinforcing the child's tantrum behaviors.

    b. they are not meeting some biological need of the child.

    c. of his or her inherited temperament.

    d. at one month of age all children are difficult to care for and hard to soothe.

8. Two-year-old Anna and her mother visit a day-care center. Seeing an interesting toy, Anna runs a few steps toward it, then stops and looks back to see if her mother is coming. Anna's behavior illustrates

    a. the crisis of autonomy versus shame and doubt.

    b. synchrony.

    c. dyssynchrony.

    d. social referencing.

9. Frankie eats, chews, and talks excessively in quest of pleasures that were denied in infancy. Freud would probably say that Frankie is

    a. anally expulsive.

    b. anally retentive.

    c. fixated in the oral stage.

    d. experiencing the crisis of trust versus mistrust.

10. A researcher at the child development center places a dot on an infant's nose and watches to see if the infant reacts to her image in a mirror by touching her nose. Evidently, the researcher is testing the child's

    a. attachment.

    b. temperament.

    c. self-awareness.

    d. social referencing.

11. Four-month-old Carl and his thirteen-month-old sister Paula are left in the care of a babysitter. As their parents are leaving, it is to be expected that

    a. Carl will become extremely upset, while Paula will calmly accept her parents' departure.

    b. Paula will become more upset over her parents' departure than will Carl.

    c. Carl and Paula will both become quite upset as their parents leave.

    d. Neither Carl nor Paula will become very upset as their parents leave.

12. You have been asked to give a presentation on "Mother–Infant Attachment" to a group of expectant mothers. Basing your presentation on the research of Mary Ainsworth, you conclude your talk by stating that mother–infant attachment depends mostly on

    a. an infant's innate temperament.

    b. the amount of time mothers spend with their infants.

    c. sensitive and responsive caregiving in the early months.

    d. whether the mother herself was securely attached as an infant.

Answer Key

Key Terms

1. The social smile—a smile of pleasure in response to a human face or voice—appears at about 6 weeks. (p. 180; objective 1)

2. A common early fear, stranger wariness (also called fear of strangers) is first noticeable at about 6 months. (p. 180; objective 2)

3. Separation anxiety, which is the infant's fear of being left by the mother or other caregiver, emerges at about 8 or 9 months, peaks at about 14 months, and then gradually subsides. (p. 181; objective 2)

4. Self-awareness refers to a person's sense of himself or herself as being distinct from other people that makes possible many new self-conscious emotions, including shame, guilt, embarrassment, and pride. (p. 181; objective 4)

5. Temperament refers to the set of innate tendencies, or dispositions, that underlie and affect each person's interactions with people, situations, and events. (p. 183; video lesson, segment 1; objective 7)

6. Goodness of fit is the match between the child's temperamental pattern and the demands of the environment. (p. 185; objective 7)

7. In Erikson's theory, the crisis of infancy is one of trust versus mistrust, in which the infant learns whether the world is a secure place in which basic needs will be met. (p. 187; video lesson, segment 1; objective 6)

8. In Erikson's theory, the crisis of toddlerhood is one of autonomy versus shame and doubt, in which toddlers strive to rule their own actions and bodies. (p. 187; video lesson, segment 1; objective 6)

9. Social learning is accomplished by observing others—both what they do and how other people respond to that behavior. (p. 188; objective 3)

10. According to cognitive theory, infants use social relationships to develop a set of assumptions called a working model that organizes their perceptions and experiences. (p. 189; objective 6)

11. An ethnotheory is a theory that underlies the values and practices of a culture, but that isn't usually apparent to people within the culture. (p. 189; objective 3)

12. Parents who focus on close, physical contact with their infants (e.g., often holding or cuddling them) are engaged in proximal parenting. (p. 190; objective 9)

13. Distal parenting is defined as a focus on intellect and conversation more than on physical contact. (p. 190; objective 9)

14. Synchrony refers to the coordinated interaction between caregiver and infant that helps infants learn to express and read emotions. (p. 193; video lesson, segment 2; objective 8)

15. The still-face technique occurs when a parent maintains an expressionless face while maintaining eye contact with their child, an experience that is very stressful for the infant. (p. 194; objective 8)

16. Attachment is the enduring emotional tie that a person or animal forms with another. (p. 195; video lesson, segment 2; objective 9)

17. A secure attachment (type B) is one in which the infant derives comfort and confidence from the "secure base" provided by a caregiver. (p. 196; video lesson, segment 2; objective 9)

18. Insecure-avoidant attachment (type A) is a form of insecure attachment in which the child is likely to disregard or avoid a caregiver. (p. 196; video lesson, segment 2; objective 9)

19. Insecure-resistant/ambivalent attachment (type C) is a form of attachment in which children become very upset when they are separated from a caregiver, yet also fail to find comfort when the primary caregiver returns. (p. 196; video lesson, segment 2; objective 9)

20. Disorganized attachment (type D) is a form of attachment in which infants display inconsistent attachment behaviors, acting both avoidantly and resistantly to their primary caregivers. (p. 196; video lesson, segment 2; objective 9)

21. The Strange Situation is a laboratory procedure developed by Mary Ainsworth for assessing attachment. Infants are observed in a playroom, in several successive episodes, while the caregiver (usually the mother) and a stranger move in and out of the room. (p. 197; video lesson, segment 2; objective 9)

22. When infants engage in social referencing, they are looking to trusted adults for emotional cues on how to interpret uncertain situations. (p. 198; video lesson, segment 2; objective 3)

23. When an adult establishes a child care center in his/her own home, it is referred to as family day care. Typically, such caregivers are paid a lower rate and care for several children of different ages at once. (p. 200; objective 10)

24. Center child care (non-parental childcare) refers to caregiving provided by day-care workers and other adults who are not the child's biological parents and/or have no legal relationship to the child. (p. 201; video lesson, segment 3; objective 10)

25. Following, approaching, and other proximity-seeking behaviors are intended to place an individual close to another person to whom he or she is attached. (video lesson, segment 2; objective 9)

26. Clinging, resisting being put down, and other contact-maintaining behaviors are intended to keep a person near another person to whom he or she is attached. (video lesson, segment 2; objective 9)

27. Insecure attachment is characterized by the infant's fear, anger, or seeming indifference toward the caregiver. (video lesson, segment 2; objective 9)

Practice Questions I

Multiple-Choice Questions

1. b. is the correct answer. (objective 1)

   a., c., & d. are incorrect. These emotions emerge later in infancy, at about the same time as self-awareness emerges.

2. a. is the correct answer. (objective 1)

3. a. is the correct answer. (objective 2)

   b. & d. are incorrect. This fear, which is also called fear of strangers, peaks by 10 to 14 months.

4. d. is the correct answer. (video lesson, segment 2; objective 3)

5. b. is the correct answer. (objective 7)

   a. is incorrect. Reinforcement and punishment have no place in the psychoanalytic perspective.

   c. is incorrect. This is Erikson's theory, which sees development as occurring through a series of basic crises.

d. is incorrect. This perspective analyzes how genes and environment contribute to development.

6. b. is the correct answer. (objectives 5 & 6)

   a. is incorrect. Orality and anality refer to personality traits that result from fixation in the oral and anal stages, respectively.

   c. is incorrect. According to Erikson, this is the crisis of toddlerhood, which corresponds to Freud's anal stage.

   d. is incorrect. This is not a developmental crisis in Erikson's theory.

7. c. is the correct answer. (video lesson, segment 1; objective 6)

8. a. is the correct answer. Anger increases with age because toddlers are able to anticipate events and realize that other people's actions sometimes block their own efforts. (objective 2)

9. b. is the correct answer. (video lesson, segment 1; objective 7)

   a. is incorrect. "Secure" and "insecure" are different forms of attachment.

   c. is incorrect. The lesson does not describe different types of parenting.

   d. is incorrect. The Strange Situation is a test of attachment, rather than of temperament.

10. a. is the correct answer. (video lesson, segment 2; objective 9)

11. a. is the correct answer. (video lesson, segment 2; objective 8)

12. d. is the correct answer. (video lesson, segment 2; objective 9)

   a. is incorrect. Self-awareness refers to the infant's developing sense of "me and mine."

   b. is incorrect. Synchrony describes the coordinated interaction between infant and caregiver.

   c. is incorrect. Affiliation describes the tendency of people at any age to seek the companionship of others.

13. b. is the correct answer. (video lesson, segment 2; objective 9)

   a. is incorrect. The lesson does not link self-awareness to secure attachment.

   c. is incorrect. On the contrary, secure attachment promotes independence in infants and children.

14. a. is the correct answer. (objective 1)

   b., c., & d. are incorrect. As infants become older, they smile more selectively.

True or False Items

15. F   Most developmentalists believe that infants are born with a tendency toward sociability as a means of survival. (objective 1)

16. F   Emotions become more intense and are manifested more quickly and more persistently. (objective 2)

17. T   (objective 2)

18. T   (objective 2)

19. F   A securely attached toddler is most likely to explore the environment, the mother's presence being enough to give him or her the courage to do so. (video lesson, segment 2; objective 9)

20. F   Many researchers believe that high-quality day care is not likely to harm the child. In fact, it is thought to be beneficial to the development of cognitive and social skills. (video lesson, segment 3; objective 10)

21. F   Temperament is a product of both nature and nurture. (objective 7)

22. T (objective 4)

23. T (video lesson, segment 2; objective 9)

24. F Experts express the greatest concerns about children who display insecure-disorganized attachment. (video lesson, segment 2; objective 9)

25. T (video lesson, segment 3; objective 10)

Practice Questions II

Multiple-Choice Questions

1. d. is the correct answer. (objective 1)

2. a. is the correct answer. (objectives 5 & 6)

3. c. is the correct answer. (objective 4)

4. a. is the correct answer. (video lesson, segment 3; objective 10)

5. c. is the correct answer. (objective 4)

   a. & b. are incorrect. The social smile, as well as temperamental characteristics, emerge well before the first signs of self-awareness.

   d. is incorrect.

6. c. is the correct answer. (objective 2)

7. c. is the correct answer. (objectives 8 & 9)

8. d. is the correct answer. (video lesson, segment 2; objective 9)

9. a. is the correct answer. (video lesson, segment 2; objective 9)

   c. & d. are incorrect. The textbook does not suggest that the consequences of secure and insecure attachment differ in boys and girls.

10. d. is the correct answer. (objective 3)

11. a. is the correct answer. (objective 5)

12. b. is the correct answer. (video lesson, segment 1; objectives 5 & 6)

    a. & c. Freud would have agreed with both of these statements.

Matching Items

13. h (video lesson, segment 1; objective 7)

14. k (video lesson, segment 1; objective 6)

15. g (video lesson, segment 2; objective 9)

16. j (video lesson, segment 2; objective 8)

17. b (video lesson, segment 1; objective 6)

18. e (objective 6)

19. a (video lesson, segment 2; objective 3)

20. c (video lesson, segment 1; objective 6)

21. l (objective 5)

22. f (video lesson, segment 2; objective 9)

23. d (video lesson, segment 2; objective 9)

24. i (video lesson, segment 2; objective 9)

Applying Your Knowledge

1. b. is the correct answer. (video lesson, segment 2; objective 9)

   a., c., & d. are incorrect. These responses are more typical of insecurely attached infants.

2. b. is the correct answer. (video lesson, segment 2; objective 3)

3. d. is the correct answer. (video lesson, segment 2; objective 9)

4. a. is the correct answer. About 50 percent of young infants can be described as "easy." (objective 7)

   b. is incorrect. About 15 percent of infants are described as "slow to warm up."

   c. is incorrect. About 10 percent of infants are described as "difficult."

5. a. is the correct answer. (objective 10)

6. c. is the correct answer. (video lesson, segment 2; objective 9)

   a. & d. are incorrect. When their mothers return following an absence, securely attached infants usually reestablish social contact (with a smile or by climbing into their laps) and then resume playing.

   b. is incorrect. There is no evidence in this example that Ethan is an abused child.

7. c. is the correct answer. (objective 10)

   a. & b. are incorrect. There is no evidence in the question that the parents are reinforcing tantrum behavior or failing to meet some biological need of the child's.

   d. is incorrect.

8. d. is the correct answer. (video lesson, segment 2; objective 3)

   a. is incorrect. According to Erikson, this is the crisis of toddlerhood.

   b. is incorrect. This describes a moment of coordinated and mutually responsive interaction between a parent and an infant.

   c. is incorrect. Dyssynchrony occurs when the coordinated pace and timing of a synchronous interaction are temporarily lost.

9. c. is the correct answer. (objective 5)

   a. & b. are incorrect. In Freud's theory, a person who is fixated in the anal stage exhibits messiness and disorganization or compulsive neatness.

   d. is incorrect. Erikson, rather than Freud, proposed crises of development.

10. c. is the correct answer. (objective 4)

11. b. is the correct answer. The fear of being left by a caregiver (separation anxiety) emerges at about 8 or 9 months, and peaks at about 14 months. For this reason, four-month-old Carl can be expected to become less upset than his older sister. (objective 2)

12. c. is the correct answer. (video lesson, segment 2; objective 9)

Lesson Review

Lesson 7

The First Two Years
Psychosocial Development

Please Note: Use this matrix to guide your study and achieve the learning objectives of this lesson. It will also help you to view the video, which defines and demonstrates important concepts and skills as they relate to everyday life.

Learning Objective	Textbook	Course Student Guide	Video Lesson
1. Describe the basic emotions expressed by infants during the first days and months.	pp. 180–181, 193–194	Key Terms: 1; Practice Questions I: 1, 2, 14, 15; Practice Questions II: 1.	
2. Describe the main developments in the emotional life of the child between 6 months and 2 years.	pp. 180–183	Key Terms: 2, 3; Practice Questions I: 3, 8, 16, 17, 18; Practice Questions II: 6; Applying Your Knowledge: 11.	
3. Discuss the concept of social referencing, including its development and role in shaping later emotions.	pp. 188–189, 198–200	Key Terms: 9, 11, 22; Practice Questions I: 4; Practice Questions II: 10, 19; Applying Your Knowledge: 2, 8.	Segment 2: *Attachment*
4. Discuss the links between an infant's emerging self-awareness and his or her continuing emotional development.	pp. 181–182	Key Terms: 4; Practice Questions I: 22; Practice Questions II: 3, 5; Applying Your Knowledge: 10.	
5. Describe how Freud's psychosexual stages can be used to explain the origins and development of personality.	pp. 181, 186–187, 199	Practice Questions I: 6; Practice Questions II: 2, 11, 12, 21; Applying Your Knowledge: 9.	Segment 1: *Development through Crises*
6. Describe how Erikson's psychosocial stages can be used to explain the origins and development of personality.	pp. 186–189	Key Terms: 7, 8, 10; Practice Questions I: 6, 7; Practice Questions II: 2, 12, 14, 17, 18, 20.	Segment 1: *Development through Crises*

Learning Objective	Textbook	Course Student Guide	Video Lesson
7. Define and describe the concept of temperament, discuss its development as an interaction of nature and nurture, and explain the significance of research on temperament for parents and caregivers.	pp. 183–186, 188	Key Terms: 5, 6; Practice Questions I: 5, 9, 21; Practice Questions II: 13; Applying Your Knowledge: 4.	Segment 1: *Development through Crises*
8. Describe the synchrony of parent–infant interaction during the first year, and discuss its significance for the developing person.	pp. 185, 193–194	Key Terms: 14, 15; Practice Questions I: 11; Practice Questions II: 7, 16.	Segment 2: *Attachment*
9. Define attachment, explain how it is measured and how it is influenced by context, and discuss the long-term consequences of secure and insecure attachment.	pp. 185, 190, 194–198	Key Terms: 12, 13, 16, 17, 18, 19, 20, 21, 25, 26, 27; Practice Questions I: 10, 12, 13, 19, 23, 24; Practice Questions II: 7, 8, 9, 15, 22, 23, 24; Applying Your Knowledge: 1, 3, 6, 12.	Segment 2: *Attachment*
10. Discuss the potential effects of day care on a baby's development, and identify the factors that define high-quality day care.	pp. 184, 200–202	Key Terms: 23, 24; Practice Questions I: 20, 25; Practice Questions II: 4; Applying Your Knowledge: 5, 7.	Segment 3: *Attachment and Day Care*

Playing and Growing

Lesson 8

The Play Years:
Biosocial Development

Preview

Lesson 8 introduces the developing person between the ages of 2 and 6. This period is called the play years, emphasizing the central importance of play to the biosocial, cognitive, and psychosocial development of preschoolers.

The lesson begins by outlining the changes in size and shape that occur from ages 2 through 6. This is followed by a look at brain growth and development and its role in the development of physical and cognitive abilities. The lesson also addresses the important issues of **injury control** and accidents, the major cause of childhood death in all but the most disease-ridden or war-torn countries. A description of the acquisition of gross and fine motor skills notes that mastery of such skills develops steadily during the play years along with intellectual growth. The lesson concludes with an in-depth exploration of **child maltreatment**, including its prevalence, contributing factors, consequences for future development, treatment, and prevention.

As you move through this lesson, think of children you know in this age range. Consider their size and shape, their eating habits, and their motor skill capabilities—what they can do with their bodies and hands. Also consider any child maltreatment cases you know of or have read about. What were the circumstances? What type of maltreatment occurred? What was the response?

Prior Course Knowledge that Will Be Used in this Lesson

• In this lesson, physical growth and the development of gross and fine motor skills during "The Play Years" will be compared to earlier development during infancy and toddlerhood (Lesson 5/Chapter 5).

• This lesson will return to the topic of brain growth and development, which was introduced in Lesson 6/Chapter 6. In children from ages 2 to 6, the growth of dendrites and axons continues, along with myelination, the insulating process that speeds up the transmission of neural impulses. This brain maturation leads to many other advances, including development of the visual pathways and eye-hand coordination that will make reading and writing possible.

Learning Objectives

Use this information to guide your reading, viewing, thinking, and studying. After successfully completing this lesson, you should be able to:

1. Describe normal physical growth during the play years, and account for variations in height and weight.
2. Describe changes in eating habits and nutritional needs during the preschool years.
3. Discuss brain growth and development and its effect on other areas of development during the play years.
4. Describe the prevalence of accidental injuries during early childhood, describe some measures that have significantly reduced accidental death rates for children, and identify several factors that contribute to this problem.
5. Discuss the development of gross and fine motor skills during the play years.
6. Identify the various categories and consequences of child maltreatment.
7. Discuss several factors that contribute to maltreatment, and describe current treatment and prevention efforts.

📖 **Read Chapter 8, "The Play Years: Biosocial Development," pages 209–235.**

◄◄ **View the video for Lesson 8, "Playing and Growing."**

Segment 1: *Body and Brain Growth*
Segment 2: *Motor Skills*
Segment 3: *Maltreatment*

Summary

Children grow steadily taller and slimmer during the preschool years, with their genetic background and nutrition being responsible for most of the variation seen in children from various parts of the world. The most significant aspect of growth is the continued maturation of the nervous system and the refinement of the visual, muscular, and cognitive skills that will be necessary for the child to function in school. The brain becomes more specialized as it matures, with the left half usually becoming the center for speech, and the right the center for visual, spatial, and artistic skills.

Gross motor skills, such as running, climbing, jumping, and throwing, improve dramatically between ages 2 and 6, making it essential that children have access to safe play space and guided practice to assist in this developmental process. Fine motor skills, such as pouring, holding a pencil, and using a knife and fork, are much harder for preschoolers to master. This difficulty is due to several factors, including incomplete myelination of the nervous system and incomplete muscular control. Of course, for young children especially, art is not limited to coloring or drawing and often includes using markers, paint brushes, clay, and other vehicles. In fact, very young children (who lack the fine motor skills required to hold a crayon, brush, or pencil) are more likely to use large arm movements (such as those involved in finger painting) in their art. Doing so, of course, is a powerful stimulus to the development of the fine motor skills, as children are drawn to practice these skills in order to produce the artistic results they desire.

Throughout childhood, accidents are the leading cause of death. The accident risk for a particular child depends on several factors. Boys, as a group, and low-socioeconomic status (SES) children suffer more serious injuries and accidental deaths than girls, and high-SES children.

Child maltreatment takes many forms, including physical, emotional, or sexual **abuse**, and emotional or physical **neglect**. Although certain conditions are almost universally harmful, some practices that are considered neglectful or abusive in one culture are acceptable in others. Two environmental aspects have been directly related to potential maltreatment. Maltreatment occurs more frequently as income level falls. Maltreatment is also especially likely to develop in isolated families in which the parents are unusually suspicious or distrustful of outsiders.

The consequences of maltreatment to children include impaired learning, self-esteem, social relationships, and emotional control. Many people erroneously believe that maltreated children automatically become adults who abuse or neglect their own children. The phenomenon of maltreated children invariably growing up to become abusive or neglectful parents themselves (**intergenerational transmission**) is a widely held, and very destructive, misconception. Experts believe that between 30 and 40 percent of children who were abused actually become child abusers themselves. Still, this rate is much higher than that in the general population, so it is safest to conclude that it is a real, although often-exaggerated, problem.

The most effective prevention strategies for maltreatment are those that enhance community support and address the specific material and emotional needs of troubled families. Foster care and kinship care provide alternative environments for maltreated children when their families are abusive or neglectful. Adoption is the final option when families are inadequate and children are young.

📖 **Review all reading assignments for this lesson.**

💻 **As assigned by your instructor, complete the optional online component for this lesson.**

Key Terms

Using your own words, write a brief definition or explanation of each of the following terms on a separate piece of paper.

1. myelination
2. corpus callosum
3. lateralization
4. perseveration
5. amygdala
6. hippocampus
7. hypothalamus
8. injury control/harm reduction
9. primary prevention
10. secondary prevention
11. tertiary prevention
12. child maltreatment
13. child abuse
14. child neglect
15. reported maltreatment
16. substantiated maltreatment
17. post-traumatic stress disorder (PTSD)
18. permanency planning
19. foster care
20. kinship care
21. adoption
22. intergenerational transmission

Practice Questions I

Multiple-Choice Questions

1. During the preschool years, the most common nutritional problem in developed countries is
   a. serious malnutrition.
   b. excessive intake of sweets.
   c. deficiencies in iron, zinc, and calcium.
   d. excessive caloric intake.

2. The brain center for language is usually located in the
   a. right hemisphere.
   b. left hemisphere.
   c. corpus callosum.
   d. space just below the right ear.

3. Childhood height and weight
   a. are consistent throughout the world.
   b. vary from one culture to another.
   c. are more pronounced in Western cultures.
   d. are more pronounced today than in the past.

4. Which of the following is **NOT** true regarding injury control?
   a. Many injuries can be avoided by taking sensible and appropriate steps.
   b. Primary prevention measures like sidewalks, speed bumps, and stoplights, help to reduce childhood injuries.
   c. Safety laws that include penalties are more effective than educational measures.
   d. Accidental deaths of one- to five-year-olds have held steady in the United States over the past two decades.

5. Like most U.S. adults, children in the United States tend to have too much _____ in their diet.
   a. iron
   b. fat
   c. sugar
   d. sodium

6. Children learn gross motor skills best
   a. when parents determine the order of learning.
   b. in small spaces.
   c. from peers.
   d. from none of the above.

7. The brain's ongoing myelination during childhood helps children
   a. control their actions more precisely.
   b. react more quickly to stimuli.
   c. focus more easily on printed letters.
   d. do all of the above.

8. The leading cause of death in childhood is
   a. accidents.
   b. untreated diabetes.
   c. malnutrition.
   d. iron deficiency anemia.

9. At age 6, the proportions of a child's body
   a. still retain the "top-heavy" look of infancy.
   b. are more adultlike in girls than in boys.
   c. are not very different from those of an adult.
   d. are influenced more by heredity than by health care or nutrition.

10. Which of the following factors is most responsible for differences in height and weight between children in developed and developing countries?
    a. the child's genetic background
    b. health care
    c. nutrition
    d. age of weaning

11. In which of the following age periods is appetite likely to be the lowest?
    a. infancy
    b. early childhood
    c. adolescence
    d. appetite remains constant across the life span

12. The relationship between accident rate and age in childhood can be described as
    a. a positive correlation.
    b. a negative correlation.
    c. curvilinear.
    d. no correlation.

13. Which of the following is true of the corpus callosum?
    a. It enables short-term memory.
    b. It connects the two halves of the brain.
    c. It must be fully myelinated before gross motor skills can be acquired.
    d. All of the above are correct.

14. Physical coordination improves during the play years, in part because
    a. the brain areas associated with this ability become more fully myelinated.
    b. the corpus callosum begins to function.
    c. fine motor skills have matured by age 2.
    d. gross motor skills have matured by age 2.

15. Foster children
    a. are mostly from low-income families.
    b. are children who have been abused or neglected.
    c. develop better in foster care.
    d. are all of the above.

True or False Items
Write T (for true) or F (for false) on the line in front of each statement.

16. _F_ Growth between ages 2 and 6 is more rapid than at any other period in the life span.

17. _T_ During childhood, the legs develop faster than any other part of the body. *brain*

18. _T_ For most people, the brain center for language is located in the left hemisphere.

19. _T_ The health care, genetic background, and nutrition of the preschool child are major influences on growth.

20. _F_ Brain growth during childhood proceeds in spurts and plateaus.

21. _F_ Fine motor skills are usually easier for preschoolers to master than are gross motor skills.

22. _T_ Most serious childhood injuries truly are "accidents." *lack of forethought*

23. _T_ Children often fare as well in kinship care as they do in conventional foster care.

24. _T_ Most child maltreatment does not involve serious physical abuse.

Practice Questions II

Multiple-Choice Questions

1. Each year from ages 2 to 6, the average child gains and grows, respectively
   a. 2 pounds and 1 inch.
   b. 3 pounds and 2 inches.
   c. 4.5 pounds and 3 inches.
   d. 6 pounds and 6 inches.

2. Impulsiveness and perseveration are

   a. are opposite behaviors.
   b. the result of an immature prefrontal cortex.
   c. both typical of three-year-old children.
   d. all of the above.

3. Which of the following does **NOT** seem to have a negative impact on a child's health?

   a. The amounts of sugar children consume.
   b. The presence of high levels of lead in the environment.
   c. A decrease in appetite during the play years.
   d. A lack of green and orange vegetables in a child's diet.

4. The portion of the brain associated with executive function is the

   a. corpus callosum.
   b. pharyngeal gland.
   c. hippocampus.
   d. prefrontal cortex.

5. Which of the following is an example of secondary prevention of child maltreatment?

   a. removing a child from an abusive home
   b. jailing a maltreating parent
   c. home visitation of families with infants by health professionals
   d. public-policy measures aimed at creating stable neighborhoods

6. When parents or caregivers do not provide adequate food, shelter, attention, or supervision, it is referred to as

   a. abuse.
   b. neglect.
   c. maltreatment.
   d. all of the above.

7. Which of the following is true of a developed nation in which many ethnic groups live together?

   a. Ethnic variations in height and weight disappear.
   b. Ethnic variations in stature persist, but are substantially smaller.
   c. Children of African descent tend to be tallest, followed by Europeans, Asians, and Latinos.
   d. Cultural patterns exert a stronger-than-normal impact on growth patterns.

8. Which of the following is an example of a fine motor skill?
   a. kicking a ball
   b. running
   c. drawing with a pencil
   d. jumping

9. During the play years, boys generally are
   a. taller and heavier than girls.
   b. shorter and heavier than girls.
   c. taller and lighter than girls.
   d. about the same weight and height as girls.

10. Most gross motor skills can be learned by healthy children by about age
    a. 2.
    b. 3.
    c. 5.
    d. 7.

11. Two of the most important factors that affect height during the play years are
    a. socioeconomic status and health care.
    b. gender and health care.
    c. heredity and nutrition.
    d. heredity and activity level.

12. Over the past two decades in the United States, the accidental death rate for children between the ages of 1 and 5 has
    a. decreased, largely as a result of new city, state, and federal safety laws.
    b. decreased, largely because parents are more knowledgeable about safety practices.
    c. increased.
    d. remained unchanged.

13. During the play years, because growth is slow, children's appetites seem _____ they were in the first two years of life.
    a. larger than
    b. smaller than
    c. about the same as
    d. erratic, sometimes smaller and sometimes larger than

Matching Items

Match each definition or description with its corresponding term.

Terms

14. _____ corpus callosum

15. _____ gross motor skills

16. _____ fine motor skills

17. _____ injury control

18. _____ child abuse

19. _____ child neglect

20. _____ primary prevention

21. _____ secondary prevention

22. _____ tertiary prevention

23. _____ permanency planning

Definitions or Descriptions

a. efforts to find a long-term living situation that will provide stability and support for a maltreated child

b. procedures to prevent child maltreatment from ever occurring

c. running and jumping

d. actions that are deliberately harmful to a child's well-being

e. procedures for spotting and treating the early warning signs of child maltreatment

f. painting a picture or tying shoelaces

g. failure to appropriately meet a child's basic needs

h. an approach emphasizing "accident" prevention

i. procedures to halt maltreatment that has already occurred

j. band of nerve fibers connecting the right and left hemispheres of the brain

Applying Your Knowledge

1. Following an automobile accident, Salma developed severe problems with her language skills. Her doctor believes that the accident injured the _____ of her brain.

    a. left side
    b. right side
    c. communication pathways
    d. corpus callosum

2. Two-year-old José is quite clumsy, falls down frequently, and often bumps into stationary objects. José most likely

    a. has a neuromuscular disorder.
    b. has an underdeveloped right hemisphere of the brain.
    c. is suffering from iron deficiency anemia.
    d. is a normal two-year-old whose gross motor skills will improve dramatically during the preschool years.

3. Climbing a fence is an example of a
    a. fine motor skill.
    b. gross motor skill.
    c. circular reaction.
    d. launching event.

4. To prevent accidental death in childhood, some experts urge forethought and planning for safety, along with measures to limit the damage of such accidents as do occur. This approach is called
    a. protective analysis.
    b. safety education.
    c. injury control.
    d. childproofing.

5. Young children may be especially likely than older children to be terrified of a "monster hiding under their bed" because
    a. they have increased amygdala activity.
    b. of a lack of brain lateralization.
    c. they use one side of the brain considerably more than the other.
    d. their underdeveloped corpus callosums limit communication between the two brain hemispheres.

6. Which of the following activities would probably be the most difficult for a five-year-old child?
    a. climbing a ladder
    b. catching a ball
    c. throwing a ball
    d. pouring juice from a pitcher without spilling it

7. Most child maltreatment
    a. does not involve serious physical abuse.
    b. involves a rare outburst from the perpetrator.
    c. involves a mentally ill perpetrator.
    d. can be predicted from the victim's personality characteristics.

8. A mayoral candidate is calling for sweeping policy changes to help ensure the well-being of children by promoting home ownership, high-quality community centers, and more stable neighborhoods. If these measures are effective in reducing child maltreatment, they would be classified as
    a. primary prevention.
    b. secondary prevention.
    c. tertiary prevention.
    d. differential response.

9. A factor that would figure very little into the development of fine motor skills, such as drawing and writing, is

   a. strength.

   b. muscular control.

   c. judgment.

   d. short, fat fingers.

10. Three-year-old Kyle's parents are concerned because Kyle, who generally seems healthy, doesn't seem to have the hefty appetite or rate of growth he had as an infant. Should they be worried?

   a. Yes, because both appetite and growth rate normally increase throughout the preschool years.

   b. Yes, because appetite (but not necessarily growth rate) normally increases during the preschool years.

   c. No, because growth rate (and hence caloric need) is less during the preschool years than during infancy.

   d. There is not enough information to determine whether Kyle is developing normally.

Answer Key

Key Terms

1. Myelination is the process by which axons and dendrites become insulated with coating of myelin, a fatty substance that speeds neural communication. (p. 213; objective 3)

2. The corpus callosum is a band of nerve fibers that connects the right and left sides of the brain. (p. 214; video lesson, segment 1; objective 3)

3. Lateralization refers to the differentiation of the two sides of the brain so that each serves specific, specialized functions. (p. 214; objective 3)

4. Perseveration is the tendency to repeat thoughts or actions, even after they have become unhelpful or inappropriate. In young children, perseveration is a normal product of immature brain functions. (p. 216; objective 3)

   Memory aid: To persevere is to continue, or persist, at something.

5. The amygdala is a brain structure in the limbic system involved in positive and negative emotions. In the play years, activity of the amygdala can overwhelm that of the prefrontal cortex, resulting in strong and sometimes irrational fears. (p. 217; objective 3)

6. The hippocampus is a brain structure in the limbic system that aids in the processing of memories, especially memories related to location. The hippocampus is also influenced by amygdala activity, helping the child form memories related to emotional experiences. (p. 217; objective 3)

7. The limbic system contains a structure called the hypothalamus, which works in conjunction with the amygdala and the hippocampus to trigger the release of hormones (e.g., stress hormones in response to a frightening experience). (p. 217; objective 3)

8. Injury control (or harm reduction) is the practice of limiting the extent of injuries by planning ahead, controlling the circumstances, preventing certain dangerous activities, and adding safety features to others. (p. 225; objective 4)

9. Primary prevention refers to public policy measures designed to prevent child maltreatment (or other harm) from ever occurring. (p. 225; objective 7)

10. Secondary prevention involves home visitation and other efforts to spot and treat the early warning signs of maltreatment before problems become severe. (p. 225; objective 7)

11. Tertiary prevention involves efforts to stop child maltreatment after it occurs and to treat the victim. Removing a child from an abusive home, jailing the perpetrator, and providing health care to the victim are examples of tertiary prevention. (p. 225; objective 7)

12. Child maltreatment is intentional harm to, or avoidable endangerment of, anyone under age 18. (p. 227; video lesson, segment 3; objectives 6 & 7)

13. Child abuse refers to deliberate actions that are harmful to a child's well-being. (p. 227; video lesson, segment 3; objectives 6 & 7)

14. Child neglect refers to failure to appropriately meet a child's basic needs. (p. 227; video lesson, segment 3; objectives 6 & 7)

15. Child maltreatment that has been officially reported to the police, or other authority, is called reported maltreatment. (p. 228; objective 6)

16. Child maltreatment that has been officially reported to authorities, and verified, is called substantiated maltreatment. (p. 228; objective 6)

17. Post-traumatic stress disorder (PTSD) is a syndrome triggered by exposure to an extreme traumatic stressor. In maltreated children, symptoms of PTSD include hyperactivity and hypervigilance, sleeplessness, and confusion between fantasy and reality. (p. 230; objective 6)

18. Because repeated changes in caregivers or schools disrupt child development, permanency planning is used to seek a long-term placement for a child where he or she will be able to live until adulthood. (p. 232; objective 7)

19. Foster care is a legally sanctioned, publicly supported arrangement in which children are removed from their biological parents and temporarily given to another adult to nurture. (p. 232; objective 7)

20. Kinship care is a form of foster care in which a relative of a maltreated child becomes the child's legal caregiver. (p. 232; objective 7)

21. An adoption is a legal proceeding in which an adult or couple unrelated to a child is granted the joy and obligations of becoming that child's parents. (p. 233; objective 7)

22. Intergenerational transmission is the assumption that mistreated children grow up to become abusive or neglectful parents themselves. (video lesson, segment 3; objective 7)

Practice Questions I

Multiple-Choice Questions

1. c. is the correct answer. (objective 2)

2. b. is the correct answer. (objective 4)

   a. & d. are incorrect. The right brain is the location of areas associated with recognition of visual configurations.

   c. is incorrect. The corpus callosum helps integrate the functioning of the two halves of the brain; it does not contain areas specialized for particular skills.

3. b. is the correct answer. (video lesson, segment 1; objective 1)

4. d. is the correct answer. Accident rates have decreased during this time period. (objective 5)
5. c. is the correct answer. (objective 2)
6. c. is the correct answer. (video lesson, segment 2; objective 5)
7. d. is the correct answer. (video lesson, segment 1; objective 3)
8. a. is the correct answer. (objective 4)
9. c. is the correct answer. (objective 1)

   b. is incorrect. The proportions are more adultlike in both girls and boys.

   d. is incorrect. Nutrition is a bigger factor in growth at this age than either heredity or health care.
10. c. is the correct answer. (video lesson, segment 1; objective 1)
11. b. is the correct answer. (objective 2)
12. b. is the correct answer. Children who are younger have higher accident rates. (objective 4)
13. b. is the correct answer. (video lesson, segment 1; objective 3)

    a. is incorrect. The corpus callosum is not directly involved in memory.

    c. is incorrect. Myelination of the central nervous system is important to the mastery of fine motor skills.
14. a. is the correct answer. (objective 3)

    b. is incorrect. The corpus callosum begins to function long before the play years.

    c. & d. are incorrect. Neither fine nor gross motor skills have fully matured by age 2.
15. d. is the correct answer. (objective 7)

True or False Items

16. F   Growth actually slows down during the play years. (video lesson, segment 1; objective 1)
17. F   During childhood, the brain develops faster than any other part of the body. (video lesson, segment 1; objectives 1 & 3)
18. T   (objective 3)
19. T   (video lesson, segment 1; objective 1)
20. T   video lesson, segment 1; objective 3)
21. F   Fine motor skills are more difficult for preschoolers to master than are gross motor skills. (video lesson, segment 2; objective 5)
22. F   Most serious accidents involve someone's lack of forethought. (objective 4)
23. T   (objective 7)
24. T   (video lesson, segment 3; objective 7)

Practice Questions II

Multiple-Choice Questions

1. c. is the correct answer. (video lesson, segment 1; objective 1)
2. a. is the correct answer. (objective 4)

   b. & c. are incorrect. The left hemisphere of the brain contains areas associated with language development.

   d. is incorrect. The corpus callosum does not contain areas for specific behaviors.

3. c. is the correct answer. (objective 2)

   b. & c. are incorrect. The left and right hemispheres develop at similar rates.

4. a. is the correct answer. (objective 3)

5. c. is the correct answer. (objective 7)

   a. & b. are incorrect. These are examples of tertiary prevention.

   d. is incorrect. This is an example of primary prevention.

6. d. is the correct answer. (video lesson, segment 3; objective 7)

7. c. is the correct answer. (objective 1)

8. c. is the correct answer. (video lesson, segment 2; objective 5)

   a., b., & d. are incorrect. These are gross motor skills.

9. a. is the correct answer. (video lesson, segment 1; objective 1)

10. c. is the correct answer. (video lesson, segment 2; objective 5)

11. c. is the correct answer. (objective 1)

12. a. is the correct answer. (objective 4)

   b. is incorrect. Although safety education is important, the decrease in accident rate is largely the result of new safety laws.

13. b. is the correct answer. (objective 2)

Matching Items

14. j (objective 3)

15. c (objective 5)

16. f (objective 5)

17. h (objective 4)

18. d (objective 6)

19. g (objective 6)

20. b (objective 7)

21. e (objective 7)

22. i (objective 7)

23. a (objective 7)

Applying Your Knowledge

1. a. is the correct answer. In most people, the left hemisphere of the brain contains centers for language, including speech. (objective 3)

2. d. is the correct answer. (objective 3)

3. b. is the correct answer. (video lesson, segment 2; objective 5)

   a. is incorrect. Fine motor skills involve small body movements, such as the hand movements used in painting.

   c. & d. are incorrect. These events were not discussed in this chapter.

4. c. is the correct answer. (objective 4)

5. a. is the correct answer. (objective 3)

6. d. is the correct answer. (video lesson, segment 2; objective 5)

   a., b., & c. are incorrect. Preschoolers find these gross motor skills easier to perform than fine motor skills such as that described in d.

7. a. is the correct answer. (video lesson, segment 3; objective 7)

8. a. is the correct answer. (objective 7)

   b. is incorrect. Had the candidate called for measures to spot the early warning signs of maltreatment, this answer would be true.

   c. is incorrect. Had the candidate called for jailing those who maltreat children or providing greater counseling and health care for victims, this answer would be true.

   d. is incorrect. Differential response is not an approach to prevention of maltreatment; rather, it refers to separate reporting procedures for high- and low-risk families.

9. a. is the correct answer. Strength is a more important factor in the development of gross motor skills. (video lesson, segment 2; objective 5)

10. c. is the correct answer. (objective 2)

Lesson Review

Lesson 8

The Play Years
Biosocial Development

Please Note: Use this matrix to guide your study and achieve the learning objectives of this lesson. It will also help you to view the video, which defines and demonstrates important concepts and skills as they relate to everyday life.

Learning Objective	Textbook	Course Student Guide	Video Lesson
1. Describe normal physical growth during the play years, and account for variations in height and weight.	pp. 209–211	Practice Questions I: 3, 9 10, 16, 17, 19; Practice Questions II: 1, 7, 9, 11.	Segment 1: *Body and Brain Growth*
2. Describe changes in eating habits and nutritional needs during the preschool years.	pp. 210–212	Practice Questions I: 1, 5, 11; Practice Questions II: 3, 13; Applying Your Knowledge: 10.	
3. Discuss brain growth and development and its effect on other areas of development during the play years.	pp. 212–219	Key Terms: 1, 2, 3, 4, 5, 6, 7; Practice Questions I: 7, 13, 14, 17, 18, 20; Practice Questions II: 4, 14; Applying Your Knowledge: 1, 2, 5.	Segment 1: *Body and Brain Growth*
4. Describe the prevalence of accidental injuries during early childhood, describe some measures that have significantly reduced accidental death rates for children, and identify several factors that contribute to this problem.	pp. 224–227	Key Terms: 8; Practice Questions I: 2, 8, 12, 22; Practice Questions II: 2, 12, 17; Applying Your Knowledge: 4.	
5. Discuss the development of gross and fine motor skills during the play years.	pp. 220–224	Practice Questions I: 4, 6, 21; Practice Questions II: 8, 10, 15, 16; Applying Your Knowledge: 3, 6, 9.	Segment 2: *Motor Skills*
6. Identify the various categories and consequences of child maltreatment.	pp. 227–230	Key Terms: 12, 13, 14, 15, 16, 17; Practice Questions II: 18, 19.	Segment 3: *Maltreatment*

Learning Objective	Textbook	Course Student Guide	Video Lesson
7. Discuss several factors that contribute to maltreatment, and describe current treatment and prevention efforts.	pp. 225–227, 231–233	Key Terms: 9, 10, 11, 12, 13, 14, 18, 19, 20, 21, 22; Practice Questions I: 15, 23, 24; Practice Questions II: 5, 6, 20, 21, 22, 23; Applying Your Knowledge: 7, 8.	Segment 3: *Maltreatment*

Playing and Learning

Lesson 9

The Play Years:
Cognitive Development

Preview

In countless everyday instances, as well as in the findings of numerous research studies, young children reveal themselves to be remarkably thoughtful, insightful, and perceptive thinkers whose memory of the past and mastery of language are sometimes astonishing. Lesson 9 begins by comparing Jean Piaget's and Lev Vygotsky's views of cognitive development at this age. According to Piaget, young children's thought is prelogical: between the ages of 2 and 6, they are unable to use logical principles and are limited by irreversible and static thinking. Lev Vygotsky, a contemporary of Piaget, saw learning more as a product of social interaction than of individual discovery.

The lesson next focuses on what preschoolers can do, including their competence in understanding number concepts, storing and retrieving memories, and theorizing about the world. This leads into a description of language development during early childhood. Although young children demonstrate rapid improvement in vocabulary and grammar, they have difficulty with abstractions, metaphorical speech, and certain rules of grammar. The lesson concludes with a discussion of preschool education, including a description of "quality" preschool programs and an evaluation of their lifelong impact on children.

As you complete this lesson, consider the cognitive development of any children you know in this age group (2 to 6). Consider what these children understand already and what they have yet to learn. Observe how they think—how they look at the world, interpret events, draw conclusions, and make decisions. Note how these children discover knowledge on their own and how they learn new skills through the guidance of parents, caregivers, and other children. Also, consider the memory skills of these children. For instance, how well can they remember events of their day and how well can they describe them? Consider their language skills—the extent of their vocabulary and their use of grammar. Finally, do any of these children go to day care or preschool? If so, what type of care are they receiving? What sort of learning experiences are they exposed to, and how might that exposure affect their development later in life?

Prior Course Knowledge that Will Be Used in this Lesson

- This lesson will return to Piaget's theory of cognitive development (from Lesson 1/Chapter 2) with a discussion of **preoperational thought**. Recall that Piaget's theory specifies four major periods of cognitive development:
    1. Sensorimotor (birth to 2 years)

2. **Preoperational (2 to 6 years)** ← **The Play Years**
3. Concrete Operational (7 to 11 years)
4. Formal Operational (12 years through adulthood)

- This lesson will return to the sociocultural theories of Lev Vygotsky (from Lesson 1/Chapter 2). Recall that Vygotsky emphasized the importance of guided participation, a process in which an individual learns through social interaction with a mentor who offers assistance, models strategies, and provides explicit instruction as needed.

Learning Objectives

Use this information to guide your reading, viewing, thinking, and studying. After successfully completing this lesson, you should be able to:

1. Describe the major characteristics of Piaget's stage of preoperational thought/ intelligence, and explain revisions to the theory suggested by recent research.
2. Contrast Vygotsky's views on cognitive development with those of Piaget, focusing on the concept of guided participation.
3. Explain the significance of the zone of proximal development and scaffolding in promoting cognitive growth.
4. Describe Vygotsky's view of the role of language in cognitive growth.
5. Explain the typical young child's theory of mind, noting how it is affected by culture and context, and relate it to the child's developing ability to understand pretense.
6. Outline the sequence by which vocabulary and grammar develop during the play years, and discuss limitations in the young child's language abilities.
7. Explain the role of fast mapping in children's acquisition of language.
8. Identify the characteristics of a high-quality preschool program, and discuss the long-term benefits of preschool education for the child and his or her family.

📖 **Read Chapter 9, "The Play Years: Cognitive Development," pages 237–263.**

⏮ **View the video for Lesson 9, "Playing and Learning."**

Segment 1: *How Preschoolers Think*

Segment 2: *Words and Memories*

Segment 3: *Early Childhood Education*

Summary

Symbolic thinking, which enables children to form mental representations of things and events they are not immediately experiencing, develops rapidly throughout the preschool years. Both language and imagination become tools of thought, making the typical four-year-old much more verbal and creative than the one-year-old.

Although preschool children can think symbolically, they cannot perform what Jean Piaget called "logical operations." One characteristic of this **preoperational thought/ intelligence** is **irreversibility**: Preschoolers do not generally understand that reversing a process will restore the original conditions. Preoperational children also fail to correctly answer problems involving **conservation**, indicating that they do not yet understand the idea that the amount of a substance is unaffected by changes in its shape or placement.

Centration refers to the tendency of preschoolers to focus or center their analysis on one aspect of a problem, for instance, the appearance of liquid in a glass. In tests of conservation, Piaget believed, the problem is that preschoolers center on only the height of the liquid and fail to consider the shape and diameter of the glass it is in. Another example of centration is the preschooler's tendency toward **egocentrism**—to see the world only from his or her perspective.

Piaget focused on the individual child's innate curiosity. In general, he believed that children will find a way to learn when they are ready to do so. In contrast, Lev Vygotsky emphasized the impact of cultural and social factors in learning, including the effects of mentors and teachers. For instance, Vygotsky believed that—for each individual—there is a **zone of proximal development**, which represents the cognitive distance between the child's actual and potential levels of development. To encourage development, mentors can **scaffold** learning—in other words, provide structured assistance to help the child master new skills. Vygotsky also believed that language advances thinking in two ways: through **private speech** that an individual child uses to assist his or her thinking, and as **social mediation**, a tool of verbal interaction between mentor and apprentice. While these approaches are sometimes described as contradictory, a closer examination reveals that they may simply emphasize two different aspects of cognitive development.

Recent experiments have shown that preschoolers are not as illogical as Piaget believed. For example, under certain circumstances, young children can demonstrate the concept of conservation. On the other hand, young children cannot count large amounts, cannot easily add or subtract, and are not skilled at deliberately storing or retrieving memories. By about age 4, however, they do understand basic counting principles.

During the play years, children are gaining a better understanding of their own thoughts and feelings. In addition, they are beginning to develop informal theories about why other people act the way they do. In time this develops into what psychologists call a **theory of mind**, an understanding of human mental processes. This understanding helps children explain basic everyday questions, such as such as how a person's knowledge and emotions affect his or her actions and how people can have such different perceptions, intentions, and desires.

Language development during the play years includes learning 10,000 words or more, in a predictable sequence according to parts of speech. Words are often learned after only one hearing, through the process called **fast mapping**. By age 3, children demonstrate extensive grammatical knowledge, although they often apply grammatical rules even when they should not (**overregularization**).

Changes in family composition and work patterns have resulted in great increases in early-childhood education programs. A high-quality preschool program is characterized by a low teacher-child ratio, a staff with training and credentials in early-childhood education, a curriculum geared toward cognitive development rather than behavioral control, and an organization of space that facilitates creative and constructive play.

While children in the play years are developing rapidly, it's important to focus their learning experiences on age-appropriate activities and not force them into tasks that are beyond their capability. For example, before a child's brain develops the ability to link spoken and written language (at about age 5), he or she is not ready to learn to read. That's why formal instruction in reading usually begins at about age 6. (Of course, *preparation* for literacy—such as reading picture books and writing one's name—should begin much earlier.)

Lesson 9/The Play Years: Cognitive Development

📖 **Review all reading assignments for this lesson.**

💻 **As assigned by your instructor, complete the optional online component for this lesson.**

Key Terms

Using your own words, write a brief definition or explanation of each of the following terms on a separate piece of paper.

1. preoperational thought/intelligence
2. centration
3. egocentrism
4. focus on appearance
5. static reasoning
6. irreversibility
7. conservation
8. animism
9. guided participation
10. zone of proximal development (ZPD)
11. scaffolding
12. private speech
13. social mediation
14. theory-theory
15. theory of mind
16. fast mapping
17. overregularization
18. balanced bilingual
19. Montessori schools
20. Reggio Emilia
21. symbolic thinking

Practice Questions I

Multiple-Choice Questions

1. Piaget believed that children are in the preoperational stage from ages
   a. 6 months to 1 year.
   b. 1 to 3 years.
   c. 2 to 6 years.
   d. 5 to 11 years.

2. Which of the following is **NOT** a characteristic of preoperational thinking?
   a. focus on appearance
   b. static reasoning
   c. lack of imagination
   d. centration

3. Preschoolers sometimes apply the rules of grammar even when they shouldn't. This tendency is called
   a. overregularization.
   b. literal language.
   c. practical usage.
   d. single-mindedness.

4. The Russian psychologist Lev Vygotsky emphasized that
   a. language helps children form ideas.
   b. children form concepts first, then find words to express them.
   c. language and other cognitive developments are unrelated at this stage.
   d. preschoolers learn language only for egocentric purposes.

5. Private speech can be described as
   a. a way of formulating ideas to oneself.
   b. fantasy.
   c. an early learning difficulty.
   d. the beginnings of deception.

6. In later life, high-quality preschool program graduates showed
   a. better report cards, but more behavioral problems.
   b. significantly higher IQ scores.
   c. higher scores on achievement tests.
   d. alienation from their original neighborhoods and families.

7. The child who has not yet grasped the principle of conservation is likely to
   a. insist that a tall, narrow glass contains more liquid than a short, wide glass, even though both glasses actually contain the same amount.
   b. be incapable of egocentric thought.
   c. be able to reverse an event.
   d. do all of the above.

8. The best preschool programs are generally those that provide the greatest amount of
   a. behavioral control.
   b. positive teacher-child social interactions.
   c. instruction in conservation and other logical principles.
   d. demonstration of toys by professionals.

9. Compared with their rate of speech development, children's understanding of language develops
   a. more slowly.
   b. at about the same pace.
   c. more rapidly.
   d. more rapidly in some cultures than in others.

10. Relatively recent experiments have demonstrated that preschoolers can succeed at tests of conservation when
    a. they are allowed to work cooperatively with other children.
    b. the test is presented as a competition.
    c. the children are informed that their parents are observing them.
    d. the test is presented in a simple, gamelike way.

11. Through the process called fast mapping, children
    a. immediately assimilate new words by connecting them through their assumed meaning to categories of words they have already mastered.
    b. acquire the concept of conservation at an earlier age than Piaget believed.
    c. are able to move beyond egocentric thinking.
    d. become skilled in the practical use of language.

True or False Items

Write T (for true) or F (for false) on the line in front of each statement.

12. __F__ Piaget's description of cognitive development in early childhood has been universally rejected by contemporary developmentalists.

13. __T__ In conservation problems, many preschoolers cannot understand the transformation because they focus exclusively on appearances.

14. __F__ Preschoolers who use private speech have slower cognitive growth than those who do not.

15. __T__ Whether or not a preschooler demonstrates conservation in an experiment depends in part on the conditions of the experiment.

16. __F__ Piaget believed that preschoolers' acquisition of language makes possible their cognitive development.

17. __F__ With the beginning of preoperational thought, most preschoolers can understand abstract words.

18. __F__ A preschooler who says "You comed up and hurted me" is demonstrating a lack of understanding of English grammar.

19. __T__ Successful preschool programs generally have a low teacher-to-child ratio.

20. __T__ Vygotsky believed that cognitive growth is largely a social activity.

Practice Questions II

Multiple-Choice Questions

1. During the preschool years, vocabulary increases exponentially, from about 500 words
    a. at age 2 to about 7,000 at age 6.
    b. at age 2 to more than 10,000 at age 6.
    c. at age 3 to more than 20,000 at age 7.
    d. at age 3 to about 25,000 at age 7.

2. Piaget believed that preoperational children fail conservation-of-liquid tests because of their tendency to
    a. focus on appearance.
    b. fast map.
    c. overregularize.
    d. do all of the above.

3. A preschooler who focuses his or her attention on only one feature of a situation is demonstrating a characteristic of preoperational thought called
   a. centration.
   b. overregularization.
   c. reversibility.
   d. egocentrism.

4. One characteristic of preoperational thought is
   a. the ability to categorize objects.
   b. the ability to count in multiples of 5.
   c. the inability to perform logical operations.
   d. difficulty adjusting to changes in routine.

5. The zone of proximal development represents the
   a. skills or knowledge that are within the potential of the learner but are not yet mastered.
   b. influence of a child's peers on cognitive development.
   c. explosive period of language development during the play years.
   d. normal variations in children's language proficiency.

6. According to Vygotsky, language advances thinking through private speech and by
   a. helping children to review privately what they know.
   b. helping children explain events to themselves.
   c. serving as a mediator of the social interaction that is a vital part of learning.
   d. facilitating the process of fast mapping.

7. Irreversibility refers to the
   a. inability to understand that other people view the world from a different perspective than one's own.
   b. inability to think about more than one idea at a time.
   c. failure to understand that changing the arrangement of a group of objects doesn't change their number.
   d. failure to understand that undoing a process will restore the original conditions.

8. According to Piaget
   a. it is impossible for preoperational children to grasp the concept of conservation, no matter how carefully it is explained.
   b. preschoolers fail to solve conservation problems because they center their attention on the transformation that has occurred and ignore the changed appearances of the objects.
   c. with special training, even preoperational children are able to grasp some aspects of conservation.
   d. preschoolers fail to solve conservation problems because they have no theory of mind.

9. In order to scaffold a child's cognitive skills, parents
   a. simplify tasks.
   b. interpret the activity.
   c. solve problems, anticipating mistakes.
   d. do all of the above.

10. Which theorist would be most likely to agree with the statement, "Learning is a social activity more than it is a matter of individual discovery"?
    a. Piaget
    b. Vygotsky
    c. both a and b
    d. neither a nor b

11. Children first demonstrate some understanding of grammar
    a. as soon as the first words are produced.
    b. once they begin to use language for practical purposes.
    c. through the process called fast mapping.
    d. in their earliest two-word sentences.

12. Overregularization indicates that a child
    a. is clearly applying rules of grammar.
    b. persists in egocentric thinking.
    c. has not yet mastered the principle of conservation.
    d. does not yet have a theory of mind.

13. Regarding the value of preschool education, most developmentalists believe that
    a. most disadvantaged children will not benefit from an early preschool education.
    b. most disadvantaged children will benefit from an early preschool education.
    c. because of sleeper effects, the early benefits of preschool education are likely to disappear by grade 3.
    d. the relatively small benefits of antipoverty measures such as Head Start do not justify their huge costs.

Matching Items

Match each definition or description with its corresponding term.

Terms

14. _____ balanced bilingual

15. _____ scaffold

16. _____ theory of mind

17. _____ zone of proximal development (ZPD)

18. _____ overregularization

19. _____ fast mapping

20. _____ centration

21. _____ conservation

22. _____ private speech

23. _____ guided participation

Definitions or Descriptions

a. the idea that amount is unaffected by changes in shape or placement

b. a person who is fluent in two languages

c. the cognitive distance between a child's actual and potential levels of development

d. the tendency to think about one aspect of a situation at a time

e. the process whereby the child learns through social interaction with a "tutor"

f. our understanding of mental processes in ourselves and others

g. the process by which words are learned after only one hearing

h. an inappropriate application of rules of grammar

i. the internal use of language to form ideas

j. to structure a child's participation in learning encounters

Applying Your Knowledge

1. An experimenter first shows a child two rows of checkers that each have the same number of checkers. Then, with the child watching, the experimenter elongates one row and asks the child whether the two rows still have the same number of checkers. This experiment tests the child's understanding of

   a. reversibility.

   b. conservation of matter.

   c. conservation of number.

   d. centration.

2. A preschooler believes that a "party" is the one and only attribute of a birthday. She says that Daddy doesn't have a birthday because he never has a party. This thinking demonstrates the tendency Piaget called

   a. egocentrism.

   b. centration.

   c. conservation of events.

   d. mental representation.

3. A four-year-old tells the teacher that a clown should not be allowed to visit the class because "Pat is 'fraid of clowns." The four-year-old thus shows that he can anticipate how another will feel. This is evidence of the beginnings of

    a. egocentrism.
    b. deception.
    c. a theory of mind.
    d. conservation.

4. Four-year-old Rhana becomes very distressed upon finding pickles on her cheeseburger. Her mother removes the pickles but Rhana still refuses to eat the sandwich, insisting that it is yucky now. Rhana's belief that the pickles permanently damaged her sandwich is consistent with a preoperational child's belief in

    a. tertiary circular reactions.
    b. irreversibility.
    c. explicit memory.
    d. oppositionalism.

5. A nursery school teacher is given the job of selecting holiday entertainment for a group of preschool children. If the teacher agrees with the ideas of Vygotsky, she is most likely to select

    a. a simple television show that every child can understand.
    b. a hands-on experience that requires little adult supervision.
    c. action-oriented play activities that the children and teachers will perform together.
    d. holiday puzzles for children to work on individually.

6. When a child produces sentences that follow rules of word order as "the initiator of an action precedes the verb, the receiver of an action follows it," this development demonstrates a knowledge of

    a. grammar.
    b. semantics.
    c. pragmatics.
    d. phrase structure.

7. The two-year-old child who says, "We goed to the store," is making a grammatical

    a. overextension.
    b. overregularization.
    c. underextension.
    d. script.

8. An experimenter who makes two balls of clay of equal amount, then rolls one into a long, skinny rope and asks the child if the amounts are still the same, is testing the child's understanding of
   a. conservation.
   b. egocentrism.
   c. perspective.
   d. centration.

9. Dr. Jones, who believes that children's language growth greatly contributes to their cognitive growth, evidently is a proponent of the ideas of
   a. Piaget.
   b. Chomsky.
   c. Flavell.
   d. Vygotsky.

10. Jack constantly "talks down" to his three-year-old son's speech level. Jack's speech is
    a. appropriate because three-year-olds have barely begun to comprehend grammatical rules.
    b. commendable, given the importance of scaffolding in promoting cognitive growth.
    c. unnecessary because preschoolers are able to comprehend more complex grammar and vocabulary than they can produce.
    d. clearly within his son's zone of proximal development.

11. In describing the limited logical reasoning of preschoolers, a contemporary developmentalist is least likely to emphasize
    a. irreversibility.
    b. centration.
    c. egocentrism.
    d. private speech.

12. A preschooler fails to complete a difficult puzzle on her own, so her mother encourages her to try again, this time guiding her by asking questions such as, "For this space do we need a big piece or a little piece?" With Mom's help, the child completes the puzzle successfully. Vygotsky would attribute the child's success to
    a. additional practice with the puzzle pieces.
    b. imitation of her mother's behavior.
    c. the social interaction with her mother that restructured the task to make its solution more attainable.
    d. modeling and reinforcement.

13. Mark is answering an essay question that asks him to "discuss the positions of major developmental theorists regarding the relationship between language and cognitive development." To help organize his answer, Mark jots down a reminder that _____ contended that language is essential to the advancement of thinking, as private speech, and as a _____ of social interactions.

    a. Piaget; mediator
    b. Vygotsky; mediator
    c. Piaget; theory
    d. Vygotsky; theory

Answer Key

Key Terms

1. According to Piaget, thinking between ages 2 and 6 is characterized by preoperational thought/intelligence, meaning that children cannot yet perform logical operations; that is, they cannot use logical principles. (p. 237; video lesson, segment 2; objective 1)

   Memory aid: Operations are mental transformations involving the manipulation of ideas and symbols. Preoperational children, who lack the ability to perform transformations, are "before" this developmental milestone.

2. Centration is the tendency of young children to focus only on a single aspect of a situation or object. (p. 238; video lesson, segment 1; objective 1)

3. Egocentrism refers to the tendency of young children to view the world exclusively from their own perspective. (p. 238; video lesson, segment 1; objective 1)

4. Focus on appearance refers to the preoperational child's tendency to focus only on physical attributes and ignore all others. (p. 238; objective 1)

5. Preoperational thinking is characterized by static reasoning, by which is meant that the young child sees the world as unchanging. (p. 238; objective 1)

6. Irreversibility is the characteristic of preoperational thought in which young children fail to recognize that a process can be reversed to restore the original conditions of a situation. (p. 238; video lesson, segment 1; objective 1)

7. Conservation is the understanding that the amount or quantity of a substance or object is unaffected by changes in its shape or configuration. (p. 238; video lesson, segment 1; objective 1)

8. Animism is the believe that natural objects and phenomena are alive. (p. 240; objective 1)

9. According to Vygotsky, intellectual growth in young children is stimulated and directed by their guided participation in learning experiences. As guides, parents, teachers, and older children offer assistance with challenging tasks, model problem-solving approaches, provide explicit instructions as needed, and support the child's interest and motivation. (p. 241; video lesson, segment 1; objective 2)

10. According to Vygotsky, for each individual there is a zone of proximal development (ZPD), which represents the skills that are within the potential of the learner but cannot be performed independently. (p. 241; video lesson, segment 1; objective 3)

11. Tutors who scaffold structure children's learning experiences by simplifying tasks, maintaining children's interest, solving problems, and anticipating mistakes, among other things. This term can be used as a verb (e.g., "to scaffold") or a noun (e.g., "creating scaffolding"). (p. 241; video lesson, segment 1; objective 3)

12. Private speech is the internal dialogue in which a person talks to himself or herself. Preschoolers' private speech, which often is uttered aloud, helps them think, review what they know, and decide what to do. (p. 243; objective 4)

13. In Vygotsky's theory, social mediation refers to the use of speech as a tool to bridge the gap in understanding or knowledge between a child and a tutor. (p. 243; objective 4)

14. Theory-theory refers to the tendency of young children to attempt to construct theories to explain everything they experience. (p. 244; objective 5)

15. A theory of mind is an understanding of mental processes, that is, of one's own or another's emotions, perceptions, intentions, and thoughts. (p. 245; video lesson, segment 2; objective 5)

16. Fast mapping is the process by which children rapidly learn new words by quickly connecting them to words and categories that are already understood. (p. 248; video lesson, segment 2; objective 7)

17. Overregularization occurs when children apply rules of grammar when they should not. It is seen in English, for example, when children add "s" to form the plural even in irregular cases that form the plural in a different way. (p. 249; video lesson, segment 2; objective 6)

18. A balanced bilingual is a person who is so fluent in two languages that there is no audible evidence of which language was learned first. (p. 251; objective 6)

19. Montessori schools offer a form of child-centered early childhood education based on the philosophy of Maria Montessori, which emphasizes careful work and tasks that each young child can do. (p. 254; objective 8)

20. Reggio Emilia is a famous style of early education that originated in the town of Reggio Emilia, Italy, and that encourages each child's creativity in a carefully designed setting. (p. 254; objective 8)

21. Symbolic thinking involves the use of words, gestures, pictures, or actions to represent other objects, behaviors, or experiences. (video lesson, segment 1; objective 1)

Practice Questions I

Multiple-Choice Questions

1. c. is the correct answer. (video lesson, segment 1; objective 1)

2. c. is the correct answer. (objective 1)

3. a. is the correct answer. (video lesson, segment 2; objective 6)

   b. & d. are incorrect. These terms are not identified in the textbook and do not apply to the use of grammar.

   c. is incorrect. Practical usage, which also is not discussed in the textbook, refers to communication between one person and another in terms of the overall context in which language is used.

4. a. is the correct answer. (objective 4)

   b. is incorrect. This expresses the views of Piaget.

c. is incorrect. Because he believed that language facilitates thinking, Vygotsky obviously felt that language and other cognitive developments are intimately related.

d. is incorrect. Vygotsky did not hold this view.

5. a. is the correct answer. (objective 4)

6. c. is the correct answer. (objective 8)

b. is incorrect. This is not discussed in the textbook. However, although there was a slight early IQ advantage in Head Start graduates, the difference disappeared by grade 3.

a. & d. are incorrect. There was no indication of greater behavioral problems or alienation in Head Start graduates.

7. a. is the correct answer. (video lesson, segment 1; objective 1)

b., c., & d. are incorrect. Failure to conserve is the result of thinking that is centered on appearances. Egocentrism and irreversibility are also examples of centered thinking.

8. b. is the correct answer. (video lesson, segment 3; objective 8)

9. c. is the correct answer. (video lesson, segment 2; objective 6)

10. d. is the correct answer. (video lesson, segment 1; objective 1)

11. a. is the correct answer. (video lesson, segment 2; objective 8)

True or False Items

12. F   More recent research has found that children may understand conservation earlier than Piaget thought, given a more gamelike presentation. His theory has not been rejected overall, however. (video lesson, segment 1; objective 1)

13. T   (video lesson, segment 1; objective 1)

14. F   In fact, just the opposite is true. Children who have learning difficulties tend to be slower to develop private speech. (objective 4)

15. T   (video lesson, segment 1; objective 1)

16. F   Vygotsky believed that language advances thinking. (objective 1)

17. F   Preschoolers have difficulty understanding abstract words; their vocabulary consists mainly of concrete nouns and verbs. (video lesson, segment 2; objective 6)

18. F   In adding "ed" to form a past tense, the child has indicated an understanding of the grammatical rule for making past tenses in English, even though the construction in these two cases is incorrect. (video lesson, segment 2; objective 6)

19. T   (video lesson, segment 3; objective 8)

20. T   (video lesson, segment 1; objective 2)

Practice Questions II

Multiple-Choice Questions

1. b. is the correct answer. (objective 6)

2. a. is the correct answer. (objective 1)

3. a. is the correct answer. (video lesson, segment 1; objective 1)

b. is incorrect. Overregularization is the child's tendency to apply grammatical rules even when he or she shouldn't.

c. is incorrect. Reversibility is the concept that reversing an operation, such as addition, will restore the original conditions.

d. is incorrect. This term is used to refer to the young child's belief that people think as he or she does.

4. c. is the correct answer. This is why the stage is called preoperational. (video lesson, segment 1; objective 1)

5. a. is the correct answer. (video lesson, segment 1; objective 3)

6. c. is the correct answer. (objective 4)

a. & b. are incorrect. These are both advantages of private speech.

d. is incorrect. Fast mapping is the process by which new words are acquired, often after only one hearing.

7. d. is the correct answer. (video lesson, segment 1; objective 1)

a. is incorrect. This describes egocentrism.

b. is incorrect. This is the opposite of centration.

c. is incorrect. This defines conservation of number.

8. a. is the correct answer. (objective 1)

b. is incorrect. According to Piaget, preschoolers fail to solve conservation problems because they focus on the appearance of objects and ignore the transformation that has occurred.

d. is incorrect. Piaget did not relate conservation to a theory of mind.

9. d. is the correct answer. (video lesson, segment 1; objective 3)

10. b. is the correct answer. (video lesson, segment 1; objective 2)

a. is incorrect. Piaget believed that learning is a matter of individual discovery.

11. d. is the correct answer. Preschoolers almost always put subject before verb in their two-word sentences. (video lesson, segment 2; objective 6)

12. a. is the correct answer. (video lesson, segment 2; objective 6)

b., c., & d. are incorrect. Overregularization is a linguistic phenomenon rather than a characteristic type of thinking (b & d), or a logical principle (c).

13. b. is the correct answer. (objective 7)

Matching Items

14. b (objective 6)

15. j (video lesson, segment 1; objective 3)

16. f (video lesson, segment 2; objective 5)

17. c (video lesson, segment 1; objective 3)

18. h (video lesson, segment 2; objective 6)

19. g (video lesson, segment 2; objective 7)

20. d (video lesson, segment 1; objective 1)

21. a (video lesson, segment 1; objective 1)

22. i (objective 4)

23. e (video lesson, segment 1; objective 2)

Applying Your Knowledge

1. c. is the correct answer. (video lesson, segment 1; objective 1)

   a. is incorrect. A test of reversibility would ask a child to perform an operation, such as adding 4 to 3, and then reverse the process (subtract 3 from 7) to determine whether the child understood that the original condition (the number 4) was restored.

   b. is incorrect. A test of conservation of matter would transform the appearance of an object, such as a ball of clay, to determine whether the child understood that the object remained the same.

   d. is incorrect. A test of centration would involve the child's ability to see various aspects of a situation.

2. b. is the correct answer. (video lesson, segment 1; objective 1)

   a. is incorrect. Egocentrism is thinking that is self-centered.

   c. is incorrect. This is not a concept in Piaget's theory.

   d. is incorrect. Mental representation is an example of symbolic thought.

3. c. is the correct answer. (video lesson, segment 2; objective 5)

   a. is incorrect. Egocentrism is self-centered thinking.

   b. is incorrect. Although deception provides evidence of a theory of mind, the child in this example is not deceiving anyone.

   d. is incorrect. Conservation is the understanding that the amount of a substance is unchanged by changes in its shape or placement.

4. b. is the correct answer. (video lesson, segment 1; objective 1)

5. c. is the correct answer. In Vygotsky's view, learning is a social activity more than a matter of individual discovery. Thus, social interaction that provides motivation and focuses attention facilitates learning. (video lesson, segment 1; objective 2)

6. a. is the correct answer. (video lesson, segment 2; objective 6)

   b. & d. are incorrect. The textbook does not discuss these aspects of language.

   c. is incorrect. Pragmatics, which is not mentioned in the textbook, refers to the practical use of language in varying social contexts.

7. b. is the correct answer. (video lesson, segment 2; objective 6)

8. a. is the correct answer. (video lesson, segment 1; objective 1)

9. d. is the correct answer. (objective 4)

   a. is incorrect. Piaget believed that cognitive growth precedes language development.

   b. & c. are incorrect. Chomsky focused on the acquisition of language, and Flavell emphasizes cognition.

10. c. is the correct answer. (objective 6)

11. d. is the correct answer. (objective 4)

12. c. is the correct answer. (objective 3)

13. b. is the correct answer. (objective 4)

Lesson Review

Lesson 9

The Play Years
Cognitive Development

Please Note: Use this matrix to guide your study and achieve the learning objectives of this lesson. It will also help you to view the video, which defines and demonstrates important concepts and skills as they relate to everyday life.

Learning Objective	Textbook	Course Student Guide	Video Lesson
1. Describe the major characteristics of Piaget's stage of preoperational thought/intelligence, and explain revisions to the theory suggested by recent research.	pp. 237–240	Key Terms: 1, 2, 3, 4, 5, 6, 7, 8, 21; Practice Questions I: 1, 2, 7, 10, 12, 13, 15, 16; Practice Questions II: 2, 3, 4, 7, 8, 20, 21; Applying Your Knowledge: 1, 2, 4, 8.	Segment 1: *How Preschoolers Think* Segment 2: *Words and Memories*
2. Contrast Vygotsky's views on cognitive development with those of Piaget, focusing on the concept of guided participation.	pp. 240–241	Key Terms: 9; Practice Questions I: 20; Practice Questions II: 10, 23; Applying Your Knowledge: 5.	Segment 1: *How Preschoolers Think;*
3. Explain the significance of the zone of proximal development and scaffolding in promoting cognitive growth.	pp. 241–242	Key Terms: 10, 11; Practice Questions II: 5, 9, 15, 17; Applying Your Knowledge: 12.	Segment 1: *How Preschoolers Think*
4. Describe Vygotsky's view of the role of language in cognitive growth.	pp. 243–244	Key Terms: 12, 13; Practice Questions I: 4, 5, 14; Practice Questions II: 6, 22; Applying Your Knowledge: 9, 11, 13.	
5. Explain the typical young child's theory of mind, noting how it is affected by culture and context, and relate it to the child's developing ability to understand pretense.	pp. 245–247	Key Terms: 14, 15; Practice Questions II: 16; Applying Your Knowledge: 3.	Segment 2: *Words and Memories*

Learning Objective	Textbook	Course Student Guide	Video Lesson
6. Outline the sequence by which vocabulary and grammar develop during the play years, and discuss limitations in the young child's language abilities.	pp. 247–251	Key Terms: 17, 18; Practice Questions I: 3, 9, 17, 18; Practice Questions II: 1, 11, 12, 14, 18; Applying Your Knowledge: 6, 7, 10.	Segment 2: *Words and Memories*
7. Explain the role of fast mapping in children's acquisition of language.	pp. 248–249	Key Terms: 16; Practice Questions II: 13, 19.	Segment 2: *Words and Memories*
8. Identify the characteristics of a high-quality preschool program, and discuss the long-term benefits of preschool education for the child and his or her family.	pp. 252–261	Key Terms: 19, 20; Practice Questions I: 6, 8, 11, 19 .	Segment 2: *Words and Memories* Segment 3: *Early Childhood Education*

Playing and Socializing

Lesson 10

The Play Years:
Psychosocial Development

Preview

Lesson 10 explores the ways in which young children begin to relate to others in an ever-widening social environment. The lesson begins where social understanding begins, with the emergence of the sense of self. With their increasing social awareness, children become more concerned with how others evaluate them and better able to regulate their emotions.

Next, the lesson explores the origins of helpful, cooperative behaviors in young children, as well as aggression and other hurtful behaviors. These social skills reflect many influences, including the quality of early attachments and learning from playmates through various types of play, as well as from television.

The lesson also describes the increasing complexity of children's interactions with others, paying special attention to the different styles of parenting and how factors such as the cultural, ethnic, and community contexts influence parenting.

The lesson concludes with a description of children's emerging awareness of male-female differences and gender identity. The major theories of gender-role development are considered.

As you complete this lesson, consider the psychosocial development of one or more preschoolers you know. Consider their self-understanding—what do they think and feel about themselves? How do they interact with adults and other children? What sort of play activities do they engage in, and how might this affect their development? How good are they at controlling their own emotions and behavior? Finally, consider the relationship these children have with their parents. How do the parents support and guide their kids, and how to they handle discipline and punishment?

Prior Course Knowledge that Will Be Used in this Lesson

- This lesson will return to Erik Erikson's theory (introduced in Lesson 1/Chapter 2) that specifies eight stages of psychosocial development, each of which is characterized by a particular challenge, or developmental crisis, which is central to that stage of life and must be resolved:
    1. Trust vs. Mistrust (birth to 1 year)
    2. Autonomy vs. Shame and Doubt (1 to 3 years)
    3. **Initiative vs. Guilt (3 to 6 years) ← The Play Years**
    4. Industry vs. Inferiority (7 to 11 years)
    5. Identity vs. Role Confusion (adolescence)
    6. Intimacy vs. Isolation (adulthood)
    7. Generativity vs. Stagnation (adulthood)
    8. Integrity vs. Despair (adulthood)

- This lesson will use the concept of theory of mind in its discussion of social awareness and the role of play during this period of development. Recall that theory of mind refers to a person's understanding of human mental processes, including the thoughts, feelings, and motivations of others.

- Five major developmental theories (from Lesson 1/Chapter 2) will be used to help explain gender-role development during the play years. Recall that:
    1. Freud's theory specifies stages of psychosexual development, during which the child battles unconscious, biological impulses.
    2. Learning theory emphasizes the effect of conditioning, as the child responds to stimuli, reinforcement, and modeling in his or her immediate environment.
    3. Cognitive theory emphasizes how the child's intellectual processes and thinking affect his or her beliefs and actions.
    4. Sociocultural theory reminds us that development is embedded in a rich cultural context, and is often influenced by the guidance of parents and mentors.
    5. Epigenetic theory emphasizes the interaction of biological and environmental forces that affect each person.

Learning Objectives

Use this information to guide your reading, viewing, thinking, and studying. After successfully completing this lesson, you should be able to:

1. Discuss the relationship between the child's developing self-concept and social awareness.
2. Discuss the importance of positive self-evaluation during this period, noting the role of mastery in gaining self-esteem.
3. Discuss emotional development during early childhood, focusing on emotional regulation.
4. Describe prosocial behavior, offer examples, and discuss its connection with rough-and-tumble and sociodramatic play.
5. Describe the different forms of aggression demonstrated by young children, and discuss the role of television in encouraging these and other maladaptive behaviors.

6. Discuss the pros and cons of physical punishment, and describe the most effective methods for disciplining a child.

7. Compare the four styles of parenting, and discuss the factors that might account for variations in parenting style.

8. Distinguish between sex differences and gender differences, and describe the developmental progression of gender awareness in young children.

9. Summarize five theories of gender-role development during the play years, noting important contributions of each.

📖 **Read Chapter 10, "The Play Years: Psychosocial Development," pages 265–290.**

◄◄ **View the video for Lesson 10, "Playing and Socializing."**

 Segment 1: *Social Awareness*

 Segment 2: *Emotional Regulation*

 Segment 3: *Parenting Styles*

Summary

During the preschool years, a child's self-confidence, social skills, and social roles become more fully developed. This growth coincides with the child's increased capacity for communication, imagination, and understanding of his or her social context. Much of this development occurs through play activities.

Play provides crucial experiences not only for motor and cognitive development but also for self-understanding and social interaction. This growth is first apparent in mastery play, as children repeatedly practice a skill until they are proficient at it. Other important types of play include **rough-and-tumble play**, in which children mimic aggression but actually have no intent to harm, and **sociodramatic play**, in which children act out various roles and themes in stories of their own creation. This exploration through play enables children to test their ability to convince others of their ideas and examine personal concerns in a nonthreatening manner.

In Erik Erikson's theory, the crisis of the play years is **initiative versus guilt**. The child is turning away from an exclusive attachment to parents and moving toward membership in the larger culture. A key factor in this developmental progression is learning **emotional regulation**—a key aspect of the child's developing emotional intelligence. Because of brain maturation, children gain a much greater ability to direct or modify their feelings, particularly feelings of fear, frustration, and anger.

Some of the emotions that mature during the preschool years lead to **prosocial behaviors** such as sharing and cooperating, which are performed to benefit other people; for some children, however, **antisocial behaviors** such as hitting or insulting may also emerge. Antisocial behaviors are those that are intended to hurt someone else. Developmental psychologists differentiate among four types of aggression: **instrumental aggression**, **reactive aggression**, **relational aggression**, and **bullying aggression**.

The three classic styles of parenting include **authoritarian** parents, whose word is law and who often show little affection or nurturance; **permissive** parents, who make few demands on their children but are affectionate and communicative; and **authoritative** parents, who set limits and enforce rules but do so more democratically by listening to their children's ideas and being willing to make compromises. A fourth style, **neglectful/uninvolved parenting**, are parents who seem unaware of what their children are doing. Among the reasons for parenting variations are culture, religion, ethnicity, and the family's economic well-being. Culture plays a large role in the choice of parenting style.

Even at age 2, children know whether they are boys or girls and apply gender labels consistently. Each of the major developmental theories has a somewhat different explanation for gender differences. Psychoanalytic theorists focus on fears and fantasies that motivate children to initially adore their opposite-sex parent and then later identify with their same-sex parent. Behaviorists maintain that gender roles are instilled because parents and society provide models and reinforcement for appropriate gender-role behavior and punishment for inappropriate behavior. In explaining gender identity and gender-role development, cognitive theorists focus on children's growing understanding of male-female differences. Sociocultural theorists emphasize the influence of cultural differences, and evolutionary theorists point out the biological tendencies that influence the child's brain patterns and behavior.

📖 **Review all reading assignments for this lesson.**

💻 **As assigned by your instructor, complete the optional online component for this lesson.**

Key Terms

Using your own words, write a brief definition or explanation of each of the following terms on a separate piece of paper.

1. emotional regulation
2. initiative versus guilt
3. self-concept
4. intrinsic motivation
5. extrinsic motivation
6. psychopathology
7. externalizing problems
8. internalizing problems
9. rough-and-tumble play
10. sociodramatic play
11. authoritarian parenting
12. permissive parenting
13. authoritative parenting
14. neglectful/uninvolved parenting
15. empathy
16. antipathy
17. prosocial behavior
18. antisocial behavior
19. instrumental aggression
20. reactive aggression
21. relational aggression
22. bullying aggression
23. psychological control
24. time-out
25. sex differences
26. gender differences
27. phallic stage
28. Oedipus complex
29. superego
30. Electra complex
31. identification
32. gender schema
33. self-esteem

Practice Questions I

Multiple-Choice Questions

1. Preschool children have a clear (but not necessarily accurate) concept of self. Typically, the preschooler believes that she or he
   a. owns all objects in sight.
   b. is great at almost everything.
   c. is much less competent than peers and older children.
   d. is more powerful than her or his parents.

2. According to Freud, the third stage of psychosexual development, during which the penis is the focus of psychological concern and pleasure, is the
   a. oral stage.
   b. anal stage.
   c. phallic stage.
   d. latency period.

3. Because it helps children rehearse social roles, work out fears and fantasies, and learn cooperation, an important form of social play is
   a. sociodramatic play.
   b. mastery play.
   c. rough-and-tumble play.
   d. sensorimotor play.

4. The three basic patterns of parenting described by Diana Baumrind are
   a. hostile, loving, and harsh.
   b. authoritarian, permissive, and authoritative.
   c. positive, negative, and punishing.
   d. indulgent, neglecting, and traditional.

5. Authoritative parents are receptive and loving, but they also normally
   a. set limits and enforce rules.
   b. have difficulty communicating.
   c. withhold praise and affection.
   d. encourage aggressive behavior.

6. Acting out emotions in an impulsive, angry way may be indicative of
   a. externalizing problems.
   b. internalizing problems.
   c. neuronal switch.
   d. a developmental disorder.

7. According to Erikson, during the play years, a child's self-concept is defined largely by his or her

    a. expanding range of skills and competencies.

    b. physical appearance.

    c. gender.

    d. relationship with family members.

8. Learning theorists emphasize the importance of _____ in the development of the preschool child.

    a. identification

    b. praise and blame

    c. initiative

    d. a theory of mind

9. Children apply gender labels, and have definite ideas about how boys and girls behave, as early as age

    a. 3.

    b. 4.

    c. 5.

    d. 7.

10. Children who are spanked

    a. stop their immediate misbehavior.

    b. are more likely to become bullies.

    c. are less likely to advance cognitively.

    d. do all of the above.

11. Five-year-old Leonardo loves rough-and-tumble play. Leonardo is

    a. on his way to becoming a bully.

    b. wasting his time playing when he should be learning.

    c. engaging in an unsafe behavior.

    d. typical of children his age.

True or False Items

Write T (for true) or F (for false) on the line in front of each statement.

12. __F__ According to Diana Baumrind, only authoritarian parents make maturity demands on their children.

13. __F__ Children of authoritative parents tend to be successful, happy with themselves, and generous with others.

14. __T__ True sex differences are more apparent in childhood than in adulthood.

15. __T__ Spanking is associated with higher rates of aggression toward peers.

16. __F__ Many gender differences are genetically based.

17. __F__ Children from feminist or nontraditional homes seldom have stereotypic ideas about feminine and masculine roles.

18. __T__ Developmentalists do not agree about how children acquire gender roles.

19. __T__ Identification was defined by Freud as a defense mechanism in which people identify with others who may be stronger and more powerful than they.

Practice Questions II

Multiple-Choice Questions

1. Children of permissive parents are most likely to lack
   a. social skills.
   b. self-control.
   c. initiative and guilt.
   d. care and concern.

2. Children learn reciprocity, nurturance, and cooperation most readily from their interaction with
   a. their mothers.
   b. their fathers.
   c. friends.
   d. others of the same sex.

3. The initial advantages of parenting style
   a. do not persist past middle childhood.
   b. remain apparent through adolescence.
   c. are likely to be even stronger over time.
   d. have an unpredictable impact later in children's lives.

4. Which of the following best summarizes the current view of developmentalists regarding gender differences?
   a. Some gender differences are biological in origin.
   b. Most gender differences are biological in origin.
   c. Nearly all gender differences are cultural in origin.
   d. There is no consensus among developmentalists regarding the origin of gender differences.

5. According to Freud, a young boy's jealousy of his father's relationship with his mother, and the guilt feelings that result, are part of the
   a. Electra complex.
   b. Oedipus complex.
   c. phallic complex.
   d. penis envy complex.

6. The style of parenting in which the parents make few demands on children, the discipline is lax, and the parents are nurturant and accepting is
   a. authoritarian.
   b. authoritative.
   c. permissive.
   d. rejecting-neglecting.

7. Cooperating with a playmate is to _____ as insulting a playmate is to _____.
   a. antisocial behavior; prosocial behavior
   b. prosocial behavior; antisocial behavior
   c. emotional regulation; antisocial behavior
   d. prosocial behavior; emotional regulation

8. Young children are most likely to witness acts of extreme violence
   a. on television.
   b. in their neighborhoods.
   c. while playing with friends.
   d. under none of the above circumstances.

9. Which of the following theories advocates the development of gender identification as a means of avoiding guilt over feelings for the opposite-sex parent?
   a. learning
   b. sociocultural
   c. psychoanalytic
   d. social learning

10. The preschooler's readiness to learn new tasks and play activities reflects his or her
    a. emerging competency and self-awareness.
    b. theory of mind.
    c. relationship with parents.
    d. growing identification with others.

11. Emotional regulation is in part related to maturation of a specific portion of the brain known as the
    a. prefrontal cortex.
    b. parietal cortex.
    c. temporal lobe.
    d. occipital lobe.

12. In which style of parenting is the parents' word law and misbehavior strictly punished?
    a. permissive
    b. authoritative
    c. authoritarian
    d. traditional

13. Erikson noted that preschoolers eagerly begin many new activities but are vulnerable to criticism and feelings of failure; they experience the crisis of

    a. identity versus role confusion.
    b. initiative versus guilt.
    c. basic trust versus mistrust.
    d. efficacy versus helplessness.

Matching Items

Match each theorist, term, or concept with its corresponding description or definition.

Theorists, Terms, and Concepts

14. _____ rough-and-tumble play
15. _____ relational aggression
16. _____ sociodramatic play
17. _____ prosocial behavior
18. _____ antisocial behavior
19. _____ Electra complex
20. _____ Oedipus complex
21. _____ authoritative
22. _____ authoritarian
23. _____ identification
24. _____ instrumental aggression

Descriptions or Definitions

a. aggressive behavior whose purpose is to obtain an object desired by another
b. Freudian theory that every daughter secretly wishes to replace her mother
c. parenting style associated with high maturity demands and low parent–child communication
d. an action performed for the benefit of another person without the expectation of reward
e. Freudian theory that every son secretly wishes to replace his father
f. parenting style associated with high maturity demands and high parent–child communication
g. two children wrestle without serious hostility
h. an action that is intended to harm someone else
i. two children act out roles in a story of their own creation
j. a defense mechanism through which children cope with their feelings of guilt during the phallic stage
k. nonphysical acts such as insults or social rejection, aimed at harming the social connection between the victim and other people

Applying Your Knowledge

1. According to Freud, Yolanda eventually copes with the fear and anger she feels over her hatred of her mother and love of her father by

    a. identifying with her mother.
    b. copying her brother's behavior.
    c. adopting her father's moral code.
    d. competing with her brother for her father's attention.

2. A little girl who says she wants her mother to go on vacation so that she can marry her father is voicing a fantasy consistent with the _____ described by Freud.

    a. Oedipus complex
    b. Electra complex
    c. theory of mind
    d. crisis of initiative versus guilt

3. According to Erikson, *before* the preschool years children are incapable of feeling guilt because

    a. guilt depends on a sense of self, which is not sufficiently established in toddlerhood.
    b. they do not yet understand that they are male or female for life.
    c. this emotion is unlikely to have been reinforced at such an early age.
    d. guilt is associated with the resolution of the Oedipus complex, which occurs later in life.

4. Parents who are strict and aloof are most likely to make their children

    a. cooperative and trusting.
    b. obedient but unhappy.
    c. violent.
    d. withdrawn and anxious.

5. When four-year-old Hai grabs for Tho's beanie baby, Tho slaps her hand away, displaying an example of

    a. bullying aggression.
    b. reactive aggression.
    c. instrumental aggression.
    d. relational aggression.

6. The belief that almost all sexual patterns are learned rather than inborn would find its strongest adherents among

    a. cognitive theorists.
    b. behaviorists.
    c. psychoanalytic theorists.
    d. epigenetic systems theorists.

7. In explaining the origins of gender distinctions, Dr. Christie notes that every society teaches children its values and attitudes regarding preferred behavior for men and women. Dr. Christie is evidently a proponent of

    a. gender-schema theory.
    b. sociocultural theory.
    c. epigenetic systems theory.
    d. psychoanalytic theory.

Answer Key

Key Terms

1. Emotional regulation is the ability to manage and modify one's feelings, particularly feelings of fear, frustration, and anger. (p. 265; video lesson, segment 2; objective 3)

2. According to Erikson, the crisis of the preschool years is initiative versus guilt. In this crisis, young children eagerly take on new tasks and play activities and feel guilty when their efforts result in failure or criticism. (p. 265; objective 2)

3. Self-concept refers to what a child thinks about him- or herself; it is the child's answer to the question, "who am I?" (p. 266; video lesson, segment 2; objective 1)

4. Intrinsic motivation is the drive to do something because of the pleasure the activity brings. A child who plays with blocks because they simply enjoy doing so is intrinsically motivated. (p. 266; objective 1)

5. When one is motivated to do something because of the promise of some external reward, the individual is acting out of extrinsic motivation. (p. 267; objective 1)

6. An illness or disorder of the mind. (p. 268; objective 3)

7. Externalizing problems are outwardly expressed emotional problems such as injuring others, destroying property, and defying authority. (p. 268; objective 1)

8. Children who have internalizing problems tend to be fearful and withdrawn as a consequence of their tendencies to keep their emotions bottled up inside themselves. (p. 268; objective 1)

9. Rough-and-tumble play is physical play that often mimics aggression, but involves no intent to harm. (p. 270; video lesson, segment 1; objective 4)

10. In sociodramatic play, children act out roles and themes in stories of their own creation, allowing them to examine personal concerns in a nonthreatening manner. (pp. 270–271; video lesson, segment 1; objective 4)

11. Authoritarian parenting is a style of child rearing in which the parents show little affection or nurturance for their children; maturity demands are high and parent–child communication is low. (p. 273; video lesson, segment 3; objective 7)

    Memory aid: Someone who is an authoritarian demands unquestioning obedience and acts in a dictatorial way.

12. Permissive parenting is a style of parenting in which the parents make few demands on their children, yet are nurturant and accepting, and communicate well with their children. (p. 273; video lesson, segment 3; objective 7)

13. Authoritative parenting is a style of parenting in which the parents set limits and enforce rules but do so more democratically than do authoritarian parents. (p. 273; video lesson, segment 3; objective 7)

    Memory aid: Authoritative parents act as authorities do on a subject—by discussing and explaining why certain family rules are in place.

14. An approach to child-rearing in which the parents are indifferent towards their children and unaware of what's going on in their children's lives. (p. 274; objective 7)

15. Empathy is a person's ability to understand the emotions of another person. (p. 279; objective 3)

16. Antipathy is referred to as intense dislike or hated of others. (p. 279; objective 4)

17. Prosocial behavior is an action, such as cooperating or sharing, which is performed to benefit another person without the expectation of reward. (p. 279; video lesson, segment 2; objective 4)

18. Antisocial behavior is an action, such as hitting or insulting, which is intended to hurt another person. (p. 279; video lesson, segment 2; objective 5)

19. Instrumental aggression is an action whose purpose is to obtain or retain an object desired by another. (p. 279; objective 5)

20. Reactive aggression is aggressive behavior that is an angry retaliation for some intentional or incidental act by another person. (p. 279; objective 5)

    Memory aid: Instrumental aggression is behavior that is instrumental in allowing a child to retain a favorite toy. Reactive aggression is a reaction to another child's behavior.

21. Nonphysical acts such as insults or social rejection, aimed at harming the social connection between the victim and other people. (p. 279; objective 3)

22. An unprovoked attack on another child is an example of bullying aggression. (p. 279; objective 5)

23. Psychological control is exerted by parents when the discipline is meant to provoke a sense of guilt or a fear of the parents' withdrawal of love. (p. 281; objective 6)

24. A time-out is a disciplinary technique in which the child is required to stop all activity and sit in a corner or stay indoors for a few minutes. (p. 282; objective 6)

25. Sex differences are biological differences between females and males. (p. 284; objective 8)

26. Gender differences are cultural differences in the roles and behavior of males and females. (p. 284; objective 8)

27. In psychoanalytic theory, the phallic stage is the third stage of psychosexual development, in which the penis becomes the focus of psychological concerns and physiological pleasure. (p. 285; objective 9)

28. According to Freud, boys in the phallic stage of psychosexual development develop a collection of feelings, known as the Oedipus complex, that center on sexual attraction to the mother and resentment of the father. (p. 285; objective 9)

29. In psychoanalytic theory, the superego is the self-critical and judgmental part of personality that internalizes the moral standards set by parents and society. (p. 285; objective 9)

30. According to Freud, girls in the phallic stage may develop a collection of feelings, known as the Electra complex, that center on sexual attraction to the father and resentment of the mother. (p. 285; objective 9)

31. In Freud's theory, identification is the defense mechanism through which a person takes on the role and attitudes of a person more powerful than himself or herself. (p. 285; objective 9)

32. A gender schema is a child's cognitive understanding of what it means to be a boy or a girl. (p. 287; objective 9)

33. Self-esteem refers to how a child *feels* about himself or herself; it has to do with how lovable the child feels. (video lesson, segment 2; objective 2)

Practice Questions I

Multiple-Choice Questions

1. b. is the correct answer. (video lesson, segment 2; objective 2)

2. c. is the correct answer. (objective 9)

   a. & b. are incorrect. In Freud's theory, the oral and anal stages are associated with infant and early childhood development, respectively.

   d. is incorrect. In Freud's theory, the latency period is associated with development during the school years.

3. a. is the correct answer. (video lesson, segment 1; objective 4)

   b. is incorrect. Mastery play is play that helps children develop new physical and intellectual skills.

   c. is incorrect. Rough-and-tumble play is physical play that mimics aggression.

   d. is incorrect. Sensorimotor play captures the pleasures of using the senses and motor skills.

4. b. is the correct answer. (video lesson, segment 3; objective 7)

   d. is incorrect. Traditional is a variation of the basic styles uncovered by later research. Indulgent and neglecting are not discussed in the textbook.

5. a. is the correct answer. (video lesson, segment 3; objective 7)

   b. & c. are incorrect. Authoritative parents communicate very well and are quite affectionate.

   d. is incorrect. This is not typical of authoritative parents.

6. a. is the correct answer. (objective 3)

7. a. is the correct answer. (objective 1)

8. b. is the correct answer. (objective 9)

   a. is incorrect. This is the focus of Freud's phallic stage.

   c. is incorrect. This is the focus of Erikson's psychosocial theory.

   d. is incorrect. This is the focus of cognitive theorists.

9. a. is the correct answer. (objective 8)

10. d. is the correct answer. (objective 6)

11. d. is the correct answer. (video lesson, segment 1; objective 4)

True or False Items

12. F   Most parents make some maturity demands on their children; maturity demands are high in both the authoritarian and authoritative parenting styles. (video lesson, segment 3; objective 7)

13. T   (video lesson, segment 3; objective 7)

14. F   Just the opposite is true. (objective 8)

15. T   (objective 6)

16. T   (objectives 8 & 9)

17. F   Children raised in feminist or nontraditional homes often surprise their parents by expressing stereotypic ideas about feminine and masculine roles. (objective 8)

18. T   (objective 9)

19. T   (objective 9)

Practice Questions II

Multiple-Choice Questions

1. b. is the correct answer. (objective 7)

2. c. is the correct answer. (video lesson, segment 1; objective 4)

    a. & b. are incorrect. Friends often provide better instruction than adults because they are likely to guide, challenge, and encourage a child's social interactions more frequently and intimately.

    d. is incorrect.

3. c. is the correct answer. (objective 7)

4. a. is the correct answer. Recent research has found that the sexes are different in part because of subtle differences in brain development. (objectives 8 & 9)

5. b. is the correct answer. (objective 9)

    a. & d. are incorrect. These are Freud's versions of phallic-stage development in little girls.

    c. is incorrect. There is no such thing as the "phallic complex."

6. c. is the correct answer. (video lesson, segment 3; objective 7)

    a. & b. are incorrect. Both authoritarian and authoritative parents make high demands on their children.

    d. is incorrect. Rejecting-neglecting parents are quite cold and unengaged.

7. b. is the correct answer. (video lesson, segment 2; objectives 4 & 5)

8. a. is the correct answer. (objective 5)

9. c. is the correct answer. (objective 9)

    a. & d. are incorrect. Learning and social learning theories emphasize that children learn about gender by rewards and punishments and by observing others.

    b. is incorrect. Sociocultural theory focuses on the impact of the environment on gender identification.

10. a. is the correct answer. (video lesson, segment 1; objective 1)

    b. is incorrect. This viewpoint is associated only with cognitive theory.

    c. is incorrect. Although parent–child relationships are important to social development, they do not determine readiness.

    d. is incorrect. Identification is a Freudian defense mechanism.

11. a. is the correct answer. (objective 3)

12. c. is the correct answer. (video lesson, segment 3; objective 7)

13. b. is the correct answer. (objective 2)

    a. & c. are incorrect. According to Erikson, these are the crises of adolescence and infancy, respectively.

    d. is incorrect. This is not a crisis described by Erikson.

Matching Items

14. g (video lesson, segment 1; objective 4)

15. k (objective 3)

16. i (video lesson, segment 1; objective 4)

17. d (video lesson, segment 2; objective 4)

18. h (video lesson, segment 2; objective 5)

19. b (objective 9)

20. e (objective 9)
21. f (video lesson, segment 3; objective 7)
22. c (video lesson, segment 3; objective 7)
23. j (objective 9)
24. a (objective 5)

Applying Your Knowledge

1. a. is the correct answer. (objective 9)

2. b. is the correct answer. (objective 9)

   a. is incorrect. According to Freud, the Oedipus complex refers to the male's sexual feelings toward his mother and resentment toward his father.

   c. & d. are incorrect. These are concepts introduced by cognitive theorists and Erik Erikson, respectively.

3. a. is the correct answer. (objective 2)

   b. is incorrect. Erikson did not equate gender constancy with the emergence of guilt.

   c. & d. are incorrect. These reflect the viewpoints of learning theory and Freud, respectively.

4. b. is the correct answer. (objective 7)

5. c. is the correct answer. The purpose of Tho's action is clearly to retain the beanie baby, rather than to retaliate (b, which is incorrect), or bully Hai (a, which is incorrect). (objective 5)

   d. is incorrect. Relational aggression takes the form of a verbal insult.

6. b. is the correct answer. (objective 9)

7. b. is the correct answer. (objective 9)

Lesson Review

Lesson 10

The Play Years
Psychosocial Development

Please Note: Use this matrix to guide your study and achieve the learning objectives of this lesson. It will also help you to view the video, which defines and demonstrates important concepts and skills as they relate to everyday life.

Learning Objective	Textbook	Course Student Guide	Video Lesson
1. Discuss the relationship between the child's developing self concept and social awareness.	pp. 265–267	Key Terms: 3, 4, 5, 7, 8; Practice Questions I: 7; Practice Questions II: 10.	Segment 1: *Social Awareness*; Segment 2: *Emotional Regulation*
2. Discuss the importance of positive self-evaluation during this period, noting the role of mastery in gaining self-esteem.	pp. 265–266	Key Terms: 2, 33; Practice Questions I: 1; Practice Questions II: 13; Applying Your Knowledge: 3.	Segment 2: *Emotional Regulation*
3. Discuss emotional development during early childhood, focusing on emotional regulation.	pp. 265–269	Key Terms: 1, 6, 15, 21; Practice Questions I: 6; Practice Questions II: 11, 15.	Segment 2: *Emotional Regulation*
4. Describe prosocial behavior, offer examples, and discuss its connection with rough-and-tumble and sociodramatic play.	pp. 270–273, 279	Key Terms: 9, 10, 16, 17; Practice Questions I: 3, 11; Practice Questions II: 2, 7, 14, 16, 17;	Segment 1: *Social Awareness*; Segment 2: *Emotional Regulation*
5. Describe the different forms of aggression demonstrated by young children, and discuss the role of television in encouraging these and other maladaptive behaviors.	pp. 276–277, 279	Key Terms: 18, 19, 20, 22; Practice Questions II: 7, 8, 18, 24; Applying Your Knowledge: 5.	Segment 2: *Emotional Regulation*
6. Discuss the pros and cons of physical punishment, and describe the most effective methods for disciplining a child.	pp. 280–283	Key Terms: 23, 24; Practice Questions I: 10, 15.	

Learning Objective	Textbook	Course Student Guide	Video Lesson
7. Compare the four styles of parenting, and discuss the factors that might account for variations in parenting style.	pp. 273–276	Key Terms: 11, 12, 13, 14; Practice Questions I: 4, 5, 12, 13; Practice Questions II: 1, 3, 6, 12, 21, 22; Applying Your Knowledge: 4.	Segment 3: *Parenting Styles*
8. Distinguish between sex differences and gender differences, and describe the developmental progression of gender awareness in young children.	p. 284	Key Terms: 25, 26; Practice Questions I: 9, 14, 16, 17; Practice Questions II: 4.	
9. Summarize five theories of gender-role development during the play years, noting important contributions of each.	pp. 285–288	Key Terms: 27, 28, 29, 30, 31, 32; Practice Questions I: 2, 8, 16, 18, 19; Practice Questions II: 4, 5, 9, 19, 20, 23; Applying Your Knowledge: 1, 2, 6, 7.	

The Golden Years of Childhood

Lesson 11

The School Years:
Biosocial Development

Preview

This lesson introduces biosocial development in middle childhood, the years from age 6 or 7 to age 11. Changes in physical size and shape are described first, and the growing problem of childhood obesity is addressed. The discussion then turns to the continuing development of motor skills during the school years. While growth tends to slow down during this period, children become much better at controlling their bodies.

During the school years, children often take tests. This lesson will discuss different types of tests, including **IQ tests** designed to measure intelligence, and why their use is controversial. As you will find, intelligence is both dynamic and multidimensional, so it is difficult to measure with a single score.

One reason for children to be tested at this age is to identify potential problems or disorders. The final section of this lesson examines the experiences of **children with special needs**, such as those diagnosed with **autism** or **attention-deficit/ hyperactivity disorder (ADHD)**. The causes of and treatments for these problems are discussed, with emphasis placed on insights arising from the new **developmental psychopathology** perspective. This perspective makes it clear that "abnormality" is really quite normal in development, and the manifestations of any special childhood problem will change as the child grows older.

As you complete this lesson, think about any children you know in this age range. Consider their height and weight relative to other children of the same age (and younger). Are any of these children overweight? If so, speculate on the possible causes. Also, observe the motor skills of these children—how does their coordination compare with younger and older children? Interview these children or their parents about any tests they've taken recently. Ask them to describe the experience. Have any of these kids taken an IQ test? If so, what was the result? Would you characterize this child as being "intelligent?" Why or why not? Do any of these children have a special problem or disorder, such as autism or ADHD? If so, how are they being treated? What kind of special services or treatment do they receive at school?

Prior Course Knowledge that Will Be Used in this Lesson
* Biosocial development during infancy and toddlerhood (Lesson 5), as well as that during early childhood (Lesson 8), will be referred to as we discuss variations in physique and the development of motor skills during middle childhood.

- This lesson will return to the concept of *self-esteem* (Lesson 10), how a child feels about him- or herself. A child's perception of his or her biological development (especially relative to peers) can affect self-evaluation in both positive and negative ways.

Learning Objectives

Use this information to guide your reading, viewing, thinking, and studying. After successfully completing this lesson, you should be able to:

1. Describe physical growth and health during middle childhood, noting variations and their causes, and discuss the importance of physical activity to children of this age.

2. Describe the problem of childhood obesity, outline its major causes and best approaches for treatment, and discuss the potential effects of obesity on a child's physical and psychological health.

3. Describe the causes of and treatments for childhood asthma, and discuss its potential impact on development.

4. Describe brain development during the school years, focusing on how it relates to motor-skill and cognitive development.

5. Explain how achievement and aptitude tests are used in evaluating individual differences in cognitive growth, and discuss why use of such tests is controversial.

6. Describe Sternberg's and Gardner's theories of multiple intelligences, and explain the significance of these theories.

7. Describe the developmental psychopathology perspective, and discuss its value in treating children with special needs.

8. Identify the symptoms of autism and discuss its possible causes.

9. Discuss the characteristics and possible causes of learning disabilities.

10. Describe the symptoms and possible causes of attention-deficit/hyperactivity disorder (ADHD) and bipolar disorder, and discuss the types of treatment available for children with these disorders.

11. Summarize techniques that have been tried in efforts to educate children with special needs.

📖 **Read Chapter 11, "The School Years: Biosocial Development," pages 293–319.**

⏮ **View the video for Lesson 11, "The Golden Years of Childhood."**

      Segment 1: *Physical Growth*

      Segment 2: *Motor-Skill Development*

      Segment 3: *Special Needs*

Summary

For most boys and girls, the years of middle childhood are a time when biosocial development is smooth and uneventful. Body maturation coupled with sufficient practice enables school-age children to master many motor skills. Although malnutrition limits the growth of children in some regions of the world, most of the variations in physical development in developed countries are due to heredity. Diet does exert its influence, however, by interacting with heredity, activity level, and other factors. In some cases, the result is obesity—a growing problem in North American children during the school years. Another condition of concern is asthma, which is also thought to be caused by a combination of genetic and environmental factors.

The fact that growth is relatively slow in middle childhood may be part of the reason children become so much more skilled at controlling their bodies. With few exceptions, boys and girls are just about equal in physical abilities during the school years. Boys have somewhat greater upper-arm strength, whereas girls have greater overall flexibility. Expertise in specific skills depends primarily on motivation, guidance, and many hours of practice.

Motor habits that rely on coordinating both sides of the body improve because the corpus callosum between the brain's hemispheres continues to mature. In addition, rough-and-tumble play may help boys overcome their tendencies toward hyperactivity and learning disabilities because it helps with regulation in the frontal lobes of the brain. Motor-skill development is also influenced by culture, national policies, and genetic endowment. Children are said to have a **learning disability** when their difficulty with a particular skill is in surprising contrast with their overall intelligence level. One of the most puzzling problems in childhood is **attention-deficit/hyperactivity disorder (ADHD)**, a behavior problem characterized by excessive activity, an inability to concentrate, and impulsive, sometimes aggressive behavior. ADHD may arise from several factors, including genetic differences, teratogens, and family and environmental influences. Also puzzling is the high rate of **autism**, a disorder in which the child is unable to socially connect with others.

Children with these challenges often receive special education during which schools address their particular learning needs in the **least restrictive environment (LRE)** possible.

📖   **Review all reading assignments for this lesson.**

🖥   **As assigned by your instructor, complete the optional online component for this lesson.**

Key Terms

Using your own words, write a brief definition or explanation of each of the following terms on a separate piece of paper.

1. middle childhood
2. BMI (body mass index)
3. overweight
4. obesity
5. asthma
6. reaction time
7. selective attention
8. automatization
9. aptitude
10. IQ test
11. achievement test
12. Flynn effect
13. multiple intelligences
14. developmental psychopathology
15. comorbid
16. attention-deficit/hyperactivity disorder (ADHD)
17. bipolar disorder
18. learning disability
19. dyslexia
20. autism
21. autism spectrum disorder
22. least restrictive environment (LRE)
23. response to intervention
24. individual education plan (IEP)
25. mainstream

Practice Questions I

Multiple-Choice Questions

1. As children move into middle childhood,
   a. the rate of accidental death increases.
   b. sexual urges intensify.
   c. the rate of weight gain increases.
   d. biological growth slows and steadies.

2. To help obese children, nutritionists usually recommend
   a. strenuous dieting to counteract early overfeeding.
   b. the use of amphetamines and other drugs.
   c. more exercise.
   d. no specific actions.

3. Dyslexia is a learning disability that affects the ability to
   a. do math.
   b. read.
   c. write.
   d. speak.

4. Childhood obesity that continues into adolescence and beyond creates an increased risk for
   a. low blood pressure.
   b. genetic malformation.
   c. muscle injury.
   d. low self-esteem.

5. The developmental psychopathology perspective is characterized by its
   a. contextual approach.
   b. emphasis on individual therapy.
   c. emphasis on the cognitive domain of development.
   d. concern with all of the above.

6. The time—usually measured in fractions of a second—it takes for a person to respond to a particular stimulus is called
   a. the interstimulus interval.
   b. reaction time.
   c. the stimulus-response interval.
   d. response latency.

7. The underlying problem in attention-deficit/hyperactivity disorder (ADHD) appears to be
   a. low overall intelligence.
   b. a neurological difficulty in paying attention.
   c. a learning disability in a specific academic skill.
   d. the existence of a conduct disorder.

8. Autistic children generally have severe deficiencies in all but which of the following?
   a. social skills
   b. imaginative play
   c. motor skills
   d. communication ability

9. Psychoactive drugs are most effective in treating attention-deficit/hyperactivity disorder (ADHD) when they are administered
   a. before the diagnosis becomes certain.
   b. for several years after the basic problem has abated.
   c. as part of the labeling process.
   d. with psychological support or therapy.

10. In the earliest aptitude tests, a child's score was calculated by dividing the child's _____ age by the _____ age to find the _____ quotient.
    a. mental; chronological; intelligence
    b. chronological; mental; intelligence
    c. intelligence; chronological; mental
    d. intelligence; mental; chronological

11. Tests that measure a child's potential to learn a new subject are measuring
    a. aptitude.
    b. achievement.
    c. vocational skills.
    d. intelligence.

True or False Items

Write T (for true) or F (for false) on the line in front of each statement.

12. __F__ Because asthma has genetic roots, there is little we can do for asthmatic children.

13. __F__ Childhood obesity usually does not correlate with adult obesity.

14. __T__ Hours spent watching television and obesity rates in children have both increased during the past 30 to 50 years.

F 15. __T__ The quick reaction time that is crucial in some sports can be readily achieved with practice. *depends on brain maturation*

16. __F__ Despite the efforts of teachers and parents, most children with learning disabilities can expect their disabilities to persist and even worsen as they enter adulthood.

17. __F__ The best way for children to lose weight is through strenuous dieting.

F 18. __T__ Most learning disabilities are caused by a difficult birth or other early trauma to the child. *difficult to pinpoint and can not be specified w/ certainty*

19. __F__ Girls experience symptoms of ADHD more frequently than boys.

20. __T__ The drugs sometimes given to children to reduce hyperactive behaviors have a reverse effect on adults.

Practice Questions II

Multiple-Choice Questions

1. During the years from age 6 to 11, the average child
   a. grows slowly and steadily.
   b. gains about 12 pounds a year.
   c. has decreased lung capacity.
   d. is more likely to become obese than at any other period in the life span.

2. Among the factors that are known to contribute to obesity are activity level, quantity and types of food eaten, and
   a. participation in organized sports.
   b. parental occupation.
   c. solitary play.
   d. genetic propensity.

3. A specific learning disability that becomes apparent when a child experiences unusual difficulty in learning to read is
   a. dyslexia.
   b. dyscalcula.
   c. ADHD.
   d. ADHDA.

4. Problems in learning to write, read, and do math are collectively referred to as
   a. learning disabilities.
   b. attention-deficit/hyperactivity disorder (ADHD).
   c. hyperactivity.
   d. dyscalcula.

5. A measure of obesity in which weight in kilograms is divided by the square of height in meters is the
   a. basal metabolic rate (BMR).
   b. body mass index (BMI).
   c. body fat index (BFI).
   d. basal fat ratio (BFR).

6. The most effective form of help for children with ADHD is
   a. medication.
   b. psychological therapy.
   c. environmental change.
   d. a combination of some or all of the above.

7. A key factor in reaction time is
   a. whether the child is male or female.
   b. brain maturation.
   c. whether the stimulus to be reacted to is an auditory or visual one.
   d. all of the above.

8. Which of the following is true of children with a diagnosed learning disability?
   a. They are, in most cases, average in intelligence.
   b. They often have a specific physical handicap, such as hearing loss.
   c. They often lack basic educational experiences.
   d. All of the above are true.

9. There is evidence asthma can be prevented or reduced by
   a. removing allergens in the environment.
   b. breastfeeding during the early months.
   c. better ventilation of schools and homes.
   d. all of the above.

10. Children with bipolar disorder
    a. are easily diagnosed.
    b. have extreme mood swings.
    c. should be prescribed the same medication as for ADHD.
    d. get over it by adulthood.

11. One out of 150 eight-year-olds is diagnosed with
    a. ADHD.
    b. autism spectrum disorder.
    c. a learning disability.
    d. bipolar disorder.

12. Bipolar disorder and ADHD
    a. both display unusual brain patterns.
    b. can produce similar behaviors.
    c. are likely to have a genetic component.
    d. do all of the above.

13. Aptitude and achievement testing are controversial because
    a. most tests are unreliable with respect to the individual scores they yield.
    b. test performance can be affected by many factors other than the child's intellectual potential or academic achievement.
    c. they often fail to identify serious learning problems.
    d. all of the above reasons.

14. Tests that measure what a child has already learned are called _____ tests.
    a. aptitude
    b. vocational
    c. achievement
    d. intelligence

15. Which of the following is **NOT** a type of intelligence identified in Robert Sternberg's theory?
    a. academic
    b. practical
    c. achievement
    d. creative

Matching Items

Match each term or concept with its corresponding description or definition.

Terms or Concepts

16. ___G___ dyslexia
17. ___J___ automatization
18. ___F___ autism
19. ___A___ learning disability
20. ___H___ asthma
21. ___B___ Flynn effect

22. ___D___ individual education plan (IEP)
23. ___K___ developmental psychopathology
24. ___C___ response to intervention
25. ___E___ mainstream
26. ___I___ attention-deficit/hyperactivity disorder (ADHD)

Descriptions or Definitions

a. an unexpected difficulty with one or more academic skills
b. the finding that IQ test scores have increased across the decades suggesting that intelligence is influenced by environmental factors.
c. an educational strategy to help under-achieving children in the early grades
d. legal document that specifies the educational goals for a child with special needs
e. system in which learning-disabled children are taught in general education classrooms
f. disorder characterized by the absence of a theory of mind
g. difficulty in reading
h. chronic inflammation of the airways
i. behavior problem involving difficulty in concentrating, as well as excitability and impulsivity
j. tasks performed repeatedly until the action becomes automatic
k. applies insights from studies of normal development to the study of childhood disorders

Applying Your Knowledge

1. According to developmentalists, the best game for a typical group of eight-year-olds would be
   a. football or baseball.
   b. basketball.
   c. one in which reaction time is not crucial.
   d. a game involving one-on-one competition.

2. Dr. Rutter, who believes that "we can learn more about an organism's normal functioning by studying its pathology and, likewise, more about its pathology by studying its normal condition," evidently is working from which of the following perspectives?
   a. clinical psychology
   b. developmental psychopathology
   c. behaviorism
   d. psychoanalysis

3. Nine-year-old John has difficulty concentrating on his class work for more than a few moments, repeatedly asks his teacher irrelevant questions, and is constantly disrupting the class with loud noises. If his difficulties persist, John is likely to be diagnosed as suffering from

    a. dyslexia.

    b. dyscalcula.

    c. autism.

    d. attention-deficit/hyperactivity disorder (ADHD).

4. Ten-year-old Jonathan is inattentive, easily frustrated, and highly impulsive. Jonathan may be suffering from

    a. dyslexia.

    b. dyscalcula.

    c. conduct disorder.

    d. attention-deficit/hyperactivity disorder (ADHD).

5. Because eleven-year-old Christopher is obese, he runs a greater risk of developing

    a. orthopedic problems.

    b. respiratory problems.

    c. psychological problems.

    d. all of the above.

6. Of the following individuals, who is likely to have the fastest reaction time?

    a. a seven-year-old

    b. a nine-year-old

    c. an eleven-year-old

    d. a sixteen-year-old

7. In determining whether an eight-year-old has a learning disability, a teacher looks primarily for

    a. marked poor accomplishment in a particular area.

    b. the exclusion of other explanations.

    c. both a and b.

    d. none of the above.

8. Mary doesn't say "hello," "please," or "thank you" like other children do. However, she has an amazing memory for details about dinosaurs. Mary probably has

    a. attention-deficit/hyperactivity disorder (ADHD).

    b. Asperger syndrome.

    c. dyslexia.

    d. depression.

9. Danny is having difficulty in math but plays the flute well. Danny
   a. has below-average intelligence.
   b. excels in musical intelligence but not in logic-mathematical intelligence.
   c. can raise his math grade by giving up flute.
   d. is academically gifted.

10. In concluding her presentation entitled "Facts and falsehoods regarding childhood obesity," Cheryl states that, _____ is not a common cause of childhood obesity.
    a. activity level
    b. cultural background
    c. overeating of high-fat foods
    d. a prenatal teratogen

11. Ayme was born in 1984. In 1992, she scored 125 on an intelligence test. Using the original formulation, what was Ayme's mental age when she took the test?
    a. 6
    b. 8
    c. 10
    d. 12

12. Howard Gardner and Robert Sternberg would probably be most critical of traditional aptitude and achievement test because they
    a. inadvertently reflect certain nonacademic competencies.
    b. do not reflect knowledge of cultural ideas.
    c. measure only a limited set of abilities.
    d. underestimate the intellectual potential of disadvantaged children.

Answer Key

Key Terms
1. Middle childhood is generally defined as the period from age 7 to 11. (p. 295; objective 1)
2. BMI (body mass index) is a measure of obesity in which a person's weight in kilograms is divided by his or her height squared in meters (p. 300; video lesson, segment 1; objective 2)
3. A person is overweight if they weigh 20–29 percent above the ideal for a person of the same age and height. (p. 300; objective 2)
4. A person is obese if they weigh 30 percent or more above the ideal for a person of the same age and height. (p. 300; objective 2)
5. Asthma is a disorder in which the airways are chronically inflamed. (p. 302; objective 3)
6. Reaction time is the length of time it takes a person to respond to a particular stimulus. (p. 305; objective 4)
7. Focusing one's attention on certain stimuli, while ignoring other stimuli, is referred to as selective attention. (p. 305; objective 4)

8. Automatization is the process by which thoughts and actions are repeated so often that they become almost automatic, requiring little or no conscious thought. (p. 305; objective 4)

9. Aptitude refers to potential, what people are capable of, rather than actual accomplishment. (p. 306; objective 5)

10. IQ tests are special aptitude tests designed to measure a person's intelligence, hence the name IQ or intelligence quotient. (p. 306; objective 5)

11. Achievement tests are designed to measure how much a person has learned or achieved in a specific subject area. (p. 307; objective 5)

12. The gradual increase in intelligence scores is referred to as the Flynn effect. This suggests that intelligence is influenced by environmental factors. (p. 307; objective 5)

13. The idea that human intelligence is comprised of a varied set of abilities rather than a single, all-encompassing ability is called multiple intelligences. (p. 307; objective 6)

14. Developmental psychopathology is a new field that applies the insights from studies of normal development to the study and treatment of childhood disorders, and vice versa. (p. 309; video lesson, segment 3; objective 7)

15. Comorbid refers to a condition when an individual has two or more separate diseases or disorders at the same time. (p. 309; objective 10)

16. Attention-deficit hyperactivity disorder (ADHD) is a behavior problem in which the individual has great difficulty concentrating, is often excessively excitable and impulsive, and is sometimes aggressive. (p. 310; video lesson, segment 3; objective 10)

17. Bipolar disorder is a condition characterized by extreme mood swings that are not related to outside experiences. (p. 311; objective 10)

18. A learning disability is a difficulty in a particular cognitive skill that is not attributable to an overall intellectual slowness, a physical handicap, a severely stressful living condition, or a lack of basic education. (p. 313; video lesson, segment 3; objective 9)

19. Dyslexia is a learning disability in reading. (p. 313; video lesson, segment 3; objective 9)

20. Autism is a severe disturbance of early childhood characterized by inability or unwillingness to communicate, poor social skills, and diminished imagination. (p. 313; objective 8)

21. Disorders characterized by poor social skills, unusual play patterns, and problems with communication are referred to as autistic spectrum disorder. (p. 314; objective 8)

22. The least restrictive environment (LRE) is a legally required school setting that allows children with special needs to benefit from the instruction available to most children (often in traditional classrooms). (p. 316; objective 11)

23. The educational strategy that uses a series of special interventions to help under-achieving children learn is called a response to intervention. (p. 316; objective 11)

24. An individual education plan (IEP) is a legal document that specifies the educational goals for a child with special needs. (p. 316; objective 11)

25. Mainstreaming is an educational approach in which children with special needs are included in regular classrooms. (video lesson, segment 3; objective 11)

Practice Questions I

Multiple-Choice Questions

1. d. is the correct answer. (video lesson, segment 1; objective 1)

2. c. is the correct answer. (video lesson, segment 1; objective 2)

   a. is incorrect. Strenuous dieting can be physically harmful and often makes children irritable, listless, and even sick—adding to the psychological problems of the obese child.

   b. is incorrect. The use of amphetamines to control weight is not recommended at any age.

3. b. is the correct answer. (video lesson, segment 3; objective 9)

   a. is incorrect. This is dyscalculia.

   c. & d. are incorrect. The textbook does not give labels for learning disabilities in writing or speaking.

4. d. is the correct answer. (video lesson, segment 1; objective 2)

5. a. is the correct answer. (video lesson, segment 3; objective 7)

   b. & c. are incorrect. Because of its contextual approach, developmental psychopathology emphasizes group therapy and all domains of development.

6. b. is the correct answer. (objective 4)

7. b. is the correct answer. (video lesson, segment 3; objective 10)

8. c. is the correct answer. (objective 8)

9. d. is the correct answer. (objective 10)

10. a. is the correct answer. (objective 5)

11. a. is the correct answer. (objective 5)

    b. is incorrect. Achievement tests measure what has already been learned.

    c. is incorrect. Vocational tests, which, as their name implies, measure what a person has learned about a particular trade, are achievement tests.

    d. in incorrect. Intelligence tests measure general aptitude, rather than aptitude for a specific subject.

True or False Items

12. F   Much can be done to alleviate their symptoms, including the removal of allergens and better ventilated buildings.(objective 3)

13. F   If obesity is established in middle childhood, it tends to continue into adulthood. (video lesson, segment 1; objective 2)

14. T   (objective 2)

15. F   Reaction time depends on brain maturation and is not readily affected by practice. (objective 4)

16. F   With the proper assistance, many children with learning disabilities develop into adults who are virtually indistinguishable from other adults in their educational and occupational achievements. (video lesson, segment 3; objective 9)

17. F   Strenuous dieting during childhood can be dangerous. The best way to get children to lose weight is by increasing their activity level. (video lesson, segment 1; objective 2)

18. F   The causes of learning disabilities are difficult to pinpoint and cannot be specified with certainty. (video lesson, segment 3; objective 9)

19. F   (objective 10)
20. T   (objective 10)

Practice Questions II
Multiple-Choice Questions

1. a. is the correct answer. (video lesson, segment 1; objective 1)

   b. & c. are incorrect. During this period children gain about 5 pounds per year and experience increased lung capacity.

   d. is incorrect. Although childhood obesity is a common problem, the textbook does not indicate that a person is more likely to become obese at this age than at any other.

2. d. is the correct answer. (objective 2)

3. a. is the correct answer. (video lesson, segment 3; objective 9)

   b. is incorrect. This learning disability involves math rather than reading.

   c. & d. are incorrect. These disorders do not manifest themselves in a particular academic skill but instead appear in psychological processes that affect learning in general.

4. a. is the correct answer. (video lesson, segment 3; objective 9)

   b. & c. are incorrect. ADHD is a general learning disability that usually does not manifest itself in specific subject areas. Hyperactivity is a facet of this disorder.

   d. is incorrect. Dyscalculia is a learning disability in math only.

5. b. is the correct answer. (video lesson, segment 1; objective 2)

6. d. is the correct answer. (objective 10)

7. b. is the correct answer. (objective 4)

8. a. is the correct answer. (video lesson, segment 3; objective 9)

9. d. is the correct answer. (objective 3)

10. b. is the correct answer. (objective 10)

11. b. is the correct answer. (objective 8)

12. d. is the correct answer. (objective 10)

13. b. is the correct answer. (objective 5)

14. c. is the correct answer. (objective 5)

15. c. is the correct answer. (objective 6)

Matching Items

16. g (video lesson, segment 3; objective 9)
17. j (objective 4)
18. f (objective 8)
19. a (video lesson, segment 3; objective 9)
20. h (objective 3)
21. b (objective 8)
22. d (video lesson, segment 3; objective 9)
23. k (video lesson, segment 3; objective 7)
24. c (objective 11)
25. e (video lesson, segment 3; objective 11)
26. i (video lesson, segment 3; objective 10)

Applying Your Knowledge

1. c. is the correct answer. (objective 4)

   a. & b. are incorrect. Each of these games involves skills that are hardest for schoolchildren to master.

   d. is incorrect. Because one-on-one sports are likely to accentuate individual differences in ability, they may be especially discouraging to some children.

2. b. is the correct answer. (video lesson, segment 3; objective 7)

3. d. is the correct answer. (video lesson, segment 3; objective 10)

   a. & b. are incorrect. Jack's difficulty is in concentrating, not in reading (dyslexia) or math (dyscalculia).

   c. is incorrect. Autism is characterized by a lack of communication skills.

4. d. is the correct answer. (video lesson, segment 3; objective 10)

5. d. is the correct answer. (video lesson, segment 1; objective 2)

6. d. is the correct answer. (objective 4)

7. c. is the correct answer. (video lesson, segment 3; objective 9)

8. b. is the correct answer. (objective 8)

9. b. is the correct answer. (objective 6)

10. d. is the correct answer. There is no evidence that teratogens have anything to do with obesity. (objective 2)

11. c. is the correct answer. At the time she took the test, Ayme's chronological age was eight. Knowing that her IQ was 125, we can solve the equation to yield a mental age of ten. (objective 5)

12. c. is the correct answer. Both Sternberg and Gardner believe that there are multiple intelligences rather than the narrowly defined abilities measured by traditional aptitude and achievement tests. (objective 6)

    a., b., & d. are incorrect. Although these criticisms are certainly valid, they are not specifically associated with Sternberg or Gardner.

Lesson Review

Lesson 11

The School Years
Biosocial Development

Please Note: Use this matrix to guide your study and achieve the learning objectives of this lesson. It will also help you to view the video, which defines and demonstrates important concepts and skills as they relate to everyday life.

Learning Objective	Textbook	Course Student Guide	Video Lesson
1. Describe physical growth and health during middle childhood, noting variations and their causes, and discuss the importance of physical activity to children of this age.	pp. 295–300	Key Terms: 1; Practice Questions I: 1; Practice Questions II: 1.	Segment 1: *Physical Growth*
2. Describe the problem of childhood obesity, outline its major causes and best approaches for treatment, and discuss the potential effects of obesity on a child's physical and psychological health.	pp. 300–302	Key Terms: 2, 3, 4; Practice Questions I: 2, 4, 13, 14, 17; Practice Questions II: 2, 5; Applying Your Knowledge: 5, 10.	Segment 1: *Physical Growth*
3. Describe the causes of and treatments for childhood asthma, and discuss its potential impact on development.	pp. 302–304	Key Terms: 5; Practice Questions I: 12; Practice Questions II: 9, 20.	
4. Describe brain development during the school years, focusing on how it relates to motor-skill and cognitive development.	pp. 304–306	Key Terms: 6, 7, 8; Practice Questions I: 6, 15; Practice Questions II: 7, 17; Applying Your Knowledge: 1, 6.	
5. Explain how achievement and aptitude tests are used in evaluating individual differences in cognitive growth, and discuss why use of such tests is controversial.	pp. 306–307	Key Terms: 9, 10, 11, 12; Practice Questions I: 10, 11; Practice Questions II: 13, 14; Applying Your Knowledge: 11.	
6. Describe Sternberg's and Gardner's theories of multiple intelligences, and explain the significance of these theories.	pp. 307–308	Key Terms: 13; Practice Questions II: 15; Applying Your Knowledge: 9, 12.	

Learning Objective	Textbook	Course Student Guide	Video Lesson
7. Describe the developmental psychopathology perspective, and discuss its value in treating children with special needs.	pp. 309–310	Key Terms: 14; Practice Questions I: 5; Practice Questions II: 23; Applying Your Knowledge: 2.	Segment 3: *Special Needs*
8. Identify the symptoms of autism, and discuss its possible causes.	pp. 313–315	Key Terms: 20, 21; Practice Questions I: 8; Practice Questions II: 11, 18, 21; Applying Your Knowledge: 8.	
9. Discuss the characteristics and possible causes of learning disabilities.	p. 313	Key Terms: 18, 19; Practice Questions I: 3, 16, 18; Practice Questions II: 3, 4, 8, 16, 19, 22; Applying Your Knowledge: 7.	Segment 3: *Special Needs*
10. Describe the symptoms and possible causes of attention-deficit/hyperactivity disorder (ADHD) and bipolar disorder, and discuss the types of treatment available for children with these disorders.	pp. 310–312	Key Terms: 15, 16, 17; Practice Questions I: 7, 9, 19, 20; Practice Questions II: 6, 10, 12, 26; Applying Your Knowledge: 3, 4.	Segment 3: *Special Needs*
11. Summarize techniques that have been tried in efforts to educate children with special needs.	pp. 315–317	Key Terms: 22, 23, 24, 25; Practice Questions II: 24, 25.	Segment 3: *Special Needs*

The Age of Reason

Lesson 12

The School Years:
Cognitive Development

Preview

Lesson 12 looks at the development of cognitive abilities in children from age 7 to 11. The first part of the lesson focuses on changes in the child's selective attention, processing speed and capacity, memory strategies, **knowledge base**, and problem-solving strategies. Next, we discuss Jean Piaget's view of the child's cognitive development in this period, which involves a growing ability to use logic and reasoning.

The lesson also looks at moral reasoning and language learning in the school years. During this time, children develop a more analytic understanding of words and show a marked improvement in pragmatic skills, such as changing from one form of speech to another when the situation so demands. The linguistic and cognitive advantages of bilingualism are discussed, as are educational and environmental conditions that are conducive to fluency in a second language.

The final part of the lesson describes innovative teaching methods, which emphasize active rather than passive learning and are derived from the developmental theories of Piaget, Vygotsky, and others. Studies that contrast these methods with more traditional approaches have shown their effectiveness in reading and math education. The lesson concludes by examining measures of cognitive growth, such as tests, and variations in cultural standards.

Prior Course Knowledge that Will Be Used in this Lesson

*   This lesson will introduce "**concrete operational thought**," the third stage in Jean Piaget's theory of cognitive development (from Chapter 2/Lesson 1). Recall that Piaget's theory specifies four major periods of cognitive development:

    1. Sensorimotor (birth to 2 years)
    2. Preoperational (2 to 6 years)
    3. **Concrete Operational (7 to 11 years)← The School Years**
    4. Formal Operational (12 years through adulthood)

    During this discussion, the concepts of selective attention and conservation will continue to be explored.

*   During its exploration of school learning, this lesson will return to Lev Vygotsky's theory of development (from Chapter 2/Lesson 1). Recall that Vygotsky emphasized the importance of guided participation, a learning process in which an individual learns through social interaction with a mentor.

- This lesson also expands on the concepts of information processing theory (from Chapter 2/Lesson 1), which likens cognition to the operations that occur within a computer, including inputs, processing, and outputs.

Learning Objectives

Use this information to guide your reading, viewing, thinking, and studying. After successfully completing this lesson, you should be able to:

1. Describe how the information processing system creates memories and forms a knowledge base.
2. Discuss advances in selective attention, processing speed and capacity, and memory skills during middle childhood.
3. Identify and describe the characteristics of concrete operational thought, give examples of how this type of thinking is demonstrated by schoolchildren, and explain how recent research suggests modifications to Piaget's theory.
4. Outline Kohlberg's stage theory of moral development and describe several criticisms of the theory.
5. Compare the academic performance of children in countries around the world, and identify differences in schools that may account for differences in academic performance.
6. Describe language development during the school years, noting changing abilities in vocabulary, grammar, and code switching.
7. Identify several conditions that foster the learning of a second language, and describe different strategies for teaching another language to school-age children.
8. Describe current controversies in education, and explain how they relate to developmental theories and culture.

📖 **Read Chapter 12, "The School Years: Cognitive Development," pages 321–347. Also, read pages 369–374 in Chapter 13, "The School Years: Psychosocial Development."**

⏮ **View the video for Lesson 12, "The Age of Reason."**

Segment 1: *How School-Age Children Think*

Segment 2: *Language Development*

Summary

Cognitive development between the ages of 7 and 11 is impressive, attested to by children's improved reasoning strategies, mastery of school-related skills, and use of language. For children around the world, the transition into middle childhood marks a passage into a new phase of cognitive development some call the "age of reason." For Piaget, the age of reason begins with the 5-to-7 shift from preoperational to **concrete operational thought**. When this transition is complete, children are much better able to understand logical principles, as long as they are applied to tangible, concrete examples.

Among the logical operations schoolchildren acquire are numerous principles, two of which are the principle that an entity remains the same despite changes in its appearance (conservation) and that certain characteristics of an object remain the same when other characteristics are changed (**identity**). Two additional principles acquired are the principle that something that has been changed can be returned to its original state by reversing the process (**reversibility**), and that a change in one object can be compensated for by a corresponding change in another (**reciprocity**).

The information-processing view of cognitive development places more emphasis than Piaget does on the ways in which children process their experiences. The ability to selectively attend to, rehearse, store, organize, and retrieve information improves steadily during middle childhood. Schoolchildren also have a larger processing capacity and **knowledge base** than they did earlier. The ability to evaluate a cognitive task and to monitor one's performance, called **metacognition**, also improves during the school years. The information-processing approach emphasizes that the most effective way to teach is to adapt teaching materials and sequence of instruction to fit the needs of the individual child.

Logical thought processes also foster moral development, as school-age children become better able to grasp moral laws and ethical principles. Moral reasoning becomes more complex during middle childhood. Lawrence Kohlberg proposed that this reasoning develops through six stages of increasing complexity, from elementary **preconventional moral reasoning**, in which the individual reasons in terms of his or her own welfare; to **conventional moral reasoning**, in which the individual considers social standards and laws to be the supreme arbiters of moral values; to the recognition of universal ethical principles that characterizes **postconventional moral reasoning**.

Lawrence Kohlberg identified three levels of moral reasoning (each level including two stages):

- Preconventional: Emphasis on avoiding punishment and obtaining rewards. *Stage 1:* Might makes right. *Stage 2*: Look out for number one.
- Conventional: Emphasis on social rules. *Stage 3:* "good girl" and "nice boy." *Stage 4*: "law and order."
- Postconventional: Emphasis on moral principles. *Stage 5:* social contract. *Stage 6:* universal ethical principles.

Language development during these years is also extensive, with children showing improvement in vocabulary, grammar, and pragmatic use of language. This is clearly indicated by their newly found delight in words and their growing sophistication in telling jokes. School-age children can also easily engage in **code-switching**, from the **formal code** used with teachers to the **informal code** used with friends.

Over decades, teacher, parents and politicians have sought to find the best way to teach children in middle childhood. International tests such as **PIRLS (Progress in International Reading, Literacy Skills)** and **TIMSS (Trends in Math and Science Study)** indicate that children in the United States could be doing better. The **No Child Left Behind Act** requires that schools meet standards as measured by the **National Assessment of Educational Progress (NAEP)** test, but there is considerable controversy as to how that is best done. Discussions over the **phonics approach** and **whole language approach** to reading have been heated, as has the debate about the best approach to teaching math.

📖 **Review all reading assignments for this lesson.**

💻 **As assigned by your instructor, complete the optional online component for this lesson.**

Key Terms

Using your own words, write a brief definition or explanation of each of the following terms on a separate piece of paper.

1. concrete operational thought
2. classification
3. transitive inference
4. sensory memory
5. working memory
6. long-term memory
7. knowledge base
8. control processes
9. metacognition
10. pragmatics
11. hidden curriculum
12. immersion
13. bilingual schooling
14. ESL (English as a second language)
15. Progress in International Reading Literacy Skills (PIRLS)
16. Trends in Math and Science Study (TIMSS)
17. No Child Left Behind Act
18. National Assessment of Educational Progress (NAEP)
19. phonics approach
20. whole-language approach
21. charter school
22. voucher
23. identity
24. reversibility
25. reciprocity
26. preconventional moral reasoning
27. conventional moral reasoning
28. postconventional moral reasoning
29. code-switching

Practice Questions I

Multiple-Choice Questions

1. According to Piaget, the stage of cognitive development in which a person understands specific logical ideas and can apply them to concrete problems is called

   a. preoperational thought.
   b. operational thought.
   c. concrete operational thought.
   d. formal operational thought.

2. The idea that an object that has been transformed in some way can be restored to its original form by undoing the process is
   a. identity.
   b. reversibility.
   c. reciprocity.
   d. automatization.

3. Information-processing theorists contend that major advances in cognitive development occur during the school years because
   a. the child's mind becomes more like a computer as he or she matures.
   b. children become better able to process and analyze information.
   c. most mental activities become automatic by the time a child is about 13 years old.
   d. the major improvements in reasoning that occur during the school years involve increased long-term memory capacity.

4. The ability to adjust one's language to the situation is called
   a. metacognition.
   b. information processing.
   c. pragmatics.
   d. decentering.

5. The term for the ability to monitor one's cognitive performance—to think about thinking—is
   a. pragmatics.
   b. information processing.
   c. selective attention.
   d. metacognition.

6. Long-term memory is _____ permanent and _____ limited than working memory.
   a. more; less
   b. less; more
   c. more; more
   d. less; less

7. Transitive inference refers to the ability to
   a. link ideas and facts together in a logical way.
   b. quickly learn a second language.
   c. store a perception as a memory.
   d. code-switching.

8. The educational emphasis on the importance of active, engaged learning during mathematics instruction is most directly derived from the developmental theory of
   a. Vygotsky.
   b. Piaget.
   c. information processing.
   d. those who advocate immersion learning.

Lesson 12/The School Years: Cognitive Development   **209**

9. Critics of Piaget contend that

    a. cognitive development is more homogeneous than Piaget predicted.
    b. children's progress through the cognitive stages is more uniform than Piaget thought.
    (c.) he underestimated variability between individuals.
    d. none of the above.

10. Billy has just texted George a joke, and George responded with "LOL!" George has just demonstrated

    a. classification.
    b. control process.
    (c.) informal code.
    d. none of the above.

11. According to Lawrence Kohlberg, the three levels of moral reasoning are

    a. amoral, immoral, and moral.
    b. egocentrism, ethnocentrism, and universality.
    (c.) preconventional, conventional, and postconventional.
    d. selfishness, law-and-order, and altruistic.

True or False Items

Write T (for true) or F (for false) on the line in front of each statement.

12. __F__ One major objection to Piagetian theory is that it describes the schoolchild as an active learner, a term appropriate only for preschoolers.

13. __T__ Learning a second language fosters children's overall linguistic and cognitive development.

14. __F__ The process of telling a joke involves pragmatic language skills usually not mastered before age 7.

15. __F__ Code-switching, especially the occasional use of slang, is a behavior characteristic primarily of children in the lower social strata.

16. __T__ Most information that comes into the sensory register is lost or discarded.

17. __T__ New standards of math education in many nations emphasize problem-solving skills rather than simple memorization of formulas.

Practice Questions II

Multiple-Choice Questions

1. According to Piaget, eight- and nine-year-olds can reason only about concrete things in their lives. "Concrete" means
    a. logical.
    b. abstract.
    c. tangible or specific.
    d. mathematical or classifiable.

2. When psychologists look at the ability of children to receive, store, and organize information, they are examining cognitive development from a view based on
    a. the observations of Piaget.
    b. information processing.
    c. learning theory.
    d. the idea that the key to thinking is the sensory register.

3. The logical operations of concrete operational thought are particularly important to an understanding of the elementary-school subject(s) of
    a. spelling.
    b. reading.
    c. math and science.
    d. social studies.

4. Which of the following Piagetian ideas is **NOT** widely accepted by developmentalists today?
    a. The thinking of school-age children is characterized by a more comprehensive logic than that of preschoolers.
    b. Children are active learners.
    c. How children think is as important as what they know.
    d. Once a certain type of reasoning ability emerges in children, it is evenly apparent in all domains of thinking.

5. Which aspect of the information-processing system assumes an executive role in regulating the analysis and transfer of information?
    a. sensory register
    b. working memory
    c. long-term memory
    d. control processes

6. An example of schoolchildren's growth in metacognition is their understanding that

    a. transformed objects can be returned to their original state.

    b. rehearsal is a good strategy for memorizing, but outlining is better for understanding.

    c. objects may belong to more than one class.

    d. they can use different language styles in different situations.

7. A new approach to math education focuses on

    a. rote memorization of formulas before problems are introduced.

    b. "hands-on" materials and active discussion of concepts.

    c. one-on-one tutorials.

    d. pretesting children and grouping them by ability.

8. Regarding bilingual education, many contemporary developmentalists believe that

    a. the attempted learning of two languages is confusing to children and delays proficiency in either one or both languages.

    b. bilingual education is linguistically, culturally, and cognitively advantageous to children.

    c. second-language education is most effective when the child has not yet mastered the native language.

    d. bilingual education programs are too expensive to justify the few developmental advantages they confer.

9. In making moral choices, according to Carol Gilligan, females are more likely than males to

    a. score at a higher level in Kohlberg's system.

    b. emphasize the needs of others.

    c. judge right and wrong in absolute terms.

    d. formulate abstract principles.

Matching Items

Match each term or concept with its corresponding description or definition.

Terms or Concepts

10. _____ classification   14. _____ phonics approach

11. _____ charter school   15. _____ metacognition

12. _____ pragmatics   16. _____ immersion

13. _____ voucher

Descriptions or Definitions

    a. the process of learning language by focusing on the sounds of letters and combinations of letters

    b. a public school with its own set of standards

    c. the practical use of language that includes making adjustments for audience and context

    d. a method by which a local government would finance a child's education in a parent's school of choice

e. an educational technique in which instruction occurs entirely in the second language

f. process by which things are organized into groups based on some property they have in common

g. the ability to evaluate a cognitive task and to monitor one's performance on it

Applying Your Knowledge

1. Compared to her four-year-old sister, nine-year-old Shannon is more likely to
   a. steal candy, if she and a friend want it very badly.
   b. judge stealing as wrong, even if the perpetrator is not caught or punished.
   c. use egocentric moral reasoning.
   d. do all of the above.

2. Dr. Larsen believes that the cognitive advances of middle childhood occur because of basic changes in children's thinking speed, knowledge base, and memory retrieval skills. Dr. Larsen evidently is working from the _____ perspective.
   a. Piagetian
   b. Vygotskian
   c. information-processing
   d. psychoanalytic

3. Heather has just completed a standardized test of her math skills that will be used to compare the math achievement of students from different nations. Heather has just participated in
   a. No Child Left Behind.
   b. TIMMS.
   c. NAEP.
   d. PIRLS.

4. A child's ability to tell a joke that will amuse his or her audience always depends on
   a. the child's mastery of reciprocity and reversibility.
   b. code-switching.
   c. the child's ability to consider another's perspective.
   d. an expansion of the child's processing capacity.

5. Six-year-old Shannon attends a class where her teacher speaks in both Spanish and English. Shannon is experiencing
   a. bilingual schooling.
   b. an ESL class.
   c. the whole-language approach.
   d. pragmatics.

6. As compared with her five-year-old brother, seven-year-old Althea has learned to adjust her vocabulary to her audience. This is known as

   a. selective attention.

   b. a retrieval strategy.

   c. code-switching.

   d. classification.

7. Mr. Jones asked the class to tell him the answer to 7 × 2. He called on Bettina, who answered, "16!" Mr. Jones replied, "No. Anyone else?" He then called on Greg who answered "14!" Mr. Jones replied, "Good, Greg. That's right. The answer is 14." Mr. Jones is using a style of teaching referred to as

   a. evaluation/response/initiation.

   b. response/evaluation.

   c. initiation/evaluation.

   d. initiation/response/evaluation.

Answer Key

Key Terms

1. During Piaget's stage of concrete operational thought, lasting from ages 7 to 11, children can think logically about concrete events and objects but are not able to reason abstractly. (p. 321; video lesson, segment 1; objective 3)

2. Classification is the logical principle by which things are organized into groups, categories, or classes based on some shared feature or property. (p. 322; objective 3)

3. The ability to link facts and ideas together in a logical way is called transitive inference. (p. 322; objective 3)

4. Sensory memory (or sensory register) is the part of the information-processing system that stores incoming stimuli for a fraction of a second, after which it is passed into working memory, or discarded as unimportant. (p. 326; video lesson, segment 1; objective 1)

5. Working memory is the part of memory that handles current, conscious mental activity. (p. 326; video lesson, segment 1; objective 1)

6. Long-term memory is the part of memory that stores unlimited amounts of information for days, months, or years. (p. 327; video lesson, segment 1; objective 1)

7. The knowledge base is a body of knowledge in a particular area that has been learned and on which additional learning can be based. (p. 327; video lesson, segment 1; objective 1)

8. Control processes (such as selective attention and retrieval strategies) regulate the analysis and flow of information in memory. (p. 327; objective 2)

9. Metacognition is the ability to evaluate a cognitive task to determine what to do and to monitor one's performance on that task. (p. 327; objective 2)

10. Pragmatics refers to the practical use of language, including adjustments for audience and context. (p. 330; objective 6)

11. A hidden curriculum involves the unofficial, unstated, or implicit rules and priorities that influence the academic curriculum and all aspects of learning in school. (p. 335; objective 5)

12. Immersion is an approach to bilingual education in which the child's instruction occurs entirely in the new language. (p. 336; video lesson, segment 2; objective 7)

13. Bilingual schooling is an approach to teaching a second language in which the teacher instructs the children in school subjects using their native language as well as the second language. (p. 336; video lesson, segment 2; objective 7)

14. English as a second language (ESL) is an approach to teaching English in which all instruction is in English, and the teacher does not speak the child's native language. (p. 336; video lesson, segment 2; objective 7)

15. The reading ability of fourth graders is the focus of the long-term study referred to as Progress in International Reading Literacy Skills (PIRLS). (p. 337; objective 5)

16. An international assessment of children's achievement in math and science is undertaken by Trends in Math and Science Study (TIMSS), although cross-cultural differences in content validity and test-taking conditions make direct comparisons challenging. (p. 337; objective 5)

17. In 2001, the U.S. Congress passed a law referred to as the No Child Left Behind Act. The goal was to increase the quality of schooling by holding schools accountable for their children's progress; however, critics suggest that this federal law has had unintended negative consequences as well. (p. 339; objectives 5 & 8)

18. The National Assessment of Educational Progress (NAEP) is often referred to as "The Nation's Report Card" because it is an ongoing study that tracks children's academic achievement over time. (p. 340; objective 5)

19. The phonics approach is a method of teaching reading by having children learn the sounds of letters before they begin to learn words. (p. 342; objective 8)

20. The whole-language approach is a method of teaching reading by encouraging children to develop all their language skills simultaneously. (p. 342; objective 8)

21. A charter school is a public school funded by the state or local governments that sets their own standards. (p. 343; objective 8)

22. A voucher offers parents permission to send their child to the school of their choice with the cost all or partly paid for by the local government. (p. 344; objective 8)

23. In Piaget's theory, identity is the logical principle that certain characteristics of an object remain the same even when other characteristics change. (video lesson, segment 1; objective 3)

24. Reversibility is the logical principle that a transformation process can be reversed to restore the original conditions. (video lesson, segment 1; objective 3)

25. Reciprocity is the logical principle that a transformation in one dimension of an object can be compensated for by a transformation in another. (video lesson, segment 1; objective 3)

    Example: A child who understands reciprocity realizes that rolling a ball of clay into a thin rope makes it longer, but also skinnier, than its original shape.

26. Kohlberg's first level of moral reasoning, preconventional moral reasoning, emphasizes obedience to authority in order to avoid punishment (stage 1) and being nice to other people so they will be nice to you (stage 2). (video lesson, segment 1; objective 4)

27. Kohlberg's second level of moral reasoning, conventional moral reasoning, emphasizes winning the approval of others (stage 3) and obeying the laws set down by those in power (stage 4). (video lesson, segment 1; objective 4)

28. Kohlberg's third level, postconventional moral reasoning, emphasizes the social and contractual nature of moral principles (stage 5) and the existence of universal ethical principles (stage 6). (video lesson, segment 1; objective 4)

29. Code-switching is a pragmatic communication skill involving changing from one form of speech to another. (video lesson, segment 2; objective 6)

Practice Questions I

Multiple-Choice Questions

1. c. is the correct answer. (video lesson, segment 1; objective 3)

   a. is incorrect. Preoperational thought is "pre-logical" thinking.

   b. is incorrect. There is no such stage in Piaget's theory.

   d. is incorrect. Formal operational thought extends logical reasoning to abstract problems.

2. b. is the correct answer. (video lesson, segment 1; objective 3)

   a. is incorrect. This is the concept that certain characteristics of an object remain the same even when other characteristics change.

   c. is incorrect. This is the concept that a change in one dimension of an object can be compensated for by a change in another dimension.

   d. is incorrect. This is the process by which familiar mental activities become routine and automatic.

3. b. is the correct answer. (video lesson, segment 1; objectives 1 & 2)

   a. is incorrect. Information-processing theorists use the mind-computer metaphor at every age.

   c. is incorrect. Although increasing automatization is an important aspect of development, the information-processing perspective does not suggest that most mental activities become automatic by age 13.

   d. is incorrect. Most of the important changes in reasoning that occur during the school years are the result of the improved processing capacity of the person's working memory.

4. c. is the correct answer. (objective 6)

5. d. is the correct answer. (objective 2)

   a. is incorrect. Pragmatics refers to the practical use of language to communicate with others.

   b. is incorrect. The information-processing perspective views the mind as being like a computer.

   c. is incorrect. This is the ability to screen out distractions in order to focus on important information.

6. a. is the correct answer. (video lesson, segment 1; objective 2)

7. a. is the correct answer. (objective 3)

8. a. is the correct answer. (objective 8)

9. c. is the correct answer. (objective 3)

10. c. is the correct answer. (objective 6)

11. c. is the correct answer. (video lesson, segment 1; objective 4)

True or False Items

12. F Most educators agree that the school-age child, like the preschooler, is an active learner. (objective 8)

13. T (video lesson, segment 2; objective 7)

14. T (video lesson, segment 2; objective 6)

15. F Code-switching (including occasional use of slang) is a behavior demonstrated by all children. (video lesson, segment 2; objective 6)

16. T (video lesson, segment 1; objective 1)

17. T (objectives 5 & 8)

Practice Questions II

Multiple-Choice Questions

1. c. is the correct answer. (video lesson, segment 1; objective 3)

2. b. is the correct answer. (video lesson, segment 1; objective 1)

3. c. is the correct answer. (video lesson, segment 1; objective 3)

4. d. is the correct answer. (video lesson, segment 1; objective 3)

5. d. is the correct answer. (objective 1)

   a. is incorrect. The sensory register stores incoming information for a split second.

   b. is incorrect. Working memory is the part of memory that handles current, conscious mental activity.

   c. is incorrect. Long-term memory stores information for days, months, or years.

6. b. is the correct answer. (objective 3)

7. b. is the correct answer. (objective 8)

8. b. is the correct answer. (video lesson, segment 2; objective 7)

9. b. is the correct answer. According to Gilligan, males seem to be more concerned with not interfering with the rights of others. (video lesson, segment 1; objective 6)

Matching Items

10. f (objective 3)

11. b (objective 8)

12. c (objective 6)

13. d (objective 8)

14. a (objective 8)

15. g (objective 1)

16. e (video lesson, segment 2; objective 7)

Applying Your Knowledge

1. b. is the correct answer. (video lesson, segment 1; objective 4)

2. c. is the correct answer. (objective 2)

   a. This perspective emphasizes the logical, active nature of thinking during middle childhood.

   b. is incorrect. This perspective emphasizes the importance of social interaction in learning.

   d. is incorrect. This perspective does not address the development of cognitive skills.

3. b. is the correct answer. (objective 5)

4. c. is the correct answer. Joke-telling is one of the clearest demonstrations of schoolchildren's improved pragmatic skills, including the ability to know what someone else will think is funny. (video lesson, segment 2; objective 6)

5. a. is the correct answer. (objective 7)

6. c. is the correct answer. (video lesson, segment 2; objective 6)

7. d. is the correct answer. (objective 8)

Lesson Review

Lesson 12

The School Years
Cognitive Development

Please Note: Use this matrix to guide your study and achieve the learning objectives of this lesson. It will also help you to view the video, which defines and demonstrates important concepts and skills as they relate to everyday life.

Learning Objective	Textbook	Course Student Guide	Video Lesson
1. Describe how the information processing system creates memories and forms a knowledge base.	pp. 325–327	Key Terms: 4, 5, 6, 7; Practice Questions I: 3, 16; Practice Questions II: 2, 5, 15.	Segment 1: *How School-Age Children Think*
2. Discuss advances in selective attention, processing speed and capacity, and memory skills during middle childhood.	pp. 327–329	Key Terms: 8, 9; Practice Questions I: 3, 5, 6; Applying Your Knowledge: 2.	Segment 1: *How School-Age Children Think*
3. Identify and describe the characteristics of concrete operational thought, give examples of how this type of thinking is demonstrated by schoolchildren, and explain how recent research suggests modifications to Piaget's theory.	pp. 321–323	Key Terms: 1, 2, 3, 23, 24, 25; Practice Questions I: 1, 2, 7, 9; Practice Questions II: 1, 3, 4, 6, 10.	Segment 1: *How School-Age Children Think*
4. Outline Kohlberg's stage theory of moral development and describe several criticisms of the theory.	pp. 370–374	Key Terms: 26, 27, 28; Practice Questions I: 11; Applying Your Knowledge: 1.	Segment 1: *How School-Age Children Think*
5. Compare the academic performance of children in countries around the world, and identify differences in school that may account for differences in academic performance.	pp. 334–342	Key Terms: 11, 15, 16, 17, 18; Practice Questions I: 17; Applying Your Knowledge: 3.	
6. Describe language development during the school years, noting changing abilities in vocabulary, grammar, and code switching.	pp. 330–334	Key Terms: 10, 29; Practice Questions I: 4, 10, 14, 15; Practice Questions II: 9, 12; Applying Your Knowledge: 4, 6.	Segment 1: *How School-Age Children Think* Segment 2: *Language Development*

Learning Objective	Textbook	Course Student Guide	Video Lesson
7. Identify several conditions that foster the learning of a second language, and describe different strategies for teaching another language to school-age children.	p. 336	Key Terms: 12, 13, 14; Practice Questions I: 13; Practice Questions II: 8, 16; Applying Your Knowledge: 5.	Segment 1: *How School-Age Children Think* Segment 2: *Language Development*
8. Describe current controversies in education, and explain how they relate to developmental theories and culture.	pp. 342–345	Key Terms: 17, 19, 20, 21, 22; Practice Questions I: 8, 12, 17; Practice Questions II: 7, 11, 13, 14; Applying Your Knowledge: 7.	

A Society of Children

Lesson 13

The School Years:
Psychosocial Development

Preview

This lesson brings to a close the unit on the school years. We have seen that from ages 7 to 11, the child becomes stronger and more competent, mastering the physical and cognitive abilities that are important in his or her culture. Psychosocial accomplishments are equally impressive.

The lesson begins by exploring the growing social competence of school-age children. Starting with the theories of Freud and Erikson, it moves on to discuss the perspectives of behavioral, cognitive, sociocultural, and evolutionary systems theorists. The lesson continues with a discussion of the school-age child's growing social awareness and self-understanding.

Children's interaction with peers and others in their ever-widening social world is the subject of the next section. In addition to the changing nature of friendships, the problem of bullies and their victims is discussed.

The lesson also explores the structure and function of families during middle childhood, including the experience of parental divorce and remarriage. The lesson closes with a discussion of the ways in which children cope with stressful situations.

As you complete this lesson, recall some of your own social experiences during this age range (7 to 11). How did you spend a typical day? Who were the friends you spent time with? Did you have a school or neighborhood bully? Did you grow up in a family with both of your biological parents or in some other **family structure**? What challenges did you face during this period of life and how did you handle them?

Prior Course Knowledge that Will Be Used in this Lesson

- The developmental theory of Erik Erikson (from Lesson 2) will be used to help explain psychosocial development during the school years. Recall that Erikson's theory specifies eight stages of psychosocial development, each of which is characterized by a particular challenge, or developmental crisis, which is central to that stage of life and must be resolved. This lesson will highlight Erikson's fourth stage, "Industry vs. Inferiority":
    1. Trust vs. Mistrust (birth to 1 year)
    2. Autonomy vs. Shame and Doubt (1 to 3 years)

3. Initiative vs. Guilt (3 to 6 years)
4. **Industry vs. Inferiority (7 to 11 years)**   ←   **The School Years**
5. Identity vs. Role Confusion (adolescence)
6. Intimacy vs. Isolation (adulthood)
7. Generativity vs. Stagnation (adulthood)
8. Integrity vs. Despair (adulthood)

- This lesson will revisit the concept of *theory of mind* (from Lesson 9), an understanding of human mental processes. During the school years, children gain an increasingly better understanding of the thoughts, emotions, needs, and motivations of others—which allows them to interact more effectively in their social world.

Learning Objectives

Use this information to guide your reading, viewing, thinking, and studying. After successfully completing this lesson, you should be able to:

1. Describe the rising competence and independence of middle childhood from different theoretical perspectives, including Erikson's crisis of "industry vs. inferiority."
2. Define social cognition, and explain how children's theory of mind and emotional understanding evolve during middle childhood.
3. Describe the development of self-understanding during middle childhood and its implications for children's self-esteem.
4. Discuss the importance of peer groups, providing examples of how school-age children develop their own subculture and explaining the importance of this development.
5. Discuss how friendship circles change during the school years.
6. Describe the special problems of unpopular children, of bullies and their victims, and discuss possible ways of helping such children.
7. Identify five essential ways in which families nurture school-age children.

8. Differentiate among various family structures, describe how family structures have changed in recent decades, and discuss their impact on the development of school-age children.
9. Discuss the impact of divorce on the psychosocial development of the school-age child.

10. Identify the variables that influence the impact of stresses on schoolchildren, and discuss those factors that seem especially important in helping children to cope with stress.

📖   **Read Chapter 13, "The School Years: Psychosocial Development," pages 349–368, 375–377.**

⏮   **View the video for Lesson 13, "A Society of Children."**

Segment 1: *Peers*

Segment 2: *Family*

Segment 3: *Coping*

Summary

The major theories of development emphasize similar characteristics in describing the school-age child. They portray an individual who is much more independent, capable, and open to the challenges of the world. Erikson, for example, refers to these years as the time of industry, while Freud says that sexual concerns are latent. Erikson's "industry" refers to children being busy learning all the skills that will make them productive adults. This means that children in the school years should be busy learning how to read, write, calculate, socialize with others, and try things like sports or dance or skill-building hobbies. Learning new skills is the "work" of the school-age child.

As school-age children further develop their theory of mind and powers of social cognition, they are increasingly aware of the motives, emotions, and personality traits that are the foundation of others' behavior. As their social skills improve, school-age children also become better able to adjust their own behavior to interact appropriately with others.

The expanded social world of children in the school years is full of opportunities for growth, as children create their own subculture or "society"—complete with its own language, values, and codes of behavior—and friendships become more selective and exclusive. This expanded world also presents challenges and special problems. This lesson discusses the impact of low self-esteem, bullying, divorce, poverty, and other stresses on children's psychosocial development. Most children, however, are sufficiently resilient and resourceful to cope with the stresses they may face during middle childhood. The emotional stability of parents and the amount of attention each child receives are significant factors in their healthy adjustment to environmental stress. How well a family nurtures and supports a child depends on how well it meets the child's basic needs, encourages learning, nurtures peer relationships, provides harmony and stability, and develops the child's self-esteem. While children can thrive in almost any structure, children living with both biological parents (either in nuclear or extended families) tend to have the best opportunity to thrive.

Review all reading assignments for this lesson.

As assigned by your instructor, complete the optional online component for this lesson.

Key Terms

Using your own words, write a brief definition or explanation of each of the following terms on a separate piece of paper.

1. industry versus inferiority
2. latency
3. social comparison
4. effortful control
5. resilience
6. family function
7. family structure
8. extended family
9. nuclear family
10. single-parent family
11. polygamous family
12. society of children/culture of children
13. aggressive-rejected children
14. bullying
15. social cognition
16. withdrawn-rejected children
17. bully-victim
18. peer group

Practice Questions I

Multiple-Choice Questions

1. The best strategy for helping children who are at risk of developing serious psychological problems because of multiple stresses would be to
   a. obtain assistance from a psychiatrist.
   b. change the household situation.
   c. increase the child's competencies or social supports.
   d. reduce the peer group's influence.

2. Compared with preschoolers, older children are more likely to blame
   a. failure on bad luck.
   b. teachers and other authority figures.
   c. their parents for their problems.
   d. themselves for their shortcomings.

3. As rejected children get older,
   a. their problems often get worse.
   b. their problems usually decrease.
   c. their friendship circles typically become larger.
   d. the importance of the peer group to their self-esteem grows weaker.

4. Compared with average or popular children, rejected children tend to be
   a. brighter and more competitive.
   b. affluent and "stuck-up."
   c. economically disadvantaged.
   d. emotionally immature.

5. Divorce and parental remarriage typically prove beneficial to children when they result in
   a. greater stability for the family.
   b. greater role overload.
   c. significant changes in lifestyle.
   d. the inclusion of stepchildren as siblings.

6. Factors that may contribute to a child's bullying behavior may include
   a. brain abnormalities.
   b. insecure attachment to parents.
   c. poor emotional regulation.
   d. all of the above.

7. During the school years, children become _____ selective about their friends, and their friendship groups become _____.
   a. less; larger
   b. more; larger
   c. less; smaller
   d. more; smaller

8. Erikson sees the crisis of the school years as that of
   a. industry versus inferiority.
   b. acceptance versus rejection.
   c. initiative versus guilt.
   d. male versus female.

True or False Items
Write T (for true) or F (for false) on the line in front of each statement.

9. __F__ As they evaluate themselves according to increasingly complex self-theories, school-age children typically experience a rise in self-esteem.

F 10. __T__ During middle childhood, acceptance by the peer group is valued ~~more~~ *less* than having a close friend.

T 11. __F__ Children from high-income homes tend to have more emotional problem than children from middle-income families.

12. __F__ Blended families are better for child development than single-parent families.

13. __F__ Divorce usually adversely affects the children for at least a year or two.

14. __T__ The quality of family interaction seems to be a more powerful predictor of children's development than the actual structure of the family.

F 15. __T__ School-age children are ~~less~~ better able than younger children to cope with the chronic stresses that are troublesome at any age.

16. __F__ The problems of most rejected children nearly always disappear by adolescence.

17. __T__ Friendships become more selective and exclusive as children grow older.

18. __T__ Research has found that children in single-mother households achieve much more in school if their father regularly pays adequate child support or if the nation they live in subsidizes single parents.

Practice Questions II

Multiple-Choice Questions

1. Children who are categorized as _____ are particularly vulnerable to bullying.
   a. aggressive-rejected
   b. passive-aggressive
   c. withdrawn-rejected
   d. passive-rejected

2. The main reason for the special vocabulary, dress codes, and behaviors that flourish within the society of children is that they
   a. lead to clubs and gang behavior.
   b. are unknown to or unapproved by adults.
   c. imitate adult-organized society.
   d. provide an alternative to useful work in society.

3. In the area of social cognition, developmentalists are impressed by the school-age child's increasing ability to
   a. identify and take into account other people's viewpoints.
   b. develop an increasingly wide network of friends.
   c. relate to the opposite sex.
   d. resist social models.

4. Typically, children in middle childhood experience a decrease in self-esteem as a result of
   a. a wavering self-theory.
   b. increased awareness of personal shortcomings and failures.
   c. rejection by peers.
   d. difficulties with members of the opposite sex.

5. A ten-year-old's sense of self-esteem is most strongly influenced by his or her
   a. peers.
   b. siblings.
   c. mother.
   d. father.

6. Which of the following most accurately describes how friendships change during the school years?
   a. Friendships become more casual and less intense.
   b. Older children demand less of their friends.
   c. Older children change friends more often.
   d. Close friendships increasingly involve members of the same sex, ethnicity, and socioeconomic status.

7. Which of the following is an accurate statement about school-age bullies?
   a. They are unapologetic about their aggressive behavior.
   b. They usually have friends who abet, fear, and admire them.
   c. Their popularity fades over the years.
   d. All of the above are accurate statements.

8. Two factors that most often help the child cope well with multiple stresses are social support and
   a. social comparison.
   b. competence in a specific area.
   c. remedial education.
   d. referral to mental health professionals.

9. Family _____ is more crucial to children's well-being than family _____ is.
   a. structure; socioeconomic status (SES)
   b. socioeconomic status (SES); stability
   c. socioeconomic status (SES); structure
   d. functioning; structure

10. According to Freud, the period between ages 7 and 11 when a child's sexual drives are relatively quiet is the
    a. phallic stage.
    b. genital stage.
    c. period of latency.
    d. period of industry versus inferiority.

11. Research studies have found that children who are forced to cope with ongoing stress (for example, poverty or large family size) are
    a. more likely to develop serious psychiatric problems than children with none of these stresses.
    b. able to cope much better when provided with a consistent daily routine.
    c. more likely to develop intense, destructive friendships than other children.
    d. less likely to be accepted by their peer group.

12. The most potentially negative aspect of the culture of children is
    a. low self-esteem.
    b. latency.
    c. social comparison.
    d. deviancy training.

Matching Items
Match each term or concept with its corresponding description or definition.

Terms or Concepts
13. _____ social cognition
14. _____ peer group
15. _____ society of children/culture of children

16. _____ bullying
17. _____ aggressive-rejected
18. _____ withdrawn-rejected

Descriptions or Definitions
a. the games, vocabulary, dress codes, and culture of children
b. a perspective that highlights how schoolchildren advance in learning, cognition, and culture by building on maturation and experience to become more articulate, insightful, and competent
c. children who are disliked because of their confrontational nature
d. a group of individuals of roughly the same age and social status who play, work, or learn together
e. children who are disliked because of their timid, anxious behavior
f. repeated efforts by a single child or group of children to inflict harm on another child through physical, verbal, or social attacks

Applying Your Knowledge

1. As an advocate of Freud's psychoanalytic theory, Dr. Wayans is most likely to explain a ten-year-old child's new independence as the result of
   a. sexual urges being submerged.
   b. the acquisition of new skills.
   c. greater self-understanding.
   d. the child's need to join the wider community and the parents' need to focus on younger children.

2. Dr. Ferris believes that skill mastery is particularly important because children develop views of themselves as either competent or incompetent in skills valued by their culture. Dr. Ferris is evidently working from the perspective of
   a. behaviorism.
   b. social learning theory.
   c. Erik Erikson's theory of development.
   d. Freud's theory of development.

3. Bonnie, who is low achieving, shy, and withdrawn, is rejected by most of her peers. Her teacher, who wants to help Bonnie increase her self-esteem and social acceptance, encourages her parents to
   a. transfer Bonnie to a different school.
   b. help their daughter improve her motor skills.
   c. help their daughter learn to accept more responsibility for her academic failures.
   d. help their daughter improve her skills in relating to peers.

4. Jorge, who has no children of his own, is worried about his twelve-year-old niece because she wears unusual clothes and uses vocabulary unknown to him. What should Jorge do?
   a. Tell his niece's parents that they need to discipline their daughter more strictly.
   b. Convince his niece to find a new group of friends.
   c. Recommend that his niece's parents seek professional counseling for their daughter, because such behaviors often are the first signs of a lifelong pattern of antisocial behavior.
   d. Jorge need not necessarily be worried because children typically develop their own subculture of speech, dress, and behavior.

5. Compared with her seven-year-old brother Walter, ten-year-old Felicity is more likely to describe their cousin
   a. in terms of physical attributes.
   b. as feeling exactly the same way she does when they are in the same social situation.
   c. in terms of personality traits.
   d. in terms of their cousin's outward behavior.

6. Seven-year-old Chantal fumes after a friend compliments her new dress, thinking that the comment was intended to be sarcastic. Chantal's reaction is an example of
   a. egocentrism.
   b. feelings of inferiority.
   c. the distorted thought processes of an emotionally disturbed child.
   d. lack of prosocial skills.

7. In contrast to younger children discussing friendship, nine-year-old children will
   a. deny that friends are important.
   b. state that they prefer same-sex playmates.
   c. stress the importance of help and emotional support in friendship.
   d. be less choosy about whom they call a friend.

8. Children who have serious difficulties in peer relationships during elementary school
   a. are at a greater risk of having emotional problems later in life.
   b. usually overcome their difficulties in a year or two.
   c. later are more likely to form an intense friendship with one person than children who did not have difficulties earlier on.
   d. do both b and c.

9. Of the following children, who is likely to have the lowest overall self-esteem?
   a. Karen, age 5
   b. David, age 7
   c. Carl, age 9
   d. Cindy, age 10

10. Ten-year-old Benjamin is less optimistic and self-confident than his five-year-old sister. This may be explained in part by the tendency of older children to
   a. evaluate their abilities by comparing them with their own competencies a year or two earlier.
   b. evaluate their competencies by comparing them with those of others.
   c. be less realistic about their own abilities.
   d. do both b and c.

Answer Key

Key Terms

1. According to Erikson, the crisis of middle childhood is that of industry versus inferiority, in which children try to master many skills and develop views of themselves as either competent or incompetent and inferior. (p. 350; video lesson, introduction; objective 1)
2. In Freud's theory, middle childhood is a period of latency, during which emotional drives are quieter and psychosexual needs are repressed. (p. 351; objective 1)
3. Social comparison is the tendency to assess one's abilities, achievements, and social status by measuring them against those of others, especially those of one's peers. (p. 351; objective 3)
4. Effortful control is a cognitive ability to inhibit impulses, and gains in this ability help foster a child's growing ability to understand social situations. (p. 352; objective 2)
5. Individuals who are able to cope with stress and very difficult situations demonstrate a high degree of resilience. (p. 353; objective 10)
6. Family function refers to how a family works to meet the needs of its members, which vary with age. Schoolchildren need their families to provide such basic necessities as food, clothing, and shelter; to encourage them to learn; to develop their self-esteem; to nurture their friendships with peers; and to provide harmony and stability at home. (p. 358; objective 7)
7. Family structure refers to the legal and genetic relationships that exist between members of a particular family. (p. 359; video lesson, segment 2; objective 6)
8. An extended family is one that includes grandparents, aunts, cousins, or other relatives in addition to parents and their children. (p. 350; objective 8)
9. A nuclear family consists of two parents and their mutual biological offspring. (p. 359; video lesson, segment 2; objective 6)
10. A single-parent family consists of one parent and his or her (usually biological) children. (p. 359; video lesson, segment 2; objective 8)
11. A polygamous family is a family that consists of one man, several wives, and the biological children of the man and his wives. (p. 360; objective 8)

12. Children in middle childhood develop and transmit their own subculture, called the society of children/culture of children, which has its own games, vocabulary, dress codes, and rules of behavior. (p. 364; video lesson, introduction; objective 4)

13. The peer group shuns aggressive-rejected children because they are overly confrontational. (p. 366; video lesson, segment 1; objective 6)

14. Bullying is the repeated, systematic effort to inflict harm on a child through physical, verbal, or social attack. (p. 366; video lesson, segment 1; objective 6)

15. Social cognition involves being able to understand social interaction, including the causes and consequences of behavior. (p. 366; objective 2)

16. Withdrawn-rejected children are shunned by the peer group because of their withdrawn and anxious demeanor. (p. 366; video lesson, segment 1; objective 6)

17. A bully-victim (also known as a provocative victim) is a bully who is or has been a victim of bullying. (p. 367; objective 6)

18. A peer group is a group of individuals of roughly the same age and social status that play, work, or learn together. (video lesson, segment 1; objective 4)

Practice Questions I

Multiple-Choice Questions

1. c. is the correct answer. (video lesson, segment 3; objective 10)
2. d. is the correct answer. (video lesson, segment 1; objective 3)
   a., b., & c. Compared with preschool children, schoolchildren are more self-critical, and their self-esteem dips, so they blame themselves.
3. a. is the correct answer. (objective 6)
4. d. is the correct answer. (video lesson, segment 1; objective 6)
5. a. is the correct answer. (video lesson; segment 3; objective 9)
   b., c., & d. are incorrect. These factors are likely to increase, rather than decrease, stress, and therefore to have an adverse effect on children.
6. d. is the correct answer. (objective 6)
7. d. is the correct answer. (objective 5)
8. a. is the correct answer. (video lesson, segment 1; objective 1)

True or False Items

9. F   In fact, just the opposite is true. (objective 3)
10. F   In fact, just the opposite is true. (video lesson, segment 1; objectives 3 & 4)
11. T   (objective 8)
12. F   (objective 9)
13. T   (video lesson, segment 2; objective 9)
14. T   (video lesson, segment 2; objective 7)
15. F   Because of the coping strategies that school-age children develop, they are better able than younger children to cope with stress. (objective 9)
16. F   The problems of rejected children often get worse as they get older. (objective 6)
17. T   (video lesson, segment 1; objective 5)
18. T   (objective 8)

Practice Questions II

Multiple-Choice Questions

1. c. is the correct answer. (video lesson, segment 1; objective 6)

    a. is incorrect. These are usually bullies.

    b. & d. are incorrect. These are not subcategories of rejected children.

2. b. is the correct answer. (video lesson, introduction; objective 4)

3. a. is the correct answer. (objective 2)

    b. is incorrect. Friendship circles typically become smaller during middle childhood, as children become more choosy about their friends.

    c. & d. are incorrect. These issues are not discussed in the textbook.

4. b. is the correct answer. (objective 3)

    a. is incorrect. This tends to promote, rather than reduce, self-esteem.

    c. is incorrect. Only 10 percent of schoolchildren experience this.

    d. is incorrect. This issue becomes more important during adolescence.

5. a. is the correct answer. (video lesson, segment 1; objective 3)

6. d. is the correct answer. (objective 5)

    a., b., & c. are incorrect. In fact, just the opposite is true of friendship during the school years.

7. d. is the correct answer. (objective 6)

8. b. is the correct answer. (video lesson, segment 3; objective 10)

9. d. is the correct answer. (video lesson, segment 2; objective 7)

10. c. is the correct answer. (objective 1)

11. b. is the correct answer. (objective 10)

    c. & d. are incorrect. The textbook did not discuss how stress influences friendship or peer acceptance.

12. d. is the correct answer. (objective 4)

Matching Items

13. b (objective 2)

14. d (objective 4)

15. a (video lesson, introduction; objective 4)

16. f (objective 6)

17. c (objective 6)

18. e (objective 6)

Applying Your Knowledge

1. a. is the correct answer. (objective 1)

    d. is incorrect. This describes the epigenetic systems perspective.

    b. is incorrect. This is the viewpoint of a learning theorist.

    c. is incorrect. This is the viewpoint of a cognitive theorist.

2. c. is the correct answer. The question describes what is, for Erikson, the crisis of middle childhood: industry versus inferiority. (objective 1)

3. d. is the correct answer. (video lesson, segment 1; objective 6)

    a. is incorrect. Because it would seem to involve "running away" from her problems, this approach would likely be more harmful than helpful.

    b. is incorrect. Improving motor skills is not a factor considered in the textbook and probably has little value in raising self-esteem in such situations.

c. is incorrect. If Bonnie is like most school-age children, she is quite self-critical and already accepts responsibility for her failures.

4. d. is the correct answer. (video lesson, segment 1; objective 3)

5. c. is the correct answer. (objective 5)

   a., b., & d. are incorrect. These are more typical of preschoolers.

6. d. is the correct answer. (objective 5)

   a. is incorrect. Egocentrism is self-centered thinking. In this example, Chantal is misinterpreting her friend's comment.

   b. & c. are incorrect. There is no reason to believe that Chantal is suffering from an emotional disturbance or that she is feeling inferior.

7. b. is the correct answer. (video lesson, segment 1; objective 5)

8. a. is the correct answer. (objective 6)

9. d. is the correct answer. Self-esteem decreases throughout middle childhood. (objective 3)

10. b. is the correct answer. (objective 3)

   a. & c. are incorrect. These are more typical of preschoolers than school-age children.

Lesson Review

Lesson 13

The School Years
Psychosocial Development

Please Note: Use this matrix to guide your study and achieve the learning objectives of this lesson. It will also help you to view the video, which defines and demonstrates important concepts and skills as they relate to everyday life.

Learning Objective	Textbook	Course Student Guide	Video Lesson
1. Describe the rising competence and independence of middle childhood from different theoretical perspectives, including Erikson's crisis of "industry vs. inferiority."	pp. 350–351	Key Terms: 1, 2; Practice Questions I: 8; Practice Questions II: 10; Applying Your Knowledge: 1, 2.	Introduction; Segment 1: *Peers*
2. Define social cognition, and explain how children's theory of mind and emotional understanding evolve during middle childhood.	p. 366	Key Terms: 4, 15; Practice Questions II: 3, 13.	
3. Describe the development of self-understanding during middle childhood and its implications for children's self-esteem.	pp. 351–352	Key Terms: 3; Practice Questions I: 2, 9, 10; Practice Questions II: 4, 5; Applying Your Knowledge: 4, 9, 10.	Segment 1: *Peers*
4. Discuss the importance of peer groups, providing examples of how school-age children develop their own subculture and explaining the importance of this development.	pp. 364–365	Key Terms: 12, 18; Practice Questions I: 10; Practice Questions II: 2, 12, 14, 15.	Introduction; Segment 1: *Peers*
5. Discuss how friendship circles change during the school years.	p. 365	Practice Questions I: 7, 17; Practice Questions II: 6; Applying Your Knowledge: 5, 6, 7.	Segment 1: *Peers;*
6. Describe the special problems of unpopular children, of bullies and their victims, and discuss possible ways of helping such children.	pp. 365–369	Key Terms: 7, 9, 13, 14, 16, 17; Practice Questions I: 3, 4, 6, 16; Practice Questions II: 1, 7, 16, 17, 18; Applying Your Knowledge: 3, 8.	Segment 1: *Peers;* Segment 2: *Family*
7. Identify five essential ways in which families nurture school-age children.	pp. 358–359	Key Terms: 6; Practice Questions I: 14; Practice Questions II: 9.	Segment 2: *Family*

Learning Objective	Textbook	Course Student Guide	Video Lesson
8. Differentiate among various family structures, describe how family structures have changed in recent decades, and discuss their impact on the development of school-age children.	pp. 359–362	Key Terms: 8, 10, 11; Practice Questions I: 11, 18.	Segment 2: *Family*
9. Discuss the impact of divorce on the psychosocial development of the school-age child.	*	Practice Questions I: 5, 12, 13, 15.	Segment 2: *Family* Segment 3: *Coping*
10. Identify the variables that influence the impact of stresses on schoolchildren, and discuss those factors that seem especially important in helping children to cope with stress.	pp. 353–356; 362–363	Key Terms: 5; Practice Questions I: 1; Practice Questions II: 8, 11.	Segment 3: *Coping*

*The video for this lesson offers an excellent description of these concepts.

Explosions

Lesson 14

Adolescence:
Biosocial Development

Preview

Between the ages of 11 and 20, young people cross the great divide between childhood and adulthood that we call **adolescence**. This crossing encompasses all three domains of development—biosocial, cognitive, and psychosocial. Lesson 14 focuses on the dramatic changes that occur in the biosocial domain, beginning with **puberty** and the **growth spurt**. The biosocial metamorphosis of the adolescent is discussed in detail, with emphasis on sexual maturation, nutrition, and the effects of the timing of puberty, including possible problems arising from early or late maturation.

Although adolescence is, in many ways, a healthy time of life, this lesson addresses three health hazards that too often affect children of this age: sexual abuse, poor nutrition, and use of alcohol, tobacco, and other drugs.

As you begin this lesson, reflect on your own experience in adolescence. Recall your physical growth and development during this period (i.e., height, weight, voice changes, hair growth, developing curves/shoulders). Did you develop any earlier or later than your peers? How did these changes make you feel? How well did you eat and take care of yourself physically? What pressures did you feel regarding drugs and alcohol?

Prior Course Knowledge that Will Be Used in this Lesson
• Biosocial development during infancy (Lesson 5), early childhood (Lesson 8), and middle childhood (Lesson 11) will be referred to as we discuss physical developments during adolescence. As you'll learn, the rate of growth in adolescence is second only to the rapid growth experienced prenatally (in the womb) and postnatally (during the first year of life).

Learning Objectives

Use this information to guide your reading, viewing, thinking, and studying. After successfully completing this lesson, you should be able to:

1. Identify and describe the biological events of puberty.

2. Identify several factors that influence the onset of puberty, and explain gender differences in the influence of early or late maturation on adolescent development.

3. Describe the growth spurt experienced during adolescence by both boys and girls, including changes in weight, height, and the body's internal organ system.

4. Describe the development of sexual characteristics in males and females during puberty, and describe influences on adolescents' sexual activity.

5. Discuss the emotional and psychological impact of pubertal hormones and how this impact has changed over the decades.

6. Describe cultural, social, and individual factors that have an impact on the adolescent's development of a positive body image.

7. Describe potential sex-related problems in adolescence, including the prevalence and consequences of child sexual abuse.

8. Discuss the nutritional needs and problems of adolescents.

9. Discuss the use and abuse of alcohol, tobacco, and other drugs among adolescents today, including prevalence, significance for development, and the best methods of prevention.

10. Describe brain development during adolescence and explain how it relates to cognition, emotion, and body rhythms.

📖   **Read Chapter 14, "Adolescence: Biosocial Development," pages 379–405 and pages 454–458 in Chapter 16, "Adolescence: Psychosocial Development."**

⏮   **View the video for Lesson 14, "Explosions."**

     Segment 1: *Puberty*

     Segment 2: *Body Image*

     Segment 3: *Health*

Summary

Puberty begins when a hormonal signal from the hypothalamus stimulates hormone production in the pituitary gland, which, in turn, triggers hormone production by the adrenal glands and by the **gonads** (sex glands). The major physical changes of puberty generally occur in the same sequence for everyone and are usually complete three or four years after they have begun. Variation in growth is related to sex, genetic inheritance, nutrition, and other factors.

The sequence of growth during puberty is from the extremities inward, making many adolescents temporarily big-footed, long-legged, and short-waisted. Internal organs also grow, including the lungs (which triple in weight) and the heart (which doubles in size and slows in rate). These changes give the adolescent increased physical endurance. The lymphoid system—including the tonsils and adenoids—

decreases in size at adolescence, making teenagers less susceptible than children to respiratory ailments. The growth and maturation of the sex organs, called **primary sex characteristics**, that result in the development of reproductive potential are signaled by the first menstrual period (**menarche**) in girls and by the first ejaculation (**spermarche**) in boys.

Attitudes toward menarche and spermarche have changed over the past two decades, and—for the most part—fewer young people face these events with anxiety, embarrassment, or guilt. Young people who experience puberty at the same time as their friends tend to view the experience more positively than those who do not. The effects of early and late maturation differ for boys and girls. Girls find *early* maturation more difficult because of the added pressures that accompany sexual maturation. Boys find *late* maturation more difficult because of the correlation between peer status and a mature build.

Parents who are in conflict with each other, immature, socially isolated, alcoholic, or drug-abusing are more likely to be sexually abusive or so neglectful that their children are vulnerable to abuse from others. The psychological effects of **child sexual abuse** depend on the extent and duration of the abuse, the age of the child, and the reactions of family members and authorities once the abuse is known. Unlike younger victims of abuse, adolescents are prone to becoming self-destructive through substance abuse or eating disorders, running away from home, risking AIDS through unsafe sex, or even attempting suicide.

Drug abuse always harms physical and psychological development. **Drug use** may or may not be harmful, depending in part on how mature the drug user is and his or her reason for using the drug. Drug use is also increasing among younger adolescents. This is cause for particular concern because research has shown that early drug use is likely to disrupt the brain and body growth that occur during adolescence and can lead to long-term problems.

📖   **Review all reading assignments for this lesson.**

💻   **As assigned by your instructor, complete the optional online component for this lesson.**

Key Terms

Using your own words, write a brief definition or explanation of each of the following terms on a separate piece of paper.

1. puberty
2. menarche
3. spermarche
4. hormone
5. pituitary gland
6. adrenal glands
7. HPA axis
8. gonads
9. HPG axis
10. estradiol
11. testosterone
12. secular trend
13. leptin

14. body image
15. anorexia nervosa
16. bulimia nervosa
17. growth spurt
18. primary sex characteristics
19. secondary sex characteristics
20. child sexual abuse
21. sexually transmitted infection (STI)
22. generational forgetting
23. adolescence
24. drug use
25. drug abuse
26. drug addiction

Practice Questions I

Multiple-Choice Questions

1. Which of the following most accurately describes the sequence of pubertal development in girls?

   a. breast buds and pubic hair; growth spurt in which fat is deposited on hips and buttocks; first menstrual period; ovulation
   b. growth spurt; breast buds and pubic hair; first menstrual period; ovulation
   c. first menstrual period; breast buds and pubic hair; growth spurt; ovulation
   d. breast buds and pubic hair; growth spurt; ovulation; first menstrual period

2. Although both sexes grow rapidly during adolescence, boys typically begin their accelerated growth about

   a. a year or two later than girls.
   b. a year earlier than girls.
   c. the time they reach sexual maturity.
   d. the time facial hair appears.

3. The first readily observable sign of the onset of puberty is

   a. the voice lowers.
   b. the appearance of facial, body, and pubic hair.
   c. a change in the shape of the eyes.
   d. a lengthening of the torso.

4. More than any other group in the population, adolescent girls are likely to have
   a. asthma.
   b. acne.
   c. iron-deficiency anemia.
   d. both b and c.

5. For males, the secondary sex characteristic that usually occurs last is
   a. breast enlargement.
   b. the appearance of facial hair.
   c. growth of the testes.
   d. the appearance of pubic hair.

6. For girls, the specific event that is taken to indicate sexual maturity is
   _____; for boys, it is _____.
   a. the growth of breast buds; voice deepening
   b. menarche; spermarche
   c. an ovulation; the testosterone surge
   d. the growth spurt; pubic hair

7. The most significant hormonal changes of puberty include a marked increase
   of _____ in _____ and a marked increase of
   _____ in _____.
   a. progesterone; boys; estradiol; girls
   b. estradiol; boys; testosterone; girls
   c. progesterone; girls; estradiol; boys
   d. estradiol; girls; testosterone; boys

8. In general, adolescents are
   a. overweight.
   b. satisfied with their appearance.
   c. dissatisfied with their appearance.
   d. unaffected by cultural attitudes about beauty.

9. The damage caused by sexual abuse depends on all of the following factors **EXCEPT**
   a. repeated incidence.
   b. the gender of the perpetrator.
   c. distorted adult-child relationships.
   d. impairment of the child's ability to develop normally.

10. Early physical growth and sexual maturation
    a. tend to be equally difficult for girls and boys.
    b. tend to be more difficult for boys than for girls.
    c. tend to be more difficult for girls than for boys.
    d. are easier for both girls and boys than late maturation.

True or False Items

Write T (for true) or F (for false) on the line in front of each statement.

11. __T__   More calories are necessary during adolescence than at any other period during the life span.

12. __F__   The first indicator of reproductive potential in males is menarche.

13. __T__   Lung capacity, heart size, and total volume of blood increase significantly during adolescence.

14. __F__   Puberty generally begins sometime between ages 8 and 14.

15. __T__   Girls who mature late and are thinner than average tend to be satisfied with their weight.

16. __F__   The strong emphasis on physical appearance is unique to adolescents and finds little support from teachers, parents, and the larger culture.

17. __F__   Childhood habits of overeating and underexercising usually lessen during adolescence.

18. __T__   During emotional situations, adolescents' emotions often overwhelm reason.

Practice Questions II

Multiple-Choice Questions

1. Which of the following is the correct sequence of pubertal events in boys?

   a. growth spurt; pubic hair; first ejaculation; lowering of voice

   b. pubic hair; first ejaculation; growth spurt; lowering of voice

   c. lowering of voice; pubic hair; growth spurt; first ejaculation

   d. growth spurt; lowering of voice; pubic hair; first ejaculation

2. Which of the following statements about adolescent physical development is **NOT** true?

   a. Hands and feet generally lengthen before arms and legs.

   b. Facial features usually grow before the head itself reaches adult size and shape.

   c. Oil, sweat, and odor glands become more active.

   d. The lymphoid system increases slightly in size, and the heart increases by nearly half.

3. In puberty, a hormone that increases markedly in girls (and only somewhat in boys) is

   a. estrogen.

   b. testosterone.

   c. androgen.

   d. menarche.

4. In females, puberty is typically marked by a(n)
    a. significant widening of the shoulders.
    b. significant widening of the hips.
    c. enlargement of the torso and upper chest.
    d. decrease in the size of the eyes and nose.

5. Nonreproductive sexual characteristics, such as the deepening of the voice and the development of breasts, are called
    a. gender-typed traits.
    b. primary sex characteristics.
    c. secondary sex characteristics.
    d. pubertal prototypes.

6. Puberty is initiated when hormones are released from the _____, then from the _____, and then from the adrenal glands and the _____.
    a. hypothalamus; pituitary; gonads
    b. pituitary; gonads; hypothalamus
    c. gonads; pituitary; hypothalamus
    d. pituitary; hypothalamus; gonads

7. With regard to appearance, adolescent girls are most commonly dissatisfied with
    a. timing of maturation.
    b. eyes and other facial features.
    c. weight.
    d. legs.

8. Individuals who experiment with drugs early are
    a. typically affluent teenagers who are experiencing an identity crisis.
    b. more likely to have multiple drug-abuse problems later on.
    c. less likely to have alcohol-abuse problems later on.
    d. usually able to resist later peer pressure leading to long-term addiction.

9. Because of brain-related hormonal changes, adolescents
    a. are on a later sleep–wake cycle than adults.
    b. are skilled at using logical thinking during emotional situations.
    c. can withstand long periods of sleep deprivation with little to no effect on their health and school performance.
    d. experience a slowing down of reaction time.

10. Puberty is most accurately defined as the period
    a. of rapid physical growth that occurs during adolescence.
    b. during which sexual maturation is attained.
    c. of rapid physical growth and sexual maturation that ends childhood.
    d. during which adolescents establish identities separate from their parents.

11. Which of the following does **NOT** typically occur during puberty?
    a. The lungs increase in size and capacity.
    (b) The heart's size and rate of beating increase.
    c. Blood volume increases.
    d. The lymphoid system decreases in size.

12. Teenagers' susceptibility to respiratory ailments typically _____ during adolescence, due to a(n) _____ in the size of the lymphoid system.
    a. increases; increase
    b. increases; decrease
    c. decreases; increase
    (d) decreases; decrease

Matching Items

Match each definition or description with its corresponding term.

Terms

13. ____B____ puberty
14. ____D____ HPA axis
15. ____C____ testosterone
16. ____E____ estradiol
17. ____F____ growth spurt

18. ____I____ primary sex characteristics
19. ____A____ menarche
20. ____J____ spermarche
21. ____H____ secondary sex characteristics
22. ____G____ body image

Definitions or Descriptions

a. onset of menstruation
b. period of rapid physical growth and sexual maturation that ends childhood
c. hormone that increases dramatically in boys during puberty
d. route followed by many hormones to trigger puberty and to regulate other bodily changes
e. hormone that increases dramatically in girls during puberty
f. first sign is increased bone length and density
g. attitude toward one's physical appearance
h. physical characteristics not involved in reproduction
i. the sex organs involved in reproduction
j. first ejaculation containing sperm

Applying Your Knowledge

1. Fifteen-year-old Latoya is preoccupied with her "disgusting appearance" and seems depressed most of the time. The best thing her parents could do to help her through this difficult time would be to

   a. ignore her self-preoccupation, since their attention would only reinforce it.

   b. encourage her to "shape up" and not give in to self-pity.

   c. kid her about her appearance in the hope that she will see how silly she is acting.

   d. offer practical advice, such as clothing suggestions, to improve her body image.

2. Thirteen-year-old Rosa, an avid runner and dancer, is worried because most of her friends have begun to menstruate regularly. Her doctor tells her

   a. that she should have a complete physical exam, because female athletes usually menstruate earlier than average.

   b. not to worry, since female athletes usually menstruate later than average.

   c. that she must stop running immediately, because the absence of menstruation is a sign of a serious health problem.

   d. that the likely cause of her delayed menarche is an inadequate diet.

3. Twelve-year-old Kwan is worried because his twin sister has suddenly grown taller and more physically mature than he. His parents should

   a. reassure him that the average boy is one or two years behind the average girl in the onset of the growth spurt.

   b. tell him that within a year or less he will grow taller than his sister.

   c. tell him that one member of each fraternal twin pair is always shorter.

   d. encourage him to exercise more to accelerate the onset of his growth spurt.

4. Regarding the effects of early and late maturation on boys and girls, which of the following is **NOT** true?

   a. Early maturation is usually easier for boys to manage than it is for girls.

   b. Late maturation is usually easier for girls to manage than it is for boys.

   c. Late-maturing girls may be drawn into older peer groups and may exhibit problem behaviors such as early sexual activity.

   d. Late-maturing boys may not "catch up" physically, or in terms of their self-images, for many years.

5. Which of the following adolescents is likely to begin puberty at the earliest age?

   a. Aretha, an African-American teenager who hates exercise

   b. Todd, a football player of European ancestry

   c. Kyu, an Asian-American honors student

   d. There is too little information to make a prediction.

6. Of the following teenagers, those most likely to be distressed about their physical development are
   a. late-maturing girls.
   b. late-maturing boys.
   c. early-maturing boys.
   d. girls or boys who masturbate.

7. Thirteen-year-old Kristin seems apathetic and lazy to her parents. You tell them
   a. that Kristin is showing signs of chronic depression.
   b. that Kristin may be experiencing psychosocial difficulties.
   c. that Kristin has a poor attitude and needs more discipline.
   d. to have Kristin's iron level checked.

8. I am a hormone that causes the gonads to increase sex hormone production during puberty in both males and females. What am I?
   a. estradiol
   b. testosterone
   c. GnRH
   d. menarche

9. Eleven-year-old Linda, who has just begun to experience the first signs of puberty, laments, "When will the agony of puberty be over?" You tell her that the major events of puberty typically end about _____ after the first visible signs appear.
   a. 6 years
   b. 3 or 4 years
   c. 2 years
   d. 1 year

Answer Key

Key Terms
1. Puberty is the period of rapid physical growth and sexual maturation that ends childhood and brings the young person to adult size, shape, and sexual potential. (p. 381; video lesson, segment 1; objective 1)
2. Menarche, which refers to the first menstrual period, is the specific event that is taken to indicate fertility in adolescent girls. (p. 381; video lesson, segment 1; objective 4)
3. Spermarche, which refers to the first ejaculation of seminal fluid containing sperm, is the specific event that is taken to indicate fertility in adolescent boys. (p. 381; video lesson, segment 1; objective 4)
4. Hormones are substances created by a body tissue and transmitted through the bloodstream to other body tissues to influence a psychological function. (p. 382; objective 1)
5. The pituitary gland, under the influence of the hypothalamus, produces hormones that regulate growth and control other glands. (p. 382; objectives 1 & 2)

6. The adrenal glands secrete epinephrine and norephinephrine, hormones that prepare the body to deal with emergencies or stress. (p. 382; objectives 1 & 2)

7. The HPA axis (hypothalamus/pituitary/adrenal axis) is the route followed by many hormones to trigger puberty and to regulate stress, growth, and other bodily changes. (p. 382; objectives 1 & 2)

8. The gonads are the pair of sex glands in humans—the ovaries in girls and the testes or testicles in boys. (p. 382; video lesson, segment 1; objectives 2 & 5)

9. The HPG axis is a sequence of hormone production beginning in the hypothalamus and moving to the pituitary and then to the gonads. (p. 383; objective 2)

10. Estradiol is a sex hormone that is secreted in greater amounts by females than males. (p. 383; video lesson, segment 1; objective 2)

11. Testosterone is a sex hormone that is secreted more by males than by females. (p. 383; video lesson, segment 1; objective 2)

12. Improved medical care and nutrition has resulted in puberty occurring earlier in development than previously, a phenomenon referred to as the secular trend. (p. 386; objective 2)

13. Leptin is a hormone that affects appetite and is thought to affect the onset of puberty. Leptin levels increase throughout childhood at peak at around age 12. (p. 386; objective 2)

14. Body image refers to adolescents' mental conception of, and attitude toward, their physical appearance. (p. 390; video lesson, segment 2; objective 6)

15. Anorexia nervosa is a sometimes fatal eating disorder characterized by self-starvation, often accompanied by over-exercise. (p. 390; objective 6)

16. Bulimia nervosa is an eating disorder characterized by frequent binging followed by purging, either by self-induced vomiting or laxatives. (p. 391; objective 6)

17. The growth spurt, which begins with an increase in bone length and density and includes rapid weight gain and organ growth, is one of the many observable signs of puberty. (p. 392; video lesson, segment 1; objective 3)

18. During puberty, changes in the primary sex characteristics involve those sex organs that are directly involved in reproduction. (p. 394; video lesson, segment 1; objective 4)

19. During puberty, changes in the secondary sex characteristics involve parts of the body that are not directly involved in reproduction but that signify sexual development. (p. 394; video lesson, segment 1; objective 4)

20. Child sexual abuse is any activity in which an adult uses a child for his or her own sexual stimulation or pleasure—even if the use does not involve physical contact. (p. 397; objective 7)

21. Diseases such as HIV, chlamydia, syphilis, and others transmitted through sexual contact are referred to as sexually transmitted infections (STIs). (p. 398; objective 7)

22. The idea that each new generation "forgets" what the previous generations have learned is called generational forgetting. (p. 457; objective 9)

23. Adolescence is the period of biological, cognitive, and psychosocial transition from childhood to adulthood. (video lesson, segment 1; objective 1)

24. Drug use is the ingestion of a drug, regardless of the amount or affect of ingestion. (video lesson, segment 3; objective 9)

25. Drug abuse is the ingestion of a drug to the extent that it impairs the user's well-being. (video lesson, segment 3; objective 9)

26. Drug addiction is a person's dependence on a drug or a behavior in order to feel physically or psychologically at ease. (video lesson, segment 3; objective 9)

Practice Questions I

Multiple-Choice Questions

1. a. is the correct answer. (video lesson, segment 1; objective 1)

2. a. is the correct answer. (video lesson, segment 1; objectives 1 & 2)

3. b. is the correct answer. (video lesson, segment 1; objective 1)

4. d. is the correct answer. (objective 3)

5. b. is the correct answer. (video lesson, segment 1; objective 3)

6. b. is the correct answer. (video lesson, segment 1; objective 4)

7. d. is the correct answer. (video lesson, segment 1; objective 2)

8. c. is the correct answer. (video lesson, segment 2; objective 6)

   a. is incorrect. Although some adolescents become overweight, many diet and lose weight in an effort to attain a desired body image.

   d. is incorrect. On the contrary, cultural attitudes about beauty are an extremely influential factor in the formation of a teenager's body image.

9. b. is the correct answer. (video lesson, segment 1; objective 7)

10. c. is the correct answer. (objective 5)

True or False Items

11. T   (objective 8)

12. F   The first indicator of reproductive potential in males is ejaculation of seminal fluid containing sperm (spermarche). Menarche (the first menstrual period) is the first indication of reproductive potential in females. (video lesson, segment 1; objective 4)

13. T   (objective 3)

14. T   (video lesson, segment 1; objectives 1 & 2)

15. F   Studies show that the majority of adolescent girls, even those in the thinnest group, want to lose weight. (objective 6)

16. F   The strong emphasis on appearance is reflected in the culture as a whole; for example, teachers (and, no doubt, prospective employers) tend to judge people who are physically attractive as being more competent than those who are less attractive. (video lesson, segment 2; objective 6)

17. F   These habits generally worsen during adolescence. (objective 8)

18. T   Because of heightened activity in the amygdala, emotional experiences can hinder the adolescent's ability to think logically. (objective 10)

Practice Questions II

Multiple-Choice Questions

1. b. is the correct answer. (objective 1)

2. d. is the correct answer. During adolescence, the lymphoid system decreases in size and the heart doubles in size. (objective 3)

3. a. is the correct answer. (video lesson, segment 1; objective 2)

   b. is incorrect. Testosterone increases markedly in boys.

c. is incorrect. Androgen is another name for testosterone.

d. is incorrect. Menarche is the first menstrual period.

4. b. is the correct answer. (objective 1)

5. c. is the correct answer. (video lesson, segment 1; objective 4)

a. is incorrect. Although not a term used in the textbook, a gender-typed trait is one that is typical of one sex but not of the other.

b. is incorrect. Primary sex characteristics are those involving the reproductive organs.

d. is incorrect. This is not a term used by developmental psychologists.

6. a. is the correct answer. (video lesson, segment 1; objective 2)

7. c. is the correct answer. (video lesson, segment 2; objective 6)

a. is incorrect. If the timing of maturation differs substantially from that of the peer group, dissatisfaction is likely; however, this is not the most common source of dissatisfaction in teenage girls.

b. & d. are incorrect. Although teenage girls are more likely than boys to be dissatisfied with certain features, which body parts are troubling varies from girl to girl.

8. b. is the correct answer. (objective 9)

9. a. is the correct answer. (objective 10)

10. c. is the correct answer. (video lesson, segment 1; objective 1)

11. b. is the correct answer. Although the size of the heart increases during puberty, heart rate decreases. (objective 3)

12. d. is the correct answer. (objective 3)

Matching Items

13. b (video lesson, segment 1; objective 1)

14. d (video lesson, segment 1; objective 2)

15. c (video lesson, segment 1; objective 2)

16. e (video lesson, segment 1; objective 2)

17. f (video lesson, segment 1; objective 3)

18. i (video lesson, segment 1; objective 4)

19. a (video lesson, segment 1; objective 1)

20. j (video lesson, segment 1; objective 4)

21. h (video lesson, segment 1; objective 4)

22. g (video lesson, segment 2; objective 6)

Applying Your Knowledge

1. d. is the correct answer. (video lesson, segment 2; objective 6)

a., b., & c. are incorrect. These would likely make matters worse.

2. b. is the correct answer. (objective 2)

a. is incorrect. Because they typically have little body fat, female dancers and athletes menstruate later than average.

c. is incorrect. Delayed maturation in a young dancer or athlete is usually quite normal.

d. is incorrect. The textbook does not indicate that the age of menarche varies with diet.

3. a. is the correct answer. (objective 2)

   b. is incorrect. It usually takes longer than one year for a prepubescent male to catch up with a female who has begun puberty.

   c. is incorrect. This is not true.

   d. is incorrect. The textbook does not suggest that exercise has an effect on the timing of the growth spurt.

4. c. is the correct answer. It is early maturing girls who are often drawn into involvement with older boys. (objective 2)

5. a. is the correct answer. African Americans often begin puberty earlier than Asian Americans or Americans of European ancestry. Furthermore, females who are inactive menstruate earlier than those who are more active. (objective 2)

6. b. is the correct answer. (video lesson, segment 2; objective 3)

   a. is incorrect. Late maturation is typically more difficult for boys than for girls.

   c. is incorrect. Early maturation is generally a positive experience for boys.

   d. is incorrect. Adolescent masturbation is no longer the source of guilt or shame that it once was.

7. d. is the correct answer. Kristin's symptoms are typical of iron-deficiency anemia, which is more common in teenage girls than in any other age group. (objective 8)

8. c. is the correct answer. (objective 2)

   a. is incorrect. Only in girls do estradiol levels rise markedly during puberty.

   b. is incorrect. Only in boys do testosterone levels rise markedly during puberty.

   d. is incorrect. Menarche is the first menstrual period.

9. b. is the correct answer. (video lesson, segment 1; objective 1)

Lesson Review

Lesson 14

Adolescence
Biosocial Development

Please Note: Use this matrix to guide your study and achieve the learning objectives of this lesson. It will also help you to view the video, which defines and demonstrates important concepts and skills as they relate to everyday life.

Learning Objective	Textbook	Course Student Guide	Video Lesson
1. Identify and describe the biological events of puberty.	pp. 381–385	Key Terms: 1, 4, 5, 6, 7, 23; Practice Questions I: 1, 2, 3, 14; Practice Questions II: 1, 4, 10, 13, 19; Applying Your Knowledge: 9.	Segment 1: *Puberty*
2. Identify several factors that influence the onset of puberty, and explain gender differences in the influence of early or late maturation on adolescent development.	pp. 385–389	Key Terms: 5, 6, 7, 8, 9, 10, 11, 12, 13; Practice Questions I: 2, 7, 14; Practice Questions II: 3, 6, 14, 15, 16; Applying Your Knowledge: 2, 3, 4, 5, 8.	Segment 1: *Puberty*
3. Describe the growth spurt experienced during adolescence by both boys and girls, including changes in weight, height, and the body's internal organ system.	pp. 392–394	Key Terms: 17; Practice Questions I: 4, 5, 13; Practice Questions II: 2, 11, 12, 17; Applying Your Knowledge: 6.	Segment 1: *Puberty;* Segment 2: *Body Image*
4. Describe the development of sexual characteristics in males and females during puberty, and describe influences on adolescents' sexual activity.	pp. 394–396	Key Terms: 2, 3, 18, 19; Practice Questions I: 6, 12; Practice Questions II: 5, 18, 20, 21.	Segment 1: *Puberty*
5. Discuss the emotional and psychological impact of pubertal hormones and how this impact has changed over the decades.	p. 383	Key Terms: 8; Practice Questions I: 10.	Segment 1: *Puberty*

Learning Objective	Textbook	Course Student Guide	Video Lesson
6. Describe cultural, social, and individual factors that have an impact on the adolescent's development of a positive body image.	pp. 390–392	Key Terms: 14, 15, 16; Practice Questions I: 8, 15, 16; Practice Questions II: 7, 22; Applying Your Knowledge: 1.	Segment 2: *Body Image*
7. Describe potential sex-related problems in adolescence, including the prevalence and consequences of child sexual abuse.	pp. 396–399	Key Terms: 20, 21; Practice Questions I: 9.	Segment 1: *Puberty*
8. Discuss the nutritional needs and problems of adolescents.	pp. 389–390	Practice Questions I: 11, 17; Applying Your Knowledge: 7.	
9. Discuss the use and abuse of alcohol, tobacco, and other drugs among adolescents today, including prevalence, significance for development, and the best methods of prevention.	pp. 454–458	Key Terms: 22, 24, 25, 26; Practice Questions II: 8.	Segment 3: *Health*
10. Describe brain development during adolescence and explain how it relates to cognition, emotion, and body rhythms.	pp. 400–403	Practice Questions I: 18; Practice Questions II: 9.	

What If?

Lesson 15

Adolescence:
Cognitive Development

Preview

Lesson 15 begins by describing the cognitive advances of adolescence, especially the emerging ability to think in an adult way; that is, to be logical, to think in terms of possibilities, and to reason scientifically and abstractly.

Not all adolescents attain this level of reasoning ability, however, and even those who do spend much of their time thinking at less advanced levels. For instance, adolescents may have difficulty thinking rationally about themselves and their immediate experiences, often seeing themselves as psychologically unique and more socially significant than they really are.

The lesson also addresses the question, "What kind of school best fosters adolescent intellectual growth?" Many adolescents enter secondary school feeling less motivated and more vulnerable to self-doubt than they did in elementary school. The rigid behavioral demands and intensified competition of most secondary schools do not, unfortunately, provide a supportive learning environment for adolescents.

Throughout this lesson, recall your own cognitive development during adolescence. In what ways was your thinking more like an adult's, and in what ways was it still "youthful"? Did you think about yourself, about your interests and your future? Reflect on your experiences in middle and secondary school. Did you get what you consider to be a good education? Why or why not? Was there much academic competition in your school(s)?

Prior Course Knowledge that Will Be Used in this Lesson
- This lesson will return to Piaget's theory of cognitive development (from Lesson 1/Chapter 2). Recall that Piaget's theory specifies four major periods of development, the fourth and final stage being *formal operational thought*:
    1. Sensorimotor (birth to 2 years)
    2. Preoperational (2 to 6 years)
    3. Concrete Operational (7 to 11 years)
    4. **Formal Operational (12 years through adulthood)**

Learning Objectives

Use this information to guide your reading, viewing, thinking, and studying. After successfully completing this lesson, you should be able to:

1. Describe Piaget's concept of formal operational thinking and provide examples of adolescents' emerging ability to reason deductively and inductively.

2. Discuss adolescent egocentrism and give three examples of egocentric fantasies or fables.

3. Describe the concept of person–environment fit, explain how schools can be organized to more effectively meet adolescents' cognitive needs, and identify the main challenges adolescents face in middle school.

4. Describe the major ethnic and cultural factors that can affect adolescent schooling, and discuss factors that influence school engagement.

5. Discuss the dual-process model of adolescent thinking, and describe how it can explain common errors in adolescent reasoning.

📖 **Read Chapter 15, "Adolescence: Cognitive Development," pages 407–431.**

◀◀ **View the video for Lesson 15, "What If?"**

Segment 1: *Formal Operational Thought*

Segment 2: *Educating Adolescents*

Segment 3: *Adolescent Decision-Making*

Summary

The basic skills of thinking, learning, and remembering continue to be refined during the adolescent years. According to most developmentalists, the distinguishing feature of adolescent thought is the capacity to think in terms of possibility rather than only in terms of reality.

Piaget described the reasoning that characterizes adolescence as **formal operational thought**, which arises from maturation and experience. On the whole, adolescents are able to fantasize, speculate, and hypothesize much more readily and on a much grander scale than younger children are. With this capacity for **hypothetical thought**, the adolescent is able to consider the here and now as one among many alternative possibilities. In addition, the capacities for **deductive reasoning** (deriving conclusions from premises) and **inductive reasoning** (reasoning from one or more specific experiences or facts to a general conclusion) become refined.

Developmental psychologists have described **adolescent egocentrism** as a stage of development in which young people typically consider their own psychological experiences (love and anger, for example) to be unique. The **invincibility fable** that they are somehow immune to common dangers and the **personal fable** that their lives are unique or heroic are further examples of adolescents' egocentrism. As another part of their egocentrism, adolescents often create for themselves an **imaginary audience** that allows them to fantasize about how others will react to their appearance and behavior.

With regard to education, the optimum **person–environment fit** depends not only on the individual's developmental stage, cognitive abilities, and learning style, but also on the society's traditions, educational objectives, and future needs, which vary substantially from place to place and from time to time. Many educational settings rely on ego-involvement learning, in which grades are based solely on individual test performance and students are ranked against each other. In such competitive conditions, many students—especially girls and minority students—find it easier and psychologically safer not to compete. Some may perform better in settings based on task-involvement learning, which encourages cooperative (group) learning and measures a student's performance based on his or her mastery of the material.

Because they often think about possibilities rather than practicalities, and because egocentrism makes it difficult to plan ahead, adolescents tend not to make major decisions about their future plans on their own. On matters of personal lifestyle, however, they do make decisions, sometimes ones that involve considerable risk. Because of their sense of personal invincibility, many teens underestimate the chances of getting pregnant or of contracting a **sexually transmitted infection (STI)**. In addition, teens often fail to think through all the possible consequences of their behavior, focusing instead on immediate concerns only. Many school systems have begun to develop sex education programs that encourage thinking, role playing, and discussion about sexuality instead of focusing only on biological facts. Such programs help adolescents to understand and consider the consequences of teen sexual activity and its impact on their future.

Review all reading assignments for this lesson.

As assigned by your instructor, complete the optional online component for this lesson.

Key Terms

Using your own words, write a brief definition or explanation of each of the following terms on a separate piece of paper.

1. adolescent egocentrism
2. personal fable
3. invincibility fable
4. imaginary audience
5. formal operational thought
6. hypothetical thought
7. deductive reasoning
8. inductive reasoning

9. dual-process model
10. intuitive thought
11. analytic thought

12. sunk cost fallacy
13. base rate neglect
14. secondary education
15. middle school
16. cyberbullying
17. cutting
18. high-stakes test
19. PISA (Programme for International Student Assessment)
20. person–environment fit
21. volatile mismatch

Practice Questions I

Multiple-Choice Questions

1. Many psychologists consider the distinguishing feature of adolescent thought to be the ability to think in terms of
   a. moral issues.
   b. concrete operations.
   c. possibility, not just reality.
   d. logical principles.

2. Piaget's last stage of cognitive development is
   a. formal operational thought.
   b. concrete operational thought.
   c. universal ethical principles.
   d. symbolic thought.

3. The adolescent who takes risks and feels immune to the laws of mortality is showing evidence of the
   a. invincibility fable.
   b. personal fable.
   c. imaginary audience.
   d. death instinct.

4. Imaginary audiences, invincibility fables, and personal fables are expressions of adolescent
   a. morality.
   b. thinking games.
   c. decision making.
   d. egocentrism.

5. The typical adolescent is
   a. tough-minded.
   b. indifferent to public opinion.
   c. self-absorbed and hypersensitive to criticism.
   d. all of the above.

6. When adolescents enter secondary school, many
   a. experience a drop in their academic self-confidence.
   b. are less motivated than they were in elementary school.
   c. are less conscientious than they were in elementary school.
   d. experience all of the above.

7. Thinking that begins with a general premise and then draws logical conclusions from it is called
   a. inductive reasoning.
   b. deductive reasoning.
   c. "the game of thinking."
   d. hypothetical reasoning.

8. Serious reflection on important issues is a wrenching process for many adolescents because of their newfound ability to reason
   a. inductively.
   b. deductively.
   c. hypothetically.
   d. symbolically.

9. Many adolescents seem to believe that their own sexual behaviors will not lead to pregnancy. This belief is an expression of the
   a. personal fable.
   b. invincibility fable.
   c. imaginary audience.
   d. "game of thinking."

10. While the United States is increasing the use of high-stakes testing in education, East Asian countries are
    a. testing students on an ever-widening array of subjects.
    b. reducing high-stakes testing and encouraging innovation.
    c. discontinuing the use of high-stakes tests entirely.
    d. doing none of the above.

11. Which of the following characteristics is the most important characteristic to ensure high school graduation?
    a. intelligence
    b. persistence
    c. creativity
    d. social skills

12. The most important relationship for ensuring success during the transition into secondary schooling is that between the student and his or her
    a. coaches.
    b. parents.
    c. teachers.
    d. friends.

True or False Items

Write T (for true) or F (for false) on the line in front of each statement.

13. __T__ Adolescents are generally better able than eight-year-olds at recognizing the validity of arguments that clash with their own beliefs.

14. __F__ Everyone attains the stage of formal operational thought by adulthood.

15. __F__ The transition from primary to secondary school is stressful only when it brings about negative changes in the adolescent's life.

16. __T__ Adolescents often create an imaginary audience as they envision how others will react to their appearance and behavior.

17. __T__ One potential unintended consequence of high-stakes tests is an increase in the high school dropout rate.

18. __F__ Inductive reasoning is a hallmark of formal operational thought.

Practice Questions II

Multiple-Choice Questions

1. Adolescents who fall prey to the invincibility fable may be more likely to
   a. engage in risky behaviors.
   b. suffer from depression.
   c. have low self-esteem.
   d. drop out of school.

2. Thinking that extrapolates from a specific experience to form a general premise is called
   a. inductive reasoning.
   b. deductive reasoning.
   c. "the game of thinking."
   d. hypothetical reasoning.

3. Recent research regarding Piaget's theory has found that
   a. many adolescents arrive at formal operational thinking later than Piaget predicted.
   b. formal operational thinking is more likely to be demonstrated in certain domains than in others.
   c. individuals often demonstrate formal operational thinking in some domains while failing to demonstrate it in other domains.
   d. all of the above are true.

4. When young people overestimate their significance to others, they are displaying
   a. concrete operational thought.
   b. adolescent egocentrism.
   c. a lack of cognitive growth.
   d. immoral development.

5. The personal fable refers to adolescents imagining that
   a. they are immune to the dangers of risky behaviors.
   b. they are always being scrutinized by others.
   c. their own lives are unique, heroic, or even mythical.
   d. the world revolves around their actions.

6. The typical secondary school environment
   a. has more rigid behavioral demands than the average elementary school.
   b. does not meet the cognitive needs of the typical adolescent.
   c. emphasizes ego-involvement learning.
   d. is described by all of the above.

7. As compared to elementary schools, most secondary schools exhibit all of the following **EXCEPT**
   a. a more flexible approach to education.
   b. intensified competition.
   c. more punitive grading practices.
   d. less individualized attention.

8. The belief that time and money should be invested in something simply because time and money have *already* been invested is referred to as
   a. the invincibility fable.
   b. adolescent egocentrism.
   c. analytic reasoning.
   d. the sunk cost fallacy.

9. Which of the following is one of the hallmarks of formal operational thought?
   a. egocentrism
   b. deductive thinking
   c. symbolic thinking
   d. all of the above

10. In explaining adolescent advances in thinking, sociocultural theorists emphasize that these changes
    a. are sudden.
    b. are gradual.
    c. result from a new context.
    d. result from advanced biology.

Matching Items

Match each definition or description with its corresponding term.

Terms

11. ___B___ invincibility fable   16. ___H___ inductive reasoning

12. ___C___ imaginary audience   17. ___F___ formal operational thought

D 13. ___I___ person–environment fit   18. ___D___ volatile mismatch

14. ___E___ hypothetical thought   19. ___A___ adolescent egocentrism

15. ___G___ deductive reasoning

Definitions or Descriptions

a. the tendency of adolescents to focus on themselves to the exclusion of others

b. adolescents feel immune to the consequences of dangerous behavior

c. a creation of adolescents, who are preoccupied with how others react to their appearance and behavior

d. the match or mismatch between an adolescent's needs

e. reasoning about propositions that may or may not reflect reality

f. the last stage of cognitive development, according to Piaget

g. thinking that moves from premise to specific conclusion

h. thinking that moves from a specific experience to a general conclusion

i. a clash between a teenager's needs and the structure

Applying Your Knowledge

1. A 13-year-old can create and solve logical problems on the computer but is not usually reasonable, mature, or consistent in his or her thinking when it comes to people and social relationships. This supports the finding that

   a. some children reach the stage of formal operational thought earlier than others.

   b. the stage of formal operational thought is not attained by age 13.

   c. formal operational thinking may be demonstrated in certain domains and not in other domains.

   d. older adolescents and adults often do poorly on standard tests of formal operational thought.

2. An experimenter hides a ball in her hand and says, "Either the ball in my hand is red or it is not red." Most preadolescent children say

   a. the statement is true.

   b. the statement is false.

   c. they cannot tell if the statement is true or false.

   d. they do not understand what the experimenter means.

3. Fourteen-year-old Monica is very idealistic and often develops crushes on people she doesn't even know. This reflects her newly developed cognitive ability to

   a. deal simultaneously with two sides of an issue.

   b. take another person's viewpoint.

   c. imagine possible worlds and people.

   d. see herself as others see her.

4. Which of the following is the **BEST** example of a personal fable?

   a. Adriana imagines that she is destined for a life of fame and fortune.

   b. Ben makes up stories about his experiences to impress his friends.

   c. Kalil questions his religious beliefs when they seem to offer little help for a problem he faces.

   d. Julio believes that every girl he meets is attracted to him.

5. Which of the following is the **BEST** example of adolescents' ability to think hypothetically?

   a. Twelve-year-old Stanley feels that people are always watching him.

   b. Fourteen-year-old Mindy engages in many risky behaviors, reasoning that "nothing bad will happen to me."

   c. Fifteen-year-old Philip believes that no one understands his problems.

   d. Thirteen-year-old Josh delights in finding logical flaws in virtually everything his teachers and parents say.

6. Frustrated because of the dating curfew her parents have set, Melinda exclaims, "You just don't know how it feels to be in love!" Melinda's thinking demonstrates

   a. the invincibility fable.

   b. the personal fable.

   c. the imaginary audience.

   d. adolescent egocentrism.

7. Compared to her 13-year-old brother, 17-year-old Yolanda is likely to

   a. be more critical about herself.

   b. be more egocentric.

   c. have less confidence in her abilities.

   d. be more capable of reasoning hypothetically.

8. Nathan's fear that his friends will ridicule him because of a pimple that has appeared on his nose reflects a preoccupation with

   a. his personal fable.

   b. the invincibility fable.

   c. an imaginary audience.

   d. preconventional reasoning.

9. Thirteen-year-old Malcolm, who lately is very sensitive to the criticism of others, feels significantly less motivated and capable in middle school than when he was in elementary school. Malcolm is probably

   a. experiencing a sense of vulnerability that is common in adolescents.

   b. a lower-track student.

   c. a student in a task-involvement classroom.

   d. all of the above.

10. In presenting an argument for why her religion is the best, 14-year-old Janice is likely to emphasize _____ thought over _____ thought.

    a. intuitive; analytic

    b. analytic; intuitive

    c. deductive; inductive

    d. inductive; deductive

11. After hearing that an unusually aggressive child has been in full-time day care since he was a toddler, 16-year-old Keenan concludes that nonparental care leads to behavior problems. Keenan's conclusion is an example of

    a. inductive reasoning.

    b. deductive reasoning.

    c. hypothetical thinking.

    d. adolescent egocentrism.

12. In which of the following schools are students likely to feel most engaged?

    a. Adams High School, which has a population of 1,000 students

    b. Jasper High School, where students are encouraged to participate in extracurricular activities

    c. Franklin High School, where most teachers have a graduate degree in the topic they teach

    d. Anderson High School, where students must take an exit exam before they can graduate

Answer Key

Key Terms

1. Adolescent egocentrism refers to the tendency of adolescents to see themselves as much more socially significant than they actually are. (p. 408; video lesson, segment 1; objective 2)

2. Another example of adolescent egocentrism is the personal fable, through which adolescents imagine their own lives as unique, heroic, or even mythical. (p. 409; video lesson, segment 1; objective 2)

   Memory aid: A fable is a mythical story.

3. Adolescents who experience the invincibility fable feel that they are immune to the dangers of risky behaviors. (p. 409; video lesson, segment 1; objective 2)

4. Adolescents often create an imaginary audience for themselves, as they assume that others are as intensely interested in them as they themselves are. (p. 409; video lesson, segment 1; objective 2)

5. In Piaget's theory, the last stage of cognitive development, which arises from a combination of maturation and experience, is called formal operational thought. A hallmark of formal operational thinking is the capacity for hypothetical, logical, and abstract thought. (p. 410; video lesson, segment 1; objective 1)

6. Hypothetical thought involves reasoning about propositions and possibilities that may or may not reflect reality. (p. 411; video lesson, segment 1; objective 1)

7. Deductive reasoning is thinking that moves from the general to the specific, or from a premise to a logical conclusion. (p. 412; video lesson, segment 1; objective 1)

8. Inductive reasoning is thinking that moves from one or more specific experiences to a general conclusion. (p. 412; video lesson, segment 1; objective 1)

9. The dual-process model suggests that there are two thought processes that develop and influence one another: the emotional/intuitive process and the analytical/logical process. (p. 413; objective 5)

10. Intuitive thought is similar to having a "hunch"; it is based more on emotion and experience than on logic. (p. 414; objective 5)

11. Analytic thought stems from the careful and logical analysis of a problem. (p. 414; objective 5)

12. The sunk cost fallacy occurs when we decide to invest time and energy into projects just because we have already invested time and energy in them previously. (p. 415; objective 5)

13. When, during decision-making, a person ignores the overall frequency of a characteristic or behavior, that person is engaging in base rate neglect. (p. 415; objective 5)

14. Secondary education begins after the completion of elementary education. It typically includes middle school and high school. (p. 417; objective 3)

15. Middle schools exist to educate students who have entered adolescence, but are not yet prepared for high school. It usually begins with grade 5 or 6 and ends with grade 8. (p. 418; objective 3)

16. Cyberbullying is a type of bullying that occurs when a person spreads insults or rumors about another person using emails, cell phone videos, or texts. Social networks are another vehicle for cyberbullying. (p. 422; objective 3)

17. Cutting is an addictive form of self-mutilation prevalent among adolescents and associated with depression and drug abuse. (p. 423; objective 3)

18. A high-stakes test is a test that determines whether a student will graduate or be promoted. It is referred to as "high-stakes" because the test is expected to measure whether the student has succeeded or failed in some aspect of his/her education. (p. 424; objective 4)

19. Fifteen-year-olds in 50 countries take the PISA or Programme for International Student Assessment, a test designed to measure problem solving and cognition in daily life. (p. 426; objective 4)

20. The term person–environment fit refers to the best setting for personal growth, as in the optimum educational setting. (video lesson, segment 2; objective 3)

21. When teenagers' individual needs do not match the size, routine, and structure of their schools, a volatile mismatch may occur. (video lesson, segment 2; objective 3)

Practice Questions I

Multiple-Choice Questions

1. c. is the correct answer. (video lesson, segment 1; objective 1)

   a. is incorrect. Although moral reasoning becomes much deeper during adolescence, it is not limited to this stage of development.

   b. & d. are incorrect. Concrete operational thought, which is logical, is the distinguishing feature of childhood thinking.

2. a. is the correct answer. (video lesson, segment 1; objective 1)

   b. is incorrect. In Piaget's theory, this stage precedes formal operational thought.

   c. & d. are incorrect. These are not stages in Piaget's theory.

3. a. is the correct answer. (video lesson, segment 1; objective 2)

   b. is incorrect. This refers to adolescents' tendency to imagine their own lives as unique, heroic, or even mythical.

   c. is incorrect. This refers to adolescents' tendency to fantasize about how others will react to their appearance and behavior.

   d. is incorrect. This is a concept in Freud's theory.

4. d. is the correct answer. These thought processes are manifestations of adolescents' tendency to see themselves as being much more central and important to the social scene than they really are. (video lesson, segment 1; objective 2)

5. c. is the correct answer. (video lesson, segment 1; objective 2)

6. d. is the correct answer. (objective 3)

7. b. is the correct answer. (video lesson, segment 1; objective 1)

   a. is incorrect. Inductive reasoning moves from specific facts to a general conclusion.

   c. & d. are incorrect. The "game of thinking," which is an example of hypothetical reasoning, involves the ability to think creatively about possibilities.

8. c. is the correct answer. (video lesson, segment 3; objective 1)

9. b. is the correct answer. (objective 2)

   a. is incorrect. This refers to adolescents' tendency to imagine their own lives as unique, heroic, or even mythical.

   c. is incorrect. This refers to adolescents' tendency to fantasize about how others will react to their appearance and behavior.

   d. is incorrect. This is the adolescent ability to suspend knowledge of reality in order to think playfully about possibilities.

10. b. is the correct answer. Japanese schools are placing less emphasis on high-stakes testing than they used to. (objective 4)

11. b. is the correct answer. (objective 4)

12. c. is the answer. (objective 3)

True or False Items

13. T   (video lesson, segment 1; objective 1)

14. F   Some people never reach the stage of formal operational thought. (video lesson, segment 1; objective 1)

15. F   Even positive changes during school transition produce stress. (objective 3)

16. T   (video lesson, segment 1; objective 2)

17. T   (objective 4)

18. F   Deductive reasoning is a hallmark of formal operational thought, although adolescents continue to improve their inductive reasoning skills as well. (video lesson, segment 1; objective 1)

Practice Questions II

Multiple-Choice Questions

1. a. is the correct answer. (video lesson, segment 1; objective 2)

   b., c., & d. are incorrect. The invincibility fable leads some teens to believe that they are immune to the dangers of risky behaviors; it is not necessarily linked to depression, low self-esteem, or the likelihood that an individual will drop out of school.

2. a. is the correct answer. (video lesson, segment 1; objective 1)

   b. is incorrect. Deductive reasoning begins with a general premise and then draws logical conclusions from it.

   c. & d. are incorrect. The "game of thinking," which is an example of hypothetical reasoning, involves the ability to think creatively about possibilities.

3. d. is the correct answer. (video lesson, segment 1; objective 1)

4. b. is the correct answer. (video lesson, segment 1; objective 2)

5. c. is the correct answer. (video lesson, segment 1; objective 2)

   a. is incorrect. This describes the invincibility fable.

   b. is incorrect. This describes the imaginary audience.

   d. is incorrect. This describes adolescent egocentrism in general.

6. d. is the correct answer. (objective 3)

7. a. is the correct answer. (objective 3)

8. d. is the correct answer. (objective 5)

9. b. is the correct answer. (video lesson, segment 1; objective 1)

10. c. is the correct answer. (objective 1)

    a., b., & d. are incorrect. These are more likely to be emphasized by information-processing theorists, Piagentian theorists, or epigenetic theorists.

Matching Items

11. b (video lesson, segment 1; objective 2)

12. c (video lesson, segment 1; objective 2)

13. d (video lesson, segment 2; objective 3)

14. e (video lesson, segment 1; objective 1)

15. g (video lesson, segment 1; objective 1)

16. h (video lesson, segment 1; objective 1)

17. f (video lesson, segment 1; objective 1)

18. i (video lesson, segment 2; objective 3)

19. a (video lesson, segment 1; objective 2)

Applying Your Knowledge

1. c. is the correct answer. (video lesson, segment 1; objectives 1 & 5)

2. c. is the correct answer. Although this statement is logically verifiable, preadolescents who lack formal operational thought cannot prove or disprove it. (objective 1)

3. c. is the correct answer. (video lesson, segment 1; objective 1)

4. a. is the correct answer. (video lesson, segment 1; objective 2)

b. & d. are incorrect. These behaviors are more indicative of a preoccupation with the imaginary audience.

c. is incorrect. Kalil's questioning attitude is a normal adolescent tendency that helps foster moral reasoning.

5. d. is the correct answer. (video lesson, segment 1; objective 1)

a. is incorrect. This is an example of the imaginary audience.

b. is incorrect. This is an example of the invincibility fable.

c. is incorrect. This is an example of adolescent egocentrism.

6. d. is the correct answer. (video lesson, segment 1; objective 2)

7. d. is the correct answer. (video lesson, segment 1; objective 1)

8. c. is the correct answer. (video lesson, segment 1; objective 2)

a. is incorrect. In this fable, adolescents see themselves destined for fame and fortune.

b. is incorrect. In this fable, young people feel that they are somehow immune to the consequences of common dangers.

d. is incorrect. This is a stage of moral reasoning in Kohlberg's theory.

9. a. is the correct answer. (objective 3)

10. a. is the correct answer. (objective 5)

11. a. is the correct answer. (objective 1)

b. is incorrect. Keenan is reasoning from the specific to the general, rather than vice versa.

c. is incorrect. Keenan is thinking about an actual observation, rather than a hypothetical possibility.

d. is incorrect. Keenan's reasoning is focused outside himself, rather than being self-centered.

12. b. is the correct answer. (objective 4)

Lesson Review

Lesson 15

Adolescence
Cognitive Development

Please Note: Use this matrix to guide your study and achieve the learning objectives of this lesson. It will also help you to view the video, which defines and demonstrates important concepts and skills as they relate to everyday life.

Learning Objective	Textbook	Course Student Guide	Video Lesson
1. Describe Piaget's concept of formal operational thinking and provide examples of adolescents' emerging ability to reason deductively and inductively.	pp. 410–413	Key Terms: 5, 6, 7, 8; Practice Questions I: 1, 2, 7, 8, 13, 14, 18; Practice Questions II: 2, 3, 9, 10, 14, 15, 16, 17; Applying Your Knowledge: 1, 2, 3, 5, 7, 11.	Segment 1: *Formal Operational Thought* Segment 3: *Adolescent Decision-Making*
2. Discuss adolescent egocentrism and give three examples of egocentric fantasies or fables.	pp. 408–410	Key Terms: 1, 2, 3, 4; Practice Questions I: 3, 4, 5, 9, 16; Practice Questions II: 1, 4, 5, 11, 12, 19; Applying Your Knowledge: 4, 6, 8.	Segment 1: *Formal Operational Thought*
3. Describe the concept of person–environment fit and explain how schools can be organized to more effectively meet adolescents' cognitive needs, and identify the main challenges adolescents face in middle school.	pp. 417–424	Key Terms: 14, 15, 16, 17, 20, 21; Practice Questions I: 6, 12, 15; Practice Questions II: 6, 7, 13, 18; Applying Your Knowledge: 9.	Segment 2: *Educating Adolescents*
4. Describe the major ethnic and cultural factors that can affect adolescent schooling, and discuss factors that influence school engagement.	pp. 424–429	Key Terms: 18, 19; Practice Questions I: 10, 11, 17; Applying Your Knowledge: 12.	
5. Discuss the dual-process model of adolescent thinking, and describe how it can explain common errors in adolescent reasoning.	pp. 413–417	Key Terms: 9, 10, 11, 12, 13; Practice Questions II: 8; Applying Your Knowledge: 1, 10.	Segment 1: *Formal Operational Thought*

Who Am I?

Lesson 16

Adolescence:
Psychosocial Development

Preview

Adolescence brings a heightened quest for self-understanding, a crucial process in the transition from childhood to adulthood. This lesson focuses on the psychosocial development required for attainment of adult status and maturity, particularly the formation of **identity**, which is a consistent definition of one's self. The influences of family, peers, and society on this development are examined in some detail.

During adolescence, biological changes make reproduction possible, and cognitive changes make teenagers more capable of mature decision making. In simpler cultures, the plan of life often allows for an early transition into adult life. But, in technologically advanced societies, a decade of preparation is needed before self-reliance becomes practical. The resulting conflict can be difficult to manage.

This lesson also explores the issue of adolescent suicide and the special problem of adolescent lawbreaking. Suggestions for alleviating or treating these problems are given. While no other period of life except infancy is characterized by so many changes, for most young people, the teenage years are happy ones. In addition, serious problems in adolescence do not necessarily lead to lifelong problems.

As you complete this lesson, consider your own psychosocial development during adolescence. How would you define your identity at that time? What kind of person were you? What was your relationship with your parents like? Was there much friction or bickering? If so, over what kind of issues? Describe your social circles, your peers and friends. Did these people have a positive or negative influence on your development? Did you have any romantic relationships? What were they like? Did you or someone you know ever think about suicide during this time? What were the circumstances? Did you know someone who broke the law or got arrested? What was the situation?

Prior Course Knowledge that Will Be Used in this Lesson

- This lesson will return to Erik Erikson's theory from Lesson 1 that specifies eight stages of *psychosocial development,* each of which is characterized by a particular challenge, or *developmental crisis,* which is central to that stage of life and must be resolved. This lesson will focus on Erikson's fifth stage, called "identity vs. role confusion":

  1. Trust vs. Mistrust (birth to 1 year)
  2. Autonomy vs. Shame and Doubt (1 to 3 years)
  3. Initiative vs. Guilt (3 to 6 years)
  4. Industry vs. Inferiority (7 to 11 years)
  5. **Identity vs. Role Confusion (adolescence)**
  6. Intimacy vs. Isolation (adulthood)
  7. Generativity vs. Stagnation (adulthood)
  8. Integrity vs. Despair (adulthood)

- In a discussion of family influences during adolescence, this lesson will return to the concept of "parenting styles" introduced in Lesson 10. Recall that four basic styles include *authoritarian* (parents expect unquestioning obedience and offer little affection), *permissive* (affectionate but with few demands), *authoritative* (parents expect obedience, set appropriate limits, and offer affection), and *neglectful/uninvolved* (parents seem unaware of what their children are doing).

Learning Objectives

Use this information to guide your reading, viewing, thinking, and studying. After successfully completing this lesson, you should be able to:

1. Define the concept of identity and describe the development of identity during adolescence, incorporating Erikson's crisis of "identity versus role confusion."
2. Describe the five major identity statuses or conditions and give an example of each.
3. Discuss the influence of society and culture on identity formation, and describe the four main domains of identity development.
4. Discuss parent-child relationships during adolescence, including typical conflicts.
5. Discuss the influence of peers, friends, and romantic relationships in adolescence.
6. Discuss the causes and consequences of sadness and anger among adolescents, including the factors that contribute to adolescent suicide.
7. Discuss delinquency among adolescents today, noting its incidence and prevalence, significance for later development, and best approaches for prevention and treatment.
8. Describe adolescents' sexual development, and explain how parents, peers, and schools influence adolescent sexual behavior.

📖 **Read Chapter 16, "Adolescence: Psychosocial Development," pages 433–454.**

⏮ **View the video for Lesson 16, "Who Am I?"**

Segment 1: *Identity*

Segment 2: *Friends and Family*

Summary

Adolescence heightens the search for self-understanding because of the momentous changes that occur during the teenage years. Many adolescents experience the emergence of **possible selves**, or diverse perceptions of identity in different groups or settings.

According to Erik Erikson, the psychosocial challenge of adolescence is **identity versus role confusion**. The specific task of this challenge is the search for identity, both as an individual and as a member of the larger community. The ultimate goal, **identity achievement**, occurs when adolescents establish their own goals and values by abandoning some of those set by parents and society while accepting others.

Some adolescents form an identity prematurely, a process called **foreclosure**. Other adolescents, unable to find alternative roles that are truly their own, simply rebel and become the opposite of what is expected of them, adopting a **negative identity**. Others experience **identity diffusion**, with few commitments to goals or values, whether those of parents, peers, or the larger society. Many adolescents declare an **identity moratorium**, often by using an institutionalized time-out such as college or voluntary military service as a means of postponing final decisions about career or marriage. While identity formation is a major task of adolescence, many people don't reach identity achievement until early adulthood (or later), and most continue to shape and refine their identities throughout the life span.

For immigrants and minority adolescents, identity formation is particularly complex because they must find the right balance between their ethnic background and the values of the society at large. This may cause them to embrace a negative identity or, as is more often the case, to foreclose on identity prematurely.

Research studies demonstrate that the **generation gap** is not as wide as it is popularly assumed to be. Indeed, studies have found substantial agreement between parents and adolescents on political, religious, educational, and vocational opinions and values. However, there are **generational stakes**, which refers to the particular needs and concerns of each generation in the parent–adolescent relationship as well as the natural tendency to see the family in a certain way.

The adolescent's peer group is a social institution that eases the transition from childhood to adulthood by functioning in a variety of ways. Peer groups function as a source of information and social support, a group of contemporaries who are experiencing similar struggles. As adolescents associate themselves with a particular subgroup, peers help them define who they are by helping them define who they are not. Peer groups also serve as a sounding board for exploring and defining one's values and aspirations.

While the search for identity brings with it certain difficulties, most adolescents reach adulthood safe and secure. Others have special problems, including delinquent behavior and depression that may lead to suicide. Thinking about suicide (**suicidal ideation**) is quite common among high school students. Fortunately, most suicide attempts in adolescence do not result in death. Deliberate acts of self-destruction that do not cause death are referred to as **parasuicide**. Whether or not suicidal ideation leads to parasuicide or suicide depends on **parental monitoring**, the availability of lethal methods, the use of alcohol and other drugs, and the attitudes about suicide held by the adolescent's family, friends, and culture.

📖 **Review all reading assignments for this lesson.**

💻 **As assigned by your instructor, complete the optional online component for this lesson.**

Key Terms

Using your own words, write a brief definition or explanation of each of the following terms on a separate piece of paper.

1. identity versus role confusion
2. identity achievement
3. role confusion
4. foreclosure
5. moratorium
6. gender identity
7. bickering
8. parental monitoring
9. peer pressure
10. clique
11. crowd
12. deviancy training
13. sexual orientation
14. clinical depression
15. rumination
16. suicidal ideation
17. parasuicide
18. cluster suicides
19. life-course-persistent offender
20. adolescent-limited offender
21. identity
22. possible selves
23. negative identity
24. generation gap
25. generational stakes

Practice Questions I

Multiple-Choice Questions

1. According to Erikson, the primary task of adolescence is that of establishing
   a. basic trust.
   b. an identity.
   c. intimacy.
   d. integrity.

2. According to developmentalists who study identity formation, foreclosure involves
   a. accepting an identity prematurely, without exploration.
   b. taking time off from school, work, and other commitments.
   c. opposing parental values.
   d. failing to commit oneself to a vocational goal.

3. When adolescents adopt an identity that is the opposite of the one they are expected to adopt, they are considered to be taking on a
   a. foreclosed identity.
   b. diffused identity.
   c. negative identity.
   d. reverse identity.

4. The main sources of emotional support for most young people who are establishing independence from their parents are
   a. older adolescents of the opposite sex.
   b. older siblings.
   c. teachers.
   d. peer groups.

5. For members of minority ethnic groups, identity achievement may be particularly complicated because

    a. their cultural ideal clashes with the Western emphasis on adolescent self-determination.

    b. democratic ideology espouses a color-blind, multiethnic society in which background is irrelevant.

    c. parents and other relatives tend to emphasize ethnicity and expect teens to honor their roots.

    d. of all of the above reasons.

6. In a crime-ridden neighborhood, parents can protect their adolescents by keeping close watch over activities, friends, and so on. This practice is called

    a. generational stake.

    b. foreclosure.

    c. peer screening.

    d. parental monitoring.

7. Increased parental-adolescent conflict is likely to occur in _____ and to center on issues of _____.

    a. early adolescence; morality

    b. late adolescence; self-discipline

    c. early adolescence; self-control

    d. late adolescence; politics

8. Which of the following did Erikson identify as an area of identity development?

    a. political identity

    b. religious identity

    c. sexual/gender identity

    d. all of the above

9. Suicide is _____ common among adults than adolescents. Parasuicide is _____ common among adults than adolescents.

    a. less; less

    b. more; less

    c. less; more

    d. more; more

10. The early signs of life-course-persistent offenders include all of the following **EXCEPT**

    a. signs of brain damage early in life.

    b. antisocial school behavior.

    c. delayed sexual intimacy.

    d. use of alcohol and tobacco at an early age.

11. Regarding gender differences in self-destructive acts, the rate of parasuicide is
    _____ and the rate of suicides _____.
    a. higher in males; higher in females
    b. higher in females; higher in males
    c. the same in males and females; higher in males
    d. the same in males and females; higher in females

12. Conflict between parents and adolescent offspring is
    a. most likely to involve fathers and their late-maturing sons.
    b. more frequent in single-parent homes.
    c. more likely to involve mothers and daughters.
    d. not likely in any of the above situations.

13. Compared to adolescents 10 years ago, teens today
    a. have sex with more partners.
    b. are more likely to become pregnant.
    c. are more likely to use contraception.
    d. are more influenced by biology.

True or False Items

Write T (for true) or F (for false) on the line in front of each statement.

14. __T__ Both gay men and lesbian women report realizing their sexual
    orientation during adolescence. _during emerging adulthood_

15. __F__ Most adolescents have political views and educational values that
    are markedly different from those of their parents.

16. __F__ Peer pressure is inherently destructive to the adolescent seeking an
    identity.

17. __T__ For most adolescents, group socializing and dating precede the
    establishment of true intimacy with one member of the opposite sex.

18. __F__ Most adolescent self-destructive acts are a response to an
    immediate and specific psychological blow.

19. __T__ The rate of youth suicide in the United States has doubled since 1960.

20. __T__ In finding themselves, teens try to find an identity that is stable,
    consistent, and mature.

21. __F__ Parents who exert extreme psychological control over their teens
    have the most successful adolescents.

22. __T__ Completed suicides are more common among boys.

Practice Questions II

Multiple-Choice Questions

1. Which of the following was **NOT** identified as a factor that influences the likelihood of parasuicide or suicide?
   a. availability of lethal means
   b. lack of parental supervision
   c. use of alcohol and other drugs
   d. increased arguing with parents

2. Sex education in U.S. schools
   a. typically provides referrals for STI treatment.
   b. encourages increased sexual activity.
   c. often encourage abstinence.
   d. is rarely presented in classrooms.

3. The adolescent experiencing identity diffusion is typically
   a. very apathetic.
   b. a risk-taker, anxious to experiment with alternative identities.
   c. willing to accept parental values wholesale, without exploring alternatives.
   d. one who rebels against all forms of authority.

4. Crime statistics show that during adolescence
   a. males and females are equally likely to be arrested.
   b. males are more likely to be arrested than females.
   c. females are more likely to be arrested than males.
   d. males commit more crimes than females but are less likely to be arrested.

5. Which of the following is the most common problem among adolescents?
   a. pregnancy
   b. daily use of illegal drugs
   c. minor law-breaking
   d. attempts at suicide

6. A period during which a young person experiments with different identities, postponing important choices, is called a(n)
   a. identity foreclosure.
   b. negative identity.
   c. identity diffusion.
   d. identity moratorium.

7. When adolescents' political, religious, educational, and vocational opinions are compared with those held by their own parents, the so-called "generation gap" is

   (a.) much smaller than when the younger and older generations are compared overall.

   b. much wider than when the younger and older generations are compared overall.

   c. wider between parents and sons than between parents and daughters.

   d. wider between parents and daughters than between parents and sons.

8. Parent-teen conflict tends to center on issues related to

   a. politics and religion.

   b. education.

   c. vacations.

   (d.) daily details, such as musical tastes.

9. Researchers have found that among high school students, suicidal ideation is

   (a.) not as common among high school students as is popularly believed.

   b. more common among males than females.

   c. more common among females than among males.

   d. so common among high school students that it might be considered normal.

10. The best way to limit adolescent law-breaking in general would be to

   (a.) strengthen the family, school, and community fabric.

   b. increase the number of police officers in the community.

   c. improve the criminal justice system.

   d. establish rehabilitative facilities for law-breakers.

11. Adolescents help each other in many ways, including the development of

   a. identity.

   b. independence.

   c. social skills.

   (d.) all of the above.

Matching Items

Match each definition or description with its corresponding term.

Terms

12. ___G___ identity achievement   17. ___D___ generation gap

13. ___A___ foreclosure   18. ___I___ generational stake

14. ___J___ negative identity   19. ___F___ parental monitoring

15. ___C___ identity diffusion   20. ___B___ suicidal ideation

16. ___H___ identity moratorium   21. ___E___ parasuicide

Definitions or Descriptions

a. premature identity formation

b. contemplation of suicide

c. the adolescent has few commitments to goals or values

d. differences between the younger and older generations
e. self-destructive act that does not result in death
f. awareness of where children are and what they are doing
g. an individual's self-definition
h. a period during which adolescents experiment with alternative identities
i. family members in different developmental stages see the family in different ways
j. an identity opposite of the one an adolescent is expected to adopt

Applying Your Knowledge

1. From childhood, Sharon thought she wanted to follow in her mother's footsteps and be a homemaker. Now, at age 40 with a home and family, she admits to herself that what she really wanted to be was a medical researcher. Erik Erikson would probably say that Sharon

   a. adopted a negative identity when she was a child.
   b. experienced identity foreclosure at an early age.
   c. never progressed beyond the obvious identity diffusion she experienced as a child.
   d. took a moratorium from identity formation.

2. Fifteen-year-old David is rebelling against his devoutly religious parents by taking drugs, stealing, and engaging in other antisocial behaviors. Evidently, David has

   a. foreclosed on his identity.
   b. declared an identity moratorium.
   c. adopted a negative identity.
   d. experienced identity diffusion.

3. Fourteen-year-old Sean, who is fiercely proud of his Irish heritage, is prejudiced against members of several other ethnic groups. It is likely that, in forming his identity, Sean

   a. attained identity achievement.
   b. foreclosed on his identity.
   c. declared a lengthy moratorium.
   d. experienced identity diffusion.

4. An adolescent exaggerates the importance of differences in her values and those of her parents. Her parents see these differences as smaller and less important. This phenomenon is called the

   a. generation gap.
   b. generational stake.
   c. family enigma.
   d. parental imperative.

5. In our society, the most obvious examples of institutionalized moratoria on identity formation are

   a. the Boy Scouts and the Girl Scouts.
   b. college and the peacetime military.
   c. marriage and divorce.
   d. bar mitzvahs and baptisms.

6. First-time parents Norma and Norman are worried that, during adolescence, their healthy parental influence will be undone as their children are encouraged by peers to become sexually promiscuous, drug-addicted, or delinquent. Their wise neighbor, who is a developmental psychologist, tells them that

   a. during adolescence, peers are generally more likely to complement the influence of parents than they are to pull their friends in the opposite direction.
   b. research suggests that peers provide a negative influence in every major task of adolescence.
   c. only through authoritarian parenting can parents give children the skills they need to resist peer pressure.
   d. unless their children show early signs of learning difficulties or antisocial behavior, parental monitoring is unnecessary.

7. Thirteen-year-old Cassandra is constantly experimenting with different behaviors and possible identities. It is likely that she

   a. has low self-esteem.
   b. foreclosed prematurely on her identity.
   c. has great self-understanding.
   d. comes from a home environment in which there is considerable tension and conflict.

8. In forming an identity, the young person seeks to make meaningful connections with his or her past. This seeking is described as an unconscious striving for

   a. individual uniqueness.
   b. peer-group membership.
   c. continuity of experience.
   d. vocational identity.

9. Ray was among the first of his friends to have sex, drink alcohol, and smoke cigarettes. These attributes, together with his having been hyperactive and having poor emotional control, would suggest that Ray is at high risk of

   a. becoming an adolescent-limited offender.
   b. becoming a life-course-persistent offender.
   c. developing an antisocial personality.
   d. foreclosing his identity prematurely.

10. Carl is a typical sixteen-year-old adolescent who has no special problems. It is likely that Carl has

    a. contemplated suicide.
    b. engaged in some minor illegal act.
    c. struggled with "who he is."
    d. done all of the above.

11. Coming home from work, Malcolm hears a radio announcement warning parents to be alert for possible cluster suicide signs in their teenage children. What might have precipitated such an announcement?

    a. government statistics that suicide has been on the rise since the 1990s

    b. the highly publicized suicide of a famous rock singer

    c. the recent crash of an airliner, killing all on board

    d. any of the above

Answer Key

Key Terms

1. Erikson's term for the psychosocial crisis of adolescence, identity versus role confusion, refers to adolescents' need to combine their self-understanding and social roles into a coherent identity. (p. 434; video lesson, segment 1; objective 1)

2. In Erikson's theory, identity achievement occurs when adolescents attain their new identity by establishing their own goals and values and abandoning some of those set by their parents and culture and accepting others. (p. 434; video lesson, segment 1; objective 2)

3. Adolescents who experience identity diffusion, according to Erikson, have few commitments to goals or values and are often apathetic about trying to find an identity. (p. 434; video lesson, segment 1; objective 2)

4. In identity foreclosure, according to Erikson, the adolescent forms an identity prematurely, accepting earlier roles and parental values wholesale, without truly forging a unique personal identity. (p. 434; video lesson, segment 1; objective 2)

5. According to Erikson, in the process of finding a mature identity, many young people seem to declare an identity moratorium, a kind of time-out during which they experiment with alternative identities without trying to settle on any one. (p. 434; video lesson, segment 1; objective 2)

6. Gender identity is a person's self-identification of being female or male, including the roles and behaviors that society assigns to that sex. (p. 436; objective 3)

7. Bickering refers to the repeated, petty arguing that typically occurs in early adolescence about common, daily life activities. (p. 437; objective 4)

8. Parental monitoring is parental watchfulness about where one's child is and what he or she is doing, and with whom. (p. 440; objective 4)

9. Peer pressure refers to the social pressure to conform to one's friends in behavior, dress, and attitude. It may be positive or negative in its effects. (p. 442; video lesson, segment 2; objective 5)

10. A small group of close friends who are loyal to each other and exclude outsiders is referred to as a clique. (p. 443; objective 5)

11. A large group of individuals who have something in common (e.g., they are all members of sports teams) is referred to as a crowd. Members of a crowd may or may not be friends. (p. 443; objective 5)

12. Deviancy training is negative support provided among friends, encouraging dangerous, antisocial, or otherwise maladapative behavior. (p. 443; objective 5)

13. An individual's sexual orientation is based on whether they are romantically attached to the same sex, opposite sex, or both sexes. (p. 446; objective 3)

14. Clinical depression is defined by overwhelming feelings of sadness and worthlessness that last for at least two weeks. (p. 449; objective 6)

15. Rumination occurs when we think or talk about the same (usually negative) experience over and over again, which can lead to feelings of depression. (p. 449; objective 6)

16. Suicidal ideation refers to thinking about committing suicide, usually with some serious emotional and intellectual overtones. (p. 449; objective 6)

17. Parasuicide is a deliberate act of self-destruction that does not result in death. (p. 450; objective 6)

18. A cluster suicide refers to a series of suicides or suicide attempts that are precipitated by one initial suicide, usually that of a famous person or a well-known peer. (p. 452; objective 6)

19. Life-course-persistent offenders are adolescent lawbreakers who later become career criminals. (p. 453; objective 7)

20. Adolescent-limited offenders are juvenile delinquents, whose criminal activity stops by age 21. (p. 453; objective 7)

21. Identity, as used by Erikson, refers to a person's self-definition as a separate individual in terms of roles, attitudes, beliefs, and aspirations. (video lesson, segment 1; objective 1)

22. Many adolescents try out possible selves, or variations on who they are and who they might like to become. (video lesson, segment 1; objective 1)

23. Adolescents who take on a negative identity, according to Erikson, adopt an identity that is the opposite of the one they are expected to adopt. (video lesson, segment 1; objective 2)

24. The generation gap refers to the alleged distance between generations in values, behaviors, and knowledge. (video lesson, segment 2; objective 4)

25. Generational stakes is a term that refers to the tendency of each family member, because of that person's different developmental stage, to see the family in a certain way. (video lesson, segment 2; objective 4)

Practice Questions I

Multiple-Choice Questions

1. b. is the correct answer. (video lesson, segment 1; objective 1)

   a. is incorrect. According to Erikson, this is the crisis of infancy.

   c. & d. are incorrect. In Erikson's theory, these crises occur later in life.

2. a. is the correct answer. (video lesson, segment 1; objective 2)

   b. is incorrect. This describes an identity moratorium.

   c. is incorrect. This describes a negative identity.

   d. is incorrect. This describes identity diffusion.

3. c. is the correct answer. (video lesson, segment 1; objective 2)

4. d. is the correct answer. (video lesson, segment 2; objective 5)

5. d. is the correct answer. (video lesson, segments 1 & 2; objective 3)

6. d. is the correct answer. (objective 4)

   a. is incorrect. The generational stake refers to differences in how family members from different generations view the family.

   b. is incorrect. Foreclosure refers to the premature establishment of identity.

   c. is incorrect. Peer screening is an aspect of parental monitoring, but it was not specifically discussed in the text.

7. c. is the correct answer. (video lesson, segment 2; objective 4)

8. d. is the correct answer. (objective 3)

   b. is incorrect. This was not discussed in the textbook.

   c. is incorrect. This is true of girls.

9. b. is the correct answer. (objective 6)

10. c. is the correct answer. Most life-course-persistent offenders are among the earliest of their cohort to have sex. (objective 7)

11. b. is the correct answer. (objective 6)

12. c. is the correct answer. (objective 4)

   a. is incorrect. In fact, parent-child conflict is more likely to involve mothers and their early maturing offspring.

13. c. is the correct answer. (objective 8)

True or False Items

14. F   Gay men reporting knowing their sexual orientation around the age of 11, but lesbian women most often report realizing their sexual orientation during the years of emerging adulthood. (objective 8)

15. F   Numerous studies have shown substantial agreement between parents and their adolescent children on political opinions and educational values. (video lesson, segment 2; objective 4)

16. F   Just the opposite is true. (video lesson, segment 2; objective 5)

17. T   (video lesson, segment 2; objective 5)

18. T   (objective 6)

19. T   (objective 6)

20. T   (objective 1)

21. F   (objective 4)

22. T   (objective 6)

Practice Questions II

Multiple-Choice Questions

1. d. is the correct answer. (objective 6)

2. c. is the correct answer. For this reason, autonomy in their offspring tends to be delayed. (objective 8)

3. a. is the correct answer. (video lesson, segment 1; objective 2)

   b. is incorrect. This describes an adolescent undergoing an identity moratorium.

   c. is incorrect. This describes identity foreclosure.

   d. is incorrect. This describes an adolescent who is adopting a negative identity.

4. b. is the correct answer. (objective 7)

5. c. is the correct answer. (objective 7)

6. d. is the correct answer. (video lesson, segment 1; objective 2)

   a. is incorrect. Identity foreclosure occurs when the adolescent prematurely adopts an identity, without fully exploring alternatives.

   b. is incorrect. Adolescents who adopt an identity that is opposite to the one they are expected to develop have taken on a negative identity.

   c. is incorrect. Identity diffusion occurs when the adolescent is apathetic and has few commitments to goals or values.

7. a. is the correct answer. (video lesson, segment 2; objective 4)

8. d. is the correct answer. (objective 4)

a., b., & c. are incorrect. In fact, on these issues parents and teenagers tend to show substantial agreement.

9. d. is the correct answer. (objective 6)

10. a. is the correct answer. (objective 7)

11. d. is the correct answer. (objective 5)

Matching Items

12. g (video lesson, segment 1; objective 1)

13. a (video lesson, segment 1; objective 2)

14. j (video lesson, segment 1; objective 2)

15. c (video lesson, segment 1; objective 2)

16. h (video lesson, segment 1; objective 2)

17. d (video lesson, segment 2; objective 4)

18. i (video lesson, segment 2; objective 4)

19. f (objective 4)

20. b (objective 6)

21. e (objective 6)

Applying Your Knowledge

1. b. is the correct answer. Apparently, Sharon never explored alternatives or truly forged a unique personal identity. (video lesson, segment 1; objective 2)

a. is incorrect. Individuals who rebel by adopting an identity that is the opposite of the one they are expected to adopt have taken on a negative identity.

c. is incorrect. Individuals who experience identity diffusion have few commitments to goals or values. This was not Sharon's problem.

d. is incorrect. Had she taken a moratorium on identity formation, Sharon would have experimented with alternative identities and perhaps would have chosen that of a medical researcher.

2. c. is the correct answer. (video lesson, segment 1; objective 2)

3. b. is the correct answer. (video lesson, segment 1; objective 2)

a. is incorrect. Identity achievers often have a strong sense of ethnic identification but usually are low in prejudice.

c. & d. is incorrect. The textbook does not present research that links ethnic pride and prejudice with either identity diffusion or moratorium.

4. b. is the correct answer. (video lesson, segment 2; objective 4)

a. is incorrect. The generation gap refers to actual differences in attitudes and values between the younger and older generations. This example is concerned with how large these differences are perceived to be.

c. & d. is incorrect. These terms are not used in the textbook in discussing family conflict.

5. b. is the correct answer. (objective 2)

6. a. is the correct answer. (video lesson, segment 2; objective 5)

b. is incorrect. In fact, just the opposite is true.

c. is incorrect. Developmentalists recommend authoritative, rather than authoritarian, parenting.

d. is incorrect. Parental monitoring is important for all adolescents.

7. c. is the correct answer. (video lesson, segment 1; objective 1)

a., b., & d. are incorrect. Experimenting with possible selves is a normal sign of adolescent identity formation.

8. c. is the correct answer. (objective 1)

9. b. is the correct answer. (objective 7)

10. d. is the correct answer. (objectives 1, 6, & 7)

11. b. is the correct answer. (objective 6)

a., c., & d. are incorrect. Cluster suicides occur when the suicide of a well-known person leads others to attempt suicide.

Lesson Review

Lesson 16

Adolescence
Psychosocial Development

Please Note: Use this matrix to guide your study and achieve the learning objectives of this lesson. It will also help you to view the video, which defines and demonstrates important concepts and skills as they relate to everyday life.

Learning Objective	Textbook	Course Student Guide	Video Lesson
1. Define the concept of identity and describe the development of identity during adolescence, incorporating Erikson's crisis of "identity versus role confusion."	pp. 434–437	Key Terms: 1, 21, 22; Practice Questions I: 1, 20; Practice Questions II: 12; Applying Your Knowledge: 7, 8, 10.	Segment 1: *Identity*
2. Describe the five major identity statuses or conditions and give an example of each one.	p. 434	Key Terms: 2, 3, 4, 5, 23; Practice Questions I: 2, 3; Practice Questions II: 3, 6, 13, 14, 15, 16; Applying Your Knowledge: 1, 2, 3, 5.	Segment 1: *Identity*
3. Discuss the influence of society and culture on identity formation, and describe the four main domains of identity development.	pp. 435–437	Key Terms: 6, 13; Practice Questions I: 5, 8.	Segment 1: *Identity;* Segment 2: *Friends and Family*
4. Discuss parent-child relationships during adolescence, including typical conflicts.	pp. 437–441	Key Terms: 7, 8, 24, 25; Practice Questions I: 6, 7, 12, 15, 21; Practice Questions II: 7, 8, 17, 18, 19; Applying Your Knowledge: 4.	Segment 2: *Friends and Family*
5. Discuss the influence of peers, friends, and romantic relationships in adolescence.	pp. 442–447	Key Terms: 9, 10, 11, 12; Practice Questions I: 4, 16, 17; Practice Questions II: 11; Applying Your Knowledge: 6.	Segment 2: *Friends and Family*

Learning Objective	Textbook	Course Student Guide	Video Lesson
6. Discuss the causes and consequences of sadness and anger among adolescents, including the factors that contribute to adolescent suicide.	pp. 449–452	Key Terms: 14, 15, 16, 17, 18; Practice Questions I: 9, 11, 18, 19, 22; Practice Questions II: 1, 9, 20, 21; Applying Your Knowledge: 10, 11.	
7. Discuss delinquency among adolescents today, noting its incidence and prevalence, significance for later development, and best approaches for prevention and treatment.	pp. 452–454	Key Terms: 19, 20; Practice Questions I: 10; Practice Questions II: 4, 5, 10; Applying Your Knowledge: 9, 10.	
8. Describe adolescents' sexual development, and explain how parents, peers, and schools influence adolescent sexual behavior.	pp. 447–448	Practice Questions I: 13, 14; Practice Questions II: 2.	

Choices

Lesson 17

Early Adulthood:
Biosocial Development

Preview

In this lesson, we encounter the developing person in the prime of life. The early adult years, called **emerging adulthood,** are the best time for hard physical labor—because strength is at a peak—and for reproduction—because overall health is good and fertility is generally high. With the attainment of full maturity, however, a new aspect of physical development comes into play—that is, decline. Lesson 17 takes a look at how people perceive changes that occur as the body ages as well as how lifestyle choices can affect the course of their overall development.

The lesson begins with a description of the growth, strength, and health of the individual during adulthood—both visible age-related changes, such as wrinkling, and less obvious changes, such as declines in the efficiency of the body's systems. Sexual-reproductive health, a matter of great concern to young, emerging adults, is also discussed, with particular attention paid to trends in sexual responsiveness during adulthood and fertility problems that may develop. The final section looks at three problems that are more prevalent during emerging adulthood than at any other period of the life span: drug abuse, compulsive eating and destructive dieting, and violence.

As you complete this lesson, consider some of your own biophysical changes during adulthood. Has (or did) your body become stronger, more capable of extended activity? If you're old enough, when did you first notice signs of aging, such as wrinkles, declines in eyesight, graying hair, or a reduction in energy or endurance? Has anyone you know had trouble conceiving a child? What were the circumstances? Think of an emerging adult you know—yourself or someone else. Consider the use of alcohol, cigarettes, and other drugs during this time. Do you know anyone who has abused these substances? What effect has this had on his or her health? Has anyone you know developed an eating disorder? Did she/he seek treatment?

Prior Course Knowledge that Will Be Used in This Lesson

- This lesson will return to the subject of drug use, drug abuse, and drug addiction introduced in Lesson 14 (Adolescence: Biosocial Development). Most of those who use drugs begin in adolescence. This use tends to increase through a person's mid-20s, then decreases with age and maturity.

- Recall the concept of *body image* (also from Lesson 14). If a person has a distorted view of his or her appearance, serious eating disorders can result. These disorders often have their start in late adolescence and—if not treated—worsen in early adulthood.

Learning Objectives

Use this information to guide your reading, viewing, thinking, and studying. After successfully completing this lesson, you should be able to:

1. Describe the changes in growth, strength, and overall health that occur during early adulthood.
2. Discuss changes in the efficiency of various body functions and physical appearance, focusing on the significance of these changes for the individual.
3. Identify age-related trends in the norms for sexual activity, and describe potential consequences of sexual activity during emerging adulthood.
4. Discuss changes in substance abuse during early adulthood, and describe the causes and consequences of this abuse.
5. Identify common patterns of nutrition and exercise in emerging adulthood.
6. Describe the typical victims of anorexia nervosa and bulimia nervosa, and discuss possible explanations for these disorders.
7. Explain how social norms and gender socialization may be related to self-destructive behavior among emerging adults.
8. Discuss the factors that may determine whether a young male adult will suffer a violent death.
9. Explain why emerging adults have higher rates of mood disorders, anxiety disorders, and other psychological disorders than older adults.

📖 **Read Chapter 17, "Emerging Adulthood: Biosocial Development," pages 463–489.**

⏮ **View the video for Lesson 17, "Choices"**

Segment 1: *Growth, Strength, and Health*

Segment 2: *Health Problems*

Segment 3: *Gender Socialization and Violence*

Summary

In terms of overall health, the years of **emerging adulthood** are the prime of life. While signs of decline appear in every body system, most changes go unnoticed because physical strength and **organ reserve** are at a peak. Even athletic performance can remain high.

Biosocial development during early adulthood is not without potential problems, however. For example, drug abuse, eating disorders, and violent death are more likely during early adulthood than at any other time. A genetic temperament that includes attraction to excitement, intolerance of frustration, vulnerability to depression, and a social context that encourages drug use and abuse are major factors in determining an individual's propensity to use and respond to a given drug. Fortunately, many young adults stop abusing alcohol and illicit drugs before middle age, partly because their social context changes and partly because they become more mature.

Cultural norms and the specifics of the social context may undermine the body's natural tendency to maintain a healthy weight. Some dieters, especially those who are young and well educated, develop an obsession with food and weight control that turns into a serious eating disorder. **Anorexia nervosa** and **bulimia nervosa** can be life threatening. Young college women are especially likely to diet, take diet pills, binge, and purge.

Stereotypes about "masculine" behavior may promote violent death through suicide, homicide, and fatal accidents, particularly in young adult men. While genetic factors are important causes of masculine violence, researchers believe that social factors are at the root of the problem. Living up to the ideals of masculinity makes it hard for young men to avoid conflicts, back away from challenges, or admit that they need help.

Review all reading assignments for this lesson.

As assigned by your instructor, complete the optional online component for this lesson.

Key Terms

Using your own words, write a brief definition or explanation of each of the following terms on a separate piece of paper.

1. emerging adulthood
2. senescence
3. homeostasis
4. organ reserve
5. diathesis-stress model
6. hikikomori
7. set point
8. edgework
9. extreme sports
10. social norms approach
11. gender socialization

Practice Questions I

Multiple-Choice Questions

1. Senescence refers to
   a. a loss of efficiency in the body's regulatory systems.
   b. age-related decline.
   c. decreased physical strength.
   d. vulnerability to disease.

2. When do noticeable increases in height stop?
   a. at about the same age in men and women
   b. at an earlier age in women than in men
   c. at an earlier age in men than in women
   d. There is such diversity in physiological development that it is impossible to generalize regarding this issue

3. A difference between men and women during early adulthood is that men have
   a. a higher percentage of body fat.
   b. lower metabolism.
   c. proportionately more muscle.
   d. greater organ reserve.

4. The majority of young adults rate their own health as
   a. very good or excellent.
   b. average or fair.
   c. poor.
   d. worse than it was during adolescence.

5. The automatic adjustment of the body's systems to keep physiological functions in a state of equilibrium, even during heavy exertion, is called
   a. organ reserve.
   b. homeostasis.
   c. stress.
   d. muscle capacity.

6. Which of the following temperamental characteristics was **NOT** identified as being associated with a tendency to seek out risks?
   a. being male
   b. having a predisposition to be impulsive
   c. being extroverted
   d. being an emerging adult

7. Regarding sex, most emerging adults believe that
   a. extramarital sex is acceptable.
   b. marriage is not an important goal for their future.
   c. there is nothing wrong with premarital sex.
   d. all of the above statements are true.

8. Serial monogamy
   a. is practiced by most emerging adults in the United States.
   b. is rare among emerging adults in European nations.
   c. prevents emotional entanglements resulting from casual sex.
   d. helps explain decreasing rates of sexually transmitted infections.

9. Which of the following is a reason why emerging adults engage in sexual activity?
   a. for recreation
   b. for reproduction
   c. to enhance a relationship
   d. all of the above

10. A 50-year-old woman can expect to retain what percentage of her strength at age 20?
   a. 25
   b. 50
   c. 75
   d. 90

11. According to sociocultural explanations, the development of eating disorders such as anorexia nervosa is encouraged by
   a. societal pressures to be thin.
   b. evolutionary pressures to reproduce.
   c. the rising rates of obesity.
   d. conflict with mothers.

12. Compared to older adults, the rate of psychological disorders in emerging adults is
   a. lower.
   b. higher.
   c. about the same.
   d. more dependent on body image.

13. Which of the following was **NOT** suggested as a reason for the high rate of drug use and abuse during emerging adulthood?
   a. Young adults tend to ignore the lesson learned about drug use and abuse from older generations.
   b. Young adults are trying to imitate their parents' behavior.
   c. Young adults may use drugs as a way of relieving job or educational stress.
   d. Young adults enjoy living on the edge.

True or False Items

Write T (for true) or F (for false) on the line in front of each statement.

T 14. F Conditioned older athletes can perform much better than unconditioned younger persons.

15. T Few adults actually use all the muscle capacity that they could develop during young adulthood.

16. T The older a person is, the more likely they are to notice declines in homeostasis and organ reserve.

17. T Community-implemented designs, such as walkways, encourage more exercise and contribute to greater health among residents.

18. F Adolescents use and abuse drugs more than emerging adults.

19. F The incidence of sexually transmitted disease is lower than ever before.

F 20. T Most young adults rate their health as average or below average.

21. T College women and athletes are at particular risk for eating disorders.

22. T A healthy BMI is somewhere between 19 and 25.

23. T Young adult males are more likely to die in an accident than from a disease.

Practice Questions II

Multiple-Choice Questions

1. The early 20s are the peak years for
   a. hard physical work.
   b. problem-free reproduction.
   c. athletic performance.
   d. all of the above.

2. Of the fatal diseases, _____ is the leading cause of death in young adults.
   a. heart disease
   b. cancer
   c. diabetes
   d. multiple sclerosis

3. The main reason why emerging adults exercise is
   a. to maintain health.
   b. to maintain appearance.
   c. to avoid cancer.
   d. out of enjoyment.

4. The efficiency of the lungs

   a. remains stable throughout the 20s.
   b. begins to decline during the 20s.
   c. begins to decline during the 30s.
   d. declines significantly at about age 30.

5. Normally, the average resting heart rate for both men and women
   a. declines noticeably during the 30s.
   b. declines much faster than does the average maximum heart rate.
   c. reaches a peak at about age 30.
   d. remains stable until late adulthood.

6. Compared to older adult, emerging adults
   a. walk more.
   b. drive more.
   c. eat more fast food.
   d. eat fewer vegetables.

7. Which of the following is **NOT** a characteristic of sexual behavior in young adulthood?
   a. fewer orgasms
   b. strong sex drive
   c. high fertility
   d. high testosterone

8. The typical bulimic patient is a

   a. college-age woman.
   b. woman who starves herself to the point of emaciation.
   c. woman in her late 40s.
   d. woman who suffers from life-threatening obesity.

9. A diagnosis of anorexia nervosa may be warranted if a woman
   a. intensely fears gaining weight.
   b. has a disturbed body perception.
   c. does not menstruate.
   d. experiences all of the above.

10. Relative to all other age groups, young adult males are at increased risk for virtually every kind of
    a. eating disorder.
    b. violence.
    c. acute disease.
    d. chronic disease.

11. The heaviest use of most drugs in the United States occurs during
    a. adolescence.
    b. emerging adulthood.
    c. the 30s.
    d. late adulthood.

12. Researchers have found that athletic performance peaks earliest in sports that require
    a. fine motor skills.
    b. vigorous gross motor skills.
    c. greater flexibility than physical strength.
    d. extensive conditioning before peak performance is achieved.

Matching Items
Match each definition or description with its corresponding term.

Terms
13. ___G___ senescence
14. ___E___ homeostasis
15. ___D___ organ reserve
16. ___B___ diathesis-stress model
17. ___J___ social norms approach

18. ___C___ extreme sports
19. ___H___ set point
20. ___A___ edgework
21. ___I___ emerging adulthood
22. ___F___ hikikomori

Definitions or Descriptions
a. jobs or activities that involve significant risk or danger
b. the idea that psychological disorders result from an interaction of stress and an underlying predisposition
c. sports that involve significant risk of injury or death
d. extra capacity for responding to stressful events
e. a state of physiological equilibrium
f. an anxiety disorder characterized by isolating oneself for months or even years
g. age-related decline
h. a particular weight maintained by homeostasis
i. the early years of adulthood
j. reducing risky behavior by drawing from emerging adults' desire to follow social norms

Applying Your Knowledge

1. Your instructor asks you to summarize, in one sentence, the extent and cause of biosocial decline during early adulthood. You wisely respond
   a. "Any difficulties experienced by young adults in biosocial development are usually related to factors other than aging per se."
   b. "Significant declines in all aspects of physical well-being become apparent by the mid-20s."
   c. "With the attainment of full maturity, development is released from the constraints of heredity."
   d. "The first signs of aging are usually not apparent until middle adulthood."

2. When we are hot, we perspire in order to give off body heat. This is an example of the way our body functions maintain
   a. senescence.
   b. homeostasis.
   c. endometriosis.
   d. motility.

3. Because of a decline in organ reserve, 28-year-old Brenda
   a. has a higher resting heart rate than she did when she was younger.
   b. needs longer to recover from strenuous exercise than she did when she was younger.
   c. has a higher maximum heart rate than her younger sister.
   d. has all of the above.

4. Summarizing the results of cross-sectional research on attitudes, the lecturer states that "More young adults than older adults believe that casual sex is normal and acceptable behavior." The most likely explanation for the lecturer's statement is
   a. decreases in the desire to get married.
   b. increases in availability of effective contraception.
   c. decreases in moral reasoning.
   d. increases in rates of sexually transmitted infections.

5. If Benny is like most men, as he grows older, he will
   a. experience an increase in sexual activity.
   b. become more interested in edgework.
   c. engage in more edgework.
   d. become less likely to die a violent death.

6. Sheila dieted for several weeks until she lost ten pounds. Upon returning to a normal diet, she is horrified to find that she has gained some of the weight back. It is likely that Sheila's weight gain was caused by

    a. overconsumption of high-fat foods.

    b. too little exercise in her daily routine.

    c. her homeostatic mechanism returning to her natural set point.

    d. a low body set point.

7. Of the following, who is most likely to suffer from anorexia nervosa?

    a. Bill, a 23-year-old professional football player

    b. Florence, a 30-year-old account executive

    c. Lynn, a 20-year-old college student

    d. Carl, a professional dancer

8. Twenty-year-old Gwynn, who is nine pounds heavier than the national average for her height and build, should probably

    a. go on a crash diet, since every additional pound of fat is hazardous to her health.

    b. gradually reduce her weight to slightly below the national average.

    c. realize that because of her high body set point she will be unable to have children.

    d. not worry, since this is probably a healthy weight for her body.

9. Hiroshi, a 21-year-old Japanese male, has been too anxious to leave his room for six months. He is suffering from

    a. schizophrenia.

    b. drug abuse.

    c. hikikomori.

    d. bipolar disorder.

10. Michael, who is in his mid-20s, is most likely to seek medical attention for

    a. a common cold.

    b. a sports- or drug-related injury.

    c. a life-threatening chronic illness.

    d. infertility.

11. Which of the following is an example of a cohort influence on biosocial development during early adulthood?

    a. The number of North American women with a BMI below 19 has decreased over the past three decades.

    b. Women of European ancestry in the United States are particularly vulnerable to an obsession with thinness.

    c. Violent death is far more prevalent among young adult males than among females.

    d. Women with a family history of depression have a heightened risk of becoming anorexic.

12. Lucretia, who has a body-mass index of 24, has been trying unsuccessfully to lose ten pounds. It is likely that her difficulty has occurred because

    a. she has a glandular disorder.

    b. she suffers from bulimia nervosa.

    c. her natural weight set point is higher than she would like.

    d. her obesity is accompanied by a very low metabolic rate.

13. Nathan has a powerful attraction to excitement, a low tolerance for frustration, and a vulnerability to depression. He also may be vulnerable to

    a. alcoholism.

    b. cocaine abuse.

    c. most psychoactive drugs.

    d. none of the above.

Answer Key

Key Terms

1. The period of life between 18 and 25 is called emerging adulthood. (p. 465; objective 1)

2. Senescence is age-related decline throughout the body. (p. 468; video lesson, segment 1; objective 2)

3. Homeostasis refers to the process by which body functions are automatically adjusted to keep our physiological functioning in a state of balance. (p. 468; video lesson, segment 1; objective 2)

4. Organ reserve is the extra capacity of each body organ for responding to unusually stressful events or conditions that demand intense or prolonged effort. (p. 468; video lesson, segment 1; objective 2)

5. The view that psychological disorders, such as schizophrenia, are caused by an interaction between genetic vulnerability and stressful environmental factors and life events is called the diathesis–stress model. (p. 474; objective 9)

6. Hikikomori is an anxiety disorder common among young Japanese adults during which they "pull away" by isolating themselves. (p. 477; objective 9)

7. Set point is the specific body weight that a person's homeostatic processes strive to maintain. (p. 480; objective 1)

8. Work that involves a significant risk of harm is referred to as edgework because the person is "living on the edge" between safety and harm while engaged in these activities. (p. 481; objective 7)

9. Extreme sports, such as motorcross, involve a significant risk of danger or even death. (p. 482; objective 7)

10. The social norms approach aims to reduce risky behavior by showing individuals how common certain behaviors actually are in a given population. For example, if college students learned that most of their peers do not engage in binge drinking, this might create a social norm against binge drinking. (p. 486; objective 7)

11. Gender socialization refers to the process by which an individual acquires a masculine or feminine social role. (video lesson, segment 3; objective 7)

Practice Questions I

Multiple-Choice Questions

1. b. is the correct answer. (video lesson, segment 1; objective 2)

   a., c., & d. are incorrect. Each of these is a specific example of the more general process of senescence.

2. b. is the correct answer. (objective 1)

3. c. is the correct answer. (objective 1)

   a. & b. are incorrect. These are true of women.

   d. is incorrect.

4. a. is the correct answer. (video lesson, segment 1; objective 1)

5. b. is the correct answer. (video lesson, segment 1; objective 2)

   a. is incorrect. This is the extra capacity that each organ of the body has for responding to unusually stressful events or conditions that demand intense or prolonged effort.

   c. is incorrect. Stress, which is not defined in this lesson, refers to events or situations that tax the body's resources.

   d. is incorrect. This simply refers to a muscle's potential for work.

6. c. is the correct answer. (objective 7)

7. c. is the correct answer. (objective 3)

8. a. is the correct answer. (objective 3)

9. d. is the correct answer. (objective 3)

10. d. is the correct answer. (objective 1)

11. a. is the correct answer. (video lesson, segment 2; objective 6)

12. b. is the correct answer. (objective 9)

13. b. is the correct answer. In fact, just the opposite is true. Young adults may use drugs to express independence from their parents. (objective 4)

True or False Items

14. T   (video lesson, segment 1; objective 2)

15. T   (objective 2)

16. T   (objective 2)

17. T   (objective 5)

18. F   Just the opposite is true. (objective 4)

19. F   (objective 3)

20. F   (objective 1)

21. T   (video lesson, segment 2; objective 6)

22. T   (objective 1)

23. T   Among young European-American men, accidents are the number one cause of death. (video lesson, segment 3; objective 8)

Practice Questions II

Multiple-Choice Questions

1. d. is the correct answer. (video lesson, segment 1; objectives 1 & 2)

2. b. is the correct answer. (objective 1)

3. b. is the correct answer. (objective 5)

4. b. is the correct answer. (objective 2)

5. d. is the correct answer. (objective 2)

6. a. is the correct answer. (objective 5)

7. a. is the correct answer. (objective 3)

8. a. is the correct answer. (video lesson, segment 2; objective 6)

    b. is incorrect. This describes a woman suffering from anorexia nervosa.

    c. is incorrect. Eating disorders are much more common in younger women.

    d. is incorrect. Most women with bulimia nervosa are usually close to normal in weight.

9. d. is the correct answer. (objective 6)

10. b. is the correct answer. (video lesson, segment 3; objective 8)

    a. is incorrect. Eating disorders are more common in women than men.

    c. & d. are incorrect. Disease is relatively rare at this age.

11. b. is the correct answer. (video lesson, segment 2; objective 4)

12. b. is the correct answer. (objective 1)

Matching Items

13. g (video lesson, segment 1; objective 1)

14. e (video lesson, segment 1; objective 2)

15. d (video lesson, segment 1; objective 2)

16. b (objective 9)

17. j (objective 7)

18. c (objective 7)

19. h (objective 1)

20. a (objective 7)

21. i (objective 1)

22. f (objective 9)

Applying Your Knowledge

1. a. is the correct answer. (video lesson, segment 1; objective 1)

    b. is incorrect. Physical declines during the 20s are usually of little consequence.

    c. is incorrect. This is not true nor does it address the instructor's request.

    d. is incorrect. The first signs of aging become apparent at an earlier age.

2. b. is the correct answer. (video lesson, segment 1; objective 2)

    a. is incorrect. This is age-related decline.

    c. is incorrect. This is a common fertility problem for women.

    d. is incorrect. This refers to the swimming ability of sperm.

3. b. is the correct answer. (video lesson, segment 1; objective 2)

    a. is incorrect. Resting heart rate remains stable throughout adulthood.

    c. is incorrect. Maximum heart rate declines with age.

4. b. is the correct answer. (objective 3)

5. d. is the correct answer. (video lesson, segment 3; objective 8)

6. c. is the correct answer. (objective 1)

7. c. is the correct answer. (video lesson, segment 2; objective 6)

   a. & d. are incorrect. Eating disorders are more common in women than men.

   b. is incorrect. Eating disorders are more common in younger women.

8. d. is the correct answer. (objective 5)

9. c. is the correct answer. (objective 9)

   a. & b. are incorrect. Those who emphasize learning theory or cognitive theory would more likely offer these explanations.

   d. is incorrect. This is a sociocultural explanation of eating disorders.

10. b. is the correct answer. (video lesson, segment 1; objectives 1 & 2)

11. a. is the correct answer. (objective 1)

   b., c., & d. are incorrect. A cohort is a group of people born about the same time. These examples illustrate possible ethnic (b), gender (c), and genetic (d) influences on biosocial development.

12. c. is the correct answer. (objective 1)

   a. & d. are incorrect. There is no evidence that Lucretia has a glandular disorder or is obese. In fact, a BMI of 24 is well within the normal weight range.

   b. is incorrect. There is no evidence that Lucretia is bingeing and purging.

13. c. is the correct answer. (objective 4)

   a. & b. are incorrect. Although these are also correct, they are both psychoactive drugs, making c. the best answer.

Lesson Review

Lesson 17

Early Adulthood
Biosocial Development

Please Note: Use this matrix to guide your study and achieve the learning objectives of this lesson. It will also help you to view the video, which defines and demonstrates important concepts and skills as they relate to everyday life.

Learning Objective	Textbook	Course Student Guide	Video Lesson
1. Describe the changes in growth, strength, and overall health that occur during early adulthood.	pp. 465–467	Key Terms: 1, 7; Practice Questions I: 2, 3, 4, 10, 20, 22; Practice Questions II: 1, 2, 12, 13, 19, 21; Applying Your Knowledge: 1, 6, 10, 11, 12.	Segment 1: *Growth, Strength, and Health*
2. Discuss changes in the efficiency of various body functions and physical appearance, focusing on the significance of these changes for the individual.	pp. 468–469	Key Terms: 2, 3, 4; Practice Questions I: 1, 5, 14, 15, 16; Practice Questions II: 1, 4, 5, 14, 15; Applying Your Knowledge: 2, 3, 10.	Segment 1: *Growth, Strength, and Health*
3. Identify age-related trends in the norms for sexual activity, and describe potential consequences of sexual activity during emerging adulthood.	pp. 469–473	Practice Questions I: 7, 8, 9, 19; Practice Questions II: 7; Applying Your Knowledge: 4.	
4. Discuss changes in substance abuse during early adulthood, and describe the causes and consequences of this abuse.	pp. 483–485	Practice Questions I: 13, 18; Practice Questions II: 11; Applying Your Knowledge: 13.	Segment 2: *Health Problems*
5. Identify common patterns of nutrition and exercise in emerging adulthood.	pp. 478–481	Practice Questions I: 17; Practice Questions II: 3, 6; Applying Your Knowledge: 8.	

Learning Objective	Textbook	Course Student Guide	Video Lesson
6. Describe the typical victims of anorexia nervosa and bulimia nervosa, and discuss possible explanations for these disorders.	*	Practice Questions I: 11, 21; Practice Questions II: 8, 9.	Segment 2: *Health Problems*
7. Explain how social norms and gender socialization may be related to self-destructive behavior among emerging adults.	pp. 481–483, 485–487	Key Terms: 8, 9, 10, 11; Practice Questions I: 6; Practice Questions II: 17, 18, 20.	Segment 3: *Gender Socialization and Violence*
8. Discuss the factors that may determine whether a young male adult will suffer a violent death.	*	Practice Questions I: 23; Practice Questions II: 10; Applying Your Knowledge: 5.	Segment 3: *Gender Socialization and Violence*
9. Explain why emerging adults have higher rates of mood disorders, anxiety disorders, and other psychological disorders than older adults	pp. 473–478	Key Terms: 5, 6; Practice Questions I: 12; Practice Questions II: 16, 22; Applying Your Knowledge: 9.	

*The video for this lesson offers an excellent description of these concepts.

Decisions, Decisions

Lesson 18

Early Adulthood:
Cognitive Development

Preview

During the course of adulthood, there are many shifts in cognitive development—in the speed and efficiency with which we process information, in the focus and depth of our cognitive processes, and perhaps in the quality, or wisdom, of our thinking. Developmental psychologists use different approaches in explaining these shifts, with each approach providing insights into the nature of adult cognition. This chapter takes a *postformal approach*, describing age-related changes in an attempt to uncover patterns or predictable stages.

The lesson begins by describing how adult thinking differs from adolescent thinking. The experiences and challenges of adulthood result in a new, **postformal thought**, evidenced by more practical and adaptive thinking—the dynamic cognitive style that adults typically use to solve the problems of daily life.

Next, the lesson explores how the events of emerging adulthood and early adulthood can affect moral development and thinking about faith and religious matters.

The lesson also examines the effect of the college experience on cognitive growth; findings here indicate that years of education correlate positively with virtually every measure of cognition, as thinking becomes progressively more flexible and tolerant. A final section discusses the importance of life events—such as parenthood, job promotion, or illness—in triggering cognitive growth during young adulthood.

As you complete this lesson, consider your own cognitive development during emerging adulthood and early adulthood (or that of someone you know in this age range, 18 to 35). In what ways have your thinking and cognitive skills advanced during this period? How has your perspective on religion, faith, and morality changed (if at all)? What particular life events or experiences have been the most significant in changing the way you approach problems and think about life?

Prior Course Knowledge that Will Be Used in this Lesson
- This lesson will return to the theories of Jean Piaget (from Lessons 2 and 12). Recall that Piaget specified four age-related periods of cognitive development:
  1. Sensorimotor (birth to 2 years)
  2. Preoperational (2 to 6 years)

3. Concrete Operational (7 to 11 years)
4. Formal Operational (12 years through adulthood)

- Piaget described formal operational thought as the last stage of cognitive development, beginning in adolescence and extending into adulthood. But, as you will learn in this lesson, adults often develop a more complex, practical, and flexible type of cognition called *postformal thought*.

- For its discussion of adult moral reasoning and the development of faith, this lesson will briefly return to the ideas of Lawrence Kohlberg and Carol Gilligan (from Lesson 12). Recall that Kohlberg described three levels of moral reasoning: preconventional, conventional, and postconventional.

Learning Objectives

Use this information to guide your reading, viewing, thinking, and studying. After successfully completing this lesson, you should be able to:

1. Identify three approaches to the study of adult cognition, and describe the postformal approach.
2. Describe the main characteristics of postformal thought and discuss how it differs from formal operational thought.
3. Define and describe dialectical thought, and give examples of its usefulness.
4. Draw a conclusion about whether postformal thought represents a separate stage of development.
5. Explain the views of Carol Gilligan and others who believe that moral reasoning is influenced by culture and life experiences.
6. Briefly describe the six stages of faith outlined by James Fowler.
7. Explain how the Defining Issues Test helps relate moral development to other aspects of adult cognition and life satisfaction.
8. Discuss the relationship between cognitive growth and higher education.
9. Identify and evaluate differences between contemporary colleges and college students and their counterparts of a decade or two ago.
10. Discuss how life events may trigger new patterns of thinking and result in cognitive growth.

Read Chapter 18, "Emerging Adulthood: Cognitive Development," pages 491–517.

View the video for Lesson 18, "Decisions, Decisions."

Segment 1: *Postformal Thought*

Segment 2: *Life Experiences and Their Effects*

Segment 3: *Moral Reasoning*

Summary

As people grow from adolescence into adulthood, the commitments, demands, and responsibilities of adult life can produce a new type of thinking that is better suited than formal operations to solving the practical problems of daily life. Adult cognition has been studied in three major ways: from a postformal perspective, from a psychometric perspective, and from an information-processing perspective. The lesson focuses on the postformal perspective. **Postformal thought** is more adaptive, flexible, and dialectical. **Dialectical thought**, which some developmental psychologists consider the most advanced form of cognition, recognizes that most of life's important questions do not have single, unvarying, correct answers. It is grounded in the ability to consider both sides of an issue simultaneously.

Thinking about questions of faith and ethics may also progress during adulthood, especially in response to significant life experiences, such as participating in higher education and becoming a parent. Carol Gilligan suggests that men and women come to recognize the limitations of moral reasoning based solely on abstract principles and personal concerns, and attempt to integrate the two with life experiences to forge a more reflective, less absolute moral awareness. James Fowler has bridged the fields of psychology and religion by creating a model in which faith is broadly conceived. Building on the cognitive and personality theories of Jean Piaget and Erik Erikson, Fowler's model extends the concept of faith beyond religious faith to include whatever each person really cares about—his or her "ultimate concern." Fowler's theory describes six stages, each of which has distinct features and is classified as typical of a certain age.

Level of education is strongly correlated with virtually every measure of adult cognition. College education leads people to become more tolerant of differing views, more flexible and realistic in their attitudes, and dialectical in their reasoning. Throughout the world, the number of college students has increased, and more students are female, ethnic minorities, part-time, commuter, and older than ever before. Young adults are developing the ability to reason about emotionally charged issues, a skill that peaks in middle adulthood.

📖 **Review all reading assignments for this lesson.**

💻 **As assigned by your instructor, complete the optional online component for this lesson.**

Key Terms

Using your own words, write a brief definition or explanation of each of the following terms on a separate piece of paper.

1. postformal thought
2. delay discounting
3. subjective thought
4. objective thought
5. stereotype threat
6. dialectical thought
7. thesis
8. antithesis
9. synthesis
10. morality of care
11. morality of justice
12. Defining Issues Test (DIT)

Practice Questions I

Multiple-Choice Questions

1. Differences in the reasoning maturity of adolescents and young adults are most likely to be apparent when
   a. groups with low socioecomic status and high socioecomic status are compared.
   b. ethnic-minority adolescents and adults are compared.
   c. ethnic-majority adolescents and adults are compared.
   d. emotionally charged issues are involved.

2. Which of the following is **NOT** one of the major approaches to the study of adult cognition described in the text?

   a. the information-processing approach
   b. the postformal approach
   (c.) the systems approach
   d. the psychometric approach

3. Compared to adolescent thinking, adult thinking tends to be
   a. more flexible.
   b. more practical.
   c. more integrative.
   (d.) all of the above.

4. Experts have shown that the hallmark of adult adaptive thought is the

   (a.) ability to engage in dialectical thinking.
   b. reconciliation of both objective and subjective approaches to real-life problems.
   c. adoption of conjunctive faith.
   d. combination of all of the above.

5. According to James Fowler, the experience of college often is a springboard to

   a. intuitive-projective faith.
   b. mythic-literal faith.
   (c.) individual-reflective faith.
   d. synthetic-conventional faith.

6. Which approach to adult cognitive development focuses on life-span changes in the efficiency of encoding, storage, and retrieval?
   a. postformal
   (b.) information-processing
   c. psychometric
   d. dialectical

7. Postformal thinking is most useful for solving _____ problems.
   a. science
   b. mathematics
   (c.) everyday
   d. abstract, logical

8. The term for the kind of thinking that involves the consideration of both poles of an idea and their reconciliation, or synthesis, in a new idea is
   a. subjective thinking.
   b. postformal thought.
   c. adaptive reasoning.
   (d.) dialectical thinking.

9. Thesis is to antithesis as _____ is to _____.
   a. a new idea; an opposing idea
   b. abstract; concrete
   c. concrete; abstract
   d. provisional; absolute

10. Which of the following adjectives best describe(s) cognitive development during adulthood?
    a. multidirectional and multicontextual
    b. unidirectional and linear
    c. straightforward and stable
    d. random and patternless

11. Which of the following most accurately describes postformal thought?
    a. subjective thinking that arises from the personal experiences and perceptions of the individual
    b. objective reasoning that follows abstract, impersonal logic
    c. a form of reasoning that combines subjectivity and objectivity
    d. thinking that is rigid, inflexible, and fails to recognize the existence of other potentially valid views

12. The Defining Issues Test is a
    a. standardized test that measures postformal thinking.
    b. projective test that assesses dialectical reasoning.
    c. series of questions about moral dilemmas.
    d. test that assesses the impact of life events on cognitive growth.

13. According to Carol Gilligan,
    a. in matters of moral reasoning, females tend to be more concerned with the question of rights and justice.
    b. in matters of moral reasoning, males tend to put human needs above principles of justice.
    c. moral reasoning advances during adulthood in response to the more complex moral dilemmas that life poses.
    d. all of the above are true.

14. An important factor in determining whether college students learn to think deeply is
    a. the particular interactions between students and faculty.
    b. the college's overall religious or secular philosophy.
    c. the college's size.
    d. all of the above.

15. Research has revealed that a typical outcome of college education is that students become

    a. very liberal politically.

    b. less committed to any particular ideology.

    c. less tolerant of others' views.

    d. more tolerant of others' views.

True or False Items

Write T (for true) or F (for false) on the line in front of each statement.

16. _F_ Research shows that the main reason most young adults today attend college is to improve their thinking and reasoning skills.

17. _F_ Adult cognitive growth is more straightforward than that of childhood and adolescence.

18. _F_ Postformal thought produces conclusions by separating logical processes from emotional responses.

19. _F_ Because they recognize the changing and subjective nature of beliefs and values, dialectical thinkers avoid making personal or intellectual commitments.

20. _T_ Certain kinds of experiences during adulthood—especially those that entail assuming responsibility for others—can propel an individual from one level of moral reasoning to another.

21. _F_ In recent years, the number of female college students has dropped significantly.

22. _T_ Postformal thought is less absolute and less abstract than formal thought.

23. _F_ Mythic-literal faith, like other "lower" stages in the development of faith, is never found past adolescence.

24. _T_ In predicting an individual's level of cognitive development, it would be more helpful to know that person's educational background than his or her age.

25. _T_ The college student of today is more likely to be from a low-income background, to have children, and to attend college part-time than were the students of the previous generation.

26. _F_ Cognitive growth during college is primarily the accumulation of facts and figures.

Practice Questions II

need review of faith and moral development!

Multiple-Choice Questions

1. Which approach to adult cognitive development emphasizes the analysis of components of intelligence?
   a. postformal
   b. psychometric
   c. information-processing
   d. all of the above

2. Which approach to adult cognitive development "picks up where Piaget left off"?
   a. psychometric
   b. information-processing
   c. postformal
   d. dialectical

3. As adult thinking becomes more focused on occupational and interpersonal demands, it also becomes less inclined toward
    a. the game of thinking.
   b. dialectical thought.
   c. adaptive thought.
   d. all of the above.

4. The result of dialectical thinking is a view that
    a. one's self is an unchanging constant.
   b. few of life's important questions have single, correct answers.
   c. "everything is relative."
   d. all of the above are true.

5. The existence of a fifth, postformal stage of cognitive development during adulthood
    a. is recognized by most developmentalists.
   b. has very little empirical support.
   c. remains controversial among developmental researchers.
   d. is widely accepted in women, but not in men.

6. Formal operational thinking is most useful for solving problems that
   a. involve logical relationships or theoretical possibilities.
   b. require integrative skills.
   c. involve the synthesis of diverse issues.
   d. require seeing perspectives other than one's own.

7. College seems to make people more accepting of other people's attitudes because it

   a. boosts self-esteem.
   b. makes new ideas less threatening.
   c. promotes extroversion.
   d. does all of the above.

8. The goal of dialectical thinking is forging a(n) _____ from opposing poles of an idea.

   a. thesis
   b. antithesis
   c. synthesis
   d. hypothesis

9. Formal operational thinking is to postformal thinking as _____ is to _____.

   a. psychometric; information-processing
   b. adolescence; adulthood
   c. thesis; antithesis
   d. self-esteem; extroversion

10. Carol Gilligan suggests that during adulthood

    a. men and women come to recognize the limitations of basing moral reasoning solely on principles of justice.
    b. men and women come to recognize the limitations of basing moral reasoning solely on individual needs.
    c. men and women develop a more reflective, less absolute moral awareness.
    d. all of the above are true.

11. According to James Fowler, individual-reflective faith is marked by

    a. a willingness to accept contradictions.
    b. a burning need to enunciate universal values.
    c. a literal, wholehearted belief in myths and symbols.
    d. the beginnings of independent questioning of teachers and other figures of authority.

12. Research studies have shown that students experiencing stereotype threat

    a. have lower performance.
    b. tend to have higher achievement.
    c. are rarely female.
    d. are only affected if there is actual evidence of a prejudice against them.

13. According to James Fowler, the simplest stage of faith is the stage of

    a. universalizing faith.
    b. intuitive-projective faith.
    c. mythic-literal faith.
    d. conventional faith.

14. Many of the problems of adult life are characterized by ambiguity, partial truths, and extenuating circumstances, and therefore are often best solved using _____ thinking.
    a. formal
    b. reintegrative
    c. postformal
    d. executive

15. Which aspect of college is the primary catalyst for cognitive growth?
    a. academic work
    b. the encounter with new ideas
    c. the discussion with peers
    d. all of the above

Applying Your Knowledge

1. Concluding her comparison of postformal thinking with Piaget's cognitive stages, Lynn notes that
    a. not every adult thinks in a postformal manner.
    b. dialectical thinking is more evident in some contexts than in others.
    c. not everyone who thinks in a postformal way is also capable of formal operational thought.
    d. all of the above are true.

2. Jeff regularly uses his smartphone to email while he drives. Jeff is exhibiting
    a. dialectical thought.
    b. delay discounting.
    c. stereotype threat.
    d. a morality of care.

3. Research suggests that a college sophomore or junior is most likely to have reached a phase in which he or she
    a. believes that there are clear and perfect truths to be discovered.
    b. questions personal and social values, and even the idea of truth itself.
    c. rejects opposing ideas in the interest of finding one right answer.
    d. accepts a simplistic either/or dualism.

4. In his scheme of cognitive and ethical development (seen in Table 18.4 on page 491), researcher William Perry describes a position in which the college student says, "I see I am going to have to make my own decisions in an uncertain world with no one to tell me I'm right." This position marks the culmination of a phase of
    a. either/or dualism.
    b. modified dualism.
    c. relativism.
    d. commitments in relativism.

5. After suffering a heart attack in his 30s, Rob begins to think differently about life and its deeper meaning. This is an example of
   a. the effect of a mentor on cognitive development.
   b. having reached the reintegrative stage of adult cognition.
   c. a life event that results in cognitive growth.
   d. a biological or age-related change in intelligence.

6. Dr. Polaski studies how thinking during adulthood builds on the earlier formal thinking skills of adolescence. Evidently, Dr. Polaski follows the _____ approach to the study of development.
   a. postformal
   b. psychometric
   c. cognitive
   d. information-processing

7. Jack's uncle believes strongly in God but recognizes that other, equally moral people do not. The openness of his faith places him in which of Fowler's stages?
   a. universalizing faith
   b. conjunctive faith
   c. individual-reflective faith
   d. mythic-literal faith

8. When she was younger, May-Ling believed that "Honesty is always the best policy." She now realizes that although honesty is desirable, it is not always the best policy. May-Ling's current thinking is an example of
   a. formal thought.
   b. dialectical thinking.
   c. mythic-literal thinking.
   d. conjunctive thinking.

9. Who would be the most likely to agree with the statement, "To be truly ethical a person must have the experience of sustained responsibility for the welfare of others"?
   a. Gisela Labouvie-Vief
   b. Lawrence Kohlberg
   c. Jean Piaget
   d. James Fowler

10. Spike is in his third year at a private, religious liberal arts college, while his brother Lee is in his third year at a public, secular community college. In terms of their cognitive growth, what is the most likely outcome?
   a. Spike will more rapidly develop complex critical thinking skills.
   b. Lee will develop greater self-confidence in his abilities, since he is studying from the secure base of his home and family.
   c. All other things being equal, Spike and Lee will develop quite similarly.
   d. It is impossible to predict.

11. In concluding her presentation on "The College Student of Today," Coretta states that

    a. "The number of students in higher education has increased significantly in virtually every country worldwide."

    b. "There are more low-income and ethnic-minority students today than ever before."

    c. "More students choose specific career-based majors rather than a liberal arts education."

    d. all of the above are true.

12. In concluding his paper on postformal thinking, Stanley notes that

    a. postformal thinking is not the same kind of universal, age-related stage that Piaget described for earlier cognitive growth.

    b. very few adults attain this highest stage of reasoning.

    c. most everyday problems require sensitivity to subjective feelings and therefore do not foster postformal thinking.

    d. all of the above are true.

13. In predicting an individual's level of cognitive development, it would be most helpful to know that person's

    a. age.

    b. socioeconomic status.

    c. educational background.

    d. history of life challenges.

14. In Fowler's theory, at the highest stages of faith development, people incorporate a powerful vision of compassion for others into their lives. This stage is called

    a. conjunctive faith.

    b. individual-reflective faith.

    c. synthetic-conventional faith.

    d. universalizing faith.

Answer Key

Key Terms

1. Proposed by some developmentalists as an additional level of cognitive development, postformal thought is suited to solving real-world problems and is less abstract, less absolute, and more integrative and synthetic than formal thought. (p. 492; video lesson, segment 1; objective 2)

2. The tendency to undervalue or ignore future consequences or rewards in favor of immediate gratification is called delay discounting. (p. 493; objective 2)

3. Subjective thought is a kind of thinking that arises from the personal experiences and perceptions of an individual. (p. 494; objective 2)

4. Objective thought is a kind of thinking that follows abstract, impersonal logic. (p. 494; objective 2)

5. The possibility that one's appearance or behavior will be misused to confirm another person's oversimplified, prejudiced attitude is called stereotype threat. (p. 498; objective 2)

6. Dialectical thought is thinking that involves considering both poles of an idea (thesis and antithesis) simultaneously and then forging them into a synthesis. (p. 500; video lesson, segment 1; objectives 2 & 3)

7. The first stage of dialectical thinking, a thesis is a proposition or statement of belief. (p. 500; objective 3)

8. A statement that contradicts the thesis, an antithesis is the second stage of dialectical thinking. (p. 500; objective 3)

9. The final stage of dialectical thinking, the synthesis reconciles thesis and antithesis into a new, more comprehensive level of truth. (p. 500; objective 3)

10. Compared with men, women are more likely to develop a morality of care that is based on comparison, nurturance, and concern for the well-being of others. (p. 504; objective 6)

11. Compared with women, men are more likely to develop a morality of justice based on depersonalized standards of right and wrong. (p. 504; objective 6)

12. The Defining Issues Test (DIT) is a series of questions about moral dilemmas used to research moral reasoning. (p. 504; objective 7)

Practice Questions I

Multiple-Choice Questions

1. d. is the correct answer. (video lesson, segment 1; objective 2)

   a., b., & c. are incorrect. Socioeconomic status and ethnicity do not predict reasoning maturity.

2. c. is the correct answer. (objective 1)

3. d. is the correct answer. (video lesson, segment 1; objective 2)

4. b. is the correct answer. (video lesson, segment 1; objective 2)

5. c. is the correct answer. (objective 6)

6. b. is the correct answer. (objective 1)

   a. is incorrect. This approach emphasizes the emergence of a new stage of thinking that builds on the skills of formal operational thinking.

   c. is incorrect. This approach analyzes the measurable components of intelligence.

   d. is incorrect. This is a type of thinking rather than an approach to the study of cognitive development.

7. c. is the correct answer. (video lesson, segment 1; objective 1)

   a., b., & d. are incorrect. Because of its more analytical nature, formal thinking is most useful for solving these types of problems.

8. d. is the correct answer. (video lesson, segment 1; objective 3)

   a. is incorrect. Thinking that is subjective relies on personal reflection rather than objective observation.

   b. is incorrect. Although dialectical thinking is characteristic of postformal thought, this question refers specifically to dialectical thinking.

   c. is incorrect. Adaptive reasoning, which also is characteristic of postformal thought, goes beyond mere logic in solving problems to also explore real-life complexities and contextual circumstances.

9. a. is the correct answer. (objective 3)

10. a. is the correct answer. (objective 4)

b. & c. are incorrect. Comparatively speaking, linear and steady are more descriptive of childhood and adolescent cognitive development.

11. c. is the correct answer. (video lesson, segment 1; objective 2)

12. c. is the correct answer. (objective 7)

13. c. is the correct answer. (video lesson, segment 3; objective 5)

   a. is incorrect. In Gilligan's theory, this is more true of males than females.

   b. is incorrect. In Gilligan's theory, this is more true of females than males.

14. a. is the correct answer. (objective 8)

15. d. is the correct answer. (video lesson, segment 2; objective 8)

True or False Items

16. F   Most people today attend college primarily to secure better jobs. (video lesson, segment 2; objective 9)

17. F   Adult cognitive growth is multidirectional. (video lesson, introduction; objective 4)

18. F   (video lesson, segment 1; objective 2)

19. F   Dialectical thinkers recognize the need to make commitments to values even though these values will change over time. (objective 3)

20. T   (video lesson, segment 3; objective 5)

21. F   (objective 9)

22. T   (video lesson, segment 1; objective 4)

23. F   Many adults remain in the "lower" stages of faith, which, like "higher" stages, allow for attaining strength and wholeness. (objective 6)

24. T   (objective 8)

25. T   (objective 9)

26. F   (video lesson, segment 2; objective 10)

Practice Questions II

Multiple-Choice Questions

1. b. is the correct answer. (objective 1)

   a. is incorrect. This approach emphasizes the possible emergence in adulthood of new stages of thinking that build on the skills of earlier stages.

   c. is incorrect. This approach studies the encoding, storage, and retrieval of information throughout life.

2. c. is the correct answer. (video lesson, segment 1; objectives 1 & 2)

3. a. is the correct answer. (objective 2)

   b. & c. are incorrect. During adulthood, thinking typically becomes more dialectical and adaptive.

4. b. is the correct answer. (video lesson, segment 1; objective 3)

5. c. is the correct answer. (objective 4)

6. a. is the correct answer. (video lesson, segment 1; objective 2)

   b., c., & d. are incorrect. Postformal thought is most useful for solving problems such as these.

7. b. is the correct answer. (video lesson, segment 2; objective 8)

   a. & c. are incorrect. The impact of college on self-esteem and extroversion were not discussed. Moreover, it is unclear how such an impact would make a person more accepting of others.

8. c. is the correct answer. (video lesson, segment 1; objective 3)

a. is incorrect. A thesis is a new idea.

b. is incorrect. An antithesis is an idea that opposes a particular thesis.

d. is incorrect. Hypotheses, which are testable predictions about behavior, are not an aspect of dialectical thinking.

9. b. is the correct answer. (video lesson, segment 1; objective 2)

10. d. is the correct answer. (video lesson, segment 3; objective 5)

11. d. is the correct answer. (objective 6)

a. is incorrect. This describes conjunctive faith.

b. is incorrect. This describes universalizing faith.

c. is incorrect. This describes mythic-literal faith.

12. a. is the correct answer. (objective 2)

13. b. is the correct answer. (objective 6)

14. c. is the correct answer. (video lesson, segment 1; objective 2)

a. is incorrect. Formal thinking is best suited to solving problems that require logic and analytical thinking.

b. & d. are incorrect. These terms are not discussed in the textbook.

15. d. is the correct answer. Research has no conclusive answer. (video lesson, segment 2; objective 8)

a. is incorrect by itself.

c. is incorrect by itself.

d. is incorrect by itself.

Applying Your Knowledge

1. d. is the correct answer. (video lesson, introduction & segment 1; objectives 2, 3, & 4)

2. b. is the correct answer. (objective 2)

a. is incorrect. According to Gilligan, males tend to be more concerned with human rights and justice than with human needs and personal relationships, which are more the concern of females.

c. & d. are incorrect. These answers are incorrect because, according to Gilligan, as people mature and their experience of life expands, they begin to realize that moral reasoning based chiefly on justice principles or on individual needs is inadequate to resolve real-life moral dilemmas.

3. b. is the correct answer. (objective 8)

a. is incorrect. First-year college students are more likely to believe this is so.

c. & d. are incorrect. Over the course of their college careers, students become less likely to do either of these.

4. c. is the correct answer. (objective 8)

5. c. is the correct answer. (video lesson segment 2; objective 10)

6. a. is the correct answer. (video lesson, segment 1; objectives 1 & 2)

b. is incorrect. This approach analyzes components of intelligence such as those measured by IQ tests.

c. is incorrect. Each of these approaches is cognitive in nature.

d. is incorrect. This approach studies the encoding, storage, and retrieval of information throughout life.

7. b. is the correct answer. (objective 6)

8. b. is the correct answer. May-Ling has formed a synthesis between the thesis that honesty is the best policy and its antithesis. (video lesson, segment 1; objective 3)

a. is incorrect. This is an example of postformal rather than formal thinking.

c. & d. are incorrect. These are stages in the development of faith as proposed by James Fowler.

9. b. is the correct answer. (objective 5)

a. & c. are incorrect. Neither Labouvie-Vief nor Piaget focuses on ethics in their theories.

d. is incorrect. Fowler's theory, which identifies stages in the development of faith, does not emphasize this experience.

10. c. is the correct answer. (objective 8)

11. d. is the correct answer. (objective 9)

12. a. is the correct answer. (video lesson, introduction & segment 1; objectives 2 & 4)

b. is incorrect. Because postformal thinking is typical of adult thought, this is untrue.

c. is incorrect. It is exactly this sort of problem that fosters postformal thinking.

13. c. is the correct answer. (objective 8)

a. & b. are incorrect. Years of education are more strongly correlated with cognitive development than are age and socioeconomic status.

d. is incorrect. Although significant life events can trigger cognitive development, the textbook does not suggest that the relationship between life events and measures of cognition is predictable.

14. d. is the correct answer. (objective 6)

Lesson Review

Lesson 18

Early Adulthood
Cognitive Development

Please Note: Use this matrix to guide your study and achieve the learning objectives of this lesson. It will also help you to view the video, which defines and demonstrates important concepts and skills as they relate to everyday life.

Learning Objective	Textbook	Course Student Guide	Video Lesson
1. Identify three approaches to the study of adult cognition, and describe the postformal approach.	pp. 491–492	Practice Questions I: 2, 6, 7; Practice Questions II: 1, 2; Applying Your Knowledge: 6.	Segment 1: *Postformal Thought*
2. Describe the main characteristics of postformal thought and discuss how it differs from formal operational thought.	pp. 492–499	Key Terms: 1, 2, 3, 4, 5, 6; Practice Questions I: 1, 3, 4, 11, 18; Practice Questions II: 2, 3, 6, 9, 12, 14; Applying Your Knowledge: 1, 2, 6, 12.	Segment 1: *Postformal Thought*
3. Define and describe dialectical thought, and give examples of its usefulness.	pp. 500–502	Key Terms: 6, 7, 8, 9; Practice Questions I: 8, 9, 19; Practice Questions II: 4, 8; Applying Your Knowledge: 1, 8.	Segment 1: *Postformal Thought*
4. Draw a conclusion about whether postformal thought represents a separate stage of development.	pp. 493–494	Practice Questions I: 10, 17, 22; Practice Questions II: 5; Applying Your Knowledge: 1, 12.	Introduction; Segment 1: *Postformal Thought*
5. Explain the views of Carol Gilligan and others who believe that moral reasoning is influenced by culture and life experiences.	p. 504	Practice Questions I: 13, 20; Practice Questions II: 10; Applying Your Knowledge: 9.	Segment 3: *Moral Reasoning*
6. Briefly describe the six stages of faith outlined by James Fowler.	pp. 505–506	Key Terms: 10, 11; Practice Questions I: 5, 23; Practice Questions II: 11, 13; Applying Your Knowledge: 7, 14.	

Learning Objective	Textbook	Course Student Guide	Video Lesson
7. Explain how the Defining Issues Test helps relate moral development to other aspects of adult cognition and life satisfaction.	p. 505	Key Terms: 12; Practice Questions I: 12.	
8. Discuss the relationship between cognitive growth and higher education.	pp. 507–510	Practice Questions I: 14, 15, 24; Practice Questions II: 7, 15; Applying Your Knowledge: 3, 4, 10, 13.	Segment 2: *Life Experiences and Their Effects*
9. Identify and evaluate differences between contemporary colleges and college students and their counterparts of a decade or two ago.	pp. 510–515	Practice Questions I: 16, 21, 25; Applying Your Knowledge: 11.	Segment 2: *Life Experiences and Their Effects*
10. Discuss how life events may trigger new patterns of thinking and result in cognitive growth.	pp. 500–501	Practice Questions I: 26; Applying Your Knowledge: 5.	Segment 2: *Life Experiences and Their Effects*

Love and Work

Lesson 19

Early Adulthood:
Psychosocial Development

Preview

Biologically mature and no longer bound by parental authority, the young adult typically is now free to choose a particular path of development. Today, the options are incredibly varied. Not surprisingly, then, the hallmark of psychosocial development during early adulthood is diversity. Nevertheless, developmentalists have identified several themes or patterns that help us understand the course of development between the ages of 18 and 35.

After describing the task of identity development, the lesson turns next to the two basic psychosocial needs of adulthood, love and work. No matter what terminology is used, these two needs are recognized by almost all developmentalists.

Next, the lesson discusses the need for **intimacy** in adulthood, focusing on the development of friendship, love, and marriage. The impact of divorce is also discussed.

The final section of the lesson is concerned with **generativity**, or the motivation to be productive during adulthood, highlighting the importance of work and parenthood and addressing the special challenges facing stepparents, adoptive parents, and foster parents.

As you complete this lesson, consider your own psychosocial development during early adulthood (or that of someone you know in this age range). How strong is (was) your need to make friends, fall in love, get married, build a career, and have children? Have these needs grown over time? Have you felt any family or social pressure to move ahead in these areas? How have your friendships changed in young adulthood compared to adolescence? Consider your romantic relationships. What does intimacy mean to you? What role does it play in your life? Consider your marriage (or, if you're not married, your idea of marriage). In your opinion, what are the characteristics of a successful marriage? Do you know anyone who has been divorced? How do you think this might have affected their development? Consider your career. How important is work to you, and why? Do you or does someone you know have children? How might parenthood affect his or her development?

Prior Course Knowledge that Will Be Used in this Lesson
- Erik Erikson's theory (from Lesson 2) will be used to help explain psychosocial development during young adulthood. Recall that Erikson specifies eight stages of psychosocial development, each of which is characterized by a particular challenge, which is central to that stage of life and must be resolved:

1. Trust vs. Mistrust (birth to 1 year)
2. Autonomy vs. Shame and Doubt (1 to 3 years)
3. Initiative vs. Guilt (3 to 6 years)
4. Industry vs. Inferiority (7 to 11 years)
5. Identity vs. Role Confusion (adolescence)
6. **Intimacy vs. Isolation (adulthood)**
7. **Generativity vs. Stagnation (adulthood)**
8. Integrity vs. Despair (Adulthood)

- This lesson will also return to Erikson's challenge of "identity vs. role confusion" (from Lesson 16). Experts agree that many young adults grapple with identity issues well into their 20s (sometimes later), as they continue to work out "who they are." In other words, this challenge may not be resolved in adolescence.

Learning Objectives

Use this information to guide your reading, viewing, thinking, and studying. After successfully completing this lesson, you should be able to:

1. Describe the psychosocial tasks of identity, intimacy, and generativity, and explain how the viewpoint of most developmentalists regarding adult stages has shifted.
2. Explain how the social clock influences the timing of important events during early adulthood.
3. Review the changing nature of friendships during adulthood, noting factors that promote friendship and gender differences in friendship patterns.
4. Describe common young adult experiences with romantic relationships and identify and discuss Sternberg's three components of love.
5. Discuss the role of serious relationships and marriage in adulthood, describe the impact of cohabitation on relationships, and identify at least three factors that influence relationship success.
6. Discuss partner abuse, focusing on its forms, contributing factors, and prevention.
7. Discuss the importance of work to the individual and how the experiences of today's workers differ from those of past generations.
8. Discuss the myths, challenges, and opportunities of dual-earner family life.
9. Describe the changing relationship between emerging adults and their parents.
10. Explain variation in well-being during emerging adulthood.

📖 **Read Chapter 19, "Emerging Adulthood: Psychosocial Development," pages 519–545.**

⏮ **View the video for Lesson 19, "Love and Work."**

Segment 1: *The Tasks of Adulthood*

Segment 2: *Intimacy*

Segment 3: *Generativity*

Summary

Although psychosocial development in early adulthood is marked by diversity, two basic needs or "tasks" drive its evolution: *intimacy*, achieved through friendships and love relationships; and *generativity*, usually achieved through work and/or parenting or later.

The **social clock** is a culturally set timetable that establishes when various events and behaviors in life typically take place. The "settings" of the social clock still influence behavior, but less rigidly than in the past. For example, our current social clock would suggest that adolescents are too young to be getting married; our cultural timetable places marriage sometime during early adulthood or later.

Young adults typically form extensive and varied social networks. Whereas friendships for women may be important as a way of coping with problems, for men friendship may include elements of competition and may serve as a way of maintaining a favorable self-concept.

For most people, the deepest source of intimacy is found through an intimate relationship with a mate, typically through **cohabitation** and/or marriage. In general, the younger marriage partners are when they wed, the less likely the marriage is to succeed. Marriages between partners with similar interests and backgrounds (**homogamy**) are more likely to endure than those between dissimilar partners (**heterogamy**). The extent to which partners perceive equality in their relationship, or **marital equity**, also affects the fate of marriage.

For many adults, working is central to living for reasons that extend beyond financial security. Work is an outlet for self-expression, a source of esteem and status, and a context for mentoring. The shift from a manufacturing to a service-based economy means that workers today must acquire more flexible job skills than ever before. Another shift is that most parents today are part of **dual-earner**, dual-caregiving relationships, facing both benefits and problems that traditional families in the past did not have.

 Review all reading assignments for this lesson.

 As assigned by your instructor, complete the optional online component for this lesson.

Key Terms

Using your own words, write a brief definition or explanation of each of the following terms on a separate piece of paper.

1. intimacy versus isolation
2. hookup
3. social networks
4. choice overload
5. cohabitation
6. homogamy
7. heterogamy
8. social homogamy
9. demand/withdraw interaction
10. situational couple violence
11. intimate terrorism
12. linked lives
13. marital equity
14. dual-earner family
15. generativity versus stagnation
16. social clock
17. identity

Practice Questions I

Multiple-Choice Questions

1. According to Erik Erikson, the first basic task of adulthood is to establish
   a. a residence apart from parents.
   b. intimacy with others.
   c. generativity through work or parenthood.
   d. a career commitment.

2. Most social scientists who study adulthood emphasize that
   a. intimacy and generativity take various forms throughout adulthood.
   b. adult lives are less orderly and predictable than stage models suggest.
   c. each culture has a somewhat different social clock.
   d. all of the above are true.

3. Choosing a mate using online tools can result in
   a. incompatible marriages.
   b. a quicker establishment of intimacy.
   c. choice overload.
   d. a tendency to avoid commitment.

4. Some emerging adults are surprised to find that casual sex
   a. can lead to emotional entanglements.
   b. can produce a pregnancy.
   c. is an easy answer to the need for a sexual partner.
   d. makes it easier to establish a romance with a third party.

5. The concept of linked lives helps explain why
   a. adult children benefit from continued connections to their parents.
   b. it can be detrimental to young adults' well-being to achieve complete independence from their parents.
   c. parents remain invested in their adult child's development.
   d. all of the above are true.

6. According to Erikson, the failure to achieve intimacy during early adulthood is most likely to result in
   a. generativity.
   b. stagnation.
   c. role diffusion.
   d. isolation.

7. Regarding friendships, most young adults tend to
   a. be very satisfied.
   b. be very dissatisfied.
   c. find it difficult to form social networks.
   d. be without close friends.

8. According to Robert Sternberg, consummate love emerges
   a. as a direct response to passion.
   b. as a direct response to physical intimacy.
   c. when commitment is added to passion and intimacy.
   d. during the early years of parenthood.

9. An arrangement in which two unrelated, unmarried adults of the opposite sex live together is called
   a. cross-sex friendship.
   b. a passive-congenial pattern.
   c. cohabitation.
   d. affiliation.

10. Differences in religious customs or rituals are most likely to arise in a
    a. homogamous couple.
    b. heterogamous couple.
    c. cohabiting couple.
    d. very young married couple.

11. Identity is typically achieved
    a. after intimacy.
    b. after generativity.
    c. during adolescence.
    d. during emerging adulthood.

12. Adults who combine the roles of spouse, parent, and employee tend to report
    a. less overall happiness than other adults.
    b. more overall happiness than other adults.
    c. regrets over parental roles.
    d. problems in career advancement.

True or False Items

Write T (for true) or F (for false) on the line in front of each statement.

13. __T__ According to Erikson, adults experience a crisis of intimacy versus isolation and, after that, a crisis of generativity versus stagnation.

14. __T__ The best time to marry and have children is influenced by a cultural "social clock."

15. __F__ According to Sternberg, early in a relationship, emotional intimacy is at its highest.

16. __F__ The younger the bride and groom, the more likely their marriage is to succeed.

17. __T__ Gender diversity in the workplace is decreasing.

18. __F__ A high level of marital homogamy is extremely rare.

19. __T__ It is best for the development of emerging adults to eliminate their emotional and financial dependence on their parents.

20. __F__ Because of the complexity of the high-tech work world, most young adults can expect to remain at the same job throughout their careers.

21. __T__ When both verbal and physical abuse are taken into account, more women than men are considered abusive.

22. __F__ Friends are less important during emerging adulthood than they are in adolescence.

Practice Questions II

Multiple-Choice Questions

1. Generativity
   a. is often experienced before intimacy.
   b. describes an emerging adult's need to be independent of their parents.
   c. ensures the next generation will be cared for.
   d. produces feelings of profound aloneness or isolation.

2. Women often stay in a relationship with an abusive husband because
   a. they believe that this is the norm for marital relationships.
   b. they have been conditioned to accept the abuse.
   c. they are isolated from those who might encourage them to leave.
   d. of both b and c.

3. Which of the following was **NOT** cited in the textbook as a reason for men's friendships tending to be much less intimate than women's?
   a. The tendency of boys to be more active and girls more verbal during childhood lays the groundwork for interaction patterns in adulthood.
   b. Intimacy is grounded in mutual vulnerability, a characteristic discouraged in men.
   c. Many men fear their friendships will be associated with homosexuality.
   d. Men tend to be more focused on achievement needs than women.

4. The prime effect of the social clock is to make an individual aware of
   a. his or her socioeconomic status.
   b. the diversity of psychosocial paths during early adulthood.
   c. the means of fulfilling affiliation and achievement needs.
   d. the "right" or "best" time for assuming adult roles.

5. Which of the following statements about ethnic identity development is **FALSE**?
   a. It is a reciprocal process, involving responses to others and personal choices.
   b. It is typically established only once, during emerging adulthood.
   c. It is influenced by context, such as life circumstances.
   d. It is multi-faceted, meaning that one can accept certain aspects and reject others.

6. Cross-sex friendships provide several advantages to both men and women, including that they
   a. allow men to assist women in solving problems.
   b. expand each partner's perspective.
   c. make it acceptable for men and women to engage in good-natured teasing.
   d. allow men and women to develop sexual relationships without the bonds of marriage.

7. Whereas men's friendships tend to be based on _____, friendships between women tend to be based on _____.
   a. shared confidences; shared interests
   b. cooperation; competition
   c. shared interests; shared confidences
   d. finding support for personal problems; discussion of practical issues

8. According to Robert Sternberg, the three dimensions of love are
   a. passion, intimacy, and consummate love.
   b. physical intimacy, emotional intimacy, and consummate love.
   c. passion, commitment, and consummate love.
   d. passion, intimacy, and commitment.

9. Research on cohabitation in the United States suggests that
   a. relatively few young adults ever live with an unrelated partner of the other sex.
   b. cohabiting couples are more likely to separate than married couples.
   c. adults who cohabit tend to be happier and healthier than married people are.
   d. none of the above are true.

10. A homogamous marriage is best defined as a marriage between
    a. people who are physically similar to each other.
    b. people of similar social backgrounds.
    c. people of dissimilar socioeconomic backgrounds.
    d. two caring people of the same sex.

11. The strongest motivation to attend college is to resolve one's
    a. social homogamy.
    b. exclusion criteria.
    c. ethnic identity.
    d. vocational identity.

12. Today's workforce
    a. is less predictable than in previous years.
    b. should not expect to remain in a single career for their entire working lives.
    c. is characterized by more dual-earner couples than in previous years.
    d. is characterized by all of the above.

13. Over the years of adulthood, people who balance marital, parental, and vocational loads
    a. inevitably suffer from the stress of role overload.
    b. are far more likely to divorce.
    c. generally are happier than those who function in only one or two of these roles.
    d. experience both a and b.

14. One potential, unintended outcome of the quest for vocational identity is
    a. remaining in the same job for the majority of the adulthood years.
    b. unrealistic expectations regarding how self-fulfilled one will find one's work to be.
    c. failing to recognize the importance of education.
    d. burnout from focusing so intently on building one's résumé.

15. According to research, which of the following factors does **NOT** contribute to a happy marriage?
    a. cohabitation before marriage
    b. the degree to which a couple is homogamous or heterogamous
    c. the degree of marital equity
    d. whether identity needs have been met before marriage

Matching Items
Match each definition or description with its corresponding term.

Terms
16.	E	social clock	21.	F	hookup
17.	G	cohabitation	22.	C	social homogamy
18.	A	intimate terrorism	23.	B	linked lives
19.	D	heterogamy	24.	I	homogamy
20.	H	marital equity	25.	J	situational couple violence

Descriptions or Definitions
a. abusive relationship that often leads to violence, usually against the woman
b. lives in which relationships with other family members, including other generations, increase success, health and well-being
c. the similarity of a couple's leisure interests and role preferences
d. a marriage between people with dissimilar interests and backgrounds
e. the culturally set timetable at which key life events are deemed appropriate
f. a sexual encounter between two people who are not romantically involved
g. arrangement in which two unrelated adults of the opposite sex live together
h. the extent to which partners perceive equality in their relationship
i. a marriage between people with similar interests and backgrounds
j. fighting between couples brought on by a situation rather than personality problems

Applying Your Knowledge

1. Jack is in his mid-20s. Compared to his father, who was 25 during the late 1950s, Jack is
   a. more likely to have settled on a career.
   b. less likely to have settled on a career.
   c. likely to feel more social pressure to make decisions regarding career, marriage, and so forth.
   d. more likely to be concerned with satisfying his need for achievement at a younger age.

2. Marie is 24 years old. Compared to past generation, what is likely to be true about Marie's relationship with her parents?
   a. It is a more important and crucial influence on her development.
   b. It is not as close.
   c. It is less likely to involve financial support.
   d. None of the above are likely to be true.

3. After describing cross-cultural differences in the parent-child relationship in adulthood, Dr. Slater summarizes her research by stating,
   a. "The best role for parents to take during their child's transition to adulthood is to try and determine everything that the adult child is doing and thinking."
   b. "In developing nations, the focus during young adulthood is on continued dependence on parents."
   c. "Adults from Western nations focus on establishing independence from their parents."
   d. "Across cultures adult children develop a sense of independence while also remaining closely connected to parents."

4. To determine ways to lower the high rate of divorce, Dr. Wilson is conducting research on marital satisfaction and the factors that contribute to it. Which of the following would he consider to be important factors?
   a. homogamy
   b. social homogamy
   c. marital equity
   d. All of the above contribute to marital satisfaction.

5. Rwanda and Rodney have been dating for about a month. Their relationship is most likely characterized by
   a. strong feelings of commitment.
   b. consummate love.
   c. physical intimacy without true emotional intimacy.
   d. all of the above.

6. I am 25 years old. It is most likely that I
   a. am married.
   b. am divorced.
   c. have never been married.
   d. am divorced and remarried.

7. If asked to explain the high failure rate of marriages between young adults, Erik Erikson would most likely say that
   a. achievement goals are often more important than intimacy in early adulthood.
   b. intimacy is difficult to establish until identity is formed.
   c. divorce has almost become an expected stage in development.
   d. today's cohort of young adults has higher expectations of marriage than did previous cohorts.

8. Which of the following employer initiatives would be most likely to increase employee job satisfaction?
   a. offering higher wages
   b. offering improved worker benefits
   c. the opportunity to develop personal skills
   d. All of the above have about the same impact on employee satisfaction.

9. Which of the following would be the worst advice for a young adult entering the job market today?
   a. Seek education that fosters a variety of psychosocial and cognitive skills.
   b. Expect that educational requirements for work will shift every few years.
   c. To avoid diluting your skills, concentrate your education on preparing for one specific job.
   d. Be flexible and willing to adjust to the varied pacing and timing of today's jobs.

10. Which of the following best summarizes the research on psychological well-being during emerging adulthood?
   a. Overall emerging adulthood is a time of declining psychological well-being.
   b. Because well-being is determined by genetics, there are no clear patterns of development regarding well-being during emerging adulthood.
   c. The challenges and opportunities of emerging adulthood can lead to enhanced well-being or increased vulnerability toward psychological disorders.
   d. Emerging adults are most likely to thrive if they are encouraged to become as independent as possible.

11. Jessica would like to discuss a problem, but Mario says he doesn't have time. The more Mario avoids the discussion, the more Jessica presses him. This couple is engaged in

    a. a demand-withdraw interaction.
    b. situational couple violence.
    c. intimate terrorism.
    d. intimacy versus isolation.

12. Arthur and Mabel have been married for 5 years. According to Sternberg, if their relationship is a satisfying one, which of the following best describes their relationship?

    a. They are strongly committed to each other.
    b. They are passionately in love.
    c. They are in the throes of establishing intimacy.
    d. They are beginning to wonder why the passion has left their relationship.

13. Hamah and Oliver are recent college graduates who have been dating for three years and are considering living with each other before they get married. They should be informed that

    a. their experience of cohabitation will be very similar to their experience as a married couple.
    b. they will be unusual because most of their friends will not live together before marriage.
    c. cohabitation does not appear to solve problems in the relationship previous to marriage.
    d. cohabitation relationships tend to be more harmonious than married relationships.

Answer Key

Key Terms

1. According to Erik Erikson, the first crisis of adulthood is intimacy versus isolation, which involves the need to share one's personal life with someone else or risk profound loneliness. (p. 525; video lesson, segment 1; objective 1)

2. A sexual encounter between two people who are not in a romantic relationship, with no expectation of intimacy or commitment, is called a hookup. (p. 531; objective 3)

3. A Web site that allows users to post personal details and interact with friends is called a social network. (p. 531; objective 3)

4. Having so many possibilities that a thoughtful choice becomes difficult is called choice overload. This is particularly apparent when social networking and other technology make many potential romantic partners available. (p. 531; objective 7)

5. Increasingly common among young adults in all industrialized countries is the living pattern called cohabitation, in which two unrelated adults of the opposite sex live together. (p. 532; objective 5)

6. Homogamy refers to marriage between people who are similar in attitudes, socioeconomic background, interests, ethnicity, religion, and the like. (p. 535; video lesson, segment 2; objective 5)

7. Heterogamy refers to marriage between people who are dissimilar in attitudes, interests, socioeconomic status, religion, ethnic background, and goals. (p. 535; objective 5)

8. Social homogamy is defined as similarity in leisure interests and role preferences. (p. 535; objective 5)

9. An interaction between romantic partners in which one insists on talking about an issue while the other insists on not talking is called a demand-withdraw interaction. (p. 536; objective 5)

10. Fighting between romantic partners brought on more by the situation than personality problems is called situational couple violence. (p. 538; objective 6)

11. Intimate terrorism is the form of spouse abuse in which the husband uses violent methods of accelerating intensity to isolate, degrade, and punish the wife. (p. 538; objective 6)

12. When the accomplishments and struggles of one's life are connected to the lives of others, as is the case in the relationship between parents and adult children, this is referred to as linked lives. (p. 539; objective 9)

13. An important factor in a successful marriage, marital equity involves how much each partner perceives that the other is contributing to the relationship to help make it work. (video lesson, segment 2; objective 5)

14. Dual-earner families are those in which both spouses work at jobs outside the home. (video lesson, segment 3; objective 8)

15. In Erikson's theory, the second crisis of adulthood is generativity versus stagnation, which involves the need to be productive in some meaningful way, usually through work or parenthood. Generativity is best described as a commitment to the next generation. (video lesson, segment 1; objective 1)

16. The social clock represents the culturally set timetable that establishes when various events and behaviors in life are appropriate and called for. (video lesson, segment 1; objective 2)

17. In Erikson's theory, the crisis that begins in late adolescence and may extend into young adulthood is identity, which involves the need to find out who we are and how we fit into the adult world. (video lesson, segment 1; objective 1)

Practice Questions I

Multiple-Choice Questions

1. b. is the correct answer. (video lesson, segment 1; objective 1)

2. d. is the correct answer. (video lesson, segment 1; objectives 1 & 2)

3. c. is the correct answer. (objectives 3 & 4)

4. a. is the correct answer. (objectives 3 & 4)

5. d. is the correct answer. (objective 9)

6. d. is the correct answer. (video lesson, segment 3; objective 1)

   a. is incorrect. Generativity is a characteristic of the crisis following the intimacy crisis.

   b. is incorrect. Stagnation occurs when generativity needs are not met.

   c. is incorrect. Erikson's theory does not address this issue.

7. a. is the correct answer. (objective 3)

   c. is incorrect. Because they are mobile and tend to have fewer commitments, young adults find it relatively easy to form friendships.

   d. is incorrect. Almost never do young adults feel bereft of friendship.

8. c. is the correct answer. (objective 4)

    d. is incorrect. Sternberg's theory is not concerned with the stages of parenthood.

9. c. is the correct answer. (objective 5)

10. b. is the correct answer. (objective 5)

    a. is incorrect. By definition, homogamous couples share values, background, and the like.

    c. & d. are incorrect. These may or may not be true, depending on the extent to which such a couple is homogamous.

11. d. is the correct answer. (objective 1)

12. b. is the correct answer. (video lesson, segment 3; objective 8)

    c. is incorrect. Most parents report that they are pleased that they have had children.

True or False Items

13. T (video lesson, segment 1; objective 1)

14. T (video lesson, segment 1; objective 2)

15. F Physical intimacy and feelings of closeness are highest in the earliest stages of a relationship. (objective 4)

16. F Just the reverse is true. (objective 5)

17. F (video lesson; segment 3; objective 3)

18. T (video lesson, segment 2; objective 5)

19. F (objective 9)

20. F Most young adults should learn basic skills so that they have the flexibility to move into different jobs. (video lesson, segment 3; objective 7)

21. T (objective 6)

22. F (objective 3)

Practice Questions II

Multiple-Choice Questions

1. c. is the correct answer. (video lesson, segment 3; objective 1)

2. d. is the correct answer. (objective 6)

3. d. is the correct answer. (objective 3)

4. d. is the correct answer. (video lesson, segment 1; objective 2)

5. b. is the correct answer. (objective 1)

6. b. is the correct answer. (objective 3)

    a. is incorrect. Men are frustrated that women won't allow them to do this.

    c. is incorrect. Women become upset by such teasing.

    d. is incorrect. Men may try to make a platonic relationship sexual, women are offended when they do so.

7. c. is the correct answer. (objective 3)

8. d. is the correct answer. (objective 4)

    a., b., & c. are incorrect. According to Sternberg, consummate love emerges when commitment is added to passion and intimacy.

9. b. is the correct answer. (objective 5)

   a. is incorrect. Slightly more than half of all women aged 25 to 40 in the United States cohabit before their first marriage.

   c. is incorrect. In fact, a large study of adults found that cohabitants were much less happy and healthy than married people were.

10. b. is the correct answer. (video lesson, segment 2; objective 5)

    a. & d. are incorrect. These characteristics do not pertain to homogamy.

    c. is incorrect. This describes a heterogamous marriage.

11. d. is the correct answer. (objective 1)

12. d. is the correct answer. (video lesson, segment 3; objective 7)

13. c. is the correct answer. (video lesson, segment 3; objective 8)

14. b. is the correct answer. (objective 1)

15. a. is the correct answer. Cohabitation before marriage does not strengthen the relationship. (video lesson, segment 2; objective 5)

Matching Items

16. e (video lesson, segment 1; objective 2)

17. g (objective 5)

18. a (objective 6)

19. d (objective 5)

20. h (video lesson, segment 2; objective 5)

21. f (objective 5)

22. c (objective 5)

23. b (objective 10)

24. i (video lesson, segment 2; objective 5)

25. j (objective 6)

Applying Your Knowledge

1. b. is the correct answer. (video lesson, segment 1; objectives 1 & 7)

   c. & d. are incorrect. The video lesson does not indicate that there are cohort effects in these areas.

2. a. is the correct answer. (objective 9)

3. d. is the correct answer. (objective 9)

4. d. is the correct answer. The most successful relationships are between people of similar backgrounds and similar interests. The partners' perceptions of marital equity are also important. (video lesson, segment 2; objective 5)

5. c. is the correct answer. (objective 4)

   a. & b. are incorrect. These feelings emerge more gradually in relationships.

6. c. is the correct answer. (objective 5)

7. b. is the correct answer. (video lesson, segment 1; objective 1)

   a. is incorrect. In Erikson's theory, the crisis of intimacy precedes the need to be productive through work.

   c. & d. are incorrect. Although these items are true, Erikson's theory does not address these issues.

8. c. is the correct answer. (video lesson, segment 3; objective 7)

9. c. is the correct answer. (video lesson, segment 3; objective 7)

    a., b., & d. are incorrect. These would all be good pieces of advice for new workers today.

10. c. is the correct answer. (objective 10)

11. a. is the correct answer. (objective 5)

12. a. is the correct answer. (objective 4)

13. c. is the correct answer. (objective 5)

Lesson Review

Lesson 19

Early Adulthood
Psychosocial Development

Please Note: Use this matrix to guide your study and achieve the learning objectives of this lesson. It will also help you to view the video, which defines and demonstrates important concepts and skills as they relate to everyday life.

Learning Objective	Textbook	Course Student Guide	Video Lesson
1. Describe the psychosocial tasks of identity, intimacy and generativity, and explain how the viewpoint of most developmentalists regarding adult stages has shifted.	pp. 519–523, 525	Key Terms: 1, 15, 17; Practice Questions I: 1, 2, 6, 11, 13; Practice Questions II: 1, 5, 11, 14; Applying Your Knowledge: 1, 7.	Segment 1: *The Tasks of Adulthood;* Segment 2: *Intimacy;* Segment 3: *Generativity*
2. Explain how the social clock influences the timing of important events during early adulthood.	*	Key Terms: 16; Practice Questions I: 2, 14; Practice Questions II: 4, 16.	Segment 1: *The Tasks of Adulthood*
3. Review the changing nature of friendships during adulthood, noting factors that promote friendship and gender differences in friendship patterns.	pp. 525–527	Key Terms: 2, 3; Practice Questions I: 3, 4, 7, 17, 22; Practice Questions II: 3, 6, 7.	
4. Describe common young adult experiences with romantic relationships and identify and discuss Sternberg's three components of love.	pp. 527–531	Practice Questions I: 3, 4, 8, 15; Practice Questions II: 8; Applying Your Knowledge: 5, 12.	
5. Discuss the role of serious relationships and marriage in adulthood, describe the impact of cohabitation on relationships, and identify at least three factors that influence relationship success.	pp. 531–536	Key Terms: 5, 6, 7, 8, 9, 13; Practice Questions I: 9, 10, 16, 18; Practice Questions II: 9, 10, 15, 17, 19, 20, 21, 22, 24; Applying Your Knowledge: 4, 6, 11, 13.	Segment 2: *Intimacy*
6. Discuss spouse abuse, focusing on its forms, contributing factors, and prevention.	p. 537	Key Terms: 10, 11; Practice Questions I: 21; Practice Questions II: 2, 18, 25.	

Learning Objective	Textbook	Course Student Guide	Video Lesson
7. Discuss the importance of work to the individual and how the experiences of today's workers differ from those of past generations.	*	Key Terms: 4; Practice Questions I: 20; Practice Questions II: 12; Applying Your Knowledge: 1, 8, 9.	Segment 3: *Generativity*
8. Discuss the myths, challenges, and opportunities of dual-earner family life.	*	Key Terms: 14; Practice Questions I: 12; Practice Questions II: 13.	Segment 3: *Generativity*
9. Describe the changing relationship between emerging adults and their parents.	pp. 539–542	Key Terms: 12; Practice Questions I: 5, 19; Applying Your Knowledge: 2, 3.	
10. Explain variations in well-being during emerging adulthood, and identify characteristics of psychopathology.	pp. 523–525	Practice Questions II: 23; Applying Your Knowledge: 10.	

* The video for this lesson offers a useful exploration of this concept.

Thriving in Midlife

Lesson 20

Middle Adulthood:
Biosocial Development

Preview

This lesson deals with biosocial development between the ages of 25 and 64. It begins by describing changes in appearance and in the functioning of the sense organs and vital body systems. The potential impact of these changes for women and men is discussed. Although declines in all the body's senses and systems occur, for most adults these changes have no significant health consequences and do not interfere with daily living. Indeed, today's cohort of middle-aged adults is healthier than cohorts from previous years.

This lesson further explores health-related behaviors of the middle-aged, focusing on smoking, drinking, eating habits, and exercise. By middle age, most adults understand how lifestyle choices and health habits can affect their well-being. There is a decline in the number of smokers, as well as a tendency toward moderation in alcohol consumption. However, for a number of adults, risky lifestyle behaviors remain serious health hazards.

The lesson continues with a discussion of reasons for individual variations in health. These variations arise from a combination of many factors, including race, ethnicity, socioeconomic status, and gender. The lesson concludes with a discussion of the changes in the sexual-reproductive system that occur during adulthood and shows why many individuals find these changes less troubling than they anticipated.

Prior Course Knowledge that Will Be Used in this Lesson

• Biosocial development during the school years (Lesson 11), adolescence (Lesson 14), and early adulthood (Lesson 17) will be referred to as we discuss normal changes in adulthood and reasons for variations in health.

• BMI (body mass index) (Lesson 11) will be referred to as we discuss obesity as a risk factor for diabetes and other chronic illnesses.

Learning Objectives

Use this information to guide your reading, viewing, thinking, and studying. After successfully completing this lesson, you should be able to:

1. Identify typical physical changes of middle adulthood and discuss their impact.
2. Describe how the functions of the sense organs and vital body systems change during middle adulthood.

3. Describe the relationship between certain lifestyle factors—smoking, alcohol use, nutrition, weight, and exercise—and health.

4. Differentiate four measures of health, and explain the concept of quality-adjusted life years.

5. Explain how variations in health are related to gender, socioeconomic status, and stress.

6. Identify the typical changes that occur in the sexual-reproductive system during adulthood, and explain the potential positive and negative outcomes of these changes.

📖 **Read Chapter 20, "Adulthood: Biosocial Development," pages 547–577.**

⏮ **View the video for Lesson 20, "Thriving in Midlife."**

Segment 1: *Normal Physical Changes*

Segment 2: *Health Habits*

Segment 3: *Variations in Health*

Segment 4: *The Sexual Reproductive System*

Summary

Although the biological clock does not program a series of specific events to mark midlife, for most women and men, the years of middle adulthood bring about signs of aging that cannot be ignored. For example, the bodies of middle-aged adults have been aging for decades, but so imperceptibly that it takes years for some declines to become apparent. These signs include the graying and thinning of the hair, drying and wrinkling of the skin, and other changes in appearance. They also include noticeable losses in hearing and vision, and a reduction in organ reserve in the lungs, heart, and digestive and immune systems.

In general, middle-aged persons are healthier today than were earlier cohorts. Variations in health—measured in terms of **mortality**, **morbidity**, **disability**, and **vitality**—are related to genetic, educational, and socioeconomic factors, among others. The most important reason for individual variations in health, however, is personal lifestyle. Risk factors include cigarette smoking, alcohol consumption, poor nutrition, obesity, and lack of exercise.

Ethnicity, with its attendant genetic and cultural factors, is also a powerful influence on all four measures of health in middle age. Gender is also an important factor. Beginning at midlife, women have higher morbidity and disability rates than men, due in part to a gender bias in medical research that has paid insufficient attention to arthritis, **osteoporosis**, and other common chronic illnesses that affect far more women than men.

Most women find **menopause**, with its accompanying cessation of menstruation and decline in estrogen, much less troubling than they expected it to be. Although men do not experience sudden age-related drops in hormone levels or fertility, sexual response does slow down over time. Some experts suggest that the term **andropause** should be used to refer to these changes in the reproductive capabilities of men. Because of wide individual variations, however, past experience is a better predictor of sexual activity during middle adulthood than is aging.

📖 **Review all reading assignments for this lesson.**

💻 **As assigned by your instructor, complete the optional online component for this lesson.**

Key Terms

Using your own words, write a brief definition or explanation of each of the following terms on a separate piece of paper.

1. presbycusis
2. menopause
3. HRT (hormone replacement therapy)
4. andropause
5. stressor
6. problem-focused coping
7. emotion-focused coping
8. allostatic load
9. weathering
10. public health
11. mortality
12. morbidity
13. disability
14. DALYs (disability-adjusted life years)
15. vitality
16. QALYs (quality-adjusted life years)
17. osteoporosis

Practice Questions I

Multiple-Choice Questions

1. During the years from age 25 to age 64, the average adult
   a. becomes proportionally slimmer.
   b. gains about 5 pounds per year.
   c. gains about 1 pound per year.
   d. is more likely to be overweight.

2. The overall impact of aging depends largely on the individual's
   a. general physical health.
   b. genetic predisposition toward disease.
   c. attitudes about aging.
   d. health habits and lifestyle.

3. Age-related deficits in speech-related hearing are most noticeable for
   a. high-frequency sounds.
   b. low-frequency sounds.
   c. mid-range-frequency sounds.
   d. rapid conversation.

4. Level of disability is determined in part by
   a. the impact on a person's normal functioning.
   b. the origin of the condition.
   c. whether the person is able to engage in vigorous exercise.
   d. none of the above.

5. At midlife, individuals who _____ tend to live longer and have fewer chronic illnesses or disabilities.
   a. are relatively well educated
   b. are financially secure
   c. live in or near cities
   d. are or do all of the above

6. The term that refers to diseases of all kinds is
   a. mortality.
   b. morbidity.
   c. disability.
   d. vitality.

7. On average, women reach menopause at age
   a. 39.
   b. 42.
   c. 46.
   d. 51.

8. In explaining ethnic variations in health and illness during middle age, _____ factors are more important than _____ factors.
   a. genetic; social and psychological
   b. social and psychological; genetic
   c. intrinsic; cultural
   d. cultural; extrinsic

9. In middle age, _____ rates are higher for men than for women, whereas _____ rates are higher for women than men.
   a. mortality; morbidity
   b. morbidity; mortality
   c. vitality; disability
   d. disability; vitality

10. The leading cause(s) of mortality in both sexes include
    a. obesity and diabetes.
    b. accidents and homicides.
    c. heart disease and cancer.
    d. stroke and neurological disease.

11. The concept that indicates how many years of full physical, intellectual, and social health are lost to a particular physical disease or disability is
    a. vitality
    b. disability
    c. morbidity
    d. quality-adjusted life years.

12. Physical symptoms that accompany menopause, such as hot flashes,
    a. intensely bother most women.
    b. intensely bother a few women.
    c. slightly bother all women.
    d. don't bother any women.

13. Which of the following is true of all smoking diseases?
    a. They are a natural result of smoking for ten years or more, whether or not the person eventually quit.
    b. They are related to dosage of nicotine taken in and to length of time the person has smoked.
    c. They are all incurable.
    d. They are all based on the psychological addiction to tobacco.

14. Allostatic load is an accumulation of physiological responses that
    a. are the result of age.
    b. are the result of stress.
    c. can eventually take a physical toll, increasing the risk of disease.
    d. are all of the above.

True or False Items
Write T (for true) or F (for false) on the line in front of each statement.

F 15. __T__ Age-related trends in sexual responsiveness are similar for men and women.

16. __F__ Problem-focused coping is more effective than emotion-focused coping.

F 17. __T__ Approximately half of all middle-aged Americans are obese.

18. __F__ Moderate users of alcohol are more likely than non-drinkers to have heart attacks.

19. __T__ Those who exercise regularly have lower rates of serious illness than do sedentary people.

20. __F__ Middle-aged adults are less likely to improve their health habits than are members of any other age group.

21. __T__ During middle adulthood, sexual responses slow down, particularly in men.

F 22. __T__ Most physicians recommend that women who want to have children begin childbearing by age 35.

23. __F__ Scientists agree that there is no "male menopause."

24. __T__ A woman's culture, expectations, and attitude, more than biology, determine her psychological reaction to menopause.

Practice Questions II

Multiple-Choice Questions

1. For most people, the normal changes in appearance that occur during middle age have the greatest impact on their
   a. physical strength.
   b. flexibility.
   c. cardiovascular reserve.
   d. self-image.

2. Age-related deficits in the sense organs are most obvious in
   a. taste and touch.
   b. vision and hearing.
   c. smell and balance.
   d. balance and hearing.

3. After puberty, visual acuity is influenced more by _____ than by _____.
   a. heredity; age
   b. age; heredity
   c. overall health; heredity
   d. heredity; overall health

4. It is estimated that in the United States, infertility affects
   a. at least half of all married couples in which the woman is in her early 30s.
   b. men more than women.
   c. about one-third of all married couples.
   d. about 15 percent of all couples.

5. To be a true index of health, morbidity rates must be refined in terms of which of the following health measures?
   a. mortality rate
   b. disability and mortality rates
   c. vitality
   d. disability and vitality

6. Weathering is the result of
   a. long-term exposure to cigarette smoke.
   b. long-term exposure to stress.
   c. andropause.
   d. menopause.

7. A technique that involves fertilization of the ovum outside the uterus is referred to as
   a. endometriosis.
   b. artificial insemination.
   c. in vitro fertilization.
   d. in vivo fertilization.

8. Which of the following is **NOT** true regarding alcohol consumption?
   a. Alcohol decreases the blood's supply of high-density lipoprotein.
   b. Alcohol dependence is more common in middle adulthood.
   c. Alcohol is implicated in about half of all accidents, suicides, and homicides.
   d. Alcohol abuse is the main cause of cirrhosis of the liver.

9. Which of the following is true of sexual expressiveness in middle age?
   a. Menopause impairs a woman's sexual relationship.
   b. Men's frequency of ejaculation increases until approximately age 55.
   c. Signs of arousal in a woman are as obvious as they were at age 20.
   d. Men and women can experience fulfilling sex lives throughout this time period.

Matching Items
Match each definition or description with its corresponding term.

Terms
10. ___F___ mortality
11. ___A___ morbidity
12. ___H___ vitality
13. ___E___ osteoporosis
14. ___J___ disability
15. ___G___ menopause

16. ___C___ presbycusis
17. ___I___ disability-adjusted life years
18. ___B___ andropause
19. ___D___ hormone replacement therapy (HRT)
20. ___K___ quality-adjusted life years

Definitions or Descriptions
a. disease of all kinds
b. what some scientist argue to be the "male menopause," characterized by declining levels of testosterone
c. an age-related decline in hearing, usually not noticeable until the 60s
d. sometimes prescribed to treat the symptoms of menopause
e. a condition of thin and brittle bones
f. death; as a measure of health, it usually refers to the number of deaths each year per thousand individuals
g. the cessation of ovulation and menstruation
h. more important to quality of life than any other measure of health
i. a measure of the impact that disability has on quality of life

    j. the inability to perform normal activities

    k. concept that indicates how many years of full vitality are lost to a particular disease

Applying Your Knowledge

1. Which of the following types of exercise would be most beneficial in promoting general health and reducing risk of disease?

    a. sprinting 100 yards in 12 seconds

    b. lifting weights three times a week

    c. playing three sets of tennis twice a week

    d. cycling regularly at an intensity that raises the heart rate to 75 percent of its maximum

2. Fifty-five-year-old Harvey is concerned because sexual stimulation seems to take longer and needs to be more direct than earlier. As a friend, you should tell him

    a. "You should see a therapist. It is not normal."

    b. "See a doctor if your 'sexual prowess' doesn't improve soon. You may have some underlying physical problem."

    c. "Don't worry. This is normal for middle-aged men."

    d. "You're too old to have sex, so just give it up."

3. Coretta and Vernon Castle have been trying to conceive a baby for more than a year. Because they are both in their 40s, their physician suspects that

    a. Vernon is infertile.

    b. Coretta is infertile.

    c. neither Vernon nor Coretta is infertile.

    d. Vernon and Coretta are equally likely to be infertile.

4. Twenty-five-year-old Michelle believes that she is infertile. Because Michelle has been sexually active with a number of partners and once had gonorrhea, her doctor suspects she may have

    a. endometriosis.

    b. low motility.

    c. irregular ovulation.

    d. pelvic inflammatory disease.

5. Forty-five-year-old Cindy is the same weight she has been since college and continues to eat the same types and amounts of food she has always eaten. In order to maintain her weight through middle age, Cindy should

    a. continue to eat the same amounts and types of foods.

    b. reduce her caloric intake.

    c. eat more foods high in LDL.

    d. reduce her intake of foods high in HDL.

6. One hundred years ago, the psychological impact of menopause on women was probably

    a. about the same as it is today.

    b. less than it is today.

    c. greater than it is today.

    d. determined more by expectations and culture than it is today.

7. Fifty-year-old Peggy has a college degree and a good job and lives near Seattle, Washington. Compared to her sister, who dropped out of high school and is struggling to survive on a dairy farm in rural Wisconsin, Peggy is most likely to

    a. live longer.

    b. have fewer chronic illnesses.

    c. have fewer disabilities.

    d. do or have all of the above.

8. Morbidity is to mortality as _____ is to _____.

    a. disease; death

    b. death; disease

    c. inability to perform normal daily activities; disease

    d. disease; subjective feeling of being healthy

9. If Edgar is like most men, as he grows older, he will require

    a. less direct stimulation to become sexually excited.

    b. a shorter refractory period following each orgasm.

    c. a longer time between erection and ejaculation.

    d. all of the above.

10. Concluding her presentation on body weight and health, Lynn states that

    a. "Research consistently shows that 'you can't be too thin.'"

    b. "Animal research demonstrates that it is better to be a little overweight than underweight."

    c. "Even being slightly overweight increases the risk of virtually every cause of disease."

    d. "As long as metabolism remains normal, being overweight is not a health problem."

11. Compared to his identical twin brother, 48-year-old Jerry has lower blood pressure, better circulation, a lower ratio of body fat to body weight, and higher HDL in his blood. The most probable explanation for these differences is that Jerry

    a. doesn't smoke.

    b. eats a high-fiber diet.

    c. engages in regular aerobic exercise.

    d. does all of the above.

Answer Key

Key Terms

1. The loss of hearing that occurs as a result of senescence is referred to as presbycusis (p. 553; objective 2)

2. At menopause, ovulation and menstruation stop and the production of the hormone estrogen drops. (p. 557; video lesson, segment 3; objective 6)

3. HRT (Hormone replacement therapy) is intended to help relieve menopausal symptoms, especially in women who experience an abrupt drop in hormone levels because their ovaries are surgically removed. (p. 558; video lesson, segment 3; objective 6)

4. Andropause is a term used to describe "male menopause," a drop in testosterone that is thought to relate to a decrease in sex drive, sexual performance, and muscle mass. However, use of this term is controversial because testosterone decrease is very gradual, and other factors—such as stress or anxiety—can inflence levels of testosterone as well. (p. 558; objective 6)

5. A situation, event, experience or other stimulus that causes a person to feel stressed is known as a stressor. (p. 565; objective 3)

6. Tackling a stressful situation directly is called problem-focused coping. (p. 566; objective 3)

7. Dealing with stress by changing one's feelings about the stressor rather than changing the stressor itself is called emotion-focused coping. (p. 566; objective 3)

8. The accumulation of physiological responses to age and stress, such as blood pressure, is called a person's allostatic load. (p. 566; objective 3)

9. The gradual accumulation of stressors over a long period that wears down resilience and resistance is called weathering. (p. 566; objective 3)

10. Measures to prevent mortality, morbidity and disability in the public at large are collectively known as public health. (p. 569; objective 4)

11. Mortality means death. As a measure of health, it usually refers to the number of deaths each year per thousand individuals. (p. 569; video lesson, segment 3; objective 4)

12. Morbidity means disease. As a measure of health, it refers to the rate of diseases of all kinds, which can be sudden and severe (acute) or extend over a long time period (chronic). (p. 570; video lesson, segment 3; objective 4)

13. Disability refers to a person's inability to perform activities that most others can. (p. 572; video lesson, segment 3; objective 4)

14. DALYs (Disability-adjusted life years), which are the reciprocal of QALYs, are a measure of the impact that disability has on quality of life. (p. 572; objective 4)

15. Vitality refers to how healthy and energetic—physically, intellectually, and socially—an individual actually feels. (p. 572; video lesson, segment 3; objective 4)

16. QALYs (Quality-adjusted life years) is the concept that indicates how many years of full vitality an individual loses due to a particular disease or disability. (p. 572; video lesson, segment 3; objective 4)

17. Osteoporosis is a condition of porous and brittle bones leading to increased fractures and frailty in old age for which women who are thin, Caucasian, and postmenopausal are at increased risk. (video lesson, segment 3; objectives 1 & 6)

Practice Questions I

Multiple-Choice Questions

1. d. is the correct answer. (video lesson, segment 1; objective 1)
2. c. is the correct answer. (video lesson, segment 2; objective 1)
3. a. is the correct answer. (video lesson, segment 3; objective 2)
4. a. is the correct answer. (video lesson, segment 3; objective 2)
5. d. is the correct answer. (video lesson, segment 1; objective 5)
6. b. is the correct answer. (video lesson, segment 3; objective 4)

   a. is incorrect. This is the overall death rate.

   c. is incorrect. This refers to a person's inability to perform activities that most others can.

   d. is incorrect. This refers to how physically, intellectually, and socially healthy an individual feels.

7. d. is the correct answer. (video lesson, segment 3; objective 6)
8. b. is the correct answer. (video lesson, segment 2; objective 5)

   c. & d. are incorrect. Genes and culture are intrinsic and extrinsic factors, respectively.

9. a. is the correct answer. (video lesson, segment 3; objective 5)
10. c. is the correct answer. (objective 5)
11. d. is the correct answer. (video lesson, segment 3; objective 4)

    a. is incorrect. Vitality is a measure of how healthy and energetic a person feels.

    b. is incorrect. Disability measures only the inability to perform basic activities.

    c. is incorrect. Morbidity refers only to the rate of disease.

12. b. is the correct answer. (objective 6)
13. b. is the correct answer. (objective 3)
14. d. is the correct answer. (objective 3)

True or False Items

15. F   (objective 6)
16. F   (objective 3)
17. F   About two of every three Americans are overweight, and 2 percent of men and 1 percent of women are obese. (video lesson, segment 2; objective 3)
18. F   Moderate use of alcohol is associated with reduced risk of heart attacks. (objective 3)
19. T   (video lesson, segment 2; objective 3)
20. F   Middle-aged adults are much more likely to improve their health habits than younger adults. (video lesson, segment 2; objective 3)
21. T   (video lesson, segment 4; objective 6)
22. F   (objective 6)

23. F (objective 6)
24. T (objective 6)

Practice Questions II

Multiple-Choice Questions

1. d. is the correct answer. (objective 1)

   a., b., & c. are incorrect. For the most part, the normal physical changes of middle adulthood have no significant health consequences.

2. b. is the correct answer. (objective 2)

3. a. is the correct answer. (objective 2)

   c. & d. are incorrect. Although overall health is an important factor in all aspects of aging, the textbook does not compare the relative influences of overall health and heredity on visual acuity.

4. d. is the correct answer. (objective 6)

5. d. is the correct answer. (video lesson, segment 3; objective 4)

6. b. is the correct answer. (video lesson, segment 2; objective 3)

7. c. is the correct answer. (objective 6)

8. a. is the correct answer. Alcohol increases the blood's supply of HDL, which is one possible reason that adults who drink in moderation may live longer than "non-drinkers." (objective 3)

9. d. is the correct answer. (video lesson, segment 4; objective 6)

Matching Items

10. f (video lesson, segment 3; objective 4)

11. a (video lesson, segment 3; objective 4)

12. h (video lesson, segment 3; objective 4)

13. e (video lesson, segment 3; objectives 1 & 6)

14. j (objective 4)

15. g (video lesson, segment 3; objective 6)

16. c (objective 2)

17. i (objective 4)

18. b (objective 6)

19. d (video lesson, segment 3; objective 6)

20. k (objective 4)

Applying Your Knowledge

1. d. is the correct answer. (video lesson, segment 2; objective 3)

   a., b., & c. are incorrect. These forms of exercise will not produce the beneficial effects of regular aerobic exercise.

2. c. is the correct answer. (video lesson, segment 4; objective 6)

3. d. is the correct answer. (objective 6)

4. d. is the correct answer. (objective 6)

5. b. is the correct answer. (video lesson, segment 2; objective 3)

   a. is incorrect. As Cindy ages, her metabolism will slow down, so she should reduce her caloric intake.

   c. & d. are incorrect. Just the opposite is true. She should decrease her intake of foods high in LDL and increase her intake of foods high in HDL.

6. c. is the correct answer. (objective 6)

7. d. is the correct answer. People who are relatively well-educated, financially secure, and live in or near cities tend to receive all these benefits. (objective 5)

8. a. is the correct answer. (video lesson, segment 3; objective 4)

    b. is incorrect. This answer would be correct if the statement were "Mortality is to morbidity."

    c. is incorrect. This answer would be correct if the statement were "Disability is to morbidity."

    d. is incorrect. This answer would be correct if the statement were "Morbidity is to vitality."

9. c. is the correct answer. (objective 6)

10. c. is the correct answer. (video lesson, segment 2; objective 3)

    a. is incorrect. At least one longitudinal study found that death was as likely to occur among those who were 10 percent underweight as among those who were 30 percent overweight.

    b. is incorrect. Animal research demonstrates just the opposite.

    d. is incorrect. Metabolic rate influences the likelihood of being overweight but does not counteract its health consequences.

11. c. is the correct answer. (objective 3)

    a. & b. are incorrect. Although these behaviors promote health, only regular aerobic exercise produces all the health benefits that Jerry is experiencing.

Lesson Review

Lesson 20

Middle Adulthood
Biosocial Development

Please Note: Use this matrix to guide your study and achieve the learning objectives of this lesson. It will also help you to view the video, which defines and demonstrates important concepts and skills as they relate to everyday life.

Learning Objective	Textbook	Course Student Guide	Video Lesson
1. Identify typical physical changes of middle adulthood and discuss their impact.	pp. 550–552	Key Terms: 17; Practice Questions I: 1, 2; Practice Questions II: 1, 13.	Segment 1: *Normal Physical Changes;* Segment 2: *Health Habits* Segment 3: *Variations in Health*
2. Describe how the functions of the sense organs and vital body systems change during middle adulthood.	pp. 552–554	Key Terms: 1; Practice Questions I: 3, 4; Practice Questions II: 2, 3, 16.	Segment 3: *Variations in Health*
3. Describe the relationship between certain lifestyle factors—smoking, alcohol use, nutrition, weight, and exercise—and health.	pp. 559–569	Key Terms: 5, 6, 7, 8, 9; Practice Questions I: 13, 14, 16, 17, 18, 19, 20; Practice Questions II: 6, 8; Applying Your Knowledge: 1, 5, 10, 11.	Segment 2: *Health Habits*
4. Differentiate four measures of health, and explain the concept of quality-adjusted life years.	pp. 569–573	Key Terms: 10, 11, 12, 13, 14, 15, 16; Practice Questions I: 6, 11; Practice Questions II: 5, 10, 11, 12, 14, 17, 20; Applying Your Knowledge: 8.	Segment 3: *Variations in Health*
5. Explain how variations in health are related to gender, socioeconomic status, and stress.	pp. 573–575	Practice Questions I: 5, 8, 9, 10; Applying Your Knowledge: 7.	Segment 1: *Normal Physical Changes;* Segment 3: *Variations in Health*
6. Identify the typical changes that occur in the sexual-reproductive system during adulthood, and explain the potential positive and negative outcomes of these changes.	pp. 554–559	Key Terms: 2, 3, 4, 17; Practice Questions I: 7, 12, 15, 21, 22, 23, 24; Practice Questions II: 4, 7, 9, 13, 15, 18, 19; Applying Your Knowledge: 2, 3, 4, 6, 9.	Segment 3: *Variations in Health;* Segment 4: *The Sexual Reproductive System*

Use It or Lose It

Lesson 21
Middle Adulthood:
Cognitive Development

Preview

This lesson examines cognitive development between the ages of 25 and 65. Cognitive development was once thought to be an ability that could be measured as a single aptitude. However, as psychologists began to study intelligence, they discovered that it was much more complex. It is now considered to consist of many different abilities.

The lesson then examines the multidirectional nature of intelligence, noting that some abilities (such as short-term memory) decline with age, while others (such as vocabulary) generally increase. It also includes a discussion of the debate over whether all cognitive abilities inevitably decline during adulthood, or if some abilities may remain stable or even increase.

The lesson next focuses on the fact that intelligence is characterized more by variability among people than by consistency from person to person. Each person's cognitive development occurs in a unique context influenced by variations in genes, life experiences, and cohort effects.

The lesson also discusses cognitive expertise that often comes with experience, pointing out the ways in which expert thinking differs from that of the novice. Expert thinking is more specialized, flexible, and intuitive and is guided by more and better problem-solving strategies.

The lesson concludes with the message that during middle adulthood, individual differences are much more critical in determining the course of cognitive development than is chronological age alone.

Prior Course Knowledge that Will Be Used in this Lesson
- Cognitive development during the school years (Lesson 12) and adolescence (Lesson 15), as well as that during early adulthood (Lesson 18), will be referred to as we discuss normal changes in middle adulthood and the multidirectional and multidimensional nature of intelligence.

- Longitudinal and cross-sectional research studies (Lesson 2) will be referred to as we discuss the apparently contradictory findings of research using these methods to investigate age-related changes in intelligence.

Learning Objectives

Use this information to guide your reading, viewing, thinking, and studying. After successfully completing this lesson, you will be able to:

1. Discuss the psychometric approach to adult cognition, distinguish between fluid and crystallized intelligence, and explain how each is affected by age.

2. Differentiate the three fundamental forms of intelligence described by Robert Sternberg, and discuss how each tends to vary over the life span.

3. Explain the concept of selective optimization with compensation.

4. Outline Howard Gardner's theory of intelligence, and note the impact of genes, culture, and aging on the various dimensions of intelligence.

5. Discuss the multidirectionality of intelligence.

6. Briefly trace the history of the controversy regarding adult intelligence, including the findings of cross-sectional and longitudinal research and how cross-sequential research compensates for their shortcomings.

7. Explain how and why context and cohort affect intellectual development during adulthood.

8. Discuss the plasticity of intelligence, and describe how the cognitive processes of experts differ from those of novices.

📖 **Read Chapter 21, "Adulthood: Cognitive Development," pages 579–603, and review the "Criticisms of Testing" section of Chapter 11,, "Middle Childhood: Biosocial Development" on pages 307–308.**

⏮ **View the video for Lesson 21, "Use It or Lose It."**

   Segment 1: *Psychometric Approach*

   Segment 2: *Dimensions and Directions of Intelligence*

   Segment 3: *Contextual Influences*

   Segment 4: *Plastic Intellectual Change*

Summary

Psychologists' views of the nature and development of intelligence have changed considerably in recent years. Psychologists often use the psychometric approach to measure ability, aptitude, or skill in a variety of ways that are scientifically sound. Neuropsychological tests are also used—often in medical settings—to examine and diagnose individuals who appear to have memory problems or other problems that impair their cognitive functioning.

Historically, psychologists have considered intelligence to be a single ability, what Spearman referred to as *g*, or general intelligence. In the 1960s, researchers differentiated fluid intelligence and crystallized intelligence. **Fluid intelligence** is flexible reasoning and is made up of the basic mental abilities such as inductive reasoning, abstract thinking, and speed of thinking required for understanding any subject. **Crystallized intelligence** refers to the accumulation of facts, information, and knowledge that comes with education and experience within a particular culture.

Robert Sternberg has developed a theory regarding the **multidimensional nature of intelligence**, proposing that intelligence is composed of three distinct parts: 1) an analytic or academic aspect consisting of mental processes that foster efficient learning, remembering, and thinking; 2) a creative aspect involving the capacity to be flexible and innovative when dealing with new situations; and 3) a practical aspect that enables the person to adapt his or her abilities to contextual demands. An additional perspective on cognition suggests that the ability to strategically use one's cognitive strengths to compensate for the declining capacities associated with age (**selective optimization with compensation**) is a hallmark of successful aging.

Howard Gardner believes that there are at least eight distinct intelligences: linguistic, musical, logical-mathematical, spatial, bodily-kinesthetic, naturalistic, self-understanding, and social-understanding. The value placed on each dimension depends on the particular cultural environment and therefore on the training of the individual and on those evaluating him or her. Thus, differences associated with age in cross-sectional studies may reflect the experience of growing up during a particular time period rather than actual age-related developmental phenomena.

For most of the twentieth century, researchers believed that intellectual ability peaks during adolescence, then declines steadily as age advances. More recently, researchers have begun to doubt whether there is an inevitable decline in cognitive functioning with age. The earlier evidence of a decline in cognitive ability may be attributable to the shortcomings of **cross-sectional** research. Because it is impossible to match subjects in every aspect except age, cohort effects are inevitable.

Contemporary researchers also believe that since intellectual abilities are multidirectional, it is misleading to ask whether intelligence, in general, either increases or decreases. Intellectual development is greatly influenced by genetic heritage and life experiences, including changes in family and career responsibilities, cohort, educational level, income, marital status, and physical and mental health. Intellectual abilities are also characterized by their plasticity, which means that abilities can become enhanced or diminished, depending on how, when, and why a person uses them. Some researchers believe that as we age, our intelligence increases in specific areas that are of importance to us; that is, each of us develops an area of expertise.

📖   **Review all reading assignments for this lesson.**

🖥   **As assigned by your instructor, complete the optional online component for this lesson.**

Key Terms

Using your own words, write a brief definition or explanation of each of the following terms on a separate piece of paper.

1. general intelligence (*g*)
2. Seattle Longitudinal Study
3. fluid intelligence
4. crystallized intelligence
5. analytic intelligence
6. creative intelligence
7. practical intelligence
8. selective optimization with compensation
9. selective expert
10. automatic processing
11. women's work
12. plasticity
13. psychometric approach
14. multidimensional
15. multidirectional

Practice Questions I

Multiple-Choice Questions

1. Most of the evidence for an age-related decline in intelligence came from
   a. cross-sectional research.
   b. longitudinal research.
   c. cross-sequential research.
   d. random sampling.

2. The major flaw in cross-sectional research is the virtual impossibility of
   a. selecting subjects who are similar in every aspect except age.
   b. tracking all subjects over a number of years.
   c. finding volunteers with high IQs.
   d. testing concept mastery.

3. Because of the limitations of other research methods, K. Warner Schaie developed a new research design based on
   a. observer-participant methods.
   b. in-depth questionnaires.
   c. personal interviews.
   d. both cross-sectional and longitudinal methods.

4. Why don't traditional intelligence tests reveal age-related declines in processing speed and short-term memory during adulthood?
   a. They measure only fluid intelligence.
   b. They measure only crystallized intelligence.
   c. They separate verbal and non-verbal IQ scores, obscuring these declines.
   d. They yield a single IQ score, allowing adulthood increases in crystallized intelligence to mask these declines.

5. Which of the following is most likely to decrease with age?
   a. vocabulary
   b. accumulated facts
   c. speed of thinking
   d. practical intelligence

6. The basic mental abilities that go into learning and understanding any subject have been classified as
   a. crystallized intelligence.
   b. plastic intelligence.
   c. fluid intelligence.
   d. rote memory.

7. Some psychologists contend that intelligence consists of fluid intelligence, which _____ during adulthood, and crystallized intelligence, which _____.
   a. remains stable; declines
   b. declines; remains stable
   c. increases; declines
   d. declines; increases

8. Charles Spearman argued for the existence of a single general intelligence factor, which he referred to as
   a. g.
   b. practical intelligence.
   c. analytic intelligence.
   d. creative intelligence.

9. The plasticity of adult intellectual abilities refers primarily to the effects of
   a. fluid intelligence.
   b. experience.
   c. genetic inheritance.
   d. crystallized intelligence.

10. The shift from conscious, deliberate processing of information to a more unconscious, effortless performance requires
    a. automatic processing.
    b. subliminal execution.
    c. plasticity.
    d. encoding.

11. Concerning expertise, which of the following is true?

    a. In performing tasks, experts tend to be more set in their ways, preferring to use strategies that have worked in the past.

    b. The reasoning of experts is usually more formal, disciplined, and stereotyped than that of the novice.

    c. In performing tasks, experts tend to be more flexible and to enjoy experimentation more than novices do.

    d. Experts often have difficulty adjusting to situations that are exceptions to the rule.

12. Automatic processing takes place even when

    a. a person is a novice at that task.

    b. an individual follows directions step-by-step.

    c. the situation calls for fluid intelligence.

    d. an expert is distracted.

13. Which of the following describes the results of Nancy Bayley's follow-up study of members of the Berkeley Growth Study?

    a. Most subjects reached a plateau in intellectual functioning at age 21.

    b. The typical person at age 36 improved on two of ten subtests of the Wechsler Adult Intelligence Scale: Picture Completion and Arithmetic.

    c. The typical person at age 36 was still improving on the most important subtests of the intelligence scale.

    d. No conclusions could be reached because the sample of subjects was not representative.

14. Which of the following is **NOT** one of the general conclusions of research about intellectual changes during adulthood?

    a. In general, most intellectual abilities increase or remain stable throughout early and middle adulthood until the 60s.

    b. Cohort differences have a powerful influence on intellectual differences in adulthood.

    c. Intellectual functioning is affected by educational background.

    d. Intelligence becomes less specialized with increasing age.

15. The psychologist who has proposed that intelligence is composed of analytic, creative, and practical aspects is

    a. Charles Spearman.

    b. Howard Gardner.

    c. Robert Sternberg.

    d. K. Warner Schaie.

16. Paul Baltes and his colleagues believe that the strategy of selective optimization with compensation accounts for

    a. the ability of most middle-aged adults to increase performance levels.

    b. the ability of many older adults to maintain the performance levels of their younger years.

    c. the ability to remain physically fit.

    d. the increase in analytic intelligence.

True or False Items

Write T (for true) or F (for false) on the line in front of each statement.

17. __F__ A person's IQ is unaffected by years of schooling.

18. __F__ To date, cross-sectional research has shown a gradual increase in intellectual ability.

19. __T__ Longitudinal research usually shows that intelligence in most abilities increases throughout early and middle adulthood.

20. __F__ By age 60, most people decline in even the most basic cognitive abilities.

21. __T__ IQ scores have shown a steady upward drift over most of the twentieth century.

22. __F__ All people reach an intellectual peak in adolescence.

23. __T__ Historically, most psychologists have considered intelligence to be composed of several distinct abilities.

24. __T__ Today, most researchers studying cognitive abilities believe that intelligence is multidimensional.

25. __T__ Compared to novices, experts tend to be more intuitive and less stereotyped in their work performance.

26. __T__ Many researchers believe that a hallmark of successful aging is the ability to use intellectual strengths strategically to compensate for declining capacities.

Practice Questions II

Multiple-Choice Questions

1. The debate over the status of adult intelligence focuses on the question of its inevitable decline and on

    a. pharmacological deterrents to that decline.

    b. the accompanying decline in moral reasoning.

    c. its possible continuing growth.

    d. the validity of longitudinal versus personal-observation research.

2. The accumulation of facts that comes about with education and experience has been classified as
   a. crystallized intelligence.
   b. plastic intelligence.
   c. fluid intelligence.
   d. rote memory.

3. Thinking that is more intuitive, flexible, specialized, and automatic is characteristic of
   a. fluid intelligence.
   b. crystallized intelligence.
   c. expertise.
   d. plasticity.

4. The _____ nature of intelligence was attested to by Howard Gardner, who proposed the existence of eight different intelligences.
   a. multidirectional
   b. multidimensional
   c. plastic
   d. practical

5. The _____ nature of intelligence refers to the fact that each intellectual ability may rise, fall, or remain stable, according to its own unique developmental trajectory.
   a. multidirectional
   b. multidimensional
   c. plastic
   d. practical

6. At the present stage of research in adult cognition, which of the following statements has the most research support?
   a. Intellectual abilities inevitably decline from adolescence onward.
   b. Each person's cognitive development occurs in a unique context influenced by variations in genes, life experiences, and cohort effects.
   c. Some 90 percent of adults tested in cross-sectional studies show no decline in intellectual abilities until age 40.
   d. Intelligence becomes crystallized for most adults between ages 32 and 41.

7. Research on expertise indicates that during adulthood, intelligence
   a. increases in most primary mental abilities.
   b. increases in specific areas of interest to the person.
   c. increases only in those areas associated with the individual's career.
   d. shows a uniform decline in all areas.

8. Research indicates that during adulthood, declines occur in
   a. crystallized intelligence.
   b. fluid intelligence.
   c. both crystallized and fluid intelligence.
   d. neither crystallized nor fluid intelligence.

9. Fluid intelligence is based on all of the following **EXCEPT**
   a. short-term memory.
   b. abstract thinking.
   c. speed of thinking.
   d. general knowledge.

10. In recent years, researchers are more likely than before to consider intelligence as
    a. a single entity.
    b. primarily determined by heredity.
    c. entirely the product of learning.
    d. made up of several abilities.

11. One of the drawbacks of longitudinal studies of intelligence is that
    a. they are especially prone to the distortion of cohort effects.
    b. people who are retested may show improved performance as a result of practice.
    c. the biases of the experimenter are more likely to distort the results than is true of other research methods.
    d. all of the above are true.

12. To a developmentalist, an expert is a person who
    a. is extraordinarily gifted at a particular task.
    b. is significantly better at a task than people who have not put time and effort into performing that task.
    c. scores at the ninetieth percentile or better on a test of achievement.
    d. is none of the above.

13. One reason for the variety in patterns in adult intelligence is that during adulthood
    a. intelligence is fairly stable in some areas.
    b. intelligence increases in some areas.
    c. intelligence decreases in some areas.
    d. people develop specialized competencies in activities that are personally meaningful.

14. Selective optimization with compensation is crucial most of all in _____, where there's so much you have to compensate for, but _____ is the time when most people first start noticing that they can't do everything quite as well as they used to.
    a. late adulthood; middle adulthood
    b. middle adulthood; late adulthood
    c. middle adulthood; adolescence
    d. middle adulthood; early adulthood

Matching Items

Match each definition or description with its corresponding term.

Terms

15. __E__ fluid intelligence

16. __H__ crystallized intelligence

17. __C__ multidimensional

18. __G__ multidirectional

19. __B__ creative intelligence

20. __F__ plasticity

21. __A__ practical intelligence

22. __D__ expertise

23. __J__ selective optimization with compensation

24. __I__ analytic intelligence

Definitions or Descriptions

a. intellectual skills used in everyday problem solving

b. intelligence that involves the capacity to be intellectually flexible and innovative

c. intelligence is made up of several different abilities

d. specialized competence

e. flexible reasoning used to draw inferences

f. intellectual flexibility

g. cognitive abilities can follow different trajectories with age

h. the accumulation of facts, information, and knowledge

i. mental processes that foster efficient learning

j. theory that people look for the best way to compensate for physical and cognitive losses and to become more proficient at activities they can do well

Applying Your Knowledge

1. In identifying the multiple aspects of intelligence, Gardner held that
    a. intelligence appears in three fundamental forms.
    b. a general intelligence can be inferred from these various abilities.
    c. each intelligence has its own neurological network in a particular section of the brain.
    d. an individual is likely to excel equally at all types of intelligence.

2. In Sternberg's theory, which aspect of intelligence is most similar to the abilities constituting fluid intelligence?
    a. analytic
    b. creative
    c. practical
    d. None of the above is part of Sternberg's theory.

3. Concerning the acquisition of fluid and crystallized intelligence, most experts agree that

   a. both fluid and crystallized intelligence are primarily determined by heredity.

   b. both fluid and crystallized intelligence are primarily acquired through learning.

   c. fluid intelligence is primarily genetic, whereas crystallized intelligence is primarily learned.

   d. fluid intelligence declines with age whereas crystallized intelligence increases with age.

4. Regarding the multidirectionality of intelligence, which of the following statements has the most empirical support?

   a. Most intellectual abilities remain stable with age.

   b. Most intellectual abilities decline with age.

   c. Each intellectual ability may increase, decrease, or remain stable with age.

   d. There is a single mental capacity underlying all intellectual skills, and this capacity may rise or fall with age.

5. A psychologist has found that the mathematical ability of adults born in the 1920s is significantly different from that of those born in the 1950s. She suspects that this difference is a reflection of the different educational emphases of the two historical periods. This is an example of

   a. longitudinal research.

   b. sequential research.

   c. a cohort effect.

   d. all of the above.

6. Sharetta knows more about her field of specialization now at age 45 than she did at age 35. This increase is most likely due to

   a. an increase in crystallized intelligence.

   b. an increase in fluid intelligence.

   c. increases in both fluid and crystallized intelligence.

   d. a cohort difference.

7. A contemporary developmental psychologist is most likely to disagree with the statement that

   a. many people show increases in intelligence during middle adulthood.

   b. for many behaviors, the responses of older adults are slower than those of younger adults.

   c. intelligence peaks during adolescence and declines thereafter.

   d. intelligence is multidimensional and multidirectional.

8. Regarding their accuracy in measuring adult intellectual decline, cross-sectional research is to longitudinal research as _____ is to _____.

   a. underestimate; overestimate

   b. overestimate; underestimate

   c. accurate; inaccurate

   d. inaccurate; accurate

9. Dr. Hatfield wants to analyze the possible effects of retesting, cohort differences, and aging on adult changes in intelligence. Which research method should she use?

   a. cross-sectional

   b. longitudinal

   c. cross-sequential

   d. case study

10. Joseph has remained associated with interesting and creative people throughout his life. In contrast, James has become increasingly isolated as he has aged. Given these lifestyle differences, which aspect of intelligence will be most affected in Joseph and James?

    a. fluid intelligence

    b. crystallized intelligence

    c. overall IQ

    d. It is impossible to predict how their intelligence will be affected.

11. When Merle retired from teaching, he had great difficulty adjusting to the changes in his lifestyle. Robert Sternberg would probably say that Merle was somewhat lacking in which aspect of his intelligence?

    a. analytic

    b. creative

    c. practical

    d. plasticity

12. Compared to her 20-year-old daughter, 40-year-old Wendy is likely to perform better on measures of what type of intelligence?

    a. fluid

    b. practical

    c. analytic

    d. none of the above

13. Most developmentalists would agree with which of the following statements?

    a. Faster thinking is deeper thinking.

    b. Slower thinking is deeper thinking.

    c. Speed of thinking is a critical element of fluid intelligence.

    d. Speed of thinking is a critical element of crystallized intelligence.

Answer Key

Key Terms

1. General intelligence (*g*) is the idea that intelligence is one basic trait, underlying all cognitive abilities, according to Spearman. (p. 579; video lesson, segment 1; objective 1)

2. The Seattle Longitudinal Study, an ongoing project begun by researcher K. Warner Schaie, is the first cross-sequential study of adult intelligence. (p. 582; objective 6)

3. Fluid intelligence is made up of those basic mental abilities—inductive reasoning, abstract thinking, speed of processing, and the like—required for understanding any subject matter. (p. 585; video lesson, segment 2; objective 1)

4. Crystallized intelligence is the accumulation of facts, information, and knowledge that comes with education and experience within a particular culture. (p. 586; video lesson, segment 2; objective 1)

5. Analytic intelligence refers to mental processes that foster efficient learning, remembering, and thinking. (p. 587; video lesson, segment 2; objective 2)

6. Creative intelligence refers to the capacity to be flexible and innovative when dealing with new situations. (p. 587; video lesson, segment 2; objective 2)

7. Practical intelligence refers to a person's ability to adapt his or her abilities to changing contextual demands. (p. 588; video lesson, segment 2; objective 2)

8. A hallmark of successful aging, selective optimization with compensation is the ability to strategically use one's intellectual strengths to compensate for the declining capacities that are associated with aging. (p. 593; video lesson, segment 2; objective 3)

9. According to developmentalists, an expert is someone who is notably more skilled and knowledgeable about a specific intellectual topic or practical ability than the average person is. (p. 594; objective 8)

10. Thinking that occurs without deliberate, conscious thought is called automatic processing. (p. 597; objective 8)

11. Women's work is a term once used to denigrate tasks that were traditionally performed by females such as care-giving and domestic tasks. (p. 600; objective 7)

12. Intelligence is characterized by plasticity, meaning that abilities can become enhanced or diminished, depending on how, when, and why a person uses them. (video lesson, segment 4; objective 8)

13. The psychometric approach to intelligence focuses on measuring a person's ability, aptitude, or skill in a variety of ways that are scientifically sound. (video lesson, segment 1; objective 1)

14. The multidimensional nature of intelligence is the fact that intelligence is made up of several distinct abilities, rather than a single, general ability. (video lesson, segment 2; objective 1)

15. The multidirectional nature of intelligence is the fact that cognitive abilities often follow different trajectories with age. (video lesson, segment 2; objective 5)

Practice Questions I

Multiple-Choice Questions

1. a. is the correct answer. (video lesson, segment 3; objective 6)

   b. is incorrect. Although results from this type of research may also be misleading, longitudinal studies often demonstrate age-related increases in intelligence.

   c. is incorrect. Cross-sequential research is the technique devised by K. Warner Schaie that combines the strengths of the cross-sectional and longitudinal methods.

   d. is incorrect. Random sampling refers to the selection of subjects for a research study.

2. a. is the correct answer. (video lesson, segment 3; objective 6)

   b. is incorrect. This is a problem in longitudinal research.

   c. & d. are incorrect. Neither of these is particularly troublesome in cross-sectional research.

3. d. is the correct answer. (video lesson, segment 3; objective 7)

   a., b., & c. are incorrect. Cross-sequential research as described in this chapter is based on objective intelligence testing.

4. d. is the correct answer. (video lesson, segment 2; objective 1)

   a. & b. are incorrect. Traditional IQ tests measure both fluid and crystallized intelligence.

5. c. is the correct answer. (video lesson, segment 4; objective 1)

   a., b., & d. are incorrect. These often increase with age.

6. c. is the correct answer. (video lesson, segment 2; objective 1)

   a. is incorrect. Crystallized intelligence is the accumulation of facts and knowledge that comes with education and experience.

   b. is incorrect. Although intelligence is characterized by plasticity, "plastic intelligence" is not discussed as a specific type of intelligence.

   d. is incorrect. Rote memory is memory that is based on the conscious repetition of to-be-remembered information.

7. d. is the correct answer. (video lesson, segment 2; objectives 1 & 7)

8. a. is the correct answer. (video lesson, segment 1; objective 6)

   b. is incorrect. Practical intelligence refers to the intellectual skills used in everyday problem solving.

   c. & d. are incorrect. These are two aspects of intelligence identified in Robert Sternberg's theory.

9. b. is the correct answer. Life experiences give intelligence its flexibility and account for the variety of patterns of adult cognitive development. (video lesson, segment 2; objective 8)

10. a. is the correct answer. (objective 8)

    b. is incorrect. This was not discussed in the chapter.

    c. is incorrect. Plasticity refers to the flexible nature of intelligence.

    d. is incorrect. Encoding refers to the placing of information into memory.

11. c. is the correct answer. (video lesson, segment 4; objective 8)

    a., b., & d. are incorrect. These are more typical of novices than experts.

12. d. is the correct answer. (objectives 5 & 7)

13. c. is the correct answer. (objective 5)

    b. is incorrect. In fact, these were the only two subtests on which performance did not improve.

    d. is incorrect. No such criticism was made of Bayley's study.

14. d. is the correct answer. In fact, intelligence often becomes more specialized with age. (objectives 4 & 5)

15. c. is the correct answer. (video lesson, segment 2; objective 2)

    a. is incorrect. Charles Spearman proposed the existence of an underlying general intelligence, which he called *g*.

    b. is incorrect. Howard Gardner proposed that intelligence consists of eight autonomous abilities.

    d. is incorrect. K. Warner Schaie was one of the first researchers to recognize the potentially distorting cohort effects on cross-sectional research.

16. b. is the correct answer. (objective 3)

17. F   Intellectual functioning as measured by IQ tests is powerfully influenced by years of schooling. (video lesson, segment 1; objectives 4 & 7)

18. F   Cross-sectional research shows a decline in intellectual ability. (video lesson, segment 3; objectives 1 & 6)

19. T   (video lesson, segment 3; objectives 1 & 6)

20. F   Many adults show intellectual improvement over most of adulthood, with no decline, even by age 60. (video lesson, segment 2; objectives 5 & 7)

21. T   (objective 7)

22. F   There is agreement that intelligence does not peak in adolescence and decline thereafter. (video lesson, segment 2; objective 5)

23. F   Historically, psychologists have conceived of intelligence as a single entity. (video lesson, segment 1; objectives 2 & 4)

24. T   (video lesson, segment 1; objectives 2 & 4)

25. T   (objective 8)

26. T   (video lesson, segment 2; objective 3)

Practice Questions II

1. c. is the correct answer. (video lesson, segment 3; objective 6)

2. a. is the correct answer. (video lesson, segment 2; objective 1)

   b. is incorrect. Although intelligence is characterized by plasticity, "plastic intelligence" is not discussed as a specific type of intelligence.

   c. is incorrect. Fluid intelligence consists of the basic abilities that go into the understanding of any subject.

   d. is incorrect. Rote memory is based on the conscious repetition of to-be-remembered information.

3. c. is the correct answer. (video lesson, segment 4; objective 1)

4. b. is the correct answer. (objective 4)

5. a. is the correct answer. (video lesson, segment 2; objective 5)

   b. is incorrect. This refers to the fact that intelligence consists of multiple abilities.

   c. is incorrect. This characteristic suggests that intelligence can be molded in many ways.

   d. is incorrect. Practical intelligence refers to the skills used in everyday problem solving.

6. b. is the correct answer. (video lesson, segment 3; objectives 5 & 7)

   a. is incorrect. There is agreement that intelligence does not peak during adolescence.

   c. is incorrect. Cross-sectional research usually provides evidence of declining ability throughout adulthood.

   d. is incorrect. Crystallized intelligence refers to the accumulation of knowledge with experience; intelligence does not "crystallize" at any specific age.

7. b. is the correct answer. (objective 8)

8. b. is the correct answer. (video lesson, segment 2; objectives 1 & 6)

   a., c., & d. are incorrect. Crystallized intelligence typically increases during adulthood.

9. d. is the correct answer. This is an aspect of crystallized intelligence. (video lesson, segment 2; objective 1)

10. d. is the correct answer. (video lesson, segment 2; objectives 2 & 4)

   a. is incorrect. Contemporary researchers emphasize the multidimensional nature of intelligence.

   b. & c. are incorrect. Contemporary researchers see intelligence as the product of both heredity and learning.

11. b. is the correct answer. (video lesson, segment 3; objective 6)

   a. is incorrect. This is a drawback of cross-sectional research.

   c. is incorrect. Longitudinal studies are no more sensitive to experimenter bias than other research methods.

12. b. is the correct answer. (objective 8)

13. d. is the correct answer. (video lesson, segment 3; objective 7)

14. a. is the correct answer. (objective 3)

Matching Items

15. e (video lesson, segment 2; objective 1)

16. h (video lesson, segment 2; objective 1)

17. c (video lesson, segment 2; objectives 2, 4, & 5)

18. g (video lesson, segment 2; objectives 2, 4, & 5)

19. b (objectives 4 & 7)

20. f (video lesson, segment 4; objective 8)

21. a (video lesson; objective 2)

22. d (objective 8)

23. j (video lesson, segment 2; objective 3)

24. i (video lesson, segment 2; objective 2)

Applying Your Knowledge

1. c. is the correct answer. (video lesson, segment 2; objective 4)

   a. is incorrect. This is Sternberg's theory.

   b. is incorrect. This refers to Spearman's view of a *g* factor.

   d. is incorrect. While this is true, it is not part of Gardner's theory.

2. a. is the correct answer. This aspect consists of mental processes fostering efficient learning, remembering, and thinking. (video lesson, segment 2; objective 2)

   b. is incorrect. This aspect enables the person to accommodate successfully to changes in the environment.

   c. is incorrect. This aspect concerns the extent to which intellectual functions are applied to situations that are familiar or novel in a person's history.

3. d. is the correct answer. (objective 1)

4. c. is the correct answer. (video lesson, segment 2; objective 5)

5. c. is the correct answer. (video lesson, segment 1; objective 7)

   a. & b. are incorrect. From the information given, it is impossible to determine which research method the psychologist used.

6. a. is the correct answer. (video lesson, segment 2; objective 1)

   b. & c. are incorrect. According to the research, fluid intelligence declines markedly during adulthood.

d. is incorrect. Cohort effects refer to generational differences in life experiences.

7. c. is the correct answer. (video lesson, segment 1; objective 6)

8. b. is the correct answer. (video lesson, segment 3; objective 6)

c. & d. are incorrect. Both cross-sectional and longitudinal research are potentially misleading.

9. c. is the correct answer. (video lesson, segment 3; objectives 1 & 6)

a. & b. are incorrect. Schaie developed the cross-sequential research method to overcome the drawbacks of the cross-sectional and longitudinal methods, which were susceptible to cohort and retesting effects, respectively.

d. is incorrect. A case study focuses on a single subject and therefore could provide no information on cohort effects.

10. b. is the correct answer. Because the maintenance of crystallized intelligence depends partly on how it is used, the consequences of remaining socially involved or of being socially isolated become increasingly apparent in adulthood. (video lesson, segment 2; objectives 7 & 8)

11. b. is the correct answer. Creative intelligence enables the person to accommodate successfully to changes in the environment, such as those accompanying retirement. (video lesson, segment 2; objective 2)

a. is incorrect. This aspect of intelligence consists of mental processes that foster efficient learning, remembering, and thinking.

c. is incorrect. This aspect of intelligence concerns the extent to which intellectual functions are applied to situations that are familiar or novel in a person's history.

d. is incorrect. Plasticity refers to the flexible nature of intelligence; it is not an aspect of Sternberg's theory.

12. b. is the correct answer. (video lesson, segment 2; objective 1)

13. c. is the correct answer. (video lesson, segment 2; objective 1)

Lesson Review

Lesson 21

Middle Adulthood
Cognitive Development

Please Note: Use this matrix to guide your study and achieve the learning objectives of this lesson. It will also help you to view the video, which defines and demonstrates important concepts and skills as they relate to everyday life.

Learning Objective	Textbook	Course Student Guide	Video Lesson
1. Discuss the psychometric approach to adult cognition, distinguish between fluid and crystallized intelligence, and explain how each is affected by age.	pp. 579, 585–587	Key Terms: 1, 3, 4, 13, 14; Practice Questions I: 4, 5, 6, 7, 18, 19; Practice Questions II: 2, 3, 8, 9, 15, 16; Applying Your Knowledge: 3, 6, 9, 12, 13.	Segment 1: *Psychometric Approach;* Segment 2: *Dimensions & Directions of Intelligence*
2. Differentiate the three fundamental forms of intelligence described by Robert Sternberg, and discuss how each tends to vary over the life span.	pp. 587–592	Key Terms: 5, 6, 7; Practice Questions I: 15, 23, 24; Practice Questions II: 10, 17, 21, 24; Applying Your Knowledge: 2, 11.	Segment 2: *Dimensions & Directions of Intelligence*
3. Explain the concept of selective optimization with compensation.	pp. 593–594	Key Terms: 8; Practice Questions I: 16; Practice Questions II: 14, 23.	Segment 2: *Dimensions & Directions of Intelligence*
4. Outline Howard Gardner's theory of intelligence, and note the impact of genes, culture, and aging on the various dimensions of intelligence.	pp. 307, 585, 588–591	Practice Questions I: 14, 17, 23, 24; Practice Questions II: 4, 10, 17, 19; Applying Your Knowledge: 1.	
5. Discuss the multidirectionality of intelligence.	pp. 579–585, 593–594, 598–600	Key Terms: 15; Practice Questions I: 12, 13, 14, 20, 22; Practice Questions II: 5, 6, 17; Applying Your Knowledge: 4.	Segment 2: *Dimensions & Directions of Intelligence*

Learning Objective	Textbook	Course Student Guide	Video Lesson
6. Briefly trace the history of the controversy regarding adult intelligence, including the findings of cross-sectional and longitudinal research and how cross-sequential research compensates for their shortcomings.	pp. 579–585	Key Terms: 2; Practice Questions I: 1, 2, 8, 18, 20; Practice Questions II: 1, 8, 11; Applying Your Knowledge: 7, 8, 9.	Segment 3: *Contextual Influences*
7. Explain how and why context and cohort affect intellectual development during adulthood.	pp. 579–585	Key Terms: 11; Practice Questions I: 3, 7, 12, 17, 20, 21; Practice Questions II: 6, 13, 19; Applying Your Knowledge: 5, 10.	Segment 3: *Contextual Influences*
8. Discuss the plasticity of intelligence, and describe how the cognitive processes of experts differ from those of novices.	pp. 594–600	Key Terms: 9, 10, 12; Practice Questions I: 9, 10, 11; Practice Questions II: 7, 12, 20, 22; Applying Your Knowledge: 10.	Segment 4: *Plastic Intellectual Change*

Making Lemonade

Lesson 22

Adulthood:
Psychosocial Development

Preview

Lesson 22 is concerned with midlife, commonly believed to be a time of crisis and transition, when self-doubt, reevaluation of career goals, changes in family responsibilities, and a growing awareness of one's mortality lead to turmoil. The lesson begins with an examination of the changes that occur at midlife, showing that although middle adulthood may have its share of pressures and stress, a crisis is not inevitable.

Next, this lesson examines the question of whether there is stability of personality throughout adulthood, identifying five basic clusters of personality traits that remain fairly stable throughout adulthood. One personality trend attributed to middle age is that gender roles become less rigid; both sexes tend to take on characteristics typically reserved for the opposite sex. For instance, middle-aged women tend to become more assertive, whereas men of this age are likely to become more expressive.

The lesson then turns to a consideration of the changing dynamics between middle-aged adults and their adult children and aging parents, showing why the various demands of the younger and older generations have led the middle-aged to be called the "sandwich generation." Changes in the marital relationship are also examined.

The lesson ends with an examination of the evolution of work in the individual's life during middle adulthood. Many women and men place greater emphasis on balancing their work lives with parenthood and other life concerns by scaling back on their efforts in the workplace.

Prior Course Knowledge that Will Be Used in this Lesson

- Erik Erikson's theory (from Lesson 2) will be used to help explain psychosocial development during young adulthood. Recall that Erikson specifies eight stages of psychosocial development, each of which is characterized by a particular challenge, which is central to that stage of life and must be resolved:

    1. Trust vs. Mistrust (birth to 1 year)
    2. Autonomy vs. Shame and Doubt (1 to 3 years)
    3. Initiative vs. Guilt (3 to 6 years)
    4. Industry vs. Inferiority (7 to 11 years)
    5. Identity vs. Role Confusion (adolescence)

6. **Intimacy vs. Isolation (adulthood)**
7. **Generativity vs. Stagnation (adulthood)**
8. Integrity vs. Despair (Adulthood)

Learning Objectives

Use this information to guide your reading, viewing, thinking, and studying. After successfully completing this lesson, you should be able to:

1. Discuss the changes that normally occur during middle age, including whether midlife is inevitably a time of crisis, and explain how the social clock influences the timing of important events during adulthood.

2. Explain why middle-aged adults are considered the "sandwich generation," describe their caregiving roles, and discuss their relationships with other generations.

3. Describe the Big Five clusters of personality traits, and discuss reasons for their relative stability during adulthood.

4. Explain the concept of an ecological niche, noting how it interacts with personality.

5. Discuss how and why marital relationships tend to change during middle adulthood.

6. Discuss the impact of divorce and remarriage during middle adulthood, including reasons for the high divorce rate among the remarried.

7. Describe the components of the social convoy, and explain this convoy's increasing importance during middle adulthood.

8. Describe how the balance among work, family, and self often shifts during middle adulthood.

📖 **Read Chapter 22, "Adulthood: Psychosocial Development," pages 605–635.**

⏮ **View the video for Lesson 22, "Making Lemonade."**

Segment 1: *Personality Throughout Adulthood*

Segment 2: *Family Relationships*

Segment 3: *Work and Life*

Summary

Many personal changes occur during middle age. These include the awareness that one is beginning to grow old, the need to make adjustments in parental roles as children enter adolescence and subsequently adulthood, the reaching of a plateau in one's career, and the tendency to question choices that have been made in life thus far. Few developmentalists, however, believe that the challenges of midlife inevitably bring on a **midlife crisis**. How people react to midlife has more to do with their overall developmental history than with age.

Longitudinal and cross-sectional research finds five basic clusters of personality traits (the **Big Five**) that remain stable throughout adulthood. These include extroversion, agreeableness, neuroticism, conscientiousness, and openness. In pinpointing the reasons for the apparent consistency of some traits, researchers note the importance of genes, culture, early child rearing, and the experiences and choices made during late adolescence and early adulthood. The manifestation of these traits is usually stable by age 30, when most people have settled into an **ecological niche**—a life that they have crafted for themselves by making decisions about vocations, mates, neighborhood, and lifestyles—that evokes and reinforces their personality.

Middle-aged adults have been referred to as the **sandwich generation**, because they are often believed to be caught between or squeezed by the needs of both the older and younger generations. Recent research shows that this is largely a myth. The middle-aged adults who provide extensive help to their parents and children tend to enjoy providing assistance and may be particularly generous individuals. Although the typical contemporary American family is less likely to consist of several generations living under the same roof, this does not mean that family links have weakened. Close contact is still maintained by visits, telephone conversations, or regular correspondence.

The relationship between most middle-aged adults and their parents improves with time. This may occur because as adult children mature, they develop a more balanced view of the relationship. In addition, today's elderly are generally healthy, active, and independent, enhancing the relationship between themselves and their grown families. The middle generation, particularly women, tend to be the **kinkeepers**, maintaining the links between the generations. Parents generally maintain close relationships with their children, even when the latter are full-grown and independent. Typically, financial help and other support flows from the middle-aged parents to the young adults.

Throughout adulthood, marriage is the family relationship that seems most clearly linked to personal happiness, health, and companionship. After the first ten years or so, the longer a couple has been married, the happier they are. Several reasons have been suggested for this improvement: greater financial security of families at the empty-nest stage, the increasing sense of equity in the relationship, and increased time for shared activities once children have left home.

📖 **Review all reading assignments for this lesson.**

🖥 **As assigned by your instructor, complete the optional online component for this lesson.**

Key Terms

Using your own words, write a brief definition or explanation of each of the following terms on a separate piece of paper.

1. midlife crisis
2. Big Five
3. ecological niche
4. social convoy
5. consequential strangers
6. familism
7. fictive kin
8. empty nest
9. kinkeepers
10. sandwich generation
11. extrinsic rewards of work
12. intrinsic rewards of work
13. mentor
14. flextime
15. telecommuting
16. scaling back

Practice Questions I

Multiple-Choice Questions

1. The most important factor in how a person adjusts to middle age is his or her
   a. gender.
   b. personality history.
   c. age.
   d. race.

2. The Big Five personality factors are
   a. emotional stability, openness, introversion, sociability, locus of control.
   b. neuroticism, extroversion, openness, emotional stability, sensitivity.
   c. extroversion, agreeableness, conscientiousness, neuroticism, openness.
   d. neuroticism, gregariousness, extroversion, impulsiveness, openness.

3. Concerning the prevalence of midlife crises, which of the following statements has the greatest empirical support?
   a. Virtually all men, and most women, experience a midlife crisis.
   b. Virtually all men, and about 50 percent of women, experience a midlife crisis.
   c. Women are more likely to experience a midlife crisis than are men.
   d. Few contemporary developmentalists believe that the midlife crisis is a common experience.

4. Middle-age shifts in personality often reflect
   a. the particular traits that are valued within the culture at that time.
   b. rebellion against earlier life choices.
   c. the tightening of gender roles.
   d. all of the above.

5. Remarriages have _____ rates of divorce than first marriages even though _____.
   a. lower; the individuals are less committed
   b. higher; couples report greater happiness at first
   c. higher; they work harder to avoid divorce
   d. lower; even though adjusting to step-children can be stressful

6. Middle-aged adults who are providing care or assistance to adult children *and* aging parents are
   a. said to be in the sandwich generation.
   b. especially likely to suffer burnout.
   c. especially likely to suffer alienation.
   d. all of the above.

7. Which of the following statements best describes the relationship of most middle-aged adults to their aging parents?

   a. The relationship tends to improve with time.

   b. During middle adulthood, the relationship tends to deteriorate.

   c. For women, but not men, the relationship tends to improve with time.

   d. The relationship usually remains as good or as bad as it was in the past.

8. In families, middle-aged adults tend to function as the _____, celebrating family achievements, keeping the family together, and staying in touch with distant relatives.

   a. sandwich generation

   b. nuclear bond

   c. intergenerational gatekeepers

   d. kinkeepers

9. Jeremy is accepted by his best friend's family as if he were blood-related. To his best friend's family, Jeremy is

   a. a consequential stranger.

   b. an adopted step-brother.

   c. a linked life.

   d. fictive kin.

10. During middle adulthood, scaling back refers to the tendency of both men and women to

    a. limit their involvement in activities that take away from their careers.

    b. deliberately reduce workload in order to meet their family needs.

    c. pull away from their spouses as they reevaluate their life's accomplishments.

    d. explore the "shadow sides" of their personalities.

11. The jump in the number of homosexual couples between the 2000 and 2004 U.S. census is likely the result of

    a. legalization of same-sex marriage.

    b. prior undercounting of same-sex couples.

    c. an increase in the divorce rate.

    d. none of the above.

12. Concerning the degree of stability of personality traits, which of the following statements has the greatest research support?

    a. There is little evidence that personality traits remain stable during adulthood.

    b. In women, but less so in men, there is notable continuity in many personality characteristics.

    c. In men, but less so in women, there is notable continuity in many personality characteristics.

    d. In both men and women, there is notable continuity in many personality characteristics.

13. People who exhibit the personality dimension of _____ tend to be outgoing, active, and assertive.

   a. extroversion
   b. agreeableness
   c. conscientiousness
   d. neuroticism

14. As men and women get older the _____ become more important to them than the _____.

   a. intrinsic rewards of work; extrinsic rewards of work
   b. extrinsic rewards of work; intrinsic rewards of work
   c. increase in pay with seniority; job's satisfaction
   d. both b and c

15. Which of the following personality traits was **NOT** identified in the textbook as tending to remain stable throughout adulthood?

   a. neuroticism
   b. introversion
   c. openness
   d. conscientiousness

True or False Items

Write T (for true) or F (for false) on the line in front of each statement.

16. __F__ At least 75 percent of American men experience a significant midlife crisis between ages 38 and 43.

17. __T__ Better than age as a predictor of whether a midlife crisis will occur is an individual's personality history.

18. __T__ By age 30, most of an individual's basic personality traits become stable.

19. __F__ As people get older, they are more interested in salary and benefits than job satisfaction.

20. __T__ The extended family is typical of modern societies, such as those in North America today.

21. __F__ Today's parents are less likely to maintain close relationships with their aging parents.

22. __T__ After stressful periods early in marriage, marital happiness often rebounds once couples understand each other better.

23. __T__ Second marriages end in divorce more often than first marriages.

24. __F__ As adults mature, personality tends to improve.

25. __F__ There is no evidence that the stability of personality traits is influenced by heredity.

Practice Questions II

Multiple-Choice Questions

1. Society recognizes midlife as beginning around the age of _____ and lasting until about age _____.
   a. 35; 64
   b. 40; 70
   c. 30; 45
   d. 50; 75

2. By what age have most people settled into a particular ecological niche?
   a. 20
   b. 25
   c. 30
   d. 40

3. Which of the following factors play a role in whether grandparents will become surrogate parents?
   a. Both parents are full-time college students.
   b. The child is a rebellious school-age boy.
   c. One parent is busy establishing a career and the other does not want to assume the burden of raising a child.
   d. The parents are too old to care for a child.

4. Which of the following is true regarding the ecological niche of a middle-aged adult?
   a. It is determined by the person's characteristic traits.
   b. It depends almost entirely on the person's life experiences.
   c. It is shaped by and might interact with his or her personality traits.
   d. It prevents the person from changing during adulthood.

5. Whether a person ranks high or low in each of the Big Five personality factors is determined by
   a. heredity.
   b. temperament.
   c. his or her lifestyle.
   d. the interaction of genes, culture, and early experiences.

6. Regarding the strength of the contemporary family bond, most developmentalists believe that
   a. family links are considerably weaker in the typical contemporary American family than in earlier decades.
   b. family links are considerably weaker in the typical contemporary American family than in other cultures.
   c. both a and b are true.
   d. despite the fact that extended families are less common, family links are not weaker today.

7. Which of the following statements best describes the relationship of most middle-aged adults to their adult children?
   a. The relationship tends to improve with time.
   b. During middle adulthood, the relationship tends to deteriorate.
   c. For women, but not men, the relationship tends to improve with time.
   d. The relationship usually remains as good or as bad as it was in the past.

8. Which of the following statements explains why couples are particularly likely to report an increase in marital satisfaction during middle adulthood?
   a. Marital satisfaction is closely tied to financial security, which tends to improve during middle adulthood.
   b. The successful launching of children is a source of great pride and happiness.
   c. There often is improvement in marital equity during this period.
   d. For all of the above reasons, couples are likely to report improvement in their marriages during middle adulthood.

9. The belief that families should sacrifice personal freedom and success to care for other family members is
   a. expected in some cultures.
   b. called familism.
   c. common among European-Americans.
   d. both a and b.

10. Which of the following is **NOT** true concerning marriage during middle adulthood?
    a. Divorce at this time is more difficult than divorce in early adulthood.
    b. Most middle-aged divorced adults remarry within 5 years.
    c. Remarriages break up more often than first marriages.
    d. Remarried people report higher average levels of happiness than people in first marriages.

11. Which of the following personality traits tends to remain stable throughout adulthood?
    a. agreeableness
    b. neuroticism
    c. openness
    d. all of the above

12. A couple with an empty nest
    a. often has an improved relationship.
    b. is more likely to have financial troubles because they send money to their children.
    c. miss their children too much to enjoy life.
    d. are none of the above.

13. Concerning developmental changes in personality traits, the textbook notes that

    a. there are no significant changes in personality as people move through middle adulthood.

    b. because women are more likely than men to experience an abrupt transition in their roles, their personalities are more likely to change.

    (c.) experience often leads to self-improvement and greater generativity.

    d. b and c are true.

Matching Items

Match each definition or description with its corresponding term.

Terms

14. ___B___ consequential strangers   20. ___G___ agreeableness

15. ___F___ kinkeepers   21. ___E___ conscientiousness

16. ___I___ sandwich generation   22. ___J___ neuroticism

17. ___K___ telecommuting   23. ___C___ openness

18. ___D___ fictive kin   24. ___H___ extrinsic rewards of work

19. ___A___ extroversion   25. ___L___ social convoy

Definitions or Descriptions

a. tendency to be outgoing

b. People who are not in one's social convoy but who are nonetheless influential

c. tendency to be imaginative

d. used to describe someone who becomes accepted as part of a family to whom he or she has no blood relationship.

e. tendency to be organized

f. those who focus more on the family

g. tendency to be helpful

h. tangible rewards (e.g., payment) that one receives for employment

i. those pressured by the needs of the older and younger generations

j. tendency to be moody

k. working from home and using communications technology to stay in touch

l. group of people who form relationships with an individual through which they guide and socialize that person over the course of his or her life

Applying Your Knowledge

1. Forty-five-year-old Ken, who has been single-mindedly climbing the career ladder, now feels that he has no more opportunity for advancement and that he has neglected his family and made many wrong decisions in charting his life's course. Ken's feelings are probably signs of

    a. normal development during middle age.

    b. an unsuccessful passage through early adulthood.

    c. neuroticism.

    d. his being in the sandwich generation.

2. For her class presentation, Christine plans to discuss the Big Five personality factors. Which of the following is **NOT** a factor that Christine will discuss?

   a. extroversion

   b. openness

   c. independence

   d. agreeableness

3. It has long been researched that, for biological reasons, I will inevitably experience a midlife crisis. I am

   a. a middle-aged man.

   b. a middle-aged woman.

   c. either a middle-age man or a middle-aged woman.

   d. neither a nor b.

4. When Don and Linda's youngest child left home, the couple experienced

   a. ongoing depression because the nest was now empty.

   b. boredom that threatened their marriage.

   c. greater closeness as they rediscovered each other.

   d. greater conflict with increased time together.

5. The parents of Rebecca and her middle-aged twin, Josh, have become frail and unable to care for themselves. It is likely that

   a. Rebecca and Josh will play equal roles as caregivers for their parents.

   b. Rebecca will play a larger role in caring for their parents.

   c. Josh will play a larger role in caring for their parents.

   d. If Rebecca and Josh are well educated, their parents will be placed in a professional caregiving facility.

6. During middle adulthood, a person's overall happiness

   a. tends to decrease.

   b. strongly correlates with his or her marital happiness.

   c. tends to increase.

   d. is most strongly related to his or her career satisfaction.

7. Ben and Nancy have been married for 10 years. Although they are very happy, Nancy worries that with time this happiness will decrease. Research would suggest that Nancy's fear

   a. may or may not be reasonable, depending on whether she and her husband are experiencing a midlife crisis.

   b. is reasonable, since marital discord is most common in couples who have been married 10 years or more.

   c. is unfounded, since after the first 10 years or so, the longer a couple has been married, the happier they tend to be.

   d. is probably a sign of neuroticism.

8. Fifty-year-old Kenneth remarried this year following his divorce 3 years ago. It is likely that Kenneth will

   a. become healthier.

   b. become more social.

   c. have improved relationships with his children.

   d. experience all of the above.

9. After a painful phone call with her unhappy middle-aged mother, your college roommate confides her fear that she will not be able to handle the burdens of children, career, and caring for her aging parents. Your response is that

   a. she's right to worry, since middle-aged women who juggle these roles simultaneously almost always feel unfairly overburdened.

   b. her mother's unhappiness is a warning sign that she herself may be genetically prone toward developing a midlife crisis.

   c. Both a and b are true.

   d. If these roles are important to her, if her relationships are satisfying, and if the time demands are not overwhelming, filling these roles is likely to be a source of satisfaction.

10. All his life, Bill has been a worrier, often suffering from bouts of anxiety and depression. Which personality cluster best describes these traits?

    a. neuroticism

    b. extroversion

    c. openness

    d. conscientiousness

11. Jan and her sister Sue have experienced similar frequent changes in careers, residences, and spouses. Jan has found these upheavals much less stressful than Sue and so is probably characterized by which of the following personality traits?

    a. agreeableness

    b. conscientiousness

    c. openness

    d. extroversion

Answer Key

Key Terms
1. The midlife crisis is a period of unusual anxiety, radical reexamination, and sudden transformation that is widely associated with middle age. (p. 607; video lesson, segment 1; objective 1)

2. The Big Five are clusters of personality traits that remain quite stable throughout adulthood. (p. 608; video lesson, segment 1; objective 3)

3. Ecological niche refers to the lifestyle and social context adults settle into that are compatible with their individual personality needs and interests. (p. 609; video lesson, segment 1; objective 4)

4. A social convoy is a group of people who form relationships with an individual through which they guide and socialize that person as he or she moves through life. (p. 611; objective 7)

5. People who are not in one's social convoy but who are nevertheless influential are called inconsequential strangers. (p. 612; objective 7)

6. Familism is the idea that family members should support each other because family unity is more important than individual freedom and success. (p. 614; objective 2)

7. Someone who becomes accepted as part of a family to which he or she has no blood relation is fictive kin. (p. 614; objective 2)

8. The time in the lives of parents when their children have left the family home to pursue their own lives is called an empty nest. (p. 617; objective 5)

9. Because women tend to focus more on family than men do, they are the kinkeepers, the people who celebrate family achievements, gather the family together, and keep in touch with family members who have moved away. (p. 621; objective 2)

10. Middle-aged adults are commonly referred to as the sandwich generation because they are often squeezed by the needs of the younger and older generations. (p. 624; video lesson, segment 2; objective 2)

11. Tangible benefits such as compensation or health insurance that one receives for doing a job are called the extrinsic rewards of work. (p. 626; objective 8)

12. The intangible gratifications of doing a job, such as satisfaction and self-esteem, are called the intrinsic rewards of work. (p. 626; objective 8)

13. A mentor is a guide or teacher who helps an inexperienced person. (p. 628; video lesson, segment 3; objective 8)

14. An arrangement in which the timing of work hours is flexible so that a person can balance personal and occupational responsibilities is called flextime. (p. 630; objective 8)

15. An arrangement in which a person works at home and keeps in touch using communications technology (cell phone, computer, fax) is called telecommuting. (p. 630; objective 8)

16. Scaling back refers to the tendency of many middle-aged adults to deliberately put less than full effort into their work. (video lesson, segment 3; objective 8)

Practice Questions I

Multiple-Choice Questions

1. b. is the correct answer. (video lesson, introduction; objective 1)

2. c. is the correct answer. (video lesson, segment 1; objective 3)

3. d. is the correct answer. (video lesson, introduction; objective 1)

   a. & b. are incorrect. Recent studies have shown that the prevalence of the midlife crisis has been greatly exaggerated.

   c. is incorrect. The textbook does not suggest a gender difference in terms of the midlife crisis.

4. a. is the correct answer. (video lesson, segment 1; objective 4)

   b. is incorrect. This answer reflects the notion of a midlife crisis—a much rarer event than is popularly believed.

   c. is incorrect. Gender roles tend to loosen in middle adulthood.

5. b. is the correct answer. (objective 6)

6. a. is the correct answer. (video lesson, segment 2; objective 2)

   b. & c. are incorrect. These are job-related problems.

7. a. is the correct answer. (video lesson, segment 2; objective 2)

c. is incorrect. The relationship improves for both men and women.

d. is incorrect. Most of today's elderly are healthy, active, and independent, and this gives them and their grown children a measure of freedom and privacy that enhances the relationship between them.

8. d. is the correct answer. (objective 5)

a. is incorrect. This term describes middle-aged women and men, who are pressured by the needs of both the younger and older generations.

b. & c. are incorrect. These terms are not used in the textbook.

9. d. is the correct answer. (objective 2)

10. b. is the correct answer. (video lesson, segment 3; objective 8)

11. b. is the correct answer. (objective 2)

a. is incorrect. Though some states have legalized same-sex marriage, this has not affected national census rates.

c. is incorrect. The divorce rate is unrelated.

d. is incorrect. This pattern was common a century ago.

12. d. is the correct answer. (video lesson, segment 1; objective 3)

13. a. is the correct answer. (video lesson, segment 1; objective 3)

b. is incorrect. This is the tendency to be kind and helpful.

c. is incorrect. This is the tendency to be organized, deliberate, and conforming.

d. is incorrect. This is the tendency to be anxious, moody, and self-punishing.

14. a. is the correct answer. (objective 8)

15. b. is the correct answer. (video lesson, segment 1; objective 3)

True or False Items

16. F   Studies have found that crises at midlife are not inevitable. (video lesson, introduction; objective 1)

17. T   (video lesson, introduction; objective 1)

18. T   (video lesson, segment 1; objective 3)

19. F   (objective 8)

20. F   The extended family is typical of traditional societies, but not those in North America. (objective 2)

21. F   Just the opposite is true. (objective 2)

22. T   (objective 5)

23. T   (objective 6)

24. T   (video lesson, segment 1; objective 3)

25. F   The stability of personality is at least partly attributable to heredity. (video lesson, segment 1; objective 3)

Practice Questions II

1. a. is the correct answer. (video lesson, introduction; objective 1)

2. c. is the correct answer. (video lesson, segment 1; objective 4)

3. b. is the correct answer. Grandparents are most likely to act as surrogate parents if the parents are poor, young, unemployed, drug or alcohol addicted, or single or newly divorced, or if the child needs intensive involvement or is rebellious (as in b.). (objective 2)

4. c. is the correct answer. (video lesson, segment 1; objective 4)

5. d. is the correct answer. (video lesson, segment 1; objective 3)

6. d. is the correct answer. (objective 2)

7. a. is the correct answer. (objective 2)

   c. is incorrect. The relationship improves for both men and women.

   d. is incorrect. It generally improves, especially if the children have emerged from adolescence successfully. Most of today's elderly are healthy, active, and independent, and this gives them and their grown children a measure of freedom and privacy that enhances the relationship between them.

8. d. is the correct answer. (video lesson, segments 2 & 3; objectives 5 & 8)

9. d. is the correct answer. (objective 2)

10. d. is the correct answer. (objective 6)

11. d. is the correct answer. (video lesson, segment 1; objective 3)

12. a. is the correct answer. (objective 5)

13. c. is the correct answer. (video lesson, segment 1; objectives 3 & 4)

Matching Items

14. b (objective 7)

15. f (objectives 2 & 5)

16. i (video lesson, segment 2; objective 2)

17. k (objective 8)

18. d (objective 2)

19. a (video lesson, segment 1; objective 3)

20. g (video lesson, segment 1; objective 3)

21. e (video lesson, segment 1; objective 3)

22. j (video lesson, segment 1; objective 3)

23. c (video lesson, segment 1; objective 3)

24. h (objective 2)

25. l (objective 7)

Applying Your Knowledge

1. a. is the correct answer. (video lesson, segment 3; objective 8)

   b. & c. are incorrect. Ken's feelings are common in middle-aged male workers, and are not necessarily indicative of neuroticism.

   d. is incorrect. The sandwich generation refers to middle-aged adults being squeezed by the needs of the younger and older generations.

2. c. is the correct answer. (video lesson, segment 1; objective 3)

3. d. is the correct answer. Researchers have found no evidence that a midlife crisis is inevitable in middle adulthood. (video lesson, introduction; objective 1)

4. c. is the correct answer. (objective 5)

5. b. is the correct answer. Because women tend to be kinkeepers, Rebecca is likely to play a larger role than her brother. (objective 2)

   d. is incorrect. The relationship of education to care of frail parents is not discussed in the textbook.

6. b. is the correct answer. (video lesson, introduction; objective 1)

7. c. is the correct answer. (objective 5)

    a. is incorrect. Marital satisfaction can be an important buffer against midlife stress.

    d. is incorrect. There is no reason to believe Nancy's concern is abnormal, or neurotic.

8. d. is the correct answer. (video lesson, segment 2; objective 6)

9. d. is the correct answer. (video lesson, segments 2 & 3; objectives 2 & 8)

10. a. is the correct answer. (video lesson, segment 1; objective 3)

    b. is incorrect. This is the tendency to be outgoing.

    c. is incorrect. This is the tendency to be imaginative and curious.

    d. is incorrect. This is the tendency to be organized, deliberate, and conforming.

11. c. is the correct answer. Openness to new experiences might make these life experiences less threatening. (video lesson, segment 1; objective 3)

Lesson Review

Lesson 22

Middle Adulthood
Psychosocial Development

Please Note: Use this matrix to guide your study and achieve the learning objectives of this lesson. It will also help you to view the video, which defines and demonstrates important concepts and skills as they relate to everyday life.

Learning Objective	Textbook	Course Student Guide	Video Lesson
1. Discuss the changes that normally occur during middle age, including whether midlife is inevitably a time of crisis, and explain how the social clock influences the timing of important events during adulthood.	pp. 605–608	Key Terms: 1; Practice Questions I: 1, 3, 16, 17; Practice Questions II: 1; Applying Your Knowledge: 3, 6.	Introduction Segment 1: *Personality Throughout Adulthood*
2. Explain why middle-aged adults are considered the "sandwich generation," describe their caregiving roles, and discuss their relationships with other generations.	pp. 621–624	Key Terms: 6, 7, 9, 10; Practice Questions I: 6, 7, 9, 11, 20, 21; Practice Questions II: 3, 6, 7, 9, 15, 16, 18, 24; Applying Your Knowledge: 5, 9.	Segment 2: *Family Relationships* Segment 3: *Work and Life*
3. Describe the Big Five clusters of personality traits, and discuss reasons for their relative stability during adulthood.	pp. 608–611	Key Terms: 2; Practice Questions I: 2, 12, 13, 15, 18, 24, 25; Practice Questions II: 5, 11, 13, 19, 20, 21, 22, 23; Applying Your Knowledge: 2, 10, 11.	Segment 1: *Personality Throughout Adulthood*
4. Explain the concept of an ecological niche, noting how it interacts with personality.	pp. 609–615	Key Terms: 3; Practice Questions I: 4; Practice Questions II: 2, 4, 13.	Segment 1: *Personality Throughout Adulthood*
5. Discuss how and why marital relationships tend to change during middle adulthood.	pp. 616–619	Key Terms: 8; Practice Questions I: 8, 22; Practice Questions II: 8, 12, 15; Applying Your Knowledge: 4, 7.	Segment 2: Family Relationships Segment 3: *Work and Life*

Learning Objective	Textbook	Course Student Guide	Video Lesson
6. Discuss the impact of divorce and remarriage during middle adulthood, including reasons for the high divorce rate among the remarried.	pp. 619–620	Practice Questions I: 5, 23; Practice Questions II: 10; Applying Your Knowledge: 8.	Segment 2: *Family Relationships*
7. Describe the components of the social convoy, and explain this convoy's increasing importance during middle adulthood.	pp. 611–612	Key Terms: 4, 5; Practice Questions II: 14, 25.	
8. Describe how the balance among work, family, and self often shifts during middle adulthood.	pp. 625–632	Key Terms: 11, 12, 13, 14, 15, 16; Practice Questions I: 10, 14, 19; Practice Questions II: 8, 17; Applying Your Knowledge: 1, 9.	Segment 2: *Family Relationships* Segment 3: *Work and Life*

Accepting the Challenge

Lesson 23
Late Adulthood:
Biosocial Development

Preview

This lesson deals with biosocial development during the years from age 65 and beyond. It begins by discussing the myths and reality of this final stage of the life span. In modern U.S. society, which glorifies youth, there is a tendency to exaggerate the physical decline brought on by aging. In fact, the changes that occur during the later years are largely a continuation of those that began earlier in adulthood, and most elderly adults consider themselves to be in good health.

Nevertheless, the aging process is characterized by various changes in appearance, by an increased incidence of impaired vision and hearing, and by declines in the major body systems. These are all changes to which the individual must adjust. In addition, the incidence of chronic diseases increases significantly with age.

Several theories have been advanced to explain the aging process. The theories that are best supported focus on cellular malfunctions, declining immune function, and our genetic makeup. However, environment and lifestyle factors also play a role, as is apparent from studies of those who live a long life.

Prior Course Knowledge that Will Be Used in this Lesson
- Biosocial development during early adulthood (Lesson 17) and middle adulthood (Lesson 20) will be referred to as we discuss normal changes in late adulthood and reasons for variations in health.

- The epigenetic theory (Lesson 2) will be referred to as we discuss the maximum life span of human beings.

Learning Objectives

Use this information to guide your reading, viewing, thinking, and studying. After successfully completing this lesson, you should be able to:

1. Define ageism, and identify two reasons for changing views about old age.
2. Describe ongoing changes in the age distribution of the U.S. population.
3. Distinguish among three categories of the aged.
4. Differentiate between primary and secondary aging, and list several characteristic effects of aging on the individual's appearance, noting how the aged see themselves.
5. Describe age-related problems in vision and hearing.
6. Discuss the adjustments older adults may have to make in various areas of life in order to maintain optimal functioning.
7. Identify several reasons that the incidence of chronic disease increases significantly with age, and explain the concept of compression of morbidity.
8. Outline the wear-and-tear and cellular aging theories.
9. Explain how the immune system functions, and describe age-related changes in its functioning.
10. Explain senescence from an epigenetic theory perspective.
11. Discuss the role of genetics in aging, and explain what the Hayflick limit is and how it supports the idea of a genetic clock.
12. Identify lifestyle characteristics associated with the healthy, long-lived adult.
13. Discuss nutritional and exercise needs during late adulthood, and suggest how these might best be met.

📖 **Read Chapter 23, "Late Adulthood: Biosocial Development," pages 637–663.**

⏮ **View the video for Lesson 23, "Accepting the Challenge."**

Segment 1: *The Realities of Aging*
Segment 2: *Primary and Secondary Aging*
Segment 3: *The Genetics of Aging*
Segment 4: *Enhancing Longevity*

Summary

Most people's perception of late adulthood is much worse than the reality. **Ageism**, or prejudice against the elderly, fosters harmful stereotypes that work to seriously limit and isolate older adults. Ageism reflects modern U.S. culture's veneration of youthfulness as well as the increasing age segregation of society, which limits contact between the oldest generation and younger ones. Ironically, many professionals who work with the elderly—including those specializing in **gerontology**, the study of old age—have inadvertently fostered ageism by focusing on the difficulties and "declines" of old age, rather than on its strengths and stability. They have also tended to base their studies of the elderly on residents of nursing homes, while largely ignoring those adults who have remained active.

Today, the fastest growing age group in the United States is persons over age 75. If present trends continue, by the year 2025, we will witness a "squaring of the pyramid": the American population will be divided into thirds, with one-third below age 30, one-third between 30 and 59, and one-third age 60 and over.

Developmentalists distinguish between the irreversible changes that occur with time (primary aging) and changes that are caused by particular conditions or illness (secondary aging). Although many changes are apparent in the skin, hair, body shape, sensory organs, brain, and body systems of older adults, the aging process is not inevitably associated with disease. Aging does, however, make people more susceptible to chronic illness, due in part to the decreased efficiency of the immune system. In addition, the physical changes in appearance described above can have serious social and psychological implications for older adults if they accept ageist stereotypes and allow their behavior, attitudes, and self-concept to be defined and conditioned by their appearance. As the textbook describes, the examples of the **young-old**, **old-old**, and **oldest-old** indicate that aging may be optimal, usual, or impaired. Optimal aging requires active adjustment to body changes rather than passive acceptance. To have the most beneficial impact, medical interventions and lifestyle changes should take place during usual aging—typically during early or middle adulthood.

Many theories of aging have been proposed. More plausible than the usual wear-and-tear theories are cellular theories of senescence, including those proposing that increases in **oxygen free radicals**, declining immune function, or the eventual production of error catastrophe in cellular replication, may be instrumental in the aging process. Genetic diseases such as Down syndrome and progeria suggest the existence of a **genetic clock** that programs aging and determines the maximum life span of each species. Even when cells are cultured under ideal laboratory conditions, replication is finite—that is, constrained at a certain point, called the **Hayflick limit**.

People who live unusually long lives often share several characteristics. These include a moderate diet, daily exercise and relaxation, and life in rural, mountainous environments that promote fitness and minimize exposure to pollutants.

📖   **Review all reading assignments for this lesson.**

💻   **As assigned by your instructor, complete the optional online component for this lesson.**

Key Terms

Using your own words, write a brief definition or explanation of each of the following terms on a separate piece of paper.

1. ageism
2. elderspeak
3. gerontology
4. geriatrics
5. centenarian
6. young-old
7. old-old
8. oldest-old
9. primary aging
10. secondary aging
11. cardiovascular disease
12. compression of morbidity
13. wear-and-tear theory
14. genetic clock
15. maximum life span
16. average life expectancy
17. oxygen free radicals
18. antioxidants
19. B-cells
20. T-cells
21. Hayflick limit
22. telomeres
23. telomerase
24. calorie restriction
25. healthism
26. epigenetic systems perspective

Practice Questions I

Multiple-Choice Questions

1. Ageism is
   a. the study of aging and the aged.
   b. prejudice or discrimination against older people.
   c. the genetic disease that causes children to age prematurely.
   d. the view of aging that the body and its parts deteriorate with use.

2. The U.S. demographic pyramid is becoming more of a square because of
   a. increasing birth rates and life spans.
   b. decreasing birth rates and life spans.
   c. decreasing birth rates and increasing life spans.
   d. rapid population growth.

3. Primary aging refers to the
   a. changes that are caused by illness.
   b. changes that can be reversed or prevented.
   c. irreversible changes that occur with time.
   d. changes that are caused by poor health habits.

4. Auditory losses with age are more serious than visual losses because
   a. they affect a far larger segment of America's elderly population.
   b. they are more difficult for doctors to diagnose than are visual losses.
   c. hearing aids, in contrast to glasses, are ineffective as a corrective measure.
   d. those who suffer from them are less likely to take the necessary corrective steps.

5. Which disease involves the hardening of the eyeball due to the buildup of fluid?
   a. cataracts
   b. glaucoma
   c. senile macular degeneration
   d. myopia

6. Factors that explain the increased incidence of chronic diseases during late adulthood include all of the following **EXCEPT**
   a. increased hypochondria.
   b. accumulated risk factors.
   c. decreased efficiency of body systems.
   d. diminished immunity.

7. A direct result of damage to cellular DNA is
   a. errors in the reproduction of cells.
   b. an increase in the formation of free radicals.
   c. decreased efficiency of the immune system.
   d. the occurrence of a disease called progeria.

8. Which theory explains aging as due in part to environmental exposure to toxins?
   a. cellular accidents
   b. immune system deficiency
   c. wear and tear
   d. genetic clock

9. According to the theory of a genetic clock, aging
   a. is actually directed by the genes.
   b. occurs as a result of damage to the genes.
   c. occurs as a result of hormonal abnormalities.
   d. can be reversed through environmental changes.

10. Laboratory research on the reproduction of cells cultured from humans and animals has found that
    a. cell division cannot occur outside the organism.
    b. the number of cell divisions was the same regardless of the species of the donor.
    c. the number of cell divisions was different depending on the age of the donor.
    d. under the ideal conditions of the laboratory, cell division can continue indefinitely.

11. Which of the following is the best example of selective optimization with compensation?

    a. an older person walking more slowly to protect herself from falling

    b. a college student choosing to major in gerontology because the job prospects are good

    c. a factory worker choosing to work the night shift so that he can be home with his children during the day

    d. choosing to walk to the store instead of driving to get some exercise

12. Highly unstable atoms that have unpaired electrons and cause damage to other molecules in body cells are called

    a. B-cells.

    b. T-cells.

    c. free radicals.

    d. both a and b

13. In triggering our first maturational changes and then the aging process, our genetic makeup is in effect acting as a(n)

    a. immune system.

    b. cellular accident.

    c. demographic pyramid.

    d. genetic clock.

14. Age-related changes in the immune system include all of the following **EXCEPT**

    a. shrinkage of the thymus gland.

    b. loss of T-cells.

    c. reduced efficiency in repairing damage from B-cells.

    d. reduced efficiency of antibodies.

15. Women are more likely than men to

    a. have stronger immune systems.

    b. have smaller thymus glands.

    c. be immune to autoimmune diseases such as rheumatoid arthritis.

    d. have all of the above traits.

True or False Items

Write T (for true) or F (for false) on the line in front of each statement.

16. ___F___ Younger adults tend to underestimate the proportion of the elderly that are institutionalized.

17. ___T___ People with stronger immune systems tend to live longer than their contemporaries.

18. ___F___ Because of demographic changes, the majority of America's elderly population is now predominantly "old-old" rather than "young-old."

19. ___T___ Gerontologists focus on distinguishing aging in terms of the quality of aging, that is, in terms of young-old versus old-old.

20. __F__   Although the thymus gland shrinks with age, the efficiency of the immune system is not affected.

21. __T__   The immune system helps to control the effects of cellular damage.

22. __F__   A decline in the number of free radicals may accelerate the aging process.

23. __T__   Although average life expectancy is increasing, maximum life span has remained unchanged.

24. __T__   Eating less than 1,000 calories a day, supplemented with vitamins, minerals and other nutrients, may prolong lifespan.

25. __T__   The importance of lifestyle factors in contributing to longevity is underscored by studies of the long-lived.

Practice Questions II

Multiple-Choice Questions

1. People tend to view late adulthood more negatively than is actually the case because
   a. they are afraid of their own impending death.
   b. of the tendency to categorize and judge people on the basis of a single characteristic.
   c. of actual experiences with older people.
   d. they were taught to do so from an early age by their parents.

2. An important demographic change in the United States is that
   a. ageism is beginning to diminish.
   b. population growth has virtually ceased.
   c. the median age is falling.
   d. the number of older people in the population is increasing.

3. Changes in appearance during late adulthood include all of the following **EXCEPT** a
   a. slight reduction in height.
   b. significant increase in weight.
   c. redistribution of body fat.
   d. marked wrinkling of the skin.

4. Heart disease and cancer are
   a. caused by aging.
   b. genetic diseases.
   c. examples of secondary aging.
   d. all of the above.

5. The most effective way to extend one's lifespan is to
   a. take high doses of vitamins and minerals.
   b. limit activities to decrease wear and tear.
   c. consume at least 1800 calories per day.
   d. walk for an hour every day.

6. Regarding the body's self-healing processes, which of the following is **NOT** true?
   a. The natural hormone estrogen may offer women some protection against heart disease.
   b. Given a healthy lifestyle, cellular errors accumulate slowly, causing little harm.
   c. Aging makes cellular repair mechanisms less efficient.
   d. Women who postpone childbirth have less efficient cellular repair mechanisms.

7. The oldest age to which a human can live is ultimately limited by
   a. cellular accidents.
   b. the maximum life span.
   c. the average life expectancy.
   d. the Hayflick limit.

8. The disease called progeria, in which aging occurs prematurely in children, provides support for explanations of aging that focus on
   a. wear and tear.
   b. cellular accidents.
   c. cross-linkage.
   d. a genetic clock.

9. Senile macular degeneration is
   a. the leading cause of deafness among the elderly.
   b. an eye disease in which the retina deteriorates.
   c. experienced as a ringing or rhythmic buzzing in the ears.
   d. experienced by one-third of those older than 74.

10. In studies of three regions of the world known for the longevity of their inhabitants, the long-lived showed all of the following characteristics **EXCEPT**
   a. their diets were moderate.
   b. they were spared from doing any kind of work.
   c. they interacted frequently with family members, friends, and neighbors.
   d. they engaged in some form of exercise on a daily basis.

11. In defending itself against internal and external invaders, the immune system relies on two kinds of "attack" cells: _____, manufactured in the bone marrow, and _____, manufactured by the thymus gland.

   a. B-cells; T-cells
   b. T-cells; B-cells
   c. free radicals; T-cells
   d. B-cells; free radicals

12. The view of aging that the body and its parts deteriorate with use and with accumulated exposure to environmental stresses is known as the _____ theory.

   a. programmed senescence
   b. genetic clock
   c. cellular accidents
   d. wear-and-tear

13. The statistical study of population and population trends is called

   a. gerontology.
   b. demography.
   c. ageism.
   d. senescence.

14. In humans, average life expectancy varies according to the following

   a. historical factors.
   b. socioeconomic factors.
   c. cultural factors.
   d. all of the above.

Matching Items

Match each definition or description with its corresponding term.

Terms

15. ___F___ young-old
16. ___H___ old-old
17. ___K___ glaucoma
18. ___G___ cataracts
19. ___I___ B-cells
20. ___E___ T-cells

21. ___B___ compression of morbidity
22. ___D___ oxygen free radicals
23. ___C___ Hayflick limit
24. ___A___ primary aging
25. ___J___ secondary aging
26. ___L___ healthism

Definitions or Descriptions

   a. the universal changes that occur as we grow older
   b. limiting the time a person is ill
   c. the number of times a cell replicates before dying
   d. unstable atoms with unpaired electrons that damage cells

Lesson 23/Late Adulthood: Biosocial Development 399

e. attack infected cells and strengthen other aspects of the immune system's functioning

f. the majority of the elderly

g. thickening of the lens of the eye

h. the minority of the elderly

i. create antibodies that attack bacteria and viruses

j. age-related changes that are caused by health habits, genes, and other conditions

k. hardening of the eyeball due to the buildup of fluid

l. the idea that some aspects of aging are solely the result of bad health habits

Applying Your Knowledge

1. Which of the following is most likely to be a result of ageism?

   a. the participation of the elderly in community activities

   b. laws requiring workers to retire by a certain age

   c. an increase in multigenerational families

   d. greater interest in the study of gerontology

2. Loretta majored in psychology at the local university. Because she wanted to serve her community, she applied to a local agency to study the effects of aging on the elderly. Loretta is a

   a. psychoanalyst.

   b. behaviorist.

   c. gerontologist.

   d. demographer.

3. A 72-year-old man enjoys hiking, good health and actively participating in family and community activities. This person is best described as experiencing

   a. ageism.

   b. optimal aging.

   c. usual aging.

   d. impaired aging.

4. Concluding her presentation on demographic trends in the United States, Marisa states that, "By the year 2030,

   a. there will be more people aged 60 and older than below age 30."

   b. there will be more people aged 30 to 59 than below age 30."

   c. there will be more people below age 30 than above age 60."

   d. the U.S. population will be divided roughly into thirds—one-third below age 30, one-third aged 30 to 59, and one-third aged 60 and older."

5. Which developmental perspective suggests that each person is born with genetic possibilities that, along with other lifestyle factors, influence his or her life expectancy?

   a. sociocultural

   b. cognitive

   c. learning

   d. epigenetic

6. Given the changes and needs of late adulthood, an older person should probably

   a. avoid most forms of exercise.

   b. follow a regular but slower-paced program of exercise.

   c. exercise for longer periods than younger adults.

   d. focus on swimming and water exercises.

7. In summarizing research evidence concerning the causes of aging, you should state that

   a. "Errors in cellular duplication cannot explain primary aging."

   b. "Impairments of the immune system are closely involved in aging."

   c. "Aging is simply a mistake; species are not genetically programmed to die."

   d. All of the above statements are equally accurate.

8. A flu that younger adults readily recover from can prove fatal to older adults. The main reason for this is that older adults

   a. are often reluctant to consult doctors.

   b. have a greater genetic predisposition to the flu.

   c. have diminished immunity.

   d. are often weakened by inadequate nutrition.

9. The wear-and-tear theory might be best suited to explain

   a. the overall process of aging.

   b. the wrinkling of the skin that is characteristic of older adults.

   c. the arm and shoulder problems of a veteran baseball pitcher.

   d. the process of cell replacement by which minor cuts are healed.

10. With regard to nutrition, most elderly should probably be advised to

    a. take large doses of vitamins and, especially, antioxidants.

    b. eat foods that are high in calories.

    c. consume a varied and healthy diet.

    d. eat large meals but eat less often.

11. Charlotte wants to make sure her elderly grandmother has every nutritional advantage to keep her mind healthy. She should suggest that her grandmother

    a. increase her intake of vitamins and minerals and decrease her caloric intake.

    b. decrease her intake of vitamins and minerals and increase her caloric intake.

    c. increase the amount of medication she takes and decrease her fluid intake.

    d. decrease the amount of medication she takes and increase her fluid intake.

12. Because age is not an accurate predictor of dependency, some gerontologists prefer to use the term _____ to refer to the young-old, and the term _____ to refer to the oldest-old.

    a. optimal aging; usual aging

    b. usual aging; impaired aging

    c. impaired aging; optimal aging

    d. optimal aging; impaired aging

13. In concluding her presentation on human longevity, Katrina states that

    a. current average life expectancy is about twice what it was at the turn of the century.

    b. current maximum life span is about twice what it was at the turn of the century.

    c. both average life expectancy and maximum life span have increased since the turn of the century.

    d. although maximum life span has not increased, average life expectancy has, because infants are less likely to die.

Answer Key

Key Terms

1. Ageism is prejudice against older people. (p. 640; video lesson, segment 1; objective 1)

2. Elderspeak is a babyish way of speaking to older adults, using simple sentences, higher pitch, and repetition. (p. 642; objective 5)

3. Gerontology is the study of old age. (p. 643; video lesson, segment 1; objective 1)

4. Geriatrics is the traditional medical specialty that is devoted to aging. (p. 643; objective 1)

5. A centenarian is a person who has lived 100 years or more. (p. 643; objective 3)

6. Most elderly people in the United States can be classified as young-old, meaning that they are "healthy and vigorous, relatively well-off financially, well integrated into the lives of their families and communities, and politically active." (p. 646; objective 3)

7. Older people who are classified as old-old are those who suffer physical, mental, or social problems in later life. (p. 646; objective 3)

8. Elderly adults who are classified as oldest-old are dependent on others for almost everything. (p. 646; objective 3)

9. Primary aging refers to the universal and irreversible physical changes that occur as people get older. (p. 647; video lesson, segment 2; objective 4)

10. Secondary aging refers to changes that are more common as people age but are caused by health habits, genes, diseases, and other influences that vary from person to person. (p. 647; video lesson, segment 2; objective 4)

11. Cardiovascular disease, which is disease that involved the heart and circulatory system, is categorized as secondary aging, because it is related health habits and risk factors that vary from person to person and are not necessarily age-related. (p. 647; objective 4)

12. Researchers who are interested in improving the health of the elderly focus on a compression of morbidity, that is, a limiting of the time any person spends ill. (p. 650; video lesson, segment 2; objective 6)

13. The theory that people age because the body wears out due to aging and environmental factors is called the wear-and-tear theory. (p. 654; objective 8)

14. According to one theory of aging, our genetic makeup acts, in effect, as a genetic clock, triggering hormonal changes in the brain, regulating cellular processes, and "timing" aging and the moment of death. (p. 655; video lesson, segment 3; objective 11)

15. The maximum life span is the maximum number of years that a particular species is genetically programmed to live. For humans, the maximum life span is approximately 120 years. (p. 655; objective 11)

16. Average life expectancy is the number of years the average newborn of a particular species is likely to live. (p. 655; video lesson, segment 3; objective 11)

17. Oxygen free radicals are highly unstable atoms with unpaired electrons that are capable of reacting with other molecules in the cell, tearing them apart and possibly accelerating aging. (p. 656; objective 8)

18. Antioxidants are compounds such as vitamins E and C that nullify the effects of oxygen free radicals. (p. 657; objective 8)

19. B-cells are immune system cells that are manufactured in the bone marrow and create antibodies that attack specific invading bacteria and viruses. (p. 657; objective 9)

    Memory aid: The B-cells come from the bone marrow and attack bacteria.

20. T-cells are immune system cells that are manufactured in the thymus and produce substances that attack infected cells of the body. (p. 657; objective 9)

21. The Hayflick limit is the maximum number of times that cells cultured from humans and animals divide before dying. (p. 658; video lesson, segment 3; objective 11)

22. Telomeres are the ends of chromosomes in the cells, whose length decreases with each cell duplication and seems to correlate with longevity. (p. 658; objectives 8 & 11)

23. An enzyme that may prevent aging by lengthening telomeres is telomerase. (p. 658; objectives 8 & 11)

24. Limiting dietary energy in the form of calories—while supplementing with vitamins, minerals and other nutrients—in an effort to live longer is called calorie restriction. (p. 658; objective 12)

25. Healthism is the idea that illness and other effects of aging are solely the result of bad health habits. (video lesson, segment 1; objective 12)

26. As applied to aging, the epigenetic systems perspective is the idea that maximum life span is not only genetically determined but also influenced by lifestyle factors. (video lesson, segment 3; objective 10)

Practice Questions I

Multiple-Choice Questions

1. b. is the correct answer. (video lesson, segment 1; objective 1)

   a. is incorrect. This is gerontology.

   c. is incorrect. This is progeria.

   d. is incorrect. This is the wear-and-tear theory.

2. c. is the correct answer. (video lesson, segment 1; objective 2)
3. c. is the correct answer. (video lesson, segment 2; objective 4)

    a., b., & d. are incorrect. These are examples of secondary aging.
4. d. is the correct answer. (objective 5)

    a. is incorrect. Visual and auditory losses affect about the same number of aged persons.

    b. & c. are incorrect. Hearing losses are no more difficult to detect, or to correct, than vision losses.
5. b. is the correct answer. (objective 5)

    a. is incorrect. Cataracts are caused by a thickening of the lens.

    c. is incorrect. This disease involves deterioration of the retina.

    d. is incorrect. Myopia, which was not discussed in this lesson, is nearsightedness.
6. a. is the correct answer. (objective 7)
7. a. is the correct answer. (objective 11)

    b. is incorrect. In fact, free radicals damage DNA, rather than vice versa.

    c. is incorrect. The immune system compensates for, but is not directly affected by, damage to cellular DNA.

    d. is incorrect. This genetic disease occurs too infrequently to be considered a direct result of damage to cellular DNA.
8. c. is the correct answer. (objective 8)
9. a. is the correct answer. (video lesson, segment 3; objective 11)

    b. & c. are incorrect. According to the genetic clock theory, time, rather than genetic damage or hormonal abnormalities, regulates the aging process.

    d. is incorrect. The genetic clock theory makes no provision for environmental alteration of the genetic mechanisms of aging.
10. c. is the correct answer. (video lesson, segment 3; objective 11)
11. a. is the correct answer. (video lesson, segment 2; objective 6)
12. c. is the correct answer. (objective 8)

    a. & b. are incorrect. These are the "attack" cells of the immune system.
13. d. is the correct answer. (video lesson, segment 3; objective 11)

    a. is incorrect. This is the body's system for defending itself against bacteria and other "invaders."

    b. is incorrect. This is the theory that aging is caused by mutations in the cell structure or in the normal course of DNA repair.

    c. is incorrect. This is a metaphor for the distribution of age groups, with the largest and youngest group at the bottom, and the smallest and oldest group at the top.
14. c. is the correct answer. B-cells create antibodies that repair rather than damage cells. (objective 9)
15. a. is the correct answer. (objective 9)

    b. & c. are incorrect. Women have larger thymus glands than men. They are also more susceptible to autoimmune diseases.

True or False Items
16. F   The proportion tends to be overestimated, not underestimated. (video lesson, segment 1; objective 1)
17. T   (objective 9)

18. F   Although our population is aging, the terms old-old and young-old refer to degree of physical and social well-being, not to age. (objective 3)

19. F   (video lesson, segment 1; objective 3)

20. F   The shrinking of the thymus gland contributes to diminished immunity. (objective 4)

21. F   (objective 9)

22. F   Inasmuch as free radicals damage DNA and other molecules, it is their presence that may contribute to aging. (objective 8)

23. T   (video lesson, segment 3; objective 11)

24. T   (objective 12)

25. T   (video lesson, segments 2 & 4; objective 12)

Practice Questions II

1. b. is the correct answer. (video lesson, segment 1; objective 1)

2. d. is the correct answer. (video lesson, segment 1; objective 2)

   a. is incorrect. Ageism is prejudice, not a demographic change.

   b. is incorrect. Although birth rates have fallen, population growth has not ceased.

   c. is incorrect. Actually, with the "squaring of the pyramid," the median age is rising.

3. b. is the correct answer. Weight often decreases during late adulthood. (objective 4)

4. c. is the correct answer. (objective 7)

   a. & b. are incorrect. Over time, the interaction of accumulating risk factors with age-related weakening of the heart and relevant genetic weaknesses makes the elderly increasingly vulnerable to heart disease.

5. d. is the correct answer. (objective 12)

6. d. is the correct answer. The textbook does not discuss the impact of age of childbearing on a woman's cell repair mechanisms. However, it does present evidence that women who postpone or limit childbearing may extend life. (objective 8)

7. b. is the correct answer. (video lesson, segment 3; objective 11)

   a. is incorrect. This is a theory of aging.

   c. is incorrect. This statistic refers to the number of years the average newborn of a particular species is likely to live.

   d. is incorrect. This is the number of times a cultured cell replicates before dying.

8. d. is the correct answer. (video lesson, segment 3; objective 11)

   a. & b. are incorrect. Progeria is a genetic disease; it is not caused by the wearing out of the body or by cellular mutations.

   c. is incorrect. This explanation for aging was not discussed.

9. b. is the correct answer. (objective 5)

   a. is incorrect. Senile macular degeneration is an eye disease.

   c. is incorrect. This describes tinnitus.

   d. is incorrect. Senile macular degeneration affects one in six of those older than 80.

10. b. is the correct answer. In fact, just the opposite is true. (objective 12)

11. a. is the correct answer. (objective 9)

12. d. is the correct answer. (objective 8)

   a. & b. are incorrect. According to these theories, aging is genetically predetermined.

   c. is incorrect. This theory attributes aging and disease to the accumulation of cellular errors.

13. b. is the correct answer. (video lesson, segment 1; objective 2)

   a. is incorrect. This is the study of old age.

   c. is incorrect. This is prejudice against the elderly.

   d. is incorrect. This is the weakening and decline of the body that occurs with age.

14. b. is the correct answer. (objective 11)

Matching Items

15. f (objective 3)

16. h (objective 3)

17. k (objective 5)

18. g (objective 5)

19. i (objective 9)

20. e (objective 9)

21. b (video lesson, segment 2; objective 6)

22. d (objective 8)

23. c (video lesson, segment 3; objective 11)

24. a (video lesson, segment 2; objective 4)

25. j (video lesson, segment 2; objective 4)

26. l (video lesson, segment 1; objective 1)

Applying Your Knowledge

1. b. is the correct answer. (video lesson, segment 1; objective 1)

2. c. is the correct answer. (video lesson, segment 1; objective 2)

   a. is incorrect. A psychoanalyst does not necessarily specialize in treating the aged.

   b. is incorrect. Behaviorism describes her approach to studying, not what she is studying.

   d. is incorrect. Demographics is the study of populations.

3. b. is the correct answer. (objective 3)

4. d. is the correct answer. (video lesson, segment 1; objective 2)

5. d. is the correct answer. (video lesson, segment 3; objective 10)

6. b. is the correct answer. (objectives 6 & 13)

   c. & d. are incorrect. Older adults need not exercise longer, nor should their exercise be limited to water activities.

7. b. is the correct answer. (objective 9)

   a. is incorrect. Errors in cellular duplication do, in part, explain primary aging.

   c. is incorrect. For each species there does seem to be a genetically programmed maximum life span.

8. c. is the correct answer. (objective 9)

a. is incorrect. In fact, older adults are more likely to consult doctors.

b. is incorrect. There is no evidence that this is true.

d. is incorrect. Most older adults are adequately nourished.

9. c. is the correct answer. In this example, excessive use of the muscles of the arm and shoulder has contributed to their "wearing out." (objective 8)

10. c. is the correct answer. (objective 13)

a. is incorrect. Large doses of vitamins can be harmful.

b. is incorrect. Older adults need fewer calories to maintain body weight.

d. is incorrect. This is an unhealthy dietary regimen.

11. a. is the correct answer. (objective 13)

12. d. is the correct answer. (objective 3)

13. d. is the correct answer. (objective 11)

a. is incorrect. Current average life expectancy is twenty-eight years more than it was at the turn of the century.

b. & c. are incorrect. Maximum life span has not changed since the turn of the century.

Lesson Review

Lesson 23

Late Adulthood
Biosocial Development

Please Note: Use this matrix to guide your study and achieve the learning objectives of this lesson. It will also help you to view the video, which defines and demonstrates important concepts and skills as they relate to everyday life.

Learning Objective	Textbook	Course Student Guide	Video Lesson
1. Define ageism, and identify two reasons for changing views about old age.	pp. 640–643	Key Terms: 1, 3, 4; Practice Questions I: 1, 16; Practice Questions II: 1, 26; Applying Your Knowledge: 1.	Segment 1: *The Realities of Aging*
2. Describe ongoing changes in the age distribution of the U.S. population.	pp. 643–645	Practice Questions I: 2; Practice Questions II: 2, 13; Applying Your Knowledge: 2, 4.	Segment 1: *The Realities of Aging*
3. Distinguish among three categories of the aged.	pp. 645–646	Key Terms: 5, 6, 7, 8; Practice Questions I: 18, 19; Practice Questions II: 15, 16; Applying Your Knowledge: 3, 12.	Segment 1: *The Realities of Aging*
4. Differentiate between primary and secondary aging, and list several characteristic effects of aging on the individual's appearance, noting how the aged see themselves.	pp. 646–647	Key Terms: 9, 10, 11; Practice Questions I: 3, 20; Practice Questions II: 3, 24, 25.	Segment 2: *Primary and Secondary Aging*
5. Describe age-related problems in vision and hearing.	pp. 652–654	Key Terms: 2; Practice Questions I: 4, 5; Practice Questions II: 9, 17, 18.	
6. Discuss the adjustments older adults may have to make in various areas of life in order to maintain optimal functioning.	pp. 648–650	Key Terms: 12; Practice Questions I: 11; Practice Questions II: 21; Applying Your Knowledge: 6.	Segment 2: *Primary and Secondary Aging*

Learning Objective	Textbook	Course Student Guide	Video Lesson
7. Identify several reasons that the incidence of chronic disease increases significantly with age, and explain the concept of compression of morbidity.	pp. 647–648, 650	Practice Questions I: 6; Practice Questions II: 4.	Segment 2: *Primary and Secondary Aging*
8. Outline the wear-and-tear and cellular aging theories.	pp. 654–655, 656–658	Key Terms: 13, 17, 18, 22; Practice Questions I: 8, 12, 22; Practice Questions II: 6, 12, 22; Applying Your Knowledge: 9.	
9. Explain how the immune system functions and describe age-related changes in its functioning.	p. 657	Key Terms: 19, 20; Practice Questions I: 14, 15, 17, 21; Practice Questions II: 11, 19, 20; Applying Your Knowledge: 7, 8.	
10. Explain senescence from an epigenetic theory perspective.	pp. 655–656,	Key Terms: 26; Applying Your Knowledge: 5.	Segment 3: *The Genetics of Aging*
11. Discuss the role of genetics in aging, and explain what the Hayflick limit is and how it supports the idea of a genetic clock.	pp. 655–656, 658	Key Terms: 14, 15, 16, 21, 22, 23; Practice Questions I: 7, 9, 10, 13, 23; Practice Questions II: 7, 8, 14, 23; Applying Your Knowledge: 13.	Segment 3: *The Genetics of Aging*
12. Identify lifestyle characteristics associated with the healthy, long-lived adult.	pp. 660–661	Key Terms: 24, 25; Practice Questions I: 24, 25; Practice Questions II: 5, 10.	Segment 1: *The Realities of Aging*; Segment 2: *Primary and Secondary Aging*; Segment 4: *Enhancing Longevity*
13. Discuss nutritional and exercise needs during late adulthood, and suggest how these might best be met.	pp. 654–655, 658–661	Applying Your Knowledge: 6, 10, 11.	

Lesson 23/Late Adulthood: Biosocial Development

Making Memories

Lesson 24

Late Adulthood:
Cognitive Development

Preview

This lesson describes the changes in cognitive functioning associated with late adulthood. The lesson first reviews the parts of the information-processing system, providing experimental evidence that suggests declines in both the information-processing and the problem-solving abilities of older adults. Next, neurological and other reasons for this decline are discussed.

Despite these cognitive declines, as the lesson next points out, real-life conditions provide older adults with ample opportunity to compensate for the pattern of decline observed in the laboratory. It appears that, for most people, cognitive functioning in daily life remains essentially unimpaired.

The main exception to the generally positive picture of cognitive functioning during late adulthood is dementia, the subject of the third section of the lesson. This pathological loss of intellectual ability can be caused by a variety of diseases and circumstances; risk factors, treatment, and prognosis differ accordingly.

The final section of the lesson makes it clear that cognitive changes during late adulthood are by no means restricted to declines in intellectual functioning. For many individuals, late adulthood is a time of great aesthetic, creative, philosophical, and spiritual growth.

Prior Course Knowledge that Will Be Used in this Lesson
*   Cognitive development during early adulthood (Lesson 18) and middle adulthood (Lesson 21) will be referred to as we discuss normal changes in information processing during late adulthood.
*   The information-processing theory (Lesson 2) will be referred to as we discuss age-related changes in memory.
*   Erik Erikson's psychosocial theory of development (Lesson 2) will be referred to as we discuss new cognitive development in later life.

Learning Objectives

Use this information to guide your reading, viewing, thinking, and studying. After successfully completing this lesson, you should be able to:

1. Using the information-processing approach, summarize the laboratory findings regarding changes in the sensitivity of the sensory register/sensory threshold and the capacity of working memory during late adulthood.

2. Summarize the laboratory findings regarding changes in the older adult's ability to access the knowledge base and to use control processes efficiently.

3. Describe research methods for assessing long-term memory in older adults.

4. Suggest several reasons, other than the aging process itself, that might contribute to age-related declines in cognitive functioning.

5. Describe age-related changes in the brain's size, weight, number of cells, and speed of processing.

6. Characterize and explain discrepancies between how the elderly perform on memory and problem-solving tasks in the laboratory, on one hand, and in daily life, on the other.

7. Discuss whether age-related declines in memory and processing speed are inevitable.

8. Identify the most common forms of dementia and discuss the differences between them.

9. Identify and describe other organic causes of dementia as well as causes of reversible dementia.

10. Discuss the claims of developmentalists regarding the possibility of positive cognitive development during late adulthood, and cite several areas of life in which such development may occur.

📖 **Read Chapter 24, "Late Adulthood: Cognitive Development," pages 665–691.**

◄◄ **View the video for Lesson 24, "Making Memories."**

    Segment 1: *Changes in Information Processing*

    Segment 2: *Age-Related Changes*

    Segment 3: *Dementia*

    Segment 4: *Enhancing Cognitive Abilities*

Summary

Lesson 24 discusses the changes in information processing experienced by older adults. As measured by standardized laboratory tests (which are often biased against the older adult), some cognitive processes become slower and less efficient during late adulthood. In part, this is because laboratory techniques focus on tasks such as memorizing meaningless lists of words. This removes cultural bias but also removes the advantages of cultural knowledge, which older adults use as a memory aid to a greater extent than younger adults.

Senescence may create small decrements (gradual decreases) in the sensitivity of the sensory register. As a result, it takes longer to register sensory information and the information fades more quickly. Of all the aspects of information processing, **working** memory (short-term memory) is the component that shows the most substantial declines with age. In terms of both storage and processing functions, older adults seem to have smaller working-memory capacity than do younger adults. Older individuals are particularly likely to experience difficulty holding new information in mind while simultaneously analyzing it in complex ways. Research suggests that older adults may need more time to actively process items to be remembered, as well as to get information into storage. In adults, the knowledge base includes the subcomponents of short-term memory, which stores information for a minute or two, and long-term memory, which stores information for years or decades. Both short- and long-term memory take two distinct forms, each originating in a different area of the brain. **Implicit memory** is automatic, unconscious memory involving habits, emotional responses, routine procedures, and the senses. **Explicit memory** is conscious memory for words, data, concepts, and the like. Implicit memory is much less vulnerable to age-related deficits than explicit memory is. As people get older, differences in implicit and explicit memory might be reflected.

Age-related declines in cognitive functioning may result from the neurophysiological changes tied to aging, which include the progressive loss of brain cells and, more important, the slowing of brain processes as the result of reduced production of key neurotransmitters. Most older adults are not hampered in their daily life by cognitive difficulties. Through their use of compensating memory techniques, older adults are able to function acceptably. A hallmark of successful aging is selective optimization with compensation, or the ability to compensate for age-related declines in intellectual functioning. The rate at which thinking slows down with age can be reduced with regular exercise, which improves blood flow in the brain.

Lesson 24 also explores the loss of cognitive function suffered by victims of dementia. The most common forms of dementia are **Alzheimer's disease** and **vascular dementia (VaD) (multi-infarct dementia)**. Several other diseases can cause dementia—among them **Parkinson's disease**, Huntington's disease, and multiple sclerosis. Many other problems, such as alcohol and drug abuse and psychological illness, are misdiagnosed as dementia.

As emphasized by such theorists as Abraham Maslow and Erik Erikson, many older adults show new cognitive development during later life, developing a heightened aesthetic sense, gaining in wisdom, and becoming more philosophical.

📖 **Review all reading assignments for this lesson.**

💻 **As assigned by your instructor, complete the optional online component for this lesson.**

Key Terms

Using your own words, write a brief definition or explanation of each of the following terms on a separate piece of paper.

1. control processes
2. priming
3. terminal decline
4. ecological validity
5. dementia
6. delirium
7. Alzheimer's disease
8. beta-amyloid
9. tau
10. mild cognitive impairment
11. vascular dementia (VaD)/
    multi-infarct dementia (MID)
12. frontal lobe dementia
13. Parkinson's disease
14. Lewy body dementia
15. polypharmacy
16. self-actualization
17. life review
18. explicit memory
19. implicit memory
20. information processing
21. sensory register
22. working memory
    (short-term memory)

Practice Questions I

Multiple-Choice Questions

1. The information-processing component that is concerned with the temporary storage of incoming sensory information is
   a. working memory.
   b. long-term memory.
   c. the knowledge base.
   d. the sensory register/sensory threshold.

2. Older adults tend to have the greatest difficulty picking up sensory stimuli that are
   a. very loud or bright.
   b. ambiguous or of low intensity.
   c. abstract or meaningless.
   d. all of the above.

3. The two basic functions of working memory are
   a. storage that enables conscious use and processing of information.
   b. temporary storage and processing of sensory stimuli.
   c. automatic memories and retrieval of learned memories.
   d. permanent storage and retrieval of information.

4. Memory for skills is called
    a. explicit memory.
    b. declarative memory.
    c. episodic memory.
    d. implicit memory.

5. Strategies to retain and retrieve information in the knowledge base are part of which basic component of information processing?
    a. sensory memory (or sensory register)
    b. working memory
    c. control processes
    d. explicit memory

6. The plaques and tangles that accompany Alzheimer's disease usually begin in the
    a. temporal lobe.
    b. frontal lobe.
    c. hippocampus.
    d. cerebral cortex.

7. Secondary aging factors that may explain some declines in cognitive functioning include
    a. fewer opportunities for learning in old age.
    b. disparaging self-perceptions of cognitive abilities.
    c. difficulty with traditional methods of measuring cognitive functioning.
    d. all of the above.

8. Which of the following is a characteristic of laboratory experiments that inhibits the older adult's memory abilities?
    a. practice
    b. priming
    c. motivation
    d. the focus on memorizing materials devoid of cultural significance

9. Dementia refers to
    a. pathological loss of intellectual functioning.
    b. the increasing forgetfulness that sometimes accompanies the aging process.
    c. abnormal behavior associated with mental illness and with advanced stages of alcoholism.
    d. a genetic disorder that doesn't become overtly manifested until late adulthood.

10. Which of the following is not inevitable in late adulthood?
    a. a slow down in processing speed
    b. a loss of gray matter
    c. a decline in working memory
    d. a decline in the ability to function in everyday life

11. Alzheimer's disease is characterized by
   (a.) a proliferation of plaques and tangles in the cerebral cortex.
   b. a destruction of brain tissue as a result of strokes.
   c. rigidity and tremor of the muscles.
   d. an excess of fluid pressing on the brain.

12. Multi-infarct dementia and Alzheimer's disease differ in their progression in that
   a. multi-infarct dementia never progresses beyond the first stage.
   (b.) multi-infarct dementia is marked by sudden drops and temporary improvements, whereas decline in Alzheimer's disease is steady.
   c. multi-infarct dementia leads to rapid deterioration and death, whereas Alzheimer's disease may progress over a period of years.
   d. the progression of Alzheimer's disease may be halted or slowed, whereas the progression of multi-infarct dementia is irreversible.

13. Medication may become associated with symptoms of dementia in the elderly for which of the following reasons?
   a. Standard drug dosages are often too strong for the elderly.
   b. The elderly tend to become psychologically dependent upon drugs.
   c. Drugs sometimes have the side effect of slowing mental processes.
   (d.) All of the above explanations are true.

14. The primary purpose of the life review is to
   a. enhance one's spirituality.
   b. produce an autobiography.
   c. give advice to younger generations.
   (d.) put one's life into perspective.

True or False Items
Write T (for true) or F (for false) on the line in front of each statement.

15. __F__ As long as their vision and hearing remain unimpaired, older adults are no less efficient than younger adults at inputting information.

16. __T__ Changes in the sensory register are a major contributor to declines in information processing.

17. __F__ The difference between dementia and delirium is that delirium is chronic whereas dementia is temporary.

18. __F__ A majority of the elderly feel frustrated and hampered by memory loss in their daily lives.

19. __T__ The majority of cases of dementia are organically caused.

20. __T__ Alzheimer's disease is partly genetic.

21. __F__ Late adulthood is often associated with a narrowing of interests and an exclusive focus on the self.

22. __T__ According to Maslow, self-actualization is actually more likely to be reached during late adulthood.

Practice Questions II

Multiple-Choice Questions

1. Research suggests that aging results in
   a. increased sensitivity of the sensory register.
   b. a significant decrease in the sensitivity of the sensory register that cannot usually be compensated for.
   c. a small decrease in the sensory register's sensitivity that can usually be compensated for.
   d. no noticeable changes in the sensory register.

2. Which of the following most accurately characterizes age-related changes in working memory?
   a. Both storage capacity and processing efficiency decline.
   b. Storage capacity declines while processing efficiency remains stable.
   c. Storage capacity remains stable while processing efficiency declines.
   d. Both storage capacity and processing efficiency remain stable.

3. Information remembered for years or decades is stored in
   a. sensory register.
   b. working memory.
   c. long-term memory.
   d. short-term memory.

4. Conscious memory for words, data, and concepts is called _____ memory.
   a. sensory
   b. implicit
   c. explicit
   d. knowledge base

5. In general, with increasing age the control processes used to remember new information
   a. become more efficient.
   b. become more complex.
   c. become more intertwined.
   d. become simpler and less efficient.

6. Which type of memory is most vulnerable to age-related deficits?
   a. sensory register
   b. implicit memory
   c. explicit memory
   d. knowledge base

7. What do Parkinson disease and Lewy body dementia have in common?
   a. They are both forms of dementia.
   b. They both affect motor control.
   c. Hallucinations are symptoms of both diseases.
   d. Both a and b are common in both conditions.

8. One study tested memory in different age groups by requiring younger and older adults to remember to make telephone calls at a certain time. It was found that
   a. older adults did worse than younger adults because their memories were not as good.
   b. older adults did better than younger adults because they were able to trust their memories.
   c. older adults did better than younger adults because they didn't trust their memories and therefore used various reminders.
   d. older adults did worse than younger adults because they were less accustomed to having to do things at a certain time.

9. Laboratory studies of memory in late adulthood fail to take into account the effects of
   a. the knowledge base of older adults.
   b. ageism and bias in measuring cognition in late adulthood.
   c. the explicit memory that is central to the functioning of older adults.
   d. the ability of older adults to rely on their long-term memories.

10. Dementia
    a. is more likely to occur among the aged.
    b. has no relationship to age.
    c. cannot occur before the age of 60.
    d. is an inevitable occurrence during late adulthood.

11. The most common form of dementia is
    a. Alzheimer's disease.
    b. multi-infarct dementia.
    c. Parkinson's disease.
    d. alcoholism and depression.

12. Organic causes of dementia include all of the following **EXCEPT**
    a. Parkinson's disease.
    b. strokes.
    c. brain tumors.
    d. leukemia.

13. Of the following psychological illnesses, which is most likely to be misdiagnosed as dementia?
   a. schizophrenia
   b. depression
   c. personality disorder
   d. phobic disorders

14. On balance, it can be concluded that positive cognitive development during late adulthood
   a. occurs only for a small minority of individuals.
   b. leads to thought processes that are more appropriate to the final stage of life.
   c. makes older adults far less pragmatic than younger adults.
   d. is impossible in view of increasing deficits in cognitive functioning.

15. A key factor underlying the older adult's cognitive developments in the realms of aesthetics, philosophy, and spirituality may be
   a. the realization that one's life is drawing to a close.
   b. the despair associated with a sense of isolation from the community.
   c. the need to leave one's mark on history.
   d. a growing indifference to the outside world.

Matching Items

Match each definition or description with its corresponding term.

Terms

16. ___E___ polypharmacy
17. ___B___ tau
18. ___G___ beta-amyloid
19. ___C___ control processes
20. ___K___ frontal lobe dementia
21. ___D___ dementia

22. ___J___ Alzheimer's disease
23. ___F___ multi-infarct dementia (MID)
24. ___H___ Parkinson's disease
25. ___A___ self-actualization
26. ___I___ life review

Definitions or Descriptions

a. the final stage of Maslow's hierarchy where aesthetic, creative, philosophical and spiritual understanding are attained
b. the protein composing the tangles in the neurons of Alzheimer's patients
c. strategies for retaining and retrieving information
d. severely impaired thinking, memory, or problem-solving ability
e. the prescription of multiple medications that may produce symptoms of dementia
f. caused by a temporary obstruction of the blood vessels
g. a protein composing plaques in the tissues surrounding neurons
h. caused by a degeneration of neurons that produce dopamine

i. putting one's life into perspective

j. characterized by plaques and tangles in the cerebral cortex

k. a form of dementia caused by deterioration of the amygdala and frontal lobes

Applying Your Knowledge

1. Cognitive deficits emerge in late adulthood because primary aging causes

   a. sensory deficits.

   b. slower processing.

   c. a buildup of neuronal fluid.

   d. both a and b.

2. Depression among the elderly is a serious problem because

   a. rates of depression are far higher for the elderly than for younger adults.

   b. in late adulthood depression becomes extremely difficult to treat.

   c. depression in the elderly often goes untreated and may be mistaken for dementia.

   d. organic forms of dementia cause depression.

3. Given the nature of cognitive development, a profession in which an individual's greatest achievements are particularly likely to occur during late adulthood is

   a. medicine.

   b. philosophy.

   c. mathematics.

   d. administration.

4. Developmentalists believe that older people's tendency to reminisce

   a. represents an unhealthy preoccupation with the self and the past.

   b. is an underlying cause of age segregation.

   c. is a necessary and healthy process.

   d. is a result of a heightened aesthetic sense.

5. Because of deficits in the sensory register, older people may tend to

   a. forget the names of people and places.

   b. be distracted by irrelevant stimuli.

   c. miss details in a dimly lit room.

   d. reminisce at length about the past.

6. Holding material in your mind for a minute or two requires which type of memory?

   a. short-term memory

   b. explicit memory

   c. long-term memory

   d. sensory register

7. Which of the following represent ways of compensating for cognitive slowing in old age?

   a. Making a grocery list.

   b. Asking for an appointment reminder from the doctor's office.

   c. Setting an alarm to signal when your favorite television program is about to begin.

   d. All of the above.

8. Which type of material would 72-year-old Jessica probably have the greatest difficulty remembering?

   a. the dates of birth of family members

   b. a short series of numbers she has just heard

   c. vocabulary

   d. technical terms from her field of expertise prior to retirement

9. Which of the following is true regarding Alzheimer's disease?

   a. A serious loss of memory, such as that occurring in people with Alzheimer's disease, can be expected by most people once they reach their 60s.

   b. The risk rises steeply with age.

   c. Alzheimer's disease is much more common today than it was 50 years ago.

   d. Alzheimer's disease is less common today than it was 50 years ago.

10. In a study of wisdom, individuals were asks to respond to a series of dilemmas. Which of the following is true of the findings?

    a. Wise responses were found among people in all age ranges.

    b. Wisdom is rare at any age.

    c. Wisdom was highly correlated with age.

    d. Both a and b are true of the findings.

11. Lately, Wayne's father, who is 73, harps on the fact that he forgets small things, such as where he put the house keys, and has trouble eating and sleeping. The family doctor diagnoses Wayne's father as

    a. being in the early stages of Alzheimer's disease.

    b. being in the later stages of Alzheimer's disease.

    c. suffering from senile dementia.

    d. possibly suffering from depression.

Answer Key

Key Terms

1. Memory control processes, which include strategies for retaining information in the knowledge base, retrieval strategies for reaccessing information, selective attention, and rules or strategies that aid problem solving, tend to become simpler and less efficient with age. (p. 672; objective 2)

2. Priming involves preparation that makes it easier for an individual to perform a particular action. For example, it is easier to retireve an item from memory if we are given a clue about it beforehand. (p. 673; objective 2)

3. Terminal decline, also known as terminal drop, is an overall slowing of cognitive abilities in the days or months before death. (p. 674; objective 4)

4. The idea that cognition should be tested in realistic settings and measure abilities used in everyday life is called ecological validity. (p. 676; objective 6)

5. Dementia is severely impaired judgment, memory, or problem-solving ability. (p. 678; video lesson, segment 3; objectives 8 & 9)

6. Delirium is a temporary loss of memory, often accompanied by feelings of fear or grandiosity and irrational actions. (p. 678; objectives 4 & 9)

7. Alzheimer's disease, a progressive disorder that is the most common form of dementia, is characterized by plaques and tangles in the cerebral cortex that destroy normal brain functioning. (p. 678; video lesson, segment 3; objective 8)

8. Beta-amyloid is a protein that makes up the plaques that are found in the tissues surrounding neurons. (p. 679; objective 8)

9. Tau is a protein that makes up the tangles found in the neurons of an Alzheimer's patient. (p. 679; objective 8)

10. The forgetfulness and loss of verbal fluency in the early stage of Alzheimer's disease is referred to as mild cognitive impairment. (p. 679; objective 8)

11. Vascular dementia (VaD), or multi-infarct dementia (MID), which accounts for about 15 percent of all dementia, occurs because an infarct, or temporary obstruction of the blood vessels (often called a stroke), prevents a sufficient supply of blood from reaching an area of the brain. (p. 680; video lesson, segment 3; objective 9)

12. Dementia caused by the deterioration of the amygdala and frontal lobes is called frontal lobe dementia. (p. 681; objective 8)

13. Parkinson's disease, which produces dementia as well as muscle rigidity or tremors, is related to the degeneration of neurons that produce dopamine. (p. 681; objective 9)

14. A dementia caused by an increase of Lewy body cells in the brain and characterized by hallucinations, falling, momentary loss of attention and fainting is Lewy body dementia. (p. 681; objective 8)

15. The prescription of several medications to elderly people that may interact to cause dementia symptoms is called polypharmacy. (p. 683; objective 9)

16. The final stage in Maslow's hierarchy of needs, characterized by aesthetic, creative, philosophical and spiritual understanding is called self-actualization. (p. 686; objective 10)

17. In the life review, an older person attempts to put his or her life into perspective by recalling and recounting various aspects of life to members of the younger generations. (p. 687; objective 10)

18. Explicit memory is memory of consciously learned words, data, and concepts. This type of memory is more vulnerable to age-related decline than implicit memory. (video lesson, segment 1; objectives 1 & 2)

19. Implicit memory is unconscious or automatic memory involving habits, emotional responses, routine procedures, and the senses. (video lesson, segment 1; objectives 1 & 2)

20. Information processing is a theory or perspective of learning that focuses on the steps of thinking, including storage and retrieval, that are similar to the functions of a computer. (video lesson, segment 1; objective 1)

21. The sensory register (also referred to as sensory memory or sensory threshold) is the initial stage memory system that functions for only a fraction of a second, retraining a fleeting impression of a stimulus. (video lesson, segment 1; objective 1)

22. Working memory (also called short-term memory) is the part of memory that handles current, conscious mental activity. (video lesson, segment 1; objective 1)

Practice Questions I

Multiple-Choice Questions

1. d. is the correct answer. (video lesson, segment 1; objective 1)

   a. is incorrect. Working memory deals with mental, rather than sensory, activity.

   b. & c. are incorrect. Long-term memory, which is a subcomponent of the knowledge base, includes information that is stored for several minutes to several years.

2. b. is the correct answer. (video lesson, segment 1; objective 1)

3. a. is the correct answer. (objective 1)

   b. is incorrect. These are the functions of the sensory register.

   c. is incorrect. This refers to long-term memory's processing of implicit and explicit memories, respectively.

   d. is incorrect. This is the function of long-term memory.

4. d. is the correct answer. (video lesson, segment 1; objectives 1 & 2)

   a. & b. are incorrect. Explicit memory is memory of facts and experiences, which is why it is often called declarative memory.

   c. is incorrect. This type of memory, which is a type of explicit memory, was not discussed.

5. c. is the correct answer. (objective 2)

6. c. is the correct answer. (video lesson, segment 3; objective 8)

7. d. is the correct answer. (video lesson, segment 2; objective 4)

8. d. is the correct answer. (video lesson, segment 2; objectives 3 & 4)

9. a. is the correct answer. (video lesson, segment 3; objectives 8 & 9)

10. d. is the correct answer. (objectives 5 & 7)

11. a. is the correct answer. (video lesson, segment 3; objective 8)

    b. is incorrect. This describes multi-infarct dementia.

    c. is incorrect. This describes Parkinson's disease.

    d. is incorrect. This was not given in the textbook as a cause of dementia.

12. b. is the correct answer. (video lesson, segment 3; objectives 8 & 9)

    a. is incorrect. Because multiple infarcts typically occur, the disease is progressive in nature.

    c. is incorrect. The textbook does not suggest that MID necessarily leads to quick death.

    d. is incorrect. At present, Alzheimer's disease is untreatable.

13. d. is the correct answer. (video lesson, segment 3; objective 9)

14. d. is the correct answer. (objective 10)

True or False Items

15. F   The slowing of perceptual processes and decreases in attention associated with aging are also likely to affect efficiency of input. (objectives 1 & 5)

16. F   Small reductions in power and sensitivity of sensory register do occur, but they generally can be compensated for. (video lesson, segment 1; objective 1)

17. F   It's the opposite; dementia is chronic. (objective 8)

18. F   Most older adults perceive some memory loss but do not feel that it affects their daily functioning. (video lesson, segment 2; objective 6)

19. T   (video lesson, segment 3; objectives 8 & 9)

20. T   (video lesson, segment 3; objective 8)

21. F   Interests often broaden during late adulthood, and there is by no means exclusive focus on the self. (video lesson, segment 4; objectives 7 & 10)

22. T   (objective 10)

Practice Questions II

1. c. is the correct answer. (video lesson, segment 1; objectives 1 & 7)

2. a. is the correct answer. (video lesson, segment 1; objective 2)

3. c. is the correct answer. (objective 3)

   a. is incorrect. The sensory register stores information for a split second.

   b. is incorrect. Working memory stores information briefly.

   d. is incorrect. Short-term memory is another name for working memory.

4. c. is the correct answer. (video lesson, segment 1; objectives 1 & 2)

   a. is incorrect. Sensory memory, or the sensory register, stores incoming sensory information for only a split second.

   b. is incorrect. This is unconscious, automatic memory for skills.

   d. is incorrect. Explicit memory is only one part of the knowledge base. Another part—implicit memory—is unconscious memory for skills.

5. d. is the correct answer. (objective 2)

6. c. is the correct answer. (objectives 1, 2, & 5)

   a. & b. are incorrect. Age-related deficits in these types of memory are minimal.

   d. is incorrect. Although explicit memory is part of the knowledge base, another part—implicit memory—shows minimal age-related deficits.

7. c. is the correct answer. (objective 8)

8. c. is the correct answer. (objectives 3, 4, & 6)

9. b. is the correct answer. (objective 6)

10. a. is the correct answer. Although age is not the key factor, it is true that dementia is more likely to occur in older adults. (video lesson, segment 3; objective 8)

11. a. is the correct answer. (video lesson, segment 3; objective 8)

    b. is incorrect. MID is responsible for about 15 percent of all dementia.

    c. & d. are incorrect. Compared to Alzheimer's disease, which accounts for about 70 percent of all dementia, these account for a much lower percentage.

12. d. is the correct answer. (objective 9)

13. b. is the correct answer. (objective 9)

   a. & c. are incorrect. These psychological illnesses are less common in the elderly than in younger adults, and less common than depression among the elderly.

   d. is incorrect. This disorder was not discussed in association with dementia.

14. b. is the correct answer. (objective 10)

   a. & d. are incorrect. Positive cognitive development is typical of older adults.

   c. is incorrect. Pragmatism is one characteristic of wisdom, an attribute commonly associated with older people.

15. a. is the correct answer. (objective 10)

   b. & c. are incorrect. Although these may be true of some older adults, they are not necessarily a key factor in cognitive development during late adulthood.

   d. is incorrect. In fact, older adults are typically more concerned with the whole of human experience.

Matching Items

16. e (objective 9)
17. b (objective 8)
18. g (objective 8)
19. c (video lesson, segment 1; objective 2)
20. k (objective 8)
21. d (video lesson, segment 3; objective 8)
22. j (video lesson, segment 3; objective 8)
23. f (objective 9)
24. h (objective 9)
25. a (objective 10)
26. i (objective 10)

Applying Your Knowledge

1. d. is the correct answer. (objective 5)
2. c. is the correct answer. (objective 9)

   a. is incorrect. In general, psychological illnesses are less common in the elderly than in younger adults.

   b. is incorrect. Depression is quite treatable at any age.

   d. is incorrect. Symptoms of depression are often mistaken as signs of dementia.

3. b. is the correct answer. (objective 10)
4. c. is the correct answer. (objective 10)

   d. is incorrect. This would lead to a greater appreciation of nature and art, but not necessarily to a tendency to reminisce.

5. c. is the correct answer. (video lesson, segment 1; objective 1)

   a. & d. are incorrect. The sensory register is concerned with noticing sensory events rather than with memory.

   b. is incorrect. Age-related deficits in the sensory register are most likely for ambiguous or weak stimuli.

6. a. is the correct answer. (video lesson, segment 1; objective 2)

   b. is incorrect. Explicit memory involves words, data, concepts, and the like. It is a part of long-term memory.

   c. is incorrect. Long-term memory includes information remembered for years or decades.

   d. is incorrect. The sensory register stores information for a split second.

7. d. is the correct answer. (objective 6)

8. b. is the correct answer. Older individuals are particularly likely to experience difficulty holding new information in mind, particularly when it is essentially meaningless. (objective 6)

   a., c., & d. are incorrect. These are examples of long-term memory, which declines very little with age.

9. b. is the correct answer. (video lesson, segment 3; objective 8)

   c. & d. are incorrect. The textbook does not indicate the existence of cohort effects in the incidence of Alzheimer's disease.

10. d. is the correct answer. (objective 10)

11. d. is the correct answer. (objective 9)

   a., b., & c. are incorrect. The symptoms Wayne's father is experiencing are those of depression, which is often misdiagnosed as dementia in the elderly.

Lesson Review

Lesson 24

Late Adulthood
Cognitive Development

Please Note: Use this matrix to guide your study and achieve the learning objectives of this lesson. It will also help you to view the video, which defines and demonstrates important concepts and skills as they relate to everyday life.

Learning Objective	Textbook	Course Student Guide	Video Lesson
1. Using the information-processing approach, summarize the laboratory findings regarding changes in the sensitivity of the sensory register/sensory threshold and the capacity of working memory during late adulthood.	pp. 668–671	Key Terms: 18, 19, 20, 21, 22; Practice Questions I: 1, 2, 3, 4, 15, 16; Practice Questions II: 1, 4, 6; Applying Your Knowledge: 5.	Segment 1: *Changes in Information Processing*
2. Summarize the laboratory findings regarding changes in the older adult's ability to access the knowledge base and to use control processes efficiently.	pp. 672–673	Key Terms: 1, 2, 18, 19; Practice Questions I: 4, 5; Practice Questions II: 2, 4, 5, 6, 19; Applying Your Knowledge: 6.	Segment 1: *Changes in Information Processing*
3. Describe research methods for assessing long-term memory in older adults.	pp. 671–672	Practice Questions I: 8; Practice Questions II: 3, 8.	Segment 2: *Age-Related Changes*
4. Suggest several reasons, other than the aging process itself, that might contribute to age-related declines in cognitive functioning.	pp. 666–668	Key Terms: 3, 6; Practice Questions I: 7, 8; Practice Questions II: 8.	Segment 2: *Age-Related Changes*
5. Describe age-related changes in the brain's size, weight, number of cells, and speed of processing.	p. 667	Practice Questions I: 10, 15; Practice Questions II: 6 Applying Your Knowledge: 1.	
6. Characterize and explain discrepancies between how the elderly perform on memory and problem-solving tasks in the laboratory, on one hand, and in daily life, on the other.	pp. 676–677	Key Terms: 4; Practice Questions I: 18; Practice Questions II: 8, 9; Applying Your Knowledge: 7, 8.	Segment 2: *Age-Related Changes*

Learning Objective	Textbook	Course Student Guide	Video Lesson
7. Discuss whether age-related declines in memory and processing speed are inevitable.	pp. 674–676	Practice Questions I: 10, 21; Practice Questions II: 1.	Segment 1: *Changes in Information Processing* Segment 4: *Enhancing Cognitive Abilities*
8. Identify the most common forms of dementia and discuss the differences between them.	pp. 678–681	Key Terms: 5, 7, 8, 9, 10, 12, 14; Practice Questions I: 6, 9, 11, 12, 17, 19, 20; Practice Questions II: 7, 10, 11, 17, 18, 20, 21, 22; Applying Your Knowledge: 9.	Segment 3: *Dementia*
9. Identify and describe other organic causes of dementia as well as causes of reversible dementia.	pp. 681–685	Key Terms: 5, 6, 11, 13, 15; Practice Questions I: 9, 12, 13, 19; Practice Questions II: 12, 13, 16, 23, 24; Applying Your Knowledge: 2, 11.	Segment 3: *Dementia*
10. Discuss the claims of developmentalists regarding the possibility of positive cognitive development during late adulthood, and cite several areas of life in which such development may occur.	pp. 685–689	Key Terms: 16, 17; Practice Questions I: 14, 21, 22; Practice Questions II: 14, 15, 25, 26; Applying Your Knowledge: 3, 4, 10.	Segment 4: *Enhancing Cognitive Abilities*

Staying in the Game

Lesson 25

Late Adulthood:
Psychosocial Development

Preview

"The older you are, the more important your choices are." So begins Lesson 25, which focuses on psychosocial development during late adulthood. Because the choices we make are so different, adults in their later years are more diverse in terms of their development than at any other time. Even so, negative stereotypes about the elderly too often distort people's perceptions of the later years. Certain changes are common during this stage of the life span—retirement, the death of a spouse, and declining health—yet people respond to these experiences in vastly different ways.

Individual experiences may help to explain the fact that theories of psychosocial aging, discussed in the first part of the lesson, are often contradictory. The second section of the lesson focuses on the challenges to feeling fulfilled during late adulthood, such as finding new sources of achievement once derived from work. In the third section, the importance of marriage, friends, neighbors, and family in providing social support is discussed, as are the different experiences of married and single older adults. The lesson concludes with a discussion of the frail elderly—the minority of older adults, often poor and/or ill, who require extensive care.

Prior Course Knowledge that Will Be Used in this Lesson
- Psychosocial development during early adulthood (Lesson 19) and middle adulthood (Lesson 22) will be referred to as we discuss psychosocial development during late adulthood.
- The major theories of development (Lesson 2) will be referred to as we discuss psychosocial development in later life.

Learning Objectives

Use this information to guide your reading, viewing, thinking, and studying. After successfully completing this lesson, you should be able to:

1. Explain the central premises of self theories of psychosocial development during late adulthood.

2. Discuss Erikson's stage of integrity versus despair and the process of achieving integrity in old age.

3. Identify and describe the stratification theories of psychosocial development during late adulthood.

4. Discuss dynamic theories of late adulthood.

5. List and discuss several alternative sources of achievement during late adulthood and the impact of retirement.

6. Explain how the economic circumstances of the elderly have changed in recent years.

7. Explain the social convoy's increasing importance during late adulthood.

8. Discuss how, and why, marriage relationships tend to change as people grow old.

9. Discuss the impact of being old and single (never-married, divorced, or widowed) on both women and men.

10. Discuss friendships among older people.

11. Discuss the relationship between the generations as it exists today, and identify several reasons for the current pattern of detachment.

12. Describe the frail elderly, explain why their number is growing, and discuss some factors that may protect the elderly from frailty.

📖 **Read Chapter 25, "Late Adulthood: Psychosocial Development," pages 693–725.**

⏪ **View the video for Lesson 25, "Staying in the Game."**

Segment 1: *Theories of Late Adulthood*

Segment 2: *Keeping Socially Active*

Segment 3: *Importance of the Social Convoy*

Segment 4: *Quality of Life*

Summary

The major theories of adulthood include self-theories, stratification theories, and dynamic theories. **Self theories** emphasize the active part played by each person in fulfilling his or her potential. A central concept for self theory is that older adults set goals, assess abilities, and find a way to accomplish what they want to achieve despite age-related declines. One of the ways they may do this is through selective optimization with compensation, a process by which they optimize remaining abilities in order to compensate for declines in other abilities.

According to Erikson, the final challenge of development is that of integrity versus despair, in which older adults attempt to come to terms with the personal choices and events that have shaped their lives and integrate them into a meaningful whole.

Partly as a result of changes in appearance, health, and employment, maintaining a coherent and consistent sense of identity during late adulthood may be particularly challenging.

Stratification theories maintain that social forces are particularly powerful during late adulthood, when a person's ability to function depends largely on the person's position in society. **Disengagement theory** maintains that during late adulthood the individual and society mutually withdraw in order to prepare for the individual's impending death. Critics of disengagement theory point out that older people choose to keep their social networks small because they are interested in maximizing the quality of their social relationships. Furthermore, **activity theory** holds that the more active the elderly are, the greater their life satisfaction and the longer their lives.

Contemporary theories of adult development also focus on the impact of stratification by gender and race. **Feminist theory** points out that most social structures and economic policies have been established by men, and consequently, women's needs are often devalued. **Critical race theory** maintains that racial separation shapes the experiences and attitudes of both racial minorities and racial majorities.

Dynamic theory emphasizes the diversity of development, as each person shapes his or her life within specific social contexts that are constantly changing. According to **continuity theory**, people cope in late adulthood in much the same way that they did earlier in life. Thus, even though the social environments of adults may change as they age, those who coped well earlier in life continue to do so.

Compared to younger adults, older adults are more likely to feel a strong obligation to serve their community and become involved in volunteer work. Many older adults stay busy by maintaining their homes and yards, reflecting their desire to age in their own home. One result of this is that many of the elderly live by themselves.

The continuity of older adults' social convoy is an important affirmation of who they have been and what they will continue to be. Older people's satisfaction with life bears relatively little relationship to their contact with younger members of their own family but correlates significantly with the quantity and quality of their contact with their social convoy. Long-standing friendships are particularly cherished by older adults and correlate with feelings of well-being and self-esteem. Thus, older adults are like to have smaller social convoys, but these are the friends with whom they greatly enjoy spending time.

The **frail elderly**—the physically infirm, the very ill, or the cognitively impaired—are differentiated by their inability to perform adequately the **activities of daily life (ADLs)**, including eating, bathing, toileting, walking, and dressing. Equally important to independent living are the **instrumental activities of daily life (IADLs)** that require some intellectual competence, such as paying bills, shopping, and so forth.

In every nation the number of frail elderly is increasing. However, many elderly persons never become frail because of protective factors, including their attitude, their social network, their physical setting, and their financial resources. Although being female, a minority member, or poor puts a person at increased risk of frailty, this is not inevitable. Some people enter late adulthood with many buffers in place: family members and friends, education, a pension, a lifetime of good health habits, and so on.

📖 **Review all reading assignments for this lesson.**

💻 **As assigned by your instructor, complete the optional online component for this lesson.**

Key Terms

Using your own words, write a brief definition or explanation of each of the following terms on a separate piece of paper.

1. self theories
2. integrity vs. despair
3. compulsive hoarding
4. positivity effect
5. stratification theories
6. disengagement theory
7. activity theory
8. aging in place
9. naturally occurring retirement community (NORC)
10. AARP
11. filial responsibility
12. frail elderly
13. activities of daily life (ADLs)
14. instrumental activities of daily life (IADLs)
15. assisted living
16. dynamic theories
17. continuity theory
18. identity theory
19. feminist theory
20. critical race theory
21. socioemotional selectivity theory
22. social convoy
23. selective optimization with compensation

Practice Questions I

Multiple-Choice Questions

1. According to disengagement theory, during late adulthood people tend to
   a. become less role-centered and more passive.
   b. have regrets about how they have lived their lives.
   c. become involved in a range of new activities.
   d. exaggerate lifelong personality traits.

2. Compulsive hoarding occurs
   a. in nearly all older adults.
   b. as evidence of stratification theory.
   c. more often when adult children are far away.
   d. from the urge to cling to familiar places and possessions.

3. Longitudinal studies of monozygotic and dizygotic twins have recently found evidence that
   a. genetic influences weaken as life experiences accumulate.
   b. strongly supports disengagement theory.
   c. some inherited traits seem even more apparent in late adulthood than earlier.
   d. all of the above are true.

4. Eileen is a 70-year-old woman who has been in the same home for 45 years, as have most of her neighbors. Eileen

    a. lives in a naturally occurring retirement community (NORC).
    b. is clinging to a familiar place.
    c. is aging in place.
    d. is all of the above.

5. In general, older people are

    a. more likely to retire at a later age.
    b. likely to retire for health-related reasons.
    c. likely to retire simply because they want to.
    d. more likely to retire at their employers' request.

6. The idea that individuals set their own goals, assess their abilities, and figure out how to accomplish what they want to achieve during late adulthood is referred to as

    a. disengagement.
    b. selective optimization with compensation.
    c. dynamic life-course development.
    d. age stratification.

7. After retirement, the elderly are likely to

    a. get a part-time job.
    b. become politically involved.
    c. do volunteer work because they feel a particular commitment to their community.
    d. do any of the above.

8. Which of the following theories does **NOT** belong with the others?

    a. disengagement theory
    b. feminist theory
    c. critical race theory
    d. continuity theory

9. Which of the following is most true of the relationship between the generations today?

    a. Because parents and children often live at a distance from each other, they are not close.
    b. Older adults prefer not to interfere in their children's lives.
    c. Younger adults are eager to live their own lives and do not want to care for their parents.
    d. The generations tend to see and help each other frequently.

10. The importance of long-standing friendships is reflected in which of the following?

    a. the intensification of friendly bonds between in-laws
    b. the mother–daughter relationship becoming more like one between two friends
    c. the intensification of friendly bonds between members of the nuclear family
    d. a change in the husband–wife relationship to one of friendship

Lesson 25/Late Adulthood: Psychosocial Development   **433**

11. In general, during late adulthood the fewest problems are experienced by individuals who

    a. are married.
    b. have always been single.
    c. have long been divorced.
    d. are widowed.

12. Which of the following is true of adjustment to the death of a spouse?

    a. It is easier for men in all respects.
    b. It is initially easier for men but over the long term it is easier for women.
    c. It is generally easier for women.
    d. It is determined primarily by individual personality traits, and therefore shows very few sex differences.

13. According to dynamic theories,

    a. self-integrity is maintained throughout life.
    b. adults make choices and interpret reality in such a way as to express themselves as fully as possible.
    c. people organize themselves according to their particular characteristics and circumstances.
    d. each person's life is largely a self-propelled process, occurring within ever-changing social contexts.

14. Which of the following most accurately expresses the most recent view of developmentalists regarding stratification by age?

    a. Aging makes a person's social sphere increasingly narrow.
    b. Disengagement is always the result of ageism.
    c. Most older adults become more selective in their social contacts.
    d. Older adults need even more social activity to be happy than they did earlier in life.

True or False Items

Write T (for true) or F (for false) on the line in front of each statement.

15. __T__ As one of the most disruptive experiences in the life span, widowhood tends to have similar effects on men and women.

16. __T__ Most older adults spend a great deal of time volunteering for community organizations.

17. __F__ Older adults do not understand the social concerns of younger age groups.

18. __F__ Most developmentalists support the central premise of disengagement theory.

19. __T__ Most older people suffer significantly from a lack of close friendships.

20. __F__ Nearly one in two older adults makes a long-distance move after retirement.

21. __F__ Loneliness during late adulthood is greater for individuals who were never married than for any other group.

Practice Questions II

Multiple-Choice Questions

1. Critics of disengagement theory point out that
   a. older people want to substitute new involvements for the roles they lose with retirement.
   b. disengagement usually is not voluntary on the part of the individual.
   c. disengagement often leads to greater life satisfaction for older adults.
   d. disengagement is more common at earlier stages in the life cycle.

2. A beanpole family is one that consists of
   a. fewer generations with fewer members than in the past.
   b. fewer generations with more members than in the past.
   c. more generations than in the past but with only a few members in each generation.
   d. more generations with more members than in the past.

3. According to continuity theory, during late adulthood people
   a. become less role-centered.
   b. become more passive.
   c. become involved in a range of new activities.
   d. cope with challenges in much the same way they did earlier in life.

4. Developmentalists who believe that stratification theory provides an unfairly negative picture of women and minority groups point out that
   a. European Americans are more likely than African Americans to be placed in nursing homes.
   b. elderly women are less likely than men to be lonely and depressed.
   c. multigenerational families and churches often nurture Hispanic Americans.
   d. all of the above are true.

5. Protective factors that act as buffers for the elderly include
   a. personality and social setting.
   b. financial resources and age.
   c. attitude and social network.
   d. none of the above.

6. The major U.S. organization affecting the elderly is
   a. Elderhostel.
   b. the American Association of Retired Persons.
   c. Foster Grandparents.
   d. Service Corps of Retired Executives.

7. Which of the following would **NOT** be included as an instrumental activity of daily life?
   a. grocery shopping
   b. paying bills
   c. making phone calls
   d. taking a walk

8. One of the most important factors contributing to life satisfaction for older adults appears to be
   a. contact with friends.
   b. contact with younger family members.
   c. the number of new experiences to which they are exposed.
   d. continuity in the daily routine.

9. In general, the longer a couple has been married, the more likely they are to
   a. be happier with each other.
   b. have frequent, minor disagreements.
   c. feel the relationship is not equitable.
   d. do all of the above.

10. Adjustment to divorce in late adulthood tends to be
    a. equally easy for men and women.
    b. easier for women.
    c. easier for men.
    d. initially easier for women, but over the long term easier for men.

11. Which of the following is **NOT** a major factor contributing to an increase in the number of frail elderly?
    a. an increase in average life expectancy
    b. a research focus on acute, rather than chronic, illnesses
    c. inadequate expenditures on social services
    d. a lack of facilities in many areas to care for the elderly

12. According to Erikson, achieving integrity during late adulthood above all involves
    a. the ability to perceive one's own life as worthwhile.
    b. being open to new influences and experiences.
    c. treating other people with respect.
    d. developing a consistent and yet varied daily routine.

Matching Items

Match each definition or description with its corresponding term.

Terms

13. ___E___ disengagement theory
14. ___A___ self theories
15. ___J___ continuity theory
16. ___I___ activity theory
17. ___H___ stratification theories

18. ___C___ activities of daily life (ADLs)
19. ___F___ instrumental activities of daily life (IADLs)
20. ___D___ dynamic theories
21. ___B___ naturally occurring retirement community (NORC)
22. ___G___ compulsive hoarding

Definitions or Descriptions

a. theories such as Erik Erikson's that emphasize self-actualization

b. a neighborhood or apartment complex where most residents have lived since young adulthood

c. eating, bathing, toileting, walking, and dressing

d. theory that a person's life is an active, largely self-propelled process that occurs within ever-changing social contexts.

e. theory that people become less role-centered as they age

f. actions that require intellectual competence and forethought

g. the urge to accumulate and hold onto objects to the point of it being hazardous to one's health and safety

h. theories such as feminist theory and critical race theory that focus on the limitations on life choices created by social forces

i. theory that elderly people become socially withdrawn only involuntarily

j. theory that each person copes in late adulthood in the same way he or she did earlier in life

Applying Your Knowledge

1. Which of the following statements most accurately describes psychosocial development in late adulthood?

   a. Many leading gerontologists believe that people become more alike as they get older.

   b. Older adults generally fit into one of two distinct personality types.

   c. Many gerontologists believe that the diversity of personalities and patterns is especially pronounced among the elderly.

   d. Few changes in psychosocial development occur after middle adulthood.

2. An advocate of which of the following theories would be most likely to agree with the statement, "Because of their more passive style of interaction, older people are less likely to be chosen for new roles"?

   a. disengagement
   b. continuity
   c. self
   d. dynamic

3. An advocate for feminist theory would point out that

   a. since most social structures and economic policies have been established by men, women's needs are devalued.
   b. women in the United States make up the majority of the elderly and the elderly poor.
   c. many elderly women are expected to care for frail relatives even if it strains their own health.
   d. all of the above are true.

4. Professor Martin states that "membership in certain groups can place the elderly at risk for a number of dangers." Professor Martin evidently is an advocate of which theory of psychosocial development?

   a. self theories
   b. social stratification
   c. dynamic
   d. continuity

5. The one most likely to agree with the statement, "Older adults have an obligation to help others and serve the community," is

   a. a middle-aged adult.
   b. a younger woman.
   c. a younger man.
   d. an older adult.

6. An elderly man with dementia is most likely to be cared for by his spouse in _____ and by his children in _____.

   a. Korea; the United States
   b. the United States; Korea
   c. Japan; Sweden
   d. Sweden; Japan

7. Research indicates that the primary perpetrators of elder abuse are

   a. professional caregivers.
   b. mean-spirited strangers.
   c. other relatives.
   d. middle-aged children.

8. Which of the following best describes the relationship between the elderly and younger generations?

   a. If children move, the elderly will also move in order to continue to be near them.

   b. The elderly enjoy social contact with the younger generation and particularly enjoy having long visits from their grandchildren.

   c. Assistance typically flows from the older generation to their children.

   d. The relationship between mothers and daughters improves with age, with conflict decreasing substantially.

9. Of the following older adults, who is most likely to be involved in a network of intimate friendships?

   a. William, a 65-year-old who never married

   b. Darrel, a 60-year-old widower

   c. Florence, a 63-year-old widow

   d. Kay, a 66-year-old married woman

10. Sidney has been told that his eyesight is too bad for him to continue driving a car. Sidney's despairing response is explained by

    a. stratification theory.

    b. self-theory.

    c. continuity theory.

    d. disengagement theory.

11. Claudine is the primary caregiver for her elderly parents. The amount of stress she feels in this role depends above all on

    a. how frail her parents are.

    b. her subjective interpretation of the support she receives from others.

    c. her relationship to her parents prior to their becoming frail.

    d. her overall financial situation.

12. Wilma's elderly mother needs help in taking care of the instrumental activities of daily life. Such activities would include which of the following?

    a. bathing

    b. eating

    c. paying bills

    d. all of the above

13. In concluding her presentation on the frail elderly, Janet notes that "the number of frail elderly is currently _____ than the number who are active, financially stable, and capable; however, the frail elderly are _____ in absolute number."

    a. greater; decreasing

    b. less; increasing

    c. greater; increasing

    d. less; decreasing

14. Jack, who is 73, looks back on his life with a sense of pride and contentment; Eleanor feels unhappy with her life and that it is "too late to start over." In Erikson's terminology, Jack is experiencing _____, while Eleanor is experiencing _____.

    a. generativity; stagnation

    b. identity; emptiness

    c. integrity; despair

    d. completion; termination

Answer Key

Key Terms

1. Self theories such as Erik Erikson's theory focus on how adults make choices, confront problems, and interpret reality in such a way as to express themselves as fully as possible. (p. 694; video lesson, segment 1; objective 1)

2. In Erikson's theory, the final crisis of development is that of integrity versus despair, in which older adults attempt to integrate their personal experiences with their vision of the future of their community. (p. 694; video lesson, segment 1; objective 2)

3. The urge to accumulate and hold onto familiar items to the point of it becoming a hazard to health and safety is called compulsive hoarding. (p. 695; objective 1)

4. Positivity effect is the tendency for elderly people to perceive, prefer, and remember positive images and experiences more than negative ones. (p. 696; objective 4)

5. Stratification theories emphasize that social forces limit individual choices and affect the ability to function. (p. 697; video lesson, segment 1; objective 3)

6. According to disengagement theory, aging results in social withdrawal and passivity. (p. 697; video lesson, segment 1; objective 3)

7. Activity theory is the view that older people remain active in a variety of social spheres and become withdrawn only unwillingly. (p. 698; video lesson, segment 1; objective 3)

8. Aging in place refers to a preference to a preference of elderly people to remain in the same home and community, adjusting but not leaving when health fades. (p. 704; objective 5)

9. A neighborhood or apartment complex whose population is mostly retired people who have lived there since they were younger adults is called a naturally occurring retirement community or NORC. (p. 704; objective 5)

10. AARP is a U.S. organization of people aged 50 and older, which advocates for the elderly. It was originally called the American Association of Retired Persons, but now only the initials AARP is used, to reflect the fact that the organization's members do not have to be retired. (p. 706; objective 6)

11. Filial responsibility is the idea that adult children are obligated to care for their aging parents. (p. 709; objective 11)

12. The frail elderly are the minority of older adults who are physically infirm, very ill, or cognitively impaired. (p. 716; video lesson, segment 4; objective 12)

13. In determining frailty, gerontologists often refer to the activities of daily life (ADLs), which comprise five tasks: eating, bathing, toileting, dressing,

and transferring from a bed to a chair. (p. 716; video lesson, segment 4; objective 12)

14. The instrumental activities of daily life (IADLs) are actions that require some intellectual competence and forethought, such as shopping for food, paying bills, and taking medication. (p. 716; video lesson, segment 4; objective 12)

15. Assisted living is a living arrangement for elderly people that combines privacy and independence with medical supervision. (p. 721; objective 12)

16. According to dynamic theories, each person's life is an active, largely self-propelled process that occurs within ever-changing social contexts. (video lesson, segment 1; objective 4)

17. According to the continuity theory of aging, each person copes with late adulthood in much the same way that he or she coped with earlier periods of life. (video lesson, segment 1; objective 4)

18. An example of a self theory, identity theory emphasizes the impact of the choices adults make on their self-concepts. (video lesson, segment 1; objective 1)

19. A stratification theory, feminist theory points out that since most social structures and economic policies have been established by men, women's needs are devalued by society. (video lesson, segment 1; objective 3)

20. Another stratification theory, critical race theory maintains that racial stratification shapes the experiences and attitudes of both racial minorities and racial majorities. (video lesson, segment 1; objective 3)

21. According to socioemotional selectivity theory, as people get older they tend to have fewer, but more important, friendships and relationships. (video lesson, segment 3; objectives 7 & 10)

22. The social convoy is the network of people with whom we establish meaningful relationships as we travel through life. (video lesson, segment 3; objective 7)

23. Selective optimization with compensation is the idea that healthy aging involves assessing abilities realistically, choosing meaningful goals, and devising strategies to accomplish them, despite age-related losses and limitations. (video lesson, segment 1; objective 1)

Practice Questions I

Multiple-Choice Questions

1. a. is the correct answer. (video lesson, segment 1; objective 3)

   b. is incorrect. This answer depicts a person struggling with Erikson's crisis of integrity versus despair.

   c. is incorrect. This answer describes activity theory.

   d. is incorrect. Disengagement theory does not address this issue.

2. d. is the correct answer. (objective 1)

3. c. is the correct answer. (objective 1)

   a. is incorrect. Such studies have found that genetic influences do not weaken with age.

   b. is incorrect. This research provides support for self theories rather than disengagement theory.

4. d. is the correct answer. (objectives 1 & 5)

5. c. is the correct answer. (video lesson, segment 2; objective 5)

   a. & b. are incorrect. Workers are retiring earlier than in the past, and not always for health-related reasons.

d. is incorrect. Mandatory retirement is illegal in many nations.

6. b. is the correct answer. (objective 1)

a. is incorrect. This is the idea that the elderly withdraw from society as they get older.

c. is incorrect. This is the theory that each person's life is a self-propelled process occurring within ever-changing social contexts.

d. is incorrect. According to this theory, the oldest generation is segregated from the rest of society.

7. d. is the correct answer. Contrary to earlier views that retirement was not a happy time, researchers now know that the elderly are generally happy and productive, spending their time in various activities. (video lesson, segment 2; objective 5)

8. d. is the correct answer. Each of the other theories can be categorized as a stratification theory. (objectives 3 & 4)

9. d. is the correct answer. (objective 11)

10. c. is the correct answer. (objective 7)

a., b., & d. are incorrect. These may occur in some cases, but they are not discussed in the textbook.

11. a. is the correct answer. (objective 8)

12. c. is the correct answer. (objective 9)

13. d. is the correct answer. (video lesson, segment 1; objective 4)

a. is incorrect.

b. is incorrect. This expresses self theory.

c. is incorrect. This expresses stratification theory.

14. c. is the correct answer. (objective 3)

a. is incorrect. This is the central idea behind disengagement theory.

b. & d. are incorrect. These ideas are expressions of activity theory.

True or False Items

15. F   Women tend to be more prepared and have more friends to sympathize with them. Men, who tend to depend on their wives for basic needs and emotional support, find it hard to turn to others for help. (objective 9)

16. F   (objective 5)

17. F   In fact, older adults are willing to vote against the interests of their own group if a greater good is at stake. (objective 11)

18. F   In fact, disengagement theory has few serious defenders. (video lesson, segment 1; objective 3)

19. F   Most older adults have at least one close friend and, as compared with younger adults, are less likely to feel a need for more friendships. (video lesson, segment 3; objective 10)

20. F   A minority of older adults moves to another state. (objective 5)

21. F   If anything, loneliness tends to be less in never-married older adults. (objective 9)

Practice Questions II

Multiple-Choice Questions

1. a. is the correct answer. (video lesson, segment 1; objective 3)

b. is incorrect. If disengagement were not voluntary, this would not be a choice of the elderly.

c. & d. are incorrect. Neither of these answers is true, nor a criticism of disengagement theory.

2. c. is the correct answer. (objective 11)

3. d. is the correct answer. (video lesson, segment 1; objective 4)

a. & b. are incorrect. These answers describe disengagement theory.

c. is incorrect. This answer pertains to activity theory.

4. d. is the correct answer. (video lesson, segment 1; objective 3)

5. c. is the correct answer. (objective 12)

6. b. is the correct answer. (objective 6)

a. is incorrect. Elderhostel is an educational program for older adults.

c. & d. are incorrect. These service organizations affect a much smaller percentage of the elderly.

7. d. is the correct answer. (video lesson, segment 4; objective 12)

8. a. is the correct answer. (objective 10)

b., c., & d. are incorrect. The importance of these factors varies from one older adult to another.

9. a. is the correct answer. (objective 8)

b. & c. are incorrect. The longer a couple has been married, the less likely they are to have frequent disagreements or feel that the relationship is not equitable.

10. b. is the correct answer. (objectives 8 & 9)

11. c. is the correct answer. Many nations spend substantial money on services for the elderly. (objective 12)

a. is incorrect. As more people reach old age, the absolute numbers of frail individuals will increase.

b. is incorrect. Such research neglects the study of diseases that are nonfatal, yet disabling.

d. is incorrect. Services are relatively scarce in rural areas, where a large number of elderly people reside.

12. a. is the correct answer. (video lesson, segment 1; objective 2)

Matching Items

13. e (video lesson, segment 1; objective 3)

14. a (video lesson, segment 1; objective 1)

15. j (video lesson, segment 1; objective 4)

16. i (video lesson, segment 1; objective 3)

17. h (video lesson, segment 1; objective 3)

18. c (video lesson, segment 4; objective 12)

19. f (video lesson, segment 4; objective 12)

20. d (video lesson, segment 1; objective 4)

21. b (objective 5)

22. g (objective 1)

Applying Your Knowledge

1. c. is the correct answer. (objective 1)

2. a. is the correct answer. (video lesson, segment 1; objective 3)

   b. is incorrect. Continuity theory, a type of dynamic theory, maintains that older adults cope with aging in much the same ways as when they were younger.

   c. is incorrect. Self theories emphasize the quest for self-actualization.

   d. is incorrect. Dynamic theories emphasize that life is a self-propelled, ever-changing process within an ever-changing social context.

3. d. is the correct answer. (video lesson, segment 1; objective 3)

4. b. is the correct answer. "Groups" are the social "strata" that this theory focuses on. (video lesson, segment 1; objective 3)

   a. & c. are incorrect. These theories emphasize the efforts of the individual to reach his or her full potential (self theories) by interpreting experiences in the face of ever-changing social contexts (dynamic theories, of which continuity theory is one [d.]).

5. d. is the correct answer. (objective 5)

   a. is incorrect. Middle-aged adults tend to be more focused on individual and family needs.

   b. & c. are incorrect. The textbook does not suggest that there is a gender difference in adults' sense of obligation to serve others.

6. b. is the correct answer. (objective 12)

   c. & d. are incorrect. The textbook does not compare care for the frail elderly in these countries.

7. d. is the correct answer. (objective 12)

8. c. is the correct answer. (objective 11)

   a. is incorrect. Even if children move, their parents prefer to stay in their homes.

   b. is incorrect. Although the elderly enjoy social contact with the younger generations, they prefer shorter visits.

   d. is incorrect. Tension and conflict continues throughout life in mother–daughter relationships.

9. c. is the correct answer. (objective 9)

   a. & b. are incorrect. At every age, women have larger social circles and more intimate relationships with their friends than men.

   d. is incorrect. Widows tend to be more involved in friendship networks than married women.

10. b. is the correct answer. (objective 1)

11. b. is the correct answer. (objective 12)

12. c. is the correct answer. (video lesson, segment 4; objective 12)

    a. & b. are incorrect. These are examples of "activities of daily life."

13. b. is the correct answer. (objective 12)

14. c. is the correct answer. (video lesson, segment 1; objective 2)

    a. is incorrect. This is not the crisis of late adulthood in Erikson's theory.

    b. & d. are incorrect. These are not crises in Erikson's theory.

Lesson Review

Lesson 25

Late Adulthood
Psychosocial Development

Please Note: Use this matrix to guide your study and achieve the learning objectives of this lesson. It will also help you to view the video, which defines and demonstrates important concepts and skills as they relate to everyday life.

Learning Objective	Textbook	Course Student Guide	Video Lesson
1. Explain the central premises of self-theories of psychosocial development during late adulthood.	pp. 693–697	Key Terms: 1, 3, 18; Practice Questions I: 2, 3, 4, 6; Practice Questions II: 14, 22; Applying Your Knowledge: 1, 10.	Segment 1: *Theories of Late Adulthood*
2. Discuss Erikson's stage of integrity versus despair and the process of achieving integrity in old age.	pp. 694, 697	Key Terms: 2; Practice Questions II: 12; Applying Your Knowledge: 14.	Segment 1: *Theories of Late Adulthood*
3. Identify and describe the stratification theories of psychosocial development during late adulthood.	pp. 697–700	Key Terms: 5, 6, 7, 19, 20; Practice Questions I: 1, 8, 14, 18; Practice Questions II: 1, 4, 13, 16, 17; Applying Your Knowledge: 2, 3, 4.	Segment 1: *Theories of Late Adulthood*
4. Discuss dynamic theories of late adulthood.	*	Key Terms: 4, 16, 17; Practice Questions I: 8, 13; Practice Questions II: 3, 15, 20.	Segment 1: *Theories of Late Adulthood*
5. List and discuss several alternative sources of achievement during late adulthood and the impact of retirement.	pp. 701–706	Key Terms: 8, 9; Practice Questions I: 4, 5, 7, 16, 20; Practice Questions II: 21; Applying Your Knowledge: 5.	Segment 2: *Keeping Socially Active*
6. Explain how the economic circumstances of the elderly have changed in recent years.	p. 701	Key Terms: 10; Practice Questions II: 6.	
7. Explain the social convoy's increasing importance during late adulthood.	pp. 707–716	Key Terms: 21; Practice Questions I: 10.	Segment 3: *Importance of the Social Convoy*

*The video for this lesson offers an excellent description of these concepts.

Learning Objective	Textbook	Course Student Guide	Video Lesson
8. Discuss how, and why, marriage relationships tend to change as people grow old.	pp. 707–708	Practice Questions I: 11; Practice Questions II: 9, 10.	Segment 3: *Importance of the Social Convoy*
9. Discuss the impact of being old and single (never-married, divorced, or widowed) on both women and men.	pp. 699, 713–714	Practice Questions I: 12, 15, 21; Practice Questions II: 10; Applying Your Knowledge: 9.	
10. Discuss friendships among older people.	pp. 713–716	Key Terms: 21; Practice Questions I: 19; Practice Questions II: 8.	Segment 3: *Importance of the Social Convoy*
11. Discuss the relationship between the generations as it exists today, and identify several reasons for the current pattern of detachment.	pp. 708–712	Key Terms: 11; Practice Questions I: 9, 17; Practice Questions II: 2; Applying Your Knowledge: 8.	
12. Describe the frail elderly, explain why their number is growing, and discuss some factors that may protect the elderly from frailty.	pp. 716–722	Key Terms: 12, 13, 14, 15; Practice Questions II: 5, 7, 11, 18, 19; Applying Your Knowledge: 6, 7, 11, 12, 13.	Segment 4: *Quality of Life*

Living and Dying

Lesson 26

Epilogue:
Death and Dying

Preview

Depending upon an individual's age, experience, beliefs, and historical and cultural context, death can have many meanings. Death marks the close of the life span, and is another area that reflects the vast complexity of human development in the way people grieve, accept, or deny death due to their social, religious, and cultural differences.

The lesson begins by exploring the dying person's emotions, noting that the reactions that death prompts vary from individual to individual. Although contemporary psychologists consider the experience of dying to be variable and not subject to an unvarying sequence of stages, the pioneering work of Elisabeth Kübler-Ross was nevertheless instrumental in revealing the emotional gamut of terminally ill patients and the importance of honest communication.

Next, the lesson deals with how dying patients and their families plan for death and the controversial issue of whether and when the death of a loved one should be hastened. This section also discusses hospice and other forms of care designed to help the terminally ill patient to die "a good death."

The final section explores the social context of dying, noting that perceptions of death vary markedly according to their historical and cultural context. This section also deals with changing expressions of bereavement and how people can be aided in the process of recovery.

Learning Objectives

Use this information to guide your reading, viewing, thinking, and studying. After successfully completing this lesson, you should be able to:

1. Identify Kübler-Ross's stages of dying, and discuss these stages in light of more recent research.

2. Discuss age-related differences in the conceptualization of emotional reactions to death.

3. Discuss the steps that patients, family members, and medical personnel can take to plan for a swift, pain-free, and dignified death.

4. Explain the concept of palliative care, focusing on the advantages and disadvantages of hospices, and describe the conditions under which individuals choose to avoid medical intervention.

5. Discuss issues surrounding assisted suicide and active euthanasia, noting the Dutch experience with legislation regarding assisted dying.

6. Describe some cultural and religious variations in how death is viewed and treated.

7. Describe recent changes in the mourning process, and suggest steps that can be taken in helping someone to recover from bereavement.

📖 **Read Chapter 26, "Epilogue: Death and Dying," pages Ep-1–Ep-27.**

⏮ **View the video for Lesson 26, "Living and Dying."**

> **Segment 1: *Emotional Reactions to Death***
>
> **Segment 2: *Deciding How to Die***
>
> **Segment 3: *Social Context of Bereavement***
>
> **Segment 4: *Cycle of Life***

Summary

Elisabeth Kübler-Ross proposed that the dying go through five emotional stages, beginning with *denial*, during which the patient refuses to believe that he or she will die. Denial is followed by *anger*; *bargaining*, in which the patient tries to negotiate an alternative with God or fate; *depression*; and finally *acceptance* of death as the last stage of this life and possibly the beginning of the next. Although the theory brought needed attention to the experience of dying, recent research shows that Kübler-Ross's stages, when and if they occur, do not always occur in the sequence she proposed.

Most people agree that a "good death" is one that occurs swiftly, with little pain, and allows the individual to die with dignity, surrounded by loved ones. There is a growing consensus that the patient should be the ultimate authority regarding what life-sustaining measures should be used in terminal cases. Some people make a **living will** to indicate what medical intervention they want if they become incapable of expressing those wishes.

Individual reactions to dying vary across the life span. Young children are usually upset by the thought of dying because it suggests the idea of being separated from loved ones. Adolescents may be focused on the ways their condition may affect their appearance and social relationships. Middle-aged adults may be primarily concerned about meeting important obligations and responsibilities. An older adult's feelings about dying depend more on the situation. If one's spouse has already died, and if the illness brings pain and infirmity, death may be more readily accepted.

When medical interventions appear not to be working and terminally ill individuals are near the end of life, **palliative care** is designed to ease suffering through such methods as pain-killing medication or **DNR (do not resuscitate)** orders. Few doctors and nurses are trained to handle the psychological demands of palliative care. **Passive euthanasia** occurs when life-saving care methods are available, but are not used to allow death to occur.

The **hospice** is an alternative to hospital care that seeks to minimize suffering and to make the last days of life filled with love and meaning. Hospices provide the dying with skilled medical care but shun the use of artificial life-support systems. Both palliative care and passive euthanasia may be used in hospice. However, because candidates for the hospice program must be diagnosed as terminally ill, participation is restricted to a minority of the dying. Especially controversial are issues concerning **physician-assisted suicide**, in which someone provides the means for a person to end his or her life, and **active euthanasia**, in which someone intentionally acts to terminate the life of a suffering person.

The specific meanings attached to death vary from individual to individual, and according to their cultural and historical context. In most African traditions, elders take on an important new status through death, while in many Muslim nations, death affirms faith in Allah and caring for the dying is a holy reminder of mortality. Among Hindus and Sikhs, helping the dying to relinquish their ties to this world and prepare for the next is considered an obligation for the immediate family. Preparations for death are not emphasized in the Jewish tradition because hope for life can never be extinguished. Many Christians believe that death is the beginning of eternity in heaven or hell, and thus welcome or fear it.

The larger cultural context often has more influence on variations in death practices than religion does. Customs of **mourning** also vary tremendously. Two themes that emerge in cultural variations of death practices are that religious and spiritual concerns often reemerge and that returning to one's roots is a common urge.

In recent times, mourning has become more private, less emotional, and less religious. As a result of these trends, there is an increasing tendency toward social isolation for those who have lost a loved one and increased likelihood of physical illness. Mourning may be affected by the conditions under which the loved one died; deaths that are expected and occur after a long period of illness may be easier to cope with because they permit anticipatory **grief**. However, even those who have had time to prepare for the loss of the loved one may be surprised at how much additional grief they may experience afterwards.

Bereaved persons are comforted by social support: a friend who listens, sympathizes, and does not ignore the real pain and complicated emotions involved in the recovery process. Those who would comfort the bereaved should be aware that **bereavement** is likely to be a lengthy and demanding process that may last for months or even years. The experience of grief may vary markedly from one individual to the next, and there is no one "correct" way to deal with the loss.

📖 **Review all reading assignments for this lesson.**

💻 **As assigned by your instructor, complete the optional online component for this lesson.**

Key Terms

Using your own words, write a brief definition or explanation of each of the following terms on a separate piece of paper.

1.	thanatology	12.	health care proxy
2.	terror management theory (TMT)	13.	bereavement
3.	hospice	14.	grief
4.	palliative care	15.	mourning
5.	double effect	16.	complicated grief
6.	passive euthanasia	17.	absent grief
7.	DNR (do not resuscitate)	18.	disenfranchised grief
8.	active euthanasia	19.	incomplete grief
9.	physician-assisted suicide	20.	anticipatory grief
10.	slippery slope	21.	voluntary euthanasia
11.	living will		

Practice Questions I

Multiple-Choice Questions

1. Kübler-Ross found that doctors often chose not to inform terminally ill patients of their condition and sometimes concealed the information from families as well. Such an approach would tend to

    a. minimize possibilities for grief.

    b. increase feelings of isolation and sorrow.

    c. discourage the family from retaining memories of the deceased.

    d. maximize possibilities for passive euthanasia.

2. Medical advances have meant that death today is more often

    a. far less painful for the dying individual.

    b. emotionally far less painful for the bereaved.

    c. a solitary, lengthy, and painful experience.

    d. predictable, and therefore a less traumatic experience.

3. Kübler-Ross's stages of dying are, in order

    a. anger, denial, bargaining, depression, acceptance.

    b. depression, anger, denial, bargaining, acceptance.

    c. denial, anger, bargaining, depression, acceptance.

    d. bargaining, denial, anger, acceptance, depression.

4. Recent research regarding the emotions of terminally ill patients has found that

    a. all patients reach the stage of acceptance.

    b. emotional stages generally follow one another in an orderly sequence.

    c. age has an important effect on emotions.

    d. most experience depression.

5. Most adults hope that they will die
   a. with little pain.
   b. with dignity.
   c. swiftly.
   d. in all of the above ways.

6. A pain-free death is least likely to be experienced by
   a. the oldest-old patients in hospitals.
   b. hospice patients.
   c. children dying of cancer.
   d. patients who fail to make a living will.

7. Hospice is best defined as
   a. a document that indicates what kind of medical intervention a terminally ill person wants.
   b. mercifully allowing a person to die by not doing something that might extend life.
   c. an alternative to hospital care for the terminally ill.
   d. providing a person with the means to end his or her life.

8. Palliative care refers to
   a. heroic measures to save a life.
   b. conservative medical care to treat an illness.
   c. efforts to relieve pain and suffering.
   d. allowing a terminally ill patient to die naturally.

9. Which of the following describes a situation in which, at a patient's request, caregivers are ordered not to take extreme measures to intervene in life-threatening health events?
   a. involuntary euthanasia
   b. active euthanasia
   c. physician-assisted suicide
   d. DNR

10. Which of the following is a normal response in the bereavement process?
    a. experiencing powerful emotions
    b. culturally diverse emotions
    c. a lengthy period of grief
    d. All of the above are normal responses.

11. A "double effect" in medicine refers to a situation in which
    a. the effects of one drug on a patient interact with those of another drug.
    b. medication relieves pain and has a secondary effect of hastening death.
    c. family members disagree with a terminally ill patient's proxy.
    d. medical personnel ignore the wishes of a terminally ill patient and his or her proxy.

12. Criticisms made against hospices include all of the following **EXCEPT**
   a. the number of patients served is limited.
   b. in some cases a life is being ended that might have been prolonged.
   c. burnout and the rapid growth of hospices might limit the number of competent hospice workers.
   d. the patient is needlessly isolated from family and friends.

True or False Items

Write T (for true) or F (for false) on the line in front of each statement.

13. __T__ The terminally ill generally want to know about and discuss their condition.

14. __T__ Subsequent research has confirmed the accuracy of Kübler-Ross's findings regarding the five stages of dying.

15. __F__ Modern life-prolonging medical technologies have tended to make dying a pain-free, dignified death more difficult and less likely to occur.

16. __T__ Following the death of a loved one, the bereaved can best ensure their psychological health and well-being by increasing their social contacts and the number of activities in which they are involved.

17. __F__ To help a bereaved person, one should ignore the person's depression.

18. __F__ The line between life and death is clearly defined and unmistakeable.

19. __F__ Physician-assisted suicide and voluntary euthanasia are legal almost everywhere in the world.

20. __T__ Hospices administer pain-killing medication but do not make use of artificial life-support systems.

21. __T__ In the long run, the bereavement process may have a beneficial effect on the individual.

22. __T__ There is general consensus that hospice care is a good alternative to hospital care for the dying.

Practice Questions II

Multiple-Choice Questions

1. Kübler-Ross's primary contribution was to
   a. open the first hospice, thus initiating the hospice movement.
   b. show how the emotions of the dying occur in a series of clear-cut stages.
   c. demonstrate that varied and contradictory emotions are normal among the terminally ill.
   d. show the correlation between people's conceptualization of death and their developmental stage.

2. In recent times, mourning has become all of the following **EXCEPT**
   a. more private.
   b. less emotional.
   c. more likely to lead to social isolation.
   d. more religious.

3. Which of the following is **NOT** a limitation of hospices?
   a. Most insurance plans will not pay for hospice care unless the patient has been diagnosed as terminally ill.
   b. Hospice care can be very expensive.
   c. Almost no hospices serve children.
   d. The dying typically do not receive skilled medical care.

4. Legal experts and medical personnel increasingly agree that the ultimate authority in deciding how a terminal patient is treated should be
   a. the patient's physician.
   b. the legal system.
   c. the patient's family members.
   d. the patient.

5. Recent research reveals that Kübler-Ross's stages of dying
   a. occur in sequence in virtually all terminally ill patients.
   b. do not occur in hospice residents.
   c. are typical only in Western cultures.
   d. make feelings about death seem much more predictable and universal than they actually are.

6. Today, it may be more difficult for the terminally ill to die a swift, dignified, and pain-free death because
   a. modern medicine can sustain life beyond its time.
   b. many doctors view death as an enemy to be fended off at all costs.
   c. the dying often are in discomfort or outright pain because analgesic medications are underprescribed.
   d. of all of the above reasons.

7. Living wills are an attempt to
   a. make sure that passive euthanasia will not be used in individual cases.
   b. specify the extent of medical treatment desired in the event of terminal illness.
   c. specify conditions for the use of active euthanasia.
   d. ensure that death will occur at home rather than in a hospital.

8. _____ neither eat nor drink until the funeral pyre is extinguished.
   a. Buddhists
   b. Muslims
   c. Hindus
   d. Jews

9. The hospice made acceptable three basic principles regarding death and dying, including all of the following except that
   a. an interdisciplinary team can provide the best care for any sick person.
   b. death is a family affair.
   c. the dying person should be left alone to reconcile his or her feelings about life.
   d. palliative care is a worthy medical goal.

10. To develop the greatest understanding of variations in mourning practices, a person would do best to focus on
    a. the age and gender of terminally ill patients.
    b. religious differences among the bereaved.
    c. cultural differences among the bereaved.
    d. whether the death permitted anticipatory grief reactions among the bereaved.

11. Healing after the death of a loved one is most difficult when
    a. the death is a long, protracted one.
    b. the bereaved is not allowed to mourn in the way or she wishes.
    c. a period of grief has already elapsed.
    d. there are no other mourners.

Matching Items
Match each definition or description with its corresponding term.

Terms
12. ___C___ DNR
13. ___B___ hospice
14. ___D___ living will
15. ___H___ double effect

16. ___E___ physician-assisted suicide
17. ___A___ palliative care
18. ___F___ health care proxy
19. ___G___ anticipatory grief

Definitions or Descriptions
a. hospice treatment that relieves suffering and safeguards dignity
b. an alternative to hospital care for the terminally ill
c. hospital chart order to allow a terminally ill patient to die naturally
d. a document expressing a person's wishes for treatment should he or she become terminally ill and incapable of making such decisions
e. providing the means for a terminally ill patient to end his or her life
f. an individual chosen to make medical decisions for someone if that person is unable to do so

g. reduces shock and eases the acceptance of a loved one's death
h. situation in which a pain-relieving drug also hastens the death of a terminally ill patient

Applying Your Knowledge

1. Among my people, a deceased person is bathed by the next of kin. I am
   a. African.
   b. Muslim.
   c. Hindu.
   d. Native American.

2. Jeff has been sky-diving, bungee-jumping, rock climbing, and swimming with sharks. Some theorists believe Jeff is
   a. trying to commit suicide.
   b. in denial about the risks of his activities.
   c. trying to manage his terror about death and dying by proving he can survive even risky activities.
   d. convinced of his own immortality.

3. The terminally ill patient who promises to live a better life if spared from dying is probably in which of Kübler-Ross's stages?
   a. denial
   b. anger
   c. depression
   d. bargaining

4. The terminally ill patient who is convinced his laboratory tests must be wrong is probably in which of Kübler-Ross's stages?
   a. denial
   b. anger
   c. depression
   d. bargaining

5. Dr. Welby writes the orders DNR (do not resuscitate) on her patient's chart. Evidently the patient has requested
   a. a double effect.
   b. passive euthanasia.
   c. active euthanasia.
   d. an assisted suicide.

6. The doctor who injects a terminally ill patient with a lethal drug is practicing
   a. passive euthanasia.
   b. active euthanasia.
   c. an assisted suicide.
   d. an act that became legal in most countries in 1993.

Lesson 26/Epilogue: Death and Dying 455

7. Summarizing her presentation on the process of mourning, Rita states that most developmentalists view mourning as
   a. an unnecessary and emotionally crippling process.
   b. a disruptive force in development.
   c. a necessary and healthy process.
   d. important for some, but not all, individuals.

8. Which of the following statements would probably be the most helpful to a grieving person?
   a. "Why don't you get out more and get back into the swing of things?"
   b. "You're tough; bear up!"
   c. "If you need someone to talk to, call me any time."
   d. "It must have been his or her time to die."

9. Dr. Robinson is about to counsel her first terminally ill patient and his family. Research suggests that her most helpful strategy would be to
   a. keep most of the facts from both the patient and his family in order not to upset them.
   b. be truthful to the patient but not his family.
   c. be truthful to the family only, and swear them to secrecy.
   d. honestly inform both the patient and his family.

Answer Key

Key Terms
1. Thanatology is the study of death. (p. Ep-1; objective 7)
2. The theory that people adopt values and moral principles to overcome their own fear of death is called terror management theory (TMT). (p. Ep-4; objective 2)
3. A hospice is an institution in which terminally ill patients receive palliative care. (p. Ep-11; video lesson, segment 2; objective 4)
4. Palliative care, such as that provided in a hospice, is care that relieves suffering while safeguarding the person's dignity. (p. Ep-13; video lesson, segment 2; objective 4)
5. A double effect is a situation in which medication has the intended effect of relieving a dying person's pain and the secondary effect of hastening death. (p. Ep-13; objectives 3 & 4)
6. Passive euthanasia is a situation in which a seriously ill person is allowed to die naturally, through the cessation of medical intervention. (p. Ep-15; objective 3)
7. DNR is an acronym for "Do Not Resuscitate," which is a medical order to not use extreme measures to resuscitate a patient in the face of a life-threatening event. (p. Ep-15; objectives 4 & 5)
8. Active euthanasia is a situation in which someone takes action to bring about another person's death, with the intention of ending that person's suffering. (p. Ep-15; objective 3)
9. A physician-assisted suicide is one in which a doctor provides the means for a person to end his or her life. (p. Ep-16; video lesson, segment 2; objective 5)

10. Slippery slope is the argument that a given action will start a chain of events that will culminate in an undesirable outcome. (p. Ep-17; objectives 5 & 6)

11. A living will is a document that specifies what medical intervention a person wants if he or she becomes incapable of expressing those wishes. (p. Ep-17; video lesson, segment 2; objective 3)

12. A health care proxy is an individual chosen by another person to make medical decisions if the second person becomes unable to do so. (p. Ep-18; objective 3)

13. Bereavement is the sense of loss following a death. (p. Ep-20; objective 7)

14. Grief is an individual's emotional response to bereavement. (p. Ep-20; objective 7)

15. Mourning is the ceremonies and behaviors that a religion or culture prescribes for bereaved people. (p. Ep-20; objective 7)

16. When a person clings to sorrow and experiences contradictory emotions that impede his or her future life, the person is undergoing complicated grief. (p. Ep-22; objective 7)

17. Absent grief is a situation in which overly private people cut themselves off from the community and customers of expected grief; can lead to social isolation. (p. Ep-22; objective 7)

18. Disenfranchised grief is a situation in which certain people, although they are bereaved, are not allowed to mourn publicly. (p. Ep-22; objective 7)

19. Incomplete grief is a situation in which circumstances, such as a police investigation or an autopsy, interfere with the process of grieving. (p. Ep-23; objective 7)

20. The grief that a person feels before a loved one dies, and that reduces shock and increases acceptance of that death is called anticipatory grief. (video lesson, segment 1; objective 7)

21. Voluntary euthanasia is when, at a patient's request, someone intentionally acts to terminate his or her life. (video lesson, segment 2; objective 5)

Practice Questions I

Multiple-Choice Questions

1. b. is the correct answer. (video lesson, segment 1; objective 1)

2. c. is the correct answer. (video lesson, segment 2; objective 3)

3. c. is the correct answer. (video lesson, segment 1; objective 1)

4. c. is the correct answer. (video lesson, segment 1; objectives 1 & 2)

5. d. is the correct answer. (video lesson, segment 2; objective 2)

6. a. is the correct answer. (objective 2)

7. c. is the correct answer. (video lesson, segment 2; objective 4)

   a. is incorrect. This is a living will.

   b. & d. are incorrect. These are forms of euthanasia.

8. c. is the correct answer. (video lesson, segment 2; objective 4)

9. d. is the correct answer. (video lesson, segment 2; objective 5)

   a. is incorrect. There is no such thing as involuntary euthanasia.

   c. is incorrect. In this situation, a doctor provides the means for a patient to end his or her own life.

10. d. is the correct answer. (video lesson, segments 3 & 4; objectives 6 & 7)

11. b. is the correct answer. (objectives 3 & 4)

12. d. is the correct answer. A central feature of hospices is that the dying are not isolated from loved ones, as they might be in a hospital. (video lesson, segment 2; objective 4)

True or False Items

13. T (objectives 1 & 2)

14. F Later research has not confirmed Kübler-Ross's findings that the emotions of an individual faced with death occur in orderly stages. (video lesson, segment 1; objective 1)

15. T (objectives 3 & 4)

16. F The psychological well-being of the bereaved depends above all on their being able to openly express their grief. (objective 7)

17. F A friend should listen, sympathize, and not ignore the mourner's pain. (objective 7)

18. F (objective 4)

19. F These practices are illegal throughout most of the world. (video lesson, segment 2; objective 5)

20. T (video lesson, segment 2; objective 4)

21. T (objectives 6 & 7)

22. T (objective 4)

Practice Questions II

Multiple-Choice Questions

1. c. is the correct answer. (video lesson, segment 1; objective 1)

2. d. is the correct answer. In recent times, mourning has become less religious than formerly. (objective 7)

3. d. is the correct answer. Hospices generally do provide patients with skilled medical care. (video lesson, segment 2; objective 4)

4. d. is the correct answer. (objective 3)

5. d. is the correct answer. (video lesson; segment 1; objective 1)

   b. & c. are incorrect. There is no evidence that hospice residents experience different emotional stages than others who are dying, or that these stages are a product of Western culture.

6. d. is the correct answer. (objective 3)

7. b. is the correct answer. (video lesson, segment 2; objective 3)

8. c. is the correct answer. (video lesson, segment 4; objective 6)

9. c. is the correct answer. (objective 4)

10. c. is the correct answer. (objectives 6 & 7)

    a. is incorrect. Age is an important factor in both mourning and the dying person's emotions; gender, however was not discussed as a source of variation in dying practices.

    b. is incorrect. Culture often has more influence on variations in death practices than religion does.

    d. is incorrect. Anticipatory grief primarily influences the ease with which the bereaved are able to accept the loss of their loved one.

11. b. is the correct answer. (objective 7)

    a. & c. are incorrect.

    d. is incorrect. This issue was not discussed.

Matching Items

12. c (video lesson, segment 2; objective 4)

13. b (video lesson, segment 2; objective 4)

14. d (video lesson, segment 2; objective 3)

15. h (objective 5)

16. e (video lesson, segment 2; objective 5)

17. a (video lesson, segment 2; objective 4)

18. f (objective 3)

19. g (video lesson, segment 3; objectives 6 & 7)

Applying Your Knowledge

1. b. is the correct answer. (objective 6)

2. c. is the correct answer. (objective 2)

3. d. is the correct answer. (video lesson, segment 1; objective 1)

   a. is incorrect. People in this stage refuse to believe that their condition is terminal.

   b. is incorrect. In this stage, the dying person directs anger at others for his or her condition.

   c. is incorrect. In this stage, the dying person mourns his or her own impending death.

4. a. is the correct answer. (video lesson, segment 1; objective 1)

5. b. is the correct answer. (video lesson, segment 2; objectives 4 & 5)

6. b. is the correct answer. (video lesson, segment 2; objective 5)

7. c. is the correct answer. (objectives 6 & 7)

8. c. is the correct answer. (video lesson, segment 3; objective 7)

   a., b., & d. are incorrect. These statements discourage the bereaved person from mourning.

9. d. is the correct answer. (objective 3)

Lesson Review

Lesson 26

Epilogue
Death and Dying

Please Note: Use this matrix to guide your study and achieve the learning objectives of this lesson. It will also help you to view the video, which defines and demonstrates important concepts and skills as they relate to everyday life.

Learning Objective	Textbook	Course Student Guide	Video Lesson
1. Identify Kübler-Ross's stages of dying, and discuss these stages in light of more recent research.	pp. Ep-10–Ep-11	Practice Questions I: 1, 3, 4, 13, 14; Practice Questions II: 1, 5; Applying Your Knowledge: 3, 4.	Segment 1: *Emotional Reactions to Death*
2. Discuss age-related differences in the conceptualization of emotional reactions to death.	pp. Ep-2–Ep-7	Key Terms: 2; Practice Questions I: 4, 5, 6, 13; Applying Your Knowledge: 2.	Segment 1: *Emotional Reactions to Death* Segment 2: *Deciding How to Die*
3. Discuss the steps that patients, family members, and medical personnel can take to plan for a swift, pain-free, and dignified death.	pp. Ep-14–Ep-19	Key Terms: 5, 6, 8, 11, 12; Practice Questions I: 2, 11, 15; Practice Questions II: 4, 6, 7, 14, 18; Applying Your Knowledge: 9.	Segment 2: *Deciding How to Die*
4. Explain the concept of palliative care, focusing on the advantages and disadvantages of hospices, and describe the conditions under which individuals choose to avoid medical intervention.	pp. Ep-11–Ep-13	Key Terms: 3, 4, 5, 7; Practice Questions I: 7, 8, 11, 12, 15, 18, 20, 22; Practice Questions II: 3, 9, 12, 13, 17; Applying Your Knowledge: 5.	Segment 2: *Deciding How to Die*
5. Discuss issues surrounding assisted suicide and active euthanasia, noting the Dutch experience with legislation regarding assisted dying.	pp. Ep-14–Ep-17	Key Terms: 7, 9, 10, 21; Practice Questions I: 9, 19; Practice Questions II: 15, 16; Applying Your Knowledge: 5, 6.	Segment 2: *Deciding How to Die*

Learning Objective	Textbook	Course Student Guide	Video Lesson
6. Describe some cultural and religious variations in how death is viewed and treated.	pp. Ep-7–Ep-9	Key Terms: 10; Practice Questions I: 10, 21; Practice Questions II: 8, 10, 19; Applying Your Knowledge: 1, 7.	Segment 3: *Social Context of Bereavement* Segment 4: *Cycle of Life*
7. Describe recent changes in the mourning process, and suggest steps that can be taken in helping someone to recover from bereavement.	pp. Ep-19–Ep-25	Key Terms: 1, 13, 14, 15, 16, 17, 18, 19, 20; Practice Questions I: 10, 16, 17, 21; Practice Questions II: 2, 10, 11, 19; Applying Your Knowledge: 7, 8.	Segment 1: *Emotional Reactions to Death* Segment 3: *Social Context of Bereavement* Segment 4: *Cycle of Life*